AMERICAN POWER AND THE NEW MANDARINS

AMERICAN POWER
AND THE NEW
MANDARINS

NOAM CHOMSKY

PANTHEON BOOKS, A DIVISION OF RANDOM HOUSE
NEW YORK

First Printing. Copyright © 1967, 1969 by Noam Chomsky. All rights reserved under International and Pan-American Copyright Conventions. Published in the United States by Pantheon Books, a division of Random House, Inc., New York, and simultaneously in Canada by Random House of Canada Limited, Toronto. Library of Congress Catalog Card Number: 69-11864. Manufactured in the United States of America by The Haddon Craftsmen, Inc., Scranton, Pa. Designed by Joan Bastone.

7-7-67

To the brave young men who refuse to serve in a criminal war

Contents

Contents

AMERICAN POWER AND THE NEW MANDARINS

INTRODUCTION

Three years have passed since American intervention in a civil war in Vietnam was converted into a colonial war of the classic type. This was the decision of a liberal American administration. Like the earlier steps to enforce our will in Vietnam, it was taken with the support of leading political figures, intellectuals, and academic experts, many of whom now oppose the war because they do not believe that American repression can succeed in Vietnam and therefore urge, on pragmatic grounds, that we "take our stand" where the prospects are more hopeful. If the resistance in Vietnam were to collapse, if the situation were to revert to that of Thailand or Guatemala or Greece, where the forces of order, with our approval and assistance, are exercising a fair degree of control, then this opposition to the Vietnam war would also cease; in the words of one such spokesman, we might then "all be saluting the wisdom and statesmanship of the American government."[1] If we are forced to liquidate this enterprise—in one of the two possible ways—

3

the liberal ideologists will continue to urge that we organize and control as extensive a dominion as is feasible in what they take to be "our national interest" and in the interest of the elements in other societies that we designate as fit to rule.

As matters now stand, it appears unlikely that Vietnamese resistance will collapse. The United States seems unable to muster the military force to crush this resistance and to guarantee the dominance of the government and social institutions that we have determined to be appropriate. There is, therefore, some hope that American troops will be withdrawn and the Vietnamese left to try to reconstruct something from the wreckage. The course of history may be determined, to a very significant degree, by what the people of the United States will have learned from this catastrophe.

Three times in a generation American technology has laid waste a helpless Asian country. In 1945 this was done with a sense of moral rectitude that was, and remains, almost unchallenged. In Korea, there were a few qualms. The amazing resistance of the Vietnamese has finally forced us to ask, What have we done? There are, at last, some signs of awakening to the horrifying reality. Resistance to American violence and to the militarization of our own society has become, if not a significant force, at least a detectable one. There is hope that the struggle against racism and exploitation at home can be linked with the struggle to remove the heavy Yankee boot from the necks of oppressed people throughout the world.

Twenty years of intensive cold-war indoctrination and seventy years of myth regarding our international role make it difficult to face these issues in a serious way. There is a great deal of intellectual debris to be cleared away. Ideological pressures so overpowering that even their existence was denied must be examined and understood. The search for alternatives, for individuals, for American society, for the international order as a whole, has barely begun, and no one can guess where it will lead. Quite possibly it will lead nowhere, cut off by domestic repression or its "functional equivalent," to use a favorite term of the present administration: the dominance of a liberal technocracy who will serve the existing social order in the belief that they represent justice and humanity, fighting limited wars at home and overseas to preserve stability, promising that the future will be better if only the dispossessed will wait patiently, and supported by an apathetic, obedient majority, its mind and conscience dulled by a surfeit of commodities and by some new version of the old system of beliefs and ideas. Perhaps the worst excesses may be eliminated. Perhaps a way may be found to bring about a fundamental change in American society of a sort that can hardly be envisioned today. A great many people have been aroused by the Vietnam tragedy and the domestic crisis. There is a new mood of questioning and rebellion among the youth of the country, a very healthy and hopeful development, by and large, that few would have predicted a decade ago. The passionate involvement of students in the civil rights movement, in the movement to end the war, in resistance, in community organizing, already has changed the intellectual and moral climate of the universities at least. These stirrings of concern and commitment give some reason to hope that we will not repeat the crimes of the recent past. One thing is certain: we must never forget these crimes.

It is just half a century since Randolph Bourne, in his remarkably perceptive essays, warned that "the old philosophy, the old radicalism . . . has found a perfectly definite level, and there is no reason to think it will not remain there. Its flowering appears in the technical organization of the war by an earnest group of young liberals, who direct their course by an opportunist program of state socialism at home and a league of benevolently imperialistic nations abroad." The pragmatic liberalism "that worked when we were trying to get that material foundation for American life in which more impassioned living could flourish" was now helpless in "creating new values and setting at once a large standard to which the nations might repair." He wrote of the enthusiasm with which liberal intellectuals accepted the war, once America had joined in, of the "high mood of confidence and self-righteousness," the "keen sense of control over events."

> The war has revealed a younger intelligentsia, trained up in the pragmatic dispensation, immensely ready for the executive ordering of events, pitifully unprepared for the intellectual interpretation or the idealistic focusing of ends. . . . They have absorbed the secret of scientific method as applied to political administration. They are liberal, enlightened, aware. They are touched with creative intelligence toward the solution of political and industrial problems. They are a wholly new force in American life, the product of the swing in the colleges from a training that emphasized classical studies to one that emphasized political and economic values. Practically all this element, one would say, is lined up in service of the war technique. There seems to have been a peculiar congeniality between the war and these men. It is as if the war and they had been waiting for each other. . . . What is significant is that it is the technical side of the war that appeals to them, not the interpretative or political side. The formulation of values and ideals, the production of articulate and suggestive thinking, had not, in their education, kept pace, to any extent whatever, with their technical aptitude. . . . [Dewey's] disciples have learned all too literally the instrumental attitude toward life, and, being immensely intelligent and energetic, they are making themselves efficient instruments of the war technique, accepting with little question the ends as announced from above.[2]

Bourne is describing, not the "New Frontier," the "new mandarins" of the 1960s, but the liberal and radical intellectuals of

1917. His essay is entitled "Twilight of Idols." With the Vietnam war, twilight has turned to midnight.

In the same essay, Bourne speaks with hope of the "thorough malcontents" with their

> Irritation at things as they are, disgust at the frustrations and aridities of American life, deep dissatisfaction with self and with the groups that give themselves as hopeful—out of such moods there might be hammered new values. The malcontents would be men and women who could not stomach the war, or the reactionary idealism that has followed in its train. They are quite through with the professional critics and classicists who have let cultural values die through their own personal ineptitude. Yet these malcontents have no intention of being cultural vandals, only to slay. They are not barbarians, but seek the vital and the sincere everywhere.[8]

He speaks with hope that "a more skeptical, malicious, desperate, ironical mood may actually be the sign of more vivid and more stirring life fermenting in America today. . . . Malcontentedness may be the beginning of promise." The postwar repression all but destroyed this promise. Today, as the Cold War ideology is collapsing and American power is proving incapable of achieving dominance over Asia, there is once again the smell of repression in the air. If we can learn anything from history, we will find a way to avoid the arrogance and divisiveness that has been the curse of the left and unite to resist this repression, to realize the promise that might grow from malcontentedness, to replace "the allure of the martial in war" and "the allure of the technical" by "the allure of fresh and true ideas, of free speculation, of artistic vigor, of cultural styles, of intelligence suffused by feeling, and feeling given fibre and outline by intelligence." These words of Bourne's are no program for action, but an injunction to seek such a program and create for ourselves, for others, the understanding that can give it life. There has been little advance in this direction since he wrote. Given the present realities of American power, the challenge becomes an urgent, desperate necessity.

The essays collected here are, for the most part, highly critical of the role that American intellectuals have played in designing and implementing policy, interpreting historical events, and formulating an ideology of social change that in part falsifies, in part restricts and subverts it. Because of this critical tone, I want to make it clear at the outset that if any note of self-righteousness creeps in, it is unintended and, more important, unjustified. No one who involved himself in antiwar activities as late as 1965, as I did, has any reason for pride or satisfaction. This opposition was ten or fifteen years too late. This is one lesson we should have learned from the tragedy of Vietnam.

For the most part, these essays are elaborated versions of lectures given over the past few years. During these years, I have taken part in more conferences, debates, forums, teach-ins, meetings on Vietnam and American imperialism than I care to remember. Perhaps I should mention that, increasingly, I have had a certain feeling of falseness in these lectures and discussions. This feeling does not have to do with the intellectual issues. The basic facts are clear enough; the assessment of the situation is as accurate as I can make it. But the entire performance is emotionally and morally false in a disturbing way. It is a feeling that I have occasionally been struck by before. For example, I remember reading an excellent study of Hitler's East European policies a number of years ago in a mood of grim fascination. The author was trying hard to be cool and scholarly and objective, to stifle the only human response to a plan to enslave and destroy millions of subhuman organisms so that the inheritors of the spiritual values of Western civilization would be free to develop a higher form of society in peace. Controlling this elementary human reaction, we enter into a technical debate with the Nazi intelligentsia: Is it technically feasible to dispose of millions of bodies? What is the evidence that the Slavs are inferior beings? Must they be ground under foot or returned to their "natural" home in the East so that this great culture can flourish, to the benefit of all mankind? Is it true that the Jews are a cancer eating away at the vitality of the German people? and so on. Without awareness, I found myself drawn into this morass of insane rationality—inventing arguments to counter and demolish the constructions of the Bormanns and the Rosenbergs.

By entering into the arena of argument and counterargument, of technical feasibility and tactics, of footnotes and citations, by accepting the presumption of legitimacy of debate on certain issues, one has already lost one's humanity. This is the feeling I find almost impossible to repress when going through the motions of building a case against the American war in Vietnam. Anyone who puts a fraction of his mind to the task can construct a case that is overwhelming; surely this is now obvious. In an important way, by doing so he degrades himself, and insults beyond measure the victims of our violence and our moral blindness. There may have been a time when American policy in Vietnam was a debatable matter. This time is long past. It is no more debatable than the Italian war in Abyssinia or the Russian suppression of Hungarian freedom. The war is simply an obscenity, a depraved act by weak and miserable men, including all of us, who have allowed it to go on and on with endless fury and destruction—all of us who would have remained silent had stability and order been secured. It is not pleasant to use such words, but candor permits no less.

The things we have seen and read during these horrible years surpass belief. I have in front of me now an Associated Press photo from the *New York Times* with this caption:

> HOMELESS CHILDREN: Girl holds her wounded baby sister as South Vietnamese rangers move through their hamlet. Children had been rescued from a bunker under their house, burnt down when U.S. helicopters fired on Vietcong. The scene is the Mekong Delta, southwest of Saigon.

I cannot describe the pathos of this scene, or the expression on the face of the wounded child. How many hundreds of such pictures must we see before we begin to care and to act?

I suppose this is the first time in history that a nation has so openly and publicly exhibited its own war crimes. Perhaps this shows how well our free institutions function. Or does it simply show how immune we have become to suffering? Probably the latter. So at least it would seem, when we observe how opposition to the war has grown in recent months. There is no doubt that the primary cause for this opposition is that the cost of the war to us is too great, unacceptable. It is deplorable, but nonetheless true, that what has changed American public opinion and the domestic political picture is not the efforts of the "peace movement"—still less the declarations of any political spokesmen—but rather the Vietnamese resistance, which simply will not yield to American force. What is more, the "responsible" attitude is that opposition to the war on grounds of cost is not, as I have said, deplorable, but rather admirable, in keeping with the genius of American politics. American politics is a politics of accommodation that successfully excludes moral considerations. Therefore it is quite proper—a further demonstration of our superior acuity—that only pragmatic considerations of cost and utility guide our actions. When Martin Luther

King was assassinated, Kenneth Clark said that "you have to weep for this country." Are we to weep, or to laugh, when we read in the editorial columns of our great newspapers, and in much of the left-liberal press, that the health of our democratic system has been confirmed by Johnson's speech of March 31? With the collapse of his Vietnam policies, a serious international economic crisis, and domestic turmoil threatening to make the country impossible to govern, the President made a "noble" and "magnanimous" gesture—"the ultimate sacrifice for peace," in the words of one senator: he announced that he would not seek renomination. This proves the viability of American democracy. By these standards a still more viable democracy was that of fascist Japan in the late 1930s, where more than a dozen cabinets fell under not dissimilar circumstances. The health of our system would have been demonstrated by a change of policy caused by a recognition that what we have done in Vietnam is wrong, a criminal act, that an American "victory" would have been a tragedy. Nothing could be more remote from the American political consciousness. So long as this remains true, we are fated to relive this horror.

The primary reason for opposition to the war is its cost to us. A second cause is the feeling that the cost to its victims is too great. At first glance, this reaction seems to be at a higher moral level than the first, but this is questionable. The principle that we should retract our claws when the victim bleeds too much is hardly an elevated one. What about opposition to the war on the grounds that we have no right to stabilize or restructure Vietnamese society, or to carry out the experiments with "material and human resources control" that delight the "pacification theorist"? Such opposition is slight, and in the political arena virtually nonexistent. The pragmatic and responsible student of

11

contemporary affairs does not descend to such emotionalism.

In March 1968, the *Boston Globe* ran a series of letters from a member of the International Voluntary Services, a teacher in a Montagnard village, obviously a person of great courage and dedication. For the most part, these were nice, chatty letters about life in Vietnam and the good things we're doing for those poor people over there. Here are some selections from one letter:

> Funny thing about Vietnam, we're creating these secure islands, people are relocated, shuffled into "pacified" areas, but most of the country is a no man's land which we're rapidly turning into a desert by bombing, defoliation, etc. . . . If the Americans get their way, it'll be a country of beaches, plus a few islands of secure areas . . . and the rest'll be wasteland. Funny thing to do to a country whose economy and politics you're paying to enhance. But they say the only way to beat the guerrilla forces is to eliminate their source of life (the land and the people), ruin the land and concentrate the people into areas you can protect.[4]

I think that such a letter tells us a good deal about the mood of the country today. A member of the IVS learns that what we are trying to do is "eliminate their source of life (the land and the people)," and then goes on cheerily and dutifully to do her job, helping to restore what has been destroyed. More to the point, several hundred thousand citizens of Greater Boston—the cultural capital of the United States, they would like to believe —may have read that letter and gone on to do their jobs. Why not? It is no more harrowing than dozens of other things they have seen and read. In fact, it is doubtful whether there is anything we could do to the people of Vietnam (the Communists, that is) that would cause more than a momentary shudder.

A few weeks earlier the citizens of Boston read an article in the same place on the *Globe* editorial page by the chairman of the department of government at Harvard University, in which he described the process of urbanization in South Vietnam, an interesting sociological phenomenon which opens up a whole range of new possibilities for nation building.[5] He spares us the details of how "the United States is urbanizing the people of Vietnam," but others have described the process—for example, the IVS worker just quoted. Urbanization, of course, is that "funny thing" that we're doing to the people of Vietnam. It is the process described in the following terms by Don Luce, who resigned as director of IVS in late 1967 in protest against United States policy, after nine years in the field:

Less "fortunate" villagers [than those in "pacified" villages] have been uprooted from their traditional homes and placed in refugee camps that crowd around the cities. These bleak camps are made up almost completely of women and children who deeply resent having been torn away from their farmlands and way of life, away from their ancestral burial grounds, and even away from their husbands—who are usually with the Vietcong. Their old village usually becomes part of a free strike zone. This means that planes can drop bombs anywhere in that area and that anyone caught there will be considered a Vietcong and shot. Unfortunately, many of the refugees go back to harvest their rice or wander into these areas to gather wood or thatch. In Tuy Hoa, one of the IVS members was asked to give blood at the provincial hospital where he was working on a part-time basis. He asked an old man waiting in the hospital what had happened. The old man replied bitterly, "My son and four others went to cut wood. On their return an American helicopter hovered over. Frightened, they ran. Four were wounded; one was killed." [6]

In short, urbanization is the process by which you "eliminate their source of life (the land and the people), ruin the land and concentrate the people into areas you can protect." This everyone understands. Yet there is scarcely a ripple of protest when the chairman of the department of government at our greatest university speaks of the sociological process of urbanization, the benefits it provides for the Vietnamese, and the possibilities it offers us to win the war.

This calm and analytic attitude towards the problem of how to win the war can be illustrated with innumerable examples from the writings of responsible political analysts. To pick just one, consider some remarks by Joseph Harsch on the bombing tactics in North Vietnam.[7] Mr. Harsch discusses the frustrations of the limited-bombing policy:

> A bomb dropped into a leafy jungle produces no visible result. Even if it hits a truck carrying ammunition the pilot seldom has the satisfaction of knowing what he achieved. A hit on a big hydroelectric dam is another matter. There is a huge explosion visible from anywhere above. The dam can be seen to fall. The waters can be seen to pour through the breach and drown out huge areas of farm land, and villages, in its path. The pilot who takes out a hydroelectric dam gets back home with a feeling of accomplishment. Novels are written and films are made of such exploits. . . . The bomb which takes out the dam will flood villages, drown people, destroy crops, and knock out some electric power. . . . Bombing the dam would hurt people. Every dam taken out would give more reason for claiming that "the enemy is hurting." In theory, if he can be "hurt" enough his government should be more inclined to go to the conference table.

Despite all of these advantages of bombing dams, Harsch apparently believes that it is more reasonable to bomb trucks. The reason is that "there is no evidence that this causing of pain to civilians in North Vietnam" has had the effect of persuading their government to enter into negotiations. Furthermore, the effect of terror bombing is slight in a nonindustrialized country. Therefore, he suggests, we should not "go after the spectacular targets which cause militarily dubious pain to people in North Vietnam," but rather "after the unspectacular targets which can bring some military relief to the infantrymen in the battle on the ground," even though this is a shame for the pilots, who are missing out on the feeling of accomplishment and satisfaction that comes from flooding villages, drowning people, and destroying crops.

By coincidence, the same newspaper published an eyewitness report of the bombing of dikes in North Vietnam, just a few days later.[8] The correspondent reports:

> Dikes in the fertile Red River delta—North Vietnam's rice basket —have come under increasing air attack lately. The American bombing appears intended not only to demoralize and harass the population in the most densely populated region of the country, but also to destroy the rice crops in the vast alluvial plains with their vulnerable open spaces . . . here in the delta region, whose paddy fields provide the bulk of the rice supply of 17 million North Vietnamese, there have been almost daily attacks on dikes along the numerous small confluences of the Red River. . . . The pattern of the bombing in the delta seems evident—to interdict agricultural production. No military targets are visible in the dikes. The heaviest artillery pieces we saw were antiquated rifles of the peasant militia.

As a historical reference point, recall that German High Commissioner Seyss-Inquart was condemned to death at Nuremberg for opening the dikes in Holland at the time of the Allied invasion.[9] Since the editors of the *Christian Science Monitor* did not feel that this disclosure required editorial comment, I do not know whether they regarded Harsch's sensible argument for the bombing of trucks rather than dams as now counterbalanced by other considerations.

As a final illustration of the callousness of the American response to what the mass media reveal, consider a small item in the *New York Times* of March 18, 1968, headed, "Army Exhibit Bars Simulated Shooting at Vietnamese Hut." The item reports an attempt by the "peace movement" to disrupt an exhibit in the Chicago Museum of Science and Industry:

> Beginning today, visitors can no longer enter a helicopter for simulated firing of a machine gun at targets in a diorama of the Vietnam Central Highlands. The targets were a hut, two bridges and an ammunition dump, and a light flashed when a hit was scored.

Apparently, it was great fun for the kiddies until those damned peaceniks turned up and started one of their interminable demonstrations, even occupying the exhibit. According to the *Times* report, "demonstrators particularly objected to children being permitted to 'fire' at the hut, even though no people appear there or elsewhere in the diorama," which just shows how unreasonable peaceniks can be. Although it is small compensation for the closing of this entertaining exhibit, "visitors, however, may still test their skills elsewhere in the exhibit by simulated firing of an antitank weapon and several models of rifles."

What can one say about a country where a museum of science in a great city can feature an exhibit in which people fire machine guns from a helicopter at Vietnamese huts, with a light flashing when a hit is scored? What can one say about a country where such an idea can even be considered? You have to weep for this country.

These and a thousand other examples testify to moral degeneration on such a scale that talk about the "normal channels" of political action and protest becomes meaningless or hypocritical. We have to ask ourselves whether what is needed in the United States is dissent—or denazification. The question is a debatable one. Reasonable people may differ. The fact that the question is even debatable is a terrifying thing. To me it seems that what is needed is a kind of denazification. What is more, there is no powerful outside force that can call us to account—the change will have to come from within.

I have been speaking only of oppression overseas, but it need hardly be emphasized that there is a domestic analogue. The reaction to the suffering of oppressed minorities at home is not very different from the brutal apathy towards the misery we have imposed elsewhere in the world. Opposition to the war in Vietnam is based very largely on its cost, and on the failure of American power to crush Vietnamese resistance. It is sad, but nonetheless true, that the tiny steps to bring freedom to black Americans have been taken, for the most part, out of fear. We must recognize these facts and regret them deeply, but not be paralyzed by this recognition. Anger, outrage, confessions of overwhelming guilt may be good therapy; they can also become a barrier to effective action, which can always be made to seem incommensurable with the enormity of the crime. Nothing is easier than to adopt a new form of self-indulgence, no less debilitating than the old apathy. The danger is substantial. It is hardly a novel insight that confession of guilt can be institutionalized as a technique for evading what must be done. It is even possible to achieve a feeling of satisfaction by contemplating one's evil nature. No less insidious is the cry for "revolution," at a time when not even the germs of new institutions exist, let alone the moral and political consciousness that could lead to a basic modification of social life. If there will be a "revolution" in America today, it will no doubt be a move towards some variety of fascism. We must guard against the kind of revolutionary rhetoric that would have had Karl Marx burn down the British Museum because it was merely part of a repressive society. It would be criminal to overlook the serious flaws and inadequacies in our institutions, or to fail to utilize the substantial degree of freedom that most of us enjoy, within the framework of these flawed institutions, to modify them or even replace them by a better social order. One who pays some attention to history will not be surprised if those who cry most loudly that we must smash and destroy are later found among the administrators of some new system of repression.

Someday the war in Vietnam will end, and with it the renewed impulse it has given to self-analysis and the search for cures and alternatives. Those who were opposed to the war merely because of its costs or its atrocities will fall away. It is possible that an American defeat that cannot be disguised, or a "victory" that opens the way to new savagery, will be accompanied by a serious domestic repression that will leave little energy or will for the task of re-evaluation and reconstruction of ideology and social life. But there are also encouraging signs. There is a growing realization that it is an illusion to believe that all will be well if only today's liberal hero can be placed in the White House, and a growing awareness that isolated, competing individuals can rarely confront repressive institutions alone. At best, a few may be tolerated as intellectual gadflies. The mass, even under formal democracy, will accept "the values that have been inculcated, often accidentally and often deliberately by vested interests," values that have the status of "unconsciously acquired habits rather than choices."[10] In a fragmented, competitive society, individuals can neither discover their true interests nor act to defend them, as they cannot do so when prevented from free association by totalitarian controls. Recognition of these facts has brought young men together in various forms of resistance and has given rise to the little-known but very impressive attempts at community organizing in many parts of the country; it also apparently motivates many of the spokesmen for "black power." It is interesting to see how classical ideas of libertarian socialism have found their way into the ideology of the "New Left." Such statements as the following have become near clichés—not therefore false or unimportant: Our social system has "sacrificed the general interests of human society to the private interests of individuals, and thus systematically undermined a true relationship between men"; "Democracy with its motto of *equality of all citizens before the law* and Liberalism with its *right of man over his own person* both were wrecked on the realities of capitalist economy"; "The greatest evil of any form of power is just that it always tries to force the rich diversity of social life into definite forms and adjust it to particular norms";

> Political rights do not originate in parliaments; they are rather forced upon them from without. And even their enactment into law has for a long time been no guarantee of their security. They do not exist because they have been legally set down on a piece of paper, but only when they have become the ingrown habit of a people, and when any attempt to impair them will meet with the violent resistance of the populace. Where this is not the case, there is no help in any parliamentary opposition or any Platonic appeals to the constitution. One compels respect from others when one knows how to defend one's dignity as a human being. This is not only true in private life; it has always been the same in political life as well.[11]

To me it seems that the revival of anarchist thinking in the "New Left" and the attempts to put it into effect are the most promising development of the past years, and that if this development can solidify, it offers some real hope that the present American crisis will not become an American and world catastrophe.

In the decade of indifference, Albert Einstein once described the importance of the War Resisters' League in these terms:

. . . by union, it relieves courageous and resolute individuals of the paralyzing feeling of isolation and loneliness, and in this way gives them moral support in the fulfillment of what they consider to be their duty. The existence of such a moral elite is indispensable for the preparation of a fundamental change in public opinion, a change which, under present-day circumstances, is absolutely necessary if humanity is to survive.[12]

In the past few years the "moral elite" has grown to a considerable force among the young, and is searching for ways to unite and to act both as a political and a moral force. It remains to be seen whether this can become a creative and self-sustaining tradition, not dependent on exterior events for its survival, and whether it can unite with other forces for constructive change. If it can do so, we may be able to come to grips with the problems that plague us. We may also be able to avoid a fate that was—according to an often quoted story—outlined by Einstein on another occasion, when he was asked what sort of weapons might be used in a possible Third World War. His answer was that he did not know what weapons would be used in World War III, but he was sure that the Fourth World War would be fought with stones and clubs.

Notes

1. Arthur M. Schlesinger, Jr., *The Bitter Heritage: Vietnam and American Democracy* (Boston, Houghton Mifflin Company, 1967), p. 34.
2. "Twilight of Idols," in *The World of Randolph Bourne*, ed. Lillian Schlissel (New York, E. P. Dutton & Co., Inc., 1965), pp. 198–99.
3. *Ibid.*, p. 202.
4. *Boston Globe*, March 13, 1968.
5. Samuel P. Huntington, "Why the Viet Cong Attacked the Cities," *Boston Globe*, February 17, 1968. See page 42 below for some quotations.

Professor Huntington has since expanded on these thoughts in "The Bases of Accommodation," *Foreign Affairs,* Vol. 46, No. 4 (July 1968), pp. 642–56. He explains that the Viet Cong is "a powerful force which cannot be dislodged from its constituency so long as the constituency continues to exist." Evidently, we must therefore ensure that the constituency—the rural population—ceases to exist. A Himmler or a Streicher would have advanced one obvious solution. This liberal social scientist, however, suggests another: that we drive the peasants into the cities by force ("urbanization"), putting off until after the war the "massive government programs" that "will be required either to resettle migrants in rural areas or to rebuild the cities and promote peacetime urban employment." This policy may prove to be "the answer to 'wars of national liberation,' " an answer that we have "stumbled upon" in Vietnam, "in an absent-minded way."

Professor Huntington disputes the view of Sir Robert Thompson that peasant-based insurgency is immune "to the direct application of mechanical and conventional power." Not so: ". . . in the light of recent events, this statement needs to be seriously qualified. For if the 'direct application of mechanical and conventional power' takes place on such a massive scale as to produce a massive migration from countryside to city, the basic assumptions underlying the Maoist doctrine of revolutionary war no longer operate. The Maoist-inspired rural revolution is undercut by the American-sponsored urban revolution."

It is helpful to have this explanation, from a leading political scientist, of the "basic assumptions" underlying the American doctrine of counter-revolutionary war.

6. "The Making of a Dove," *The Progressive,* 1968, distributed by Vietnam Information Project, 100 Maryland Avenue N.E., Washington, D.C. 20002. This project consists of a group of returned IVS workers who are trying to bring to the attention of the American people some of the facts about what is happening in the villages of Vietnam. They are, in fact, the only Americans who have significant firsthand information about this matter. They are to be contrasted with the visiting political scientists who seem to believe that interviews with captured prisoners or defectors give a fair account of attitudes in rural Vietnam. It is worth mentioning that the IVS workers were, as a group, more or less committed to the American effort, and even after resigning in protest against what they had seen, did not question our

right to restructure Vietnamese society along lines that appear to us appropriate. See page 251 below.

7. "Truck Versus Dam," *Christian Science Monitor*, September 5, 1967. To the reader who suspects that this is irony, I can only propose that he read the article in full.

8. Amando Doronila, "Hanoi Food Output Held Target of U.S. Bombers," AP, *Christian Science Monitor*, September 8, 1967.

9. See the memorandum by Gabriel Kolko to the Russell Tribunal, quoted in *Liberation*, Vol. 12 (May–June 1967), p. 13. Eisenhower regarded this despicable act as "a blot on [the] military honor" of the German Commander and warned that he and his cohorts would be considered "violators of the laws of war who must face the certain consequences of their acts."

10. C. Wright Mills, *The Sociological Imagination* (New York, Oxford University Press, 1959), p. 194.

11. All quotes from Rudolf Rocker, "Anarchism and Anarcho-syndicalism," in Paul Eltzbacher, ed., *Anarchism* (London, Freedom Press, 1960), pp. 225–68. Equally characteristic of "New Left" thinking is the judgment that Rocker quotes from Kropotkin regarding Bolshevik Russia: "Russia has shown us the way in which Socialism cannot be realized. . . . The idea of workers' councils for the control of the political and economic life of the country is, in itself, of extraordinary importance . . . but so long as the country is dominated by the dictatorship of a party, the workers' and peasants' councils naturally lose their significance. They are degraded to the same passive role which the representatives of the Estates used to play in the time of the absolute Monarchy." Rocker himself comments that "the dictatorship of the proletariat paved the way not for a socialist society but for the most primitive type of bureaucratic state capitalism and a reversion to political absolutism which was long ago abolished in most countries by bourgeois revolutions."

12. Address at Princeton, N.J., August 10, 1953. Cited in John H. Bunzel, *Anti-Politics in America* (New York, Alfred A. Knopf, Inc., 1967), p. 166.

OBJECTIVITY AND LIBERAL SCHOLARSHIP

I

In a recent essay, Conor Cruise O'Brien speaks of the process of "counterrevolutionary subordination" which poses a threat to scholarly integrity in our own counterrevolutionary society, just as "revolutionary subordination," a phenomenon often noted and rightly deplored, has undermined scholarly integrity in revolutionary and postrevolutionary situations.[1] He observes that "power in our time has more intelligence in its service, and allows that intelligence more discretion as to its methods, than ever before in history," and suggests that this development is not altogether encouraging, since we have moved perceptibly towards the state of "a society maimed through the systematic

Parts of this essay were delivered as a lecture at New York University in March 1968, as part of the Albert Schweitzer Lecture Series, and will appear in *Power and Consciousness in Society,* edited by Conor Cruise O'Brien and published by New York University Press. I am indebted to Paul Potter, André Schiffrin, and William Watson for very helpful comments.

23

corruption of its intelligence." He urges that "increased and specific vigilance, not just the elaboration of general principles, is required from the intellectual community toward specific growing dangers to its integrity."

Senator Fulbright has developed a similar theme in an important and perceptive speech.[2] He describes the failure of the universities to form "an effective counterweight to the military-industrial complex by strengthening their emphasis on the traditional values of our democracy." Instead they have "joined the monolith, adding greatly to its power and influence." Specifically, he refers to the failure of the social scientists, "who ought to be acting as responsible and independent critics of the Government's policies," but who instead become the agents of these policies. "While young dissenters plead for resurrection of the American promise, their elders continue to subvert it." With "the surrender of independence, the neglect of teaching, and the distortion of scholarship," the university "is not only failing to meet its responsibilities to its students; it is betraying a public trust."

The extent of this betrayal might be argued; its existence, as a threatening tendency, is hardly in doubt. Senator Fulbright mentions one primary cause: the access to money and influence. Others might be mentioned: for example, a highly restrictive, almost universally shared ideology, and the inherent dynamics of professionalization. As to the former, Fulbright has cited elsewhere the observation of De Tocqueville: "I know of no country in which there is so little independence of mind and real freedom of discussion as in America." Free institutions certainly exist, but a tradition of passivity and conformism restricts their use—the cynic might say this is why they continue to exist. The impact of professionalization is also quite clear. The "free-floating intellectual" may occupy himself with problems because of their inherent interest and importance, perhaps to little effect. The professional, however, tends to define his problems on the basis of the technique that he has mastered, and has a natural desire to apply his skills. Commenting on this process, Senator Clark quotes the remarks of Dr. Harold Agnew, director of the Los Alamos Laboratories Weapons Division: "The basis of advanced technology is innovation and nothing is more stifling to innovation than seeing one's product not used or ruled out of consideration on flimsy premises involving public world opinion"[3]—"a shocking statement and a dangerous one," as Clark rightly comments. In much the same way, behavioral scientists who believe themselves to be in possession of certain techniques of control and manipulation will tend to search for problems to which their knowledge and skills might be relevant, defining these as the "important problems"; and it will come as no surprise that they occasionally express their contempt for "flimsy premises involving public world opinion" that restrict the application of these skills. Thus among engineers, there are the "weapons cultists" who construct their bombs and missiles, and among the behavioral scientists, we find the technicians who design and carry out "experiments with population and resources control methods" in Vietnam.[4]

These various factors—access to power, shared ideology, professionalization—may or may not be deplorable in themselves, but there can be no doubt that they interact so as to pose a serious threat to the integrity of scholarship in fields that are struggling for intellectual content and are thus particularly susceptible to the workings of a kind of Gresham's law. What is more, the subversion of scholarship poses a threat to society at large. The danger is particularly great in a society that encourages specialization and stands in awe of technical expertise. In such circumstances, the opportunities are great for the abuse of knowledge and technique—to be more exact, the claim to knowledge and technique. Taking note of these dangers, one reads with concern the claims of some social scientists that their discipline is essential for the training of those to whom they refer as "the mandarins of the future."[5] Philosophy and literature still "have their value," so Ithiel Pool informs us, but it is psychology, sociology, systems analysis, and political science that provide the knowledge by which "men of power are humanized and civilized." In no small measure, the Vietnam war was designed and executed by these new mandarins, and it testifies to the concept of humanity and civilization they are likely to bring to the exercise of power.[6]

Is the new access to power of the technical intelligentsia a delusion or a growing reality? There are those who perceive the "skeletal structure of a new society" in which the leadership will rest "with the research corporation, the industrial laboratories, the experimental stations, and the universities," with "the scientists, the mathematicians, the economists, and the engineers of the new computer technology"—"not only the best talents, but eventually the entire complex of social prestige and social status, will be rooted in the intellectual and scientific communities."[7] A careful look at the "skeletal structure" of this new society, if such it is, is hardly reassuring. As Daniel Bell points out, "it has been war rather than peace that has been largely responsible for the acceptance of planning and technocratic modes in government," and our present "mobilized society" is one that is geared to the "social goal" of "military and war preparedness." Bell's relative optimism regarding the new society comes from his assumption that the university is "the place where theoretical knowledge is sought, tested, and codified in a disinterested way" and that "the mobilized postures of the Cold War and the space race" are a temporary aberration, a reaction to Communist aggressiveness. In contrast, a strong argument can be made that the university has, to a significant degree, betrayed its public trust; that matters of foreign policy are very much "a reflex of internal political forces" as well as of economic institutions (rather than "a judgment about the national interest, involving strategy decisions based on the calculations of an opponent's strength and intentions"); that the mobilization for war is not "irony" but a natural development, given our present social and economic organization; that the technologists who achieve power are those who can perform a service for existing institutions; and that nothing but catastrophe is to be expected from still further centralization of decision making in government and a narrowing base of corporate affiliates. The experience of the past few years gives little reason to feel optimistic about these developments.

Quite generally, what grounds are there for supposing that those whose claim to power is based on knowledge and technique will be more benign in their exercise of power than those whose claim is based on wealth or aristocratic origin? On the contrary, one might expect the new mandarin to be dangerously arrogant, aggressive, and incapable of adjusting to failure, as compared with his predecessor, whose claim to power was not diminished by honesty as to the limitations of his knowledge, lack of work to do, or demonstrable mistakes.[8] In the Vietnam catastrophe, all of these factors are detectable. There is no point in overgeneralizing, but neither history nor psychology nor sociology gives us any particular reason to look forward with hope to the rule of the new mandarins.

In general, one would expect any group with access to power and affluence to construct an ideology that will justify this state of affairs on grounds of the general welfare. For just this reason, Bell's thesis that intellectuals are moving closer to the center of

27

power, or at least being absorbed more fully into the decision-making structure, is to some extent supported by the phenomenon of counterrevolutionary subordination noted earlier. That is, one might anticipate that as power becomes more accessible, the inequities of the society will recede from vision, the status quo will seem less flawed, and the preservation of order will become a matter of transcendent importance. The fact is that American intellectuals are increasingly achieving the status of a doubly privileged elite: first, as American citizens, with respect to the rest of the world; and second, because of their role in American society, which is surely quite central, whether or not Bell's prediction proves accurate. In such a situation, the dangers of counterrevolutionary subordination, in both the domestic and the international arena, are apparent. I think that O'Brien is entirely correct in pointing to the necessity for "increased and specific vigilance" towards the danger of counter-revolutionary subordination, of which, as he correctly remarks, "we hear almost nothing." I would like to devote this essay to a number of examples.

Several years ago it was enthusiastically proclaimed that "the fundamental political problems of the industrial revolution have been solved," and that "this very triumph of democratic social evolution in the West ends domestic politics for those intellectuals who must have ideologies or utopias to motivate them to social action."[9] During this period of faith in "the end of ideology," even enlightened and informed commentators were inclined to present the most remarkable evaluations of the state of American society. Daniel Bell, for example, wrote that "in the mass consumption economy all groups can easily acquire the outward badges of status and erase the visible demarcations."[10] Writing in *Commentary* in October 1964, he main-

28

tained that we have in effect already achieved "the egalitarian and socially mobile society which the 'free floating intellectuals' associated with the Marxist tradition have been calling for during the last hundred years." Granting the obvious general rise in standard of living, the judgment of Gunnar Myrdal seems far more appropriate to the actual situation when he says: "The common idea that America is an immensely rich and affluent country is very much an exaggeration. American affluence is heavily mortgaged. America carries a tremendous burden of debt to its poor people. That this debt must be paid is not only a wish of the do-gooders. Not paying it implies a risk for the social order and for democracy as we have known it."[11] Surely the claim that *all* groups can easily enter the mass-consumption economy and "erase the visible demarcations" is a considerable exaggeration.

Similar evaluations of American society appear frequently in contemporary scholarship. To mention just one example, consider the analysis that Adam Ulam gives of Marx's concept of capitalism: "One cannot blame a contemporary observer like Marx for his conviction that industrial fanaticism and self-righteousness were indelible traits of the capitalist. That the capitalist would grow more humane, that he would slacken in his ceaseless pursuit of accumulation and expansion, were not impressions readily warranted by the English social scene of the 1840's and '50's."[12] Again, granting the important changes in industrial society over the past century, it still comes as a surprise to hear that the capitalist has slackened in his ceaseless pursuit of accumulation and expansion.[13]

Remarks such as these illustrate a failure to come to grips with the reality of contemporary society which may not be directly traceable to the newly found (or at least hopefully sought) access to power and affluence, but which is, neverthe-

29

less, what one would expect in the developing ideology of a new privileged elite.

Various strands of this ideology are drawn together in a recent article by Zbigniew Brzezinski,[14] in which a number of the conceptions and attitudes that appear in recent social thought are summarized—I am tempted to say "parodied." Brzezinski too sees a "profound change" taking place in the intellectual community, as "the largely humanist-oriented, occasionally ideologically-minded intellectual-dissenter, who sees his role largely in terms of proffering social critiques, is rapidly being displaced either by experts and specialists, who become involved in special governmental undertakings, or by the generalists-integrators, who become in effect house-ideologues for those in power, providing overall intellectual integration for disparate actions." He suggests that these "organisation-oriented, application-minded intellectuals" can be expected to introduce broader and more relevant concerns into the political system—though there is, as he notes, a danger that "intellectual detachment and the disinterested search for truth" will come to an end, given the new access of the "application-minded intellectuals" to "power, prestige, and the good life." They are a new meritocratic elite, "taking over American life, utilising the universities, exploiting the latest techniques of communications, harnessing as rapidly as possible the most recent technological devices." Presumably, their civilizing impact is revealed by the great progress that has been made, in this new "historical era" that America alone has already entered, with respect to the problems that confounded the bumbling political leaders of past eras —the problems of the cities, of pollution, of waste and destructiveness, of exploitation and poverty. Under the leadership of this "new breed of politicians-intellectuals," America has become *the* creative society; the others, consciously and unconsciously, are

30

emulative." We see this, for example, in mathematics, the bio-logical sciences, anthropology, philosophy, cinema, music, historical scholarship, and so on, where other cultures, hopelessly outdistanced, merely observe and imitate what America creates. Thus we move towards a new world-wide " 'super-culture,' strongly influenced by American life, with its own universal electronic-computer language," with an enormous and growing "psycho-cultural gap" separating America from the rest of the "developed world."

It is impossible even to imagine what Brzezinski thinks a "universal electronic-computer language" may be, or what cultural values he thinks will be created by the new "technologically dominant and conditioned technetron" who, he apparently believes, may prove to be the true "repository of that indefinable quality we call human." It would hardly be rewarding to try to disentangle Brzezinski's confusions and misunderstandings. What is interesting, rather, is the way his dim awareness of current developments in science and technology is used to provide an ideological justification for the "increasing role in the key decision-making institutions of individuals with special intellectual and scientific attainments," the new "organisation-oriented, application-minded intellectuals" based in the university, "the creative eye of the massive communications complex."

Parallel to the assumption that all is basically well at home is the widely articulated belief that the problems of international society, too, would be subject to intelligent management were it not for the machinations of the Communists. One aspect of this complacence is the belief that the Cold War was entirely the result of Russian (later Chinese) aggressiveness. For example, Daniel Bell has described the origins of the Cold War in the following terms: "When the Russians began stirring up the Greek guerrilla EAM in what had been tacitly acknowledged at

Teheran as a British sphere of influence, the Communists began their cry against Anglo-American imperialism. Following the rejection of the Marshall Plan and the Communist coup in Czechoslovakia in February, 1948, the Cold War was on in earnest."[15] Clearly, this will hardly do as a balanced and objective statement of the origins of the Cold War, but the distortion it reflects is an inherent element in Bell's optimism about the new society, since it enables him to maintain that our Cold War posture is purely reactive, and that once Communist belligerence is tamed, the new technical intelligentsia can turn its attention to the construction of a more decent society.

A related element in the ideology of the liberal intellectual is the firm belief in the fundamental generosity of Western policy towards the Third World. Adam Ulam again provides a typical example: "Problems of an international society undergoing an economic and ideological revolution seem to defy . . . the generosity—granted its qualifications and errors—that has characterized the policy of the leading democratic powers of the West."[16] Even Hans Morgenthau succumbs to this illusion. He summarizes a discussion of intervention with these remarks: "We have intervened in the political, military and economic affairs of other countries to the tune of far in excess of $100 billion, and we are at present involved in a costly and risky war in order to build a nation in South Vietnam. Only the enemies of the United States will question the generosity of these efforts, which have no parallel in history."[17] Whatever one may think about the $100 billion, it is difficult to see why anyone should take seriously the professed "generosity" of our effort to build a nation in South Vietnam, any more than the similar professions of benevolence by our many forerunners in such enterprises. Generosity has never been a commodity in short supply among powers bent on extending their hegemony.

Still another strand in the ideology of the new emerging elite is the concern for order, for maintaining the status quo, which is now seen to be quite favorable and essentially just. An excellent example is the statement by fourteen leading political scientists and historians on United States Asian policy, recently distributed by the Freedom House Public Affairs Institute.[18] These scholars designate themselves as "the moderate segment of the academic community." The designation is accurate; they stand midway between the two varieties of extremism, one which demands that we destroy everyone who stands in our path, the other, that we adopt the principles of international behavior we require of every other world power. The purpose of their statement is to "challenge those among us who, overwhelmed by guilt complexes, find comfort in asserting or implying that we are always wrong, our critics always right, and that only doom lies ahead." They find our record in Asia to be "remarkably good," and applaud our demonstrated ability to rectify mistakes, our "capacity for pragmatism and self-examination," and our "healthy avoidance of narrow nationalism," capacities which distinguish us "among the major societies of this era."

The moderate scholars warn that "to avoid a major war in the Asia-Pacific region, it is essential that the United States continue to deter, restrain, and counterbalance Chinese power." True, "China has exercised great prudence in avoiding a direct confrontation with the United States or the Soviet Union" since the Korean War, and it is likely that China will "continue to substitute words for acts while concentrating upon domestic issues." Still, we cannot be certain of this and must therefore continue our efforts to tame the dragon. One of the gravest problems posed by China is its policy of "isolationist fanaticism" —obviously, a serious threat to peace. Another danger is the

33

terrifying figure of Mao Tse-tung, a romantic, who refuses to accept the "bureaucratism essential to the ordering of this enormously complex, extremely difficult society." The moderate scholars would feel much more at ease with the familiar sort of technical expert, who is committed to the "triumph of bureaucratism" and who refrains from romantic efforts to undermine the party apparatus and the discipline it imposes.

Furthermore, the moderate scholars announce their support for "our basic position" in Vietnam. A Communist victory in Vietnam, they argue, would "gravely jeopardize the possibilities for a political equilibrium in Asia, seriously damage our credibility, deeply affect the morale—and the policies—of our Asian allies and the neutrals." By a "political equilibrium," they do not, of course, refer to the status quo as of 1945–1946 or as outlined by international agreement at Geneva in 1954. They do not explain why the credibility of the United States is more important than the credibility of the indigenous elements in Vietnam who have dedicated themselves to a war of national liberation. Nor do they explain why the morale of the military dictatorships of Thailand and Taiwan must be preserved. They merely hint darkly of the dangers of a third world war, dangers which are real enough and which are increased when advocates of revolutionary change face an external counterrevolutionary force. In principle, such dangers can be lessened by damping revolutionary ardor or by withdrawing the counterrevolutionary force. The latter alternative, however, is unthinkable, irresponsible.

The crucial assumption in the program of the moderate scholars is that we must not encourage "those elements committed to the thesis that violence is the best means of effecting change." It is important to recognize that it is not violence as such to which the moderate scholars object. On the contrary, they approve of our violence in Vietnam, which, as they are well aware, enormously exceeds that of the Vietnamese enemy. To further underline this point, they cite as our greatest triumph in Southeast Asia the "dramatic changes" which have taken place in Indonesia—the most dramatic being the massacre of several hundred thousand people. But this massacre, like our extermination of Vietnamese, is not a use of violence to effect social change and is therefore legitimate. What is more, it may be that those massacred were largely ethnic Chinese and landless peasants, and that the "countercoup" in effect re-established traditional authority more firmly.[19] If so, all the more reason why we should not deplore this use of violence; and in fact, the moderate scholars delicately refrain from alluding to it in their discussion of dramatic changes in Indonesia. We must conclude that when these scholars deplore the use of violence to effect change, it is not the violence but rather steps toward social change that they find truly disturbing. Social change that departs from the course we plot is not to be tolerated. The threat to order is too great.

So great is the importance of stability and order that even reform of the sort that receives American authorization must often be delayed, the moderate scholars emphasize. "Indeed, many types of reform increase instability, however desirable and essential they may be in long-range terms. For people under siege, there is no substitute for security." The reference, needless to say, is not to security from American bombardment, but rather to security from the wrong sorts of political and social change.

The policy recommendations of the moderate scholars are based on their particular ideological bias, namely, that a certain form of stability—not that of North Vietnam or North Korea, but that of Thailand, Taiwan, or the Philippines—is so essential that we must be willing to use our unparalleled means of violence to ensure that it is preserved. It is instructive to see how other mentors of the new mandarins describe the problem of order and reform. Ithiel Pool formulates the central issue as follows:

> In the Congo, in Vietnam, in the Dominican Republic, it is clear that order depends on somehow compelling newly mobilized strata to return to a measure of passivity and defeatism from which they have recently been aroused by the process of modernization. At least temporarily, the maintenance of order requires a lowering of newly acquired aspirations and levels of political activity.[20]

This is what "we have learned in the past thirty years of intensive empirical study of contemporary societies." Pool is merely describing facts, not proposing policy. A corresponding version of the facts is familiar on the domestic scene: workers threaten the public order by striking for their demands, the impatience of the Negro community threatens the stability of the body politic. One can, of course, imagine another way in which order can be preserved in all such cases: namely, by meeting the demands, or at the very least by removing the barriers that have been placed, by force which may be latent and disguised, in the way of attempts to satisfy the "newly acquired aspirations." But this might mean that the wealthy and powerful would have to sacrifice some degree of privilege, and it is therefore excluded as a method for maintenance of order. Such proposals are likely to meet with little sympathy from Pool's new mandarins.

From the doubly privileged position of the American scholar, the transcendent importance of order, stability, and nonviolence (by the oppressed) seems entirely obvious; to others, the matter is not so simple. If we listen, we hear such voices as this, from an economist in India:

> It is disingenuous to invoke "democracy," "due process of law," "non-violence," to rationalise the absence of action. For meaningful concepts under such conditions become meaningless since, in reality, they justify the relentless pervasive exploitation of the masses; at once a denial of democracy and a more sinister form of violence perpetrated on the overwhelming majority through contractual forms.[21]

Moderate American scholarship does not seem capable of comprehending these simple truths.

It would be wrong to leave the impression that the ideology of the liberal intelligentsia translates itself into policy as a rain of cluster bombs and napalm. In fact, the liberal experts have been dismayed by the emphasis on military means in Vietnam and have consistently argued that the key to our efforts should be social restructuring and economic assistance. Correspondingly, I think that we can perceive more clearly the attitudes that are crystallizing among the new mandarins by considering the technical studies of pacification, for example, the research monograph of William Nighswonger, cited earlier (see note 4). The author, now a professor of political science, was senior United States civilian representative of the Agency for International Development in Quang Nam Province from 1962 to 1964. As he sees the situation, "the knotty problems of pacification are intricately intertwined with the issues of political development and they necessitate—at this time in history—intimate American involvement." Thus Americans must ask some "basic questions of value and obligation—questions that transcend the easy legalisms of 'self-determination' and 'nonintervention.'" These easy legalisms have little relevance to a world

37

in which the West is challenged by "the sophisticated methodology and quasi-religious motivation of Communist insurgency." It is our duty, in the interest of democracy and freedom, to apply our expertise to these twin goals: "to isolate the enemy and destroy his influence and control over the rural population, and to win the peasant's willing support through effective local administration and programs of rural improvement." "An underlying assumption is that insurgency ought to be defeated—for the sake of human rights. . . ." Despite the "remarkable achievements in economic and social development" in Russia and China, "The South Vietnamese peasant deserves something better," and we must give it to him—as we have in Latin America and the Philippines—even if this requires abandoning the easy legalisms of the past and intervening with military force.

Of course, it won't be easy. The enemy has enormous advantages. For one thing, "as in China, the insurgents in Vietnam have exploited the Confucian tenets of ethical rule both by their attacks on government corruption and by exemplary Communist behavior"; and "the Viet-Cong inherited, after Geneva, much of the popular support and sympathies previously attached to the Viet-Minh in the South." After the fall of Diem, matters became still worse: ". . . vast regions that had been under government control quickly came under the influence of the Viet-Cong." By late 1964 the pacification of Quang Nam Province had become "all but impossible," and the worst of it is that "the battle for Quang Nam was lost by the government to Viet-Cong forces recruited for the most part from within the province."[22] By 1966, the Vietcong seem so well entrenched in rural areas that "only a highly imaginative and comprehensive counterinsurgency campaign, with nearly perfect execution and substantial military support, would be capable of dislodging such a powerful and extensive insurgent apparatus."

A major difficulty we face is the "progressive social and economic results" shown by the Vietcong efforts. An AID report in March 1965 explains the problem. Comparing "our 'new life hamlets'" to the Vietcong hamlets, the report comments as follows:

> The basic differences are that the VC hamlets are well organized, clean, economically self supporting and have an active defense system. For example, a cottage industry in one hamlet was as large as has been previously witnessed anywhere in Chuong Thien province. New canals are being dug and pineapples are under cultivation. The VC also have a relocation program for younger families. These areas coincide with the areas just outside the planned GVN sphere of interest. Unless the USOM/GVN activities exhibit a more qualitative basis [sic], there is little likelihood of changing the present attitudes of the people. For example, in one area only five kilometers from the province capital, the people refused medical assistance offered by ARVN medics.

However, all is not lost. Even though "the Viet-Cong strength in the countryside has made a 'quantum leap' from its position of early 1962," there is a compensating factor, namely, "the counterinsurgent military capability was revolutionized by substantial American troop inputs." This allows us entirely new options. For example, we can implement more effectively some of the "experiments with population and resources control methods" that were tried by the USOM and the National Police as early as 1961, though with little success. Given the new possibilities for "material and human resources control," we may even recapture some of the population—a serious matter: "Given the enormous numbers of South Vietnamese citizens presently allied with the Viet-Cong (for whatever reason), the recovery of these peasants for the national cause must be made one of the central tasks of the pacification enterprise."

39

If we are going to succeed in implementing "material and human resources control," we must moderate ARVN behavior somehow. Thus, according to an AID report of February 1965, "A high incident rate of stealing, robbing, raping and obtaining free meals in the rural areas has not endeared the population towards ARVN or Regional Forces." Nor did it improve matters when many civilians witnessed a case in which an ARVN company leader killed a draft dodger, disemboweled him, "took his heart and liver out and had them cooked at a restaurant," after which "the heart and liver were eaten by a number of soldiers." Such acts cause great difficulties, especially in trying to combat an enemy so vile as to practice "exemplary Communist behavior."

More generally, "the success of pacification requires that there be survivors to be pacified," and given "the sheer magnitude of American, Korean, Australian and indigenous Vietnamese forces," which has so severely "strained the economic and social equilibrium of the nation," it is sometimes difficult to ensure this minimal condition.

There are other problems, for example, "the difficulty of denying food to the enemy" in the Mekong Delta; "the hunger for land ownership," which, for some curious reason, is never satisfied by our friends in Saigon; the corruption; occasional bombing of the "wrong" village; the pervasive "Viet-Cong infiltration of military and civilian government organization"; the fact that when we relocate peasants to new hamlets, we often leave "the fox still in the henhouse," because of inadequate police methods; and so on.

Still, we have a good "pacification theory," which involves three steps: "elimination of the Viet-Cong by search-and-destroy operations, protection and control of the population and its resources by police and military forces, and preparing and arming the peasants to defend their own communities." If we rarely reach the third stage, this is because we have not yet learned to "share the sense of urgency of the revolutionary cause," or "to nourish these attitudes" among our "Vietnamese associates." Thus *we* understand that the "real revolution" is the one we are implementing, "in contrast to the artificially stimulated and controlled revolution of Diem and the Communists," but we have difficulties in communicating this fact to the Vietnamese peasant or to our "Vietnamese associates." What is needed, clearly, is better training for American officials, and of course, true national dedication to this humanitarian task.

A grave defect in our society, this political scientist argues, is our tendency to avoid "an active American role in the fostering of democratic institutions abroad." The pacification program in Vietnam represents an attempt to meet our responsibility to foster democratic institutions abroad, through rational methods of material and human resources control. Refusal to dedicate ourselves to this task might be described as "a policy more selfish and timid than it was broad and enlightened,"[23] to use the terminology of an earlier day.

When we strip away the terminology of the behavioral sciences, we see revealed, in such work as this, the mentality of the colonial civil servant, persuaded of the benevolence of the mother country and the correctness of its vision of world order, and convinced that he understands the true interests of the backward peoples whose welfare he is to administer. In fact, much of the scholarly work on Southeast Asian affairs reflects precisely this mentality. As an example, consider the August 1967 issue of *Asian Survey,* fully devoted to a Vietnam symposium in which a number of experts contribute their thoughts on the success of our enterprise and how it can be moved forward.

The introductory essay by Samuel Huntington, chairman of the department of government at Harvard, is entitled "Social Science and Vietnam." It emphasizes the need "to develop scholarly study and understanding of Vietnam" if our "involvement" is to succeed, and expresses his judgment that the papers in this volume "demonstrate that issues and topics closely connected to policy can be presented and analyzed in scholarly and objective fashion."

Huntington's own contribution to "scholarly study and understanding of Vietnam" includes an article in the *Boston Globe*, February 17, 1968. Here he describes the "momentous changes in Vietnamese society during the past five years," specifically, the process of urbanization. This process "struck directly at the strength and potential appeal of the Viet Cong." "So long as the overwhelming mass of the people lived in the countryside, the VC could win the war by winning control of those people—and they came very close to doing so in both 1961 and 1964. But the American sponsored urban revolution undercut the VC rural revolution." The refugees fleeing from the rural areas found not only security but also "prosperity and economic well-being." "While wartime urban prosperity hurt some, the mass of the poor people benefited from it."

The sources of urbanization have been described clearly many times, for example, by this American spokesman in Vietnam: "There have been three choices open to the peasantry. One, to stay where they are; two, to move into the areas controlled by us; three, to move off into the interior towards the Vietcong. . . . Our operations have been designed to make the first choice impossible, the second attractive, and to reduce the likelihood of anyone choosing the third to zero."[24] The benefits accruing to the newly urbanized elements have also been amply described in the press, for example, by James Doyle of the

Globe, February 22, 1968: Saigon "is a rich city, the bar owners, B-girls, money changers and black marketeers all making
their fortunes while it lasts. It is a poor city, with hundreds of
thousands of refugees crammed into thatched huts and tin-
roofed shacks, more than two million people shoehorned into 21
square miles." Or Neil Sheehan, in a classic and often-quoted
article (*New York Times,* October 9, 1966):

A drive through Saigon demonstrates another fashion in which
the social system works. Virtually all the new construction consists of luxury apartments, hotels and office buildings financed by
Chinese businessmen or affluent Vietnamese with relatives or
connections within the regime. The buildings are destined to be
rented to Americans. Saigon's workers live, as they always have,
in fetid slums on the city's outskirts. . . . Bars and bordellos,
thousands of young Vietnamese women degrading themselves as
bar girls and prostitutes, gangs of hoodlums and beggars and
children selling their older sisters and picking pockets have become ubiquitous features of urban life.

Many have remarked on the striking difference between the
way in which the press and the visiting scholar describe what
they see in Vietnam. It should occasion no surprise. Each is
pursuing his own craft. The reporter's job is to describe what he
sees before his eyes; many have done so with courage and even
brilliance. The colonial administrator, on the other hand, is concerned to justify what he has done and what he hopes to do,
and—if an "expert" as well—to construct an appropriate ideological cover, to show that we are just and righteous in what we
do, and to put nagging doubts to rest. One sees moral degradation and fetid slums; the other, prosperity and well-being—and
if kindly old Uncle Sam occasionally flicks his ashes on someone
by mistake, that is surely no reason for tantrums.

Returning to the collection of scholarly and objective studies
in *Asian Survey,* the first, by Kenneth Young, president of the

43

Asia Society, describes our difficulties in "transferring innovations and institutions to the Vietnamese" and calls for the assistance of social scientists in overcoming these difficulties. Social
scientists should, he feels, study "the intricacies that effectively
inhibit or transfer what the Americans, either by government
policy or by the technician's action, want to introduce into the
mind of a Vietnamese or into a Vietnamese organization." The
problem, in short, is one of communication. For this objective
scholar, there is no question of our right to "transfer innovations
and institutions to the Vietnamese," by force if necessary, or of
our superior insight into the needed innovations or appropriate
institutions. In just the same way, Lord Cornwallis understood
the necessity of "transferring the institution" of a squirearchy to
India—as any reasonable person could see, this was the only
civilized form of social organization.

The "scholarly objectivity" that Huntington lauds is further
demonstrated in the contribution by Milton Sacks, entitled
"Restructuring Government in South Vietnam." As Sacks per-
ceives the situation, there are two forces in South Vietnam, the
"nationalists" and the "Communists." The "Communists" are the
Vietminh and the NLF; among the "nationalists," he mentions
specifically the VNQDD and the Dai Viet (and the military).
The "nationalists" have a few problems; for example, they
"were manipulated by the French, by the Japanese, by the communists and latterly by the Americans," and "too many of South
Vietnam's leading generals fought with the French against the
Vietnamese people."[25] Our problem is the weakness of the nationalists, although there was some hope during General
Khanh's government, "a most interesting effort because it was a
genuine coalition of representatives of all the major political
groups in South Vietnam." Curiously, this highly representative
government was unable to accept or even to consider "a pro-

posal for what appeared to be an authentic coalition government" coming from the National Liberation Front in mid-1964.[26] According to Douglas Pike, the proposal could not be seriously considered because none of the "non-Communists" in South Vietnam, "with the possible exception of the Buddhists, thought themselves equal in size and power to risk entering into a coalition, fearing that if they did the whale would swallow the minnow." Thus, he continues, "coalition government with a strong NLF could not be sold within South Vietnam," even to the government which, as Sacks informs us, was "a genuine coalition" of "all the major political groups in South Vietnam." Rather, the GVN and its successors continued to insist that the NLF show their sincerity by withdrawing "their armed units and their political cadres from South Vietnamese territory" (March 1, 1965).

According to Sacks, "the problem which presents itself is to devise an institutional arrangement that will tend to counteract the factors and forces which are conducive to that instability" that now plagues Vietnamese political life. This problem, of course, is one that presents itself to *us*. And, Sacks feels, it is well on its way to solution, with the new constitution and the forthcoming (September 1967) elections, which "will provide spokesmen who claim legitimacy through popular mandate and speak with authority on the issues of war and peace for their constituency." Although this "free election . . . will still leave unrepresented those who are fighting under the banner of the South Vietnam National Liberation Front and those whose candidates were not permitted to stand in the elections," we must, after all, understand that no institution in the real world can be perfect. The important thing, according to Sacks, is that for the first time since the fall of Diem, there will be elections that are not seen by the government in power simply "as a means of legitimating the power they already had, using the governmental machinery to underwrite themselves." Putting aside the remarkable naiveté regarding the forthcoming elections, what is striking is the implicit assumption that we have a right to continue our efforts to restructure the South Vietnamese government, in the interests of what we determine to be Vietnamese nationalism. In just the same way, the officers of the Kwantung Army sought to support "genuine Manchurian nationalism," thirty-five years ago.

To understand more fully what is implied by the judgment that we must defend the "nationalists" against the "Communists," we can turn again to Pike's interesting study. The nationalist groups mentioned by Sacks are the VNQDD and the Dai Viet. The former, after its virtual destruction by the French, was revived by the Chinese Nationalists in 1942. "It supported itself through banditry. It executed traitors with a great deal of publicity, and its violent acts in general were carefully conceived for their psychological value." Returning to Vietnam "with the occupying Chinese forces following World War II," it "was of some importance until mid-1946, when it was purged by the Vietminh." "The VNQDD never was a mass political party in the Western sense. At its peak of influence it numbered, by estimates of its own leaders, less than 1,500 persons. Nor was it ever particularly strong in either Central or South Vietnam. It had no formal structure and held no conventions or assemblies." As to the Dai Viet, "Dai Viet membership included leading Vietnamese figures and governmental officials who viewed Japan as a suitable model for Vietnam [N. B. fascist Japan]. The organization never made any particular obeisance either to democracy or to the rank-and-file Vietnamese. It probably never numbered more than 1,000 members and did not consider itself a mass-based organization. It turned away from

46

Western liberalism, although its economic orientation was basically socialist, in favor of authoritarianism and blind obedience." During World War II, "it was at all times strongly pro-Japanese."

In contrast to these genuine nationalists, we have the Vietminh, whose "war was anticolonial, clearly nationalistic, and concerned *all* Vietnamese," and the NLF, which regarded the rural Vietnamese not "simply as a pawn in a power struggle but as the active element in the thrust," which "maintained that its contest with the GVN and the United States should be fought out at a political level and that the use of massed military might was in itself illegitimate," until forced by the Americans and the GVN "to use counterforce to survive." In its internal documents as well as its public pronouncements the NLF insisted, from its earliest days, that its goal must be to "set up a democratic national coalition administration in South Vietnam; realize independence, democratic freedoms, and improvement of the people's living conditions; safeguard peace; and achieve national reunification on the basis of independence and democracy." "Aside from the NLF there has never been a truly mass-based political party in South Vietnam." It organized "the rural population through the instrument of self-control—victory by means of the organizational weapon," setting up a variety of self-help "functional liberation associations" based on "associational discipline" coupled with "the right of freedom of discussion and secret vote at association meetings," and generating "a sense of community, first, by developing a pattern of political thought and behavior appropriate to the social problems of the rural Vietnamese village in the midst of sharp social change and, second, by providing a basis for group action that allowed the individual villager to see that his own efforts could have meaning and effect" (obviously, a skilled and treacherous

47

enemy). This was, of course, prior to "the advent of massive American aid, and the GVN's strategic hamlet program." With the American takeover of the war, the emphasis shifted to military rather than political action, and ultimately, North Vietnamese involvement and perhaps control; "beginning in 1965, large numbers of regular army troops from North Vietnam were sent into South Vietnam."

In short, what we see is a contrast between the Dai Viet and VNQDD, representing South Vietnamese nationalism, and the NLF, an extrinsic alien force. One must bear in mind that Sacks would undoubtedly accept Pike's factual description as accurate, but, like Pike, would regard it as demonstrating nothing, since we are the ultimate arbiters of what counts as "genuine Vietnamese nationalism."

An interesting counterpoint to Sacks's exposition of nationalist versus Communist forces is provided in David Wurfel's careful analysis, in the same issue of *Asian Survey,* of the "Saigon political elite." He argues that "this elite has not substantially changed its character in the last few years" (i.e., since 1962), though there may be a few modifications: "Formerly, only among the great landlords were there those who held significant amounts of both political and economic power; grandiose corruption may have allowed others to attain that distinction in recent years." Continuing, "the military men in post-Diem cabinets all served under Bao Dai and the French in a civil or military capacity." Under the French, "those who felt most comfortable about entering the civil service were those whose families were already part of the bureaucratic-intellectual elite. By the early 1950's they saw radicalism, in the form of the Viet Minh, as a threat to their own position. The present political elite is the legacy of these developments." Although, he observes, things might change, "the South Vietnamese cabinets and perhaps most of the rest of the political elite have been constituted by a highly westernized intelligentsia. Though the people of South Vietnam seem to be in a revolutionary mood, this elite is hardly revolutionary." The NLF constitutes a "counter-elite," less Westernized: of the NLF Central Committee members, "only 3 out of 27 report studying in France."

The problem of "restructuring government" is further analyzed by Ithiel Pool, along lines that parallel Sacks's contribution to this collection of "scholarly, objective studies." He begins by formulating a general proposition: "I rule out of consideration here a large range of viable political settlements," namely, those that involve "the inclusion of the Viet Cong in a coalition government or even the persistence of the Viet Cong as a legal organization in South Vietnam." Such arrangements "are not acceptable"—to us, that is. The only acceptable settlement is one "imposed by the GVN despite the persisting great political power of the Viet Cong."

There is, of course, a certain difficulty: ". . . the Viet Cong is too strong to be simply beaten or suppressed." It follows, then, that we must provide inducements to the Vietcong activists to join our enterprise. This should not prove too difficult, he feels. The Vietcong leadership consists basically of bureaucratic types who are on the make. Cognitive dissonance theory suggests that this "discontented leadership" has "the potential for making a total break when the going gets too rough." We must therefore provide them with "a political rationalization for changing sides." The problem is ideological. We must induce a change in the "image of reality" of the Vietcong cadres, replacing their "naive ideology," which sees the GVN as "American puppets and supporters of exploiters, the tax collectors, the merchants, the big landlords, the police, and the evil men in the villages," by a more realistic conception. We can do this by emphasizing

49

hamlet home rule and preventing the use of military forces to collect rents, a suggestion which will be greeted with enthusiasm in Saigon, no doubt. The opportunity to serve as functionaries for a central government which pursues such policies will attract the Vietcong cadres and thus solve our problem, that of excluding from the political process the organization that contains the effective political leaders.

Others have expressed a rather different evaluation of the human quality and motivation of these cadres. For example, Joseph Buttinger contrasts the inability of the Diem regime to mobilize support with the success of the NLF: ". . . that people willing to serve their country were to be found in Vietnam no one could doubt. The Vietminh had been able to enlist them by the tens of thousands and to extract from them superhuman efforts and sacrifices in the struggle for independence."[27] Military reports by the dozens relate the amazing heroism and dedication of the guerrillas. Throughout history, however, colonial administrators have had their difficulties in comprehending or coming to grips with this phenomenon.

In the course of his analysis of our dilemma in Vietnam, Pool explains some of the aspects of our culture that make it difficult for us to understand such matters clearly. We live in "a guilt culture in which there is a tradition of belief in equality." For such reasons, we find it hard to understand the true nature of Vietcong land redistribution, which is primarily "a patronage operation" in which "dissatisfied peasants band together in a gang to despoil their neighbors" and "then reward the deserving members of the cabal."

This terminology recalls Franz Borkenau's description of the "streak of moral indifference" in the history of Russian revolutionism, which permitted such atrocities as the willingness "to 'expropriate,' by means of robbery, the individual property of individual bourgeois."[28] Our side, in contrast, adheres to the "tradition of belief in equality" when we implement land reform. For example, the *New York Times,* December 26, 1967, reports a recent conference of experts studying the "Taiwan success in land reform," one of the real success stories of American intervention. "The Government reimbursed the former landlords in part (30 per cent) with shares of four large public enterprises taken over from the Japanese. The remainder was paid in bonds. . . . Many speakers at the conference singled out the repayment as the shrewdest feature of the Taiwan program. It not only treated the landlords fairly, they said, but it also redirected the landlords' energies and capital towards industry," thus advancing the "wholesale restructuring of society" in the only healthy and humane direction.

In a side remark, Pool states that "in lay public debates now going on one often hears comments to the effect that Vietnamese communism, because it is anti-Chinese, would be like Yugoslav communism." It would, of course, be ridiculous to argue such a causal connection, and, in fact, I have never heard it proposed in "lay public debate" or anywhere else. Rather, what has been maintained by such laymen as Hans Morgenthau, General James Gavin, and others is that Vietnamese Communism is likely to be Titoist, in the sense that it will strive for independence from Chinese domination. Thus they reject the claim that by attacking Vietnamese Communism we are somehow "containing Chinese Communism"—a claim implied, for example, in the statement of the "Citizens Committee for Peace with Freedom in Vietnam," in which Ithiel Pool, Milton Sacks, and others, speaking for "the understanding, independent and responsible men and women who have consistently opposed rewarding international aggressors from Adolf Hitler to Mao Tse-tung," warn that if we "abandon Vietnam," then

"Peking and Hanoi, flushed with success, [will] continue their expansionist policy through many other 'wars of liberation.' " By misstating the reference to Titoist tendencies, Pool avoids the difficulty of explaining how an anti-Chinese North Vietnam is serving as the agent of Hitlerian aggression from Peking; by referring to "lay public debate," he hopes, I presume, to disguise the failure of argument by a claim to expertise.

Returning again to the *Asian Survey* Vietnam symposium, the most significant contribution is surely Edward Mitchell's discussion of his RAND Corporation study on "the significance of land tenure in the Vietnamese insurgency." In a study of twenty-six provinces, Mitchell has discovered a significant correlation between "inequality of land tenure" and "extent of Government [read: American] control." In brief, "greater inequality implies greater control." "Provinces seem to be more secure when the percentage of owner-operated land is low (tenancy is high); inequality in the distribution of farms by size is great; large, formerly French-owned estates are present; and no land redistribution has taken place." To explain this phenomenon, Mitchell turns to history and behavioral psychology. As he notes, "in a number of historical cases it has been the better-to-do peasant who has revolted, while his poorer brothers actively supported or passively accepted the existing order." The "behavioral explanation" lies "in the relative docility of poorer peasants and the firm authority of landlords in the more 'feudal' areas . . . the landlord can exercise considerable influence over his tenant's behavior and readily discourage conduct inconsistent with his own interests."

In an interview with the *New York Times* (October 15, 1967), Mitchell adds an additional explanation for the fact that the most secure areas are those that remain "essentially feudal in social structure": when the feudal structure is eliminated, "there's a vacuum and that is ideal for the Vietcong because they've got an organization to fill the vacuum." This observation points to a difficulty that has always plagued the American effort. As Joseph Buttinger points out, the Diem regime too was unable to experiment with "freely constituted organizations" because these "would have been captured by the Vietminh."[29]

Mitchell's informative study supports an approach to counterinsurgency that has been expressed by Roger Hilsman, who explains that in his view, modernization "cannot help much in a counterguerrilla program," because it "inevitably uproots established social systems [and] produces political and economic dislocation and tension." He therefore feels that popularity of governments, reform, and modernization may be "important ingredients," but that their role in counterinsurgency "must be measured more in terms of their contributions to physical security."[30]

Before leaving this symposium on social science and Vietnam, we should take note of the scholarly detachment that permits one *not* to make certain comments or draw certain conclusions. For example, John Bennett discusses the important matter of "geographic and job mobility": "Under the dual impact of improved opportunities elsewhere and deteriorating security at home, people are willing to move to a hitherto unbelievable extent." No further comment on this "willingness," which provides such interesting new opportunities for the restructuring of Vietnamese society. John Donnell discusses the unusual success of pacification in Binh Dinh Province, particularly in the areas controlled by the Koreans, who "have tended to run their own show with their own methods and sometimes have not allowed the RD teams sent from Saigon all the operational leeway desired," and who have been "extremely impressive in eliminating NLF influence." Again, no comment is given on these methods, amply reported in the press,[31] or on the significance of the fact that Koreans are eliminating NLF influence from Vietnamese villages, and not allowing the Vietnamese government cadres the leeway desired.

Mitchell draws no policy conclusions from his study, but others have seen the point: recall the remarks of the moderate scholars on the dangers of social reform. Other scholars have carried the analysis much further. For example, Charles Wolf, senior economist of the RAND Corporation, discusses the matter in a recent book.[32] Wolf considers two "theoretical models" for analyzing insurgency problems. The first is the approach of the hearts-and-minds school of counterinsurgency, which emphasizes the importance of popular support. Wolf agrees that it is no doubt "a desirable goal" to win "popular allegiance to a government that is combating an insurgent movement," but this objective, he argues, is not appropriate "as a conceptual framework for counterinsurgency programs." His alternative approach has as its "unifying theme" the concept of "influencing *behavior*, rather than attitudes." Thus, "confiscation of chickens, razing of houses, or destruction of villages have a place in counterinsurgency efforts, but only if they are done for a strong reason: namely, to penalize those who have assisted the insurgents. . . . whatever harshness is meted out by government forces [must be] unambiguously recognizable as deliberately imposed because of behavior by the population that contributes to the insurgent movement." Furthermore, it must be noted that "policies that would increase rural income by raising food prices, or projects that would increase agricultural productivity through distribution of fertilizer or livestock, may be of negative value during an insurgency . . . since they may actually facilitate guerrilla operations by increasing the availability of inputs that the guerrillas need." More generally: "In setting up economic and social improvement programs, the crucial point is to connect such programs with the kind of population behavior the government wants to promote." The principle is to reward the villages that cooperate and to provide penalties for the behavior that the government is trying to discourage. "At a broad, conceptual level, the main concern of counterinsurgency efforts should be to influence the behavior of the population rather than their loyalties and attitudes"; "the primary consideration should be whether the proposed measure is likely to increase the cost and difficulties of insurgent operations and help to disrupt the insurgent organization, rather than whether it wins popular loyalty and support, or whether it contributes to a more productive, efficient, or equitable use of resources."

Other scholars have elaborated on the advantages of Wolf's "alternative approach," which concerns itself with control of behavior rather than the mystique of popular support. For example, Morton H. Halperin, of the Harvard Center for International Affairs, writes that in Vietnam, the United States "has been able to prevent any large-scale Vietcong victories, regardless of the loyalties of the people." Thus we have an empirical demonstration of a certain principle of behavioral science, as Halperin notes:

> The events in Vietnam also illustrate the fact that most people tend to be motivated, not by abstract appeals, but rather by their perception of the course of action that is most likely to lead to their own personal security and to the satisfaction of their economic, social, and psychological desires. Thus, for example, large-scale American bombing in South Vietnam may have antagonized a number of people; but at the same time it demonstrated to these people that the Vietcong could not guarantee their security as it had been able to do before the bombing and that the belief in an imminent victory for the Vietcong might turn out to be dangerously false.[33]

55

In short, along with "confiscation of chickens, razing of houses, or destruction of villages," we can also make effective use of 100 pounds of explosives per person, 12 tons per square mile, as in Vietnam, as a technique for controlling behavior, relying on the principle, now once again confirmed by experiment, that satisfaction of desires is a more important motivation in human behavior than abstract appeals to loyalty. Surely this is extremely sane advice. It would, for example, be absurd to try to control the behavior of a rat by winning its loyalty rather than by the proper scheduling of reinforcement.

An added advantage of this new, more scientific approach is that it will "modify the attitudes with which *counter*insurgency efforts are viewed in the United States"[34] (when we turn to the United States, of course, we are concerned with people whose attitudes must be taken into account, not merely their behavior). It will help us overcome one of the main defects in the American character, the "emotional reaction" that leads us to side with "crusaders for the common man" and against a "ruthless, exploitative tyrant" ("that there may be reality as well as appearance in this role-casting is not the point"). This sentimentality "frequently interferes with a realistic assessment of alternatives, and inclines us instead toward a carping righteousness in our relations with the beleaguered government we are ostensibly supporting"; it may be overcome by concentration on control of behavior rather than modification of attitudes or the winning of hearts and minds. Hence the new approach to counterinsurgency should not only be effective in extending the control of American-approved governments, but it may also have a beneficial effect on us. The possibilities are awe-inspiring. Perhaps in this way we can even escape the confines of our "guilt culture in which there is a tradition of belief in equality."

It is extremely important, Wolf would claim, that we develop a rational understanding of insurgency, for "insurgency is probably the most likely type of politico-military threat in the third world, and surely one of the most complex and challenging problems facing United States policies and programs." The primary objective of American foreign policy in the Third World must be "the *denial* of communist control," specifically, the support of countries that are defending their "independence from external and internal communist domination." The latter problem, defending independence from internal Communist domination, is the crucial problem, particularly in Latin America. We must counter the threat by a policy of promoting economic growth and modernization (making sure, however, to avoid the risks inherent in these processes—cf. Mitchell), combined with "a responsible use of force." No question is raised about the appropriateness of our use of force in a country threatened by insurgency. The justification, were the question raised, is inherent in the assumption that we live "in a world in which loss of national independence is often synonymous with communist control, and communism is implicitly considered to be irreversible." Thus, by Orwellian logic, we are actually defending national independence when we intervene with military force to protect a ruling elite from internal insurgency.[35]

Perhaps the most interesting aspect of scholarly work such as this is the way in which behavioral-science rhetoric is used to lend a vague aura of respectability. One might construct some such chain of associations as this. Science, as everyone knows, is responsible, moderate, unsentimental, and otherwise good. Behavioral science tells us that we can be concerned only with behavior and control of behavior. Therefore we *should* be concerned only with behavior and control of behavior;[36] and it is responsible, moderate, unsentimental, and otherwise good to control behavior by appropriately applied reward and punish-

57

ment. Concern for loyalties and attitudes is emotional and un-scientific. As rational men, believers in the scientific ethic, we should be concerned with manipulating behavior in a desir-able direction, and not be deluded by mystical notions of freedom, individual needs, or popular will.

Let me make it clear that I am not criticizing the behavioral sciences because they lend themselves to such perversion. On other grounds, the "behavioral persuasion" seems to me to lack merit; it seriously mistakes the method of science and imposes pointless methodological strictures on the study of man and society, but this is another matter entirely. It is, however, fair to inquire to what extent the popularity of this approach is based on its demonstrated achievements, and to what extent its appeal is based on the ease with which it can be refashioned as a new coercive ideology with a faintly scientific tone. (In passing, I think it is worth mention that the same questions can be raised outside of politics, specifically, in connection with education and therapy.)

The assumption that the colonial power is benevolent and has the interests of the natives at heart is as old as imperialism itself. Thus the liberal Herman Merivale, lecturing at Oxford in 1840, lauded the "British policy of colonial enlightenment" which "stands in contrast to that of our ancestors," who cared little "about the internal government of their colonies, and kept them in subjection in order to derive certain supposed commer-cial advantages from them," whereas we "give them commercial advantages, and tax ourselves for their benefit, in order to give them an interest in remaining under our supremacy, that we may have the pleasure of governing them."[37] And our own John Hay in 1898 outlined "a partnership in beneficence" which would bring freedom and civilization to Cuba, Hawaii, and the Philippines, just as the Pax Britannica had brought these benefits to India, Egypt, and South Africa.[38] But although the benevolence of imperialism is a familiar refrain, the idea that the issue of benevolence is irrelevant, an improper, sentimental consideration, is something of an innovation in imperialist rhetoric, a contribution of the sort one might perhaps expect from "the new mandarins" whose claim to power is based on knowledge and technique.

Going a step beyond, notice how perverse is the entire discussion of the "conceptual framework" for counterinsurgency. The idea that we must choose between the method of "winning hearts and minds" and the method of shaping behavior presumes that we have the right to choose at all. This is to grant us a right that we would surely accord to no other world power. Yet the overwhelming body of American scholarship accords us this right. For example, William Henderson, formerly associate executive director and Far Eastern specialist for the Council on Foreign Relations, proposes that we must "prosecute a constructive, manipulative diplomacy" in order to deal with "internal subversion, particularly in the form of Communist-instigated guerrilla warfare or insurgency"—"internal aggression," as he calls it, in accordance with contemporary usage.[39] Our "historic tasks," he proclaims, are "nothing less than to assist purposefully and constructively in the processes of modern nation building in Southeast Asia, to deflect the course of a fundamental revolution into channels compatible with the long range interests of the United States." It is understood that true "nation building" is that path of development compatible with our interests; hence there is no difficulty in pursuing these historic tasks in concert. There are, however, two real stumbling-blocks in the way of the required manipulative diplomacy. The first is "a great psychological barrier." We must learn to abandon "old dogma" and pursue a "new diplomacy" that is "frankly interventionist," recognizing "that it goes counter to all the traditional conventions of diplomatic usage." Some may ask whether "we have the moral right to interfere in the properly autonomous affairs of others," but Henderson feels that the Communist threat fully justifies such interference and urges that we be ready to "use our 'special forces' when the next bell rings," with no moral qualms or hesitation. The second barrier is that "our knowledge is pitifully inadequate." He therefore calls on the academic community, which will be only too willing to oblige, to supply "the body of expertise and the corps of specialists," the knowledge, the practitioners, and the teachers, to enable us to conduct such a "resourceful diplomacy" more effectively.

Turning to the liberal wing, we find that Roger Hilsman has a rather similar message in his study of the diplomacy of the Kennedy administration, *To Move a Nation*. He informs us that the most divisive issue among the "hardheaded and pragmatic liberals" of the Kennedy team was how the United States should deal with the problem of "modern guerrilla warfare, as the Communists practice it." The problem is that this "is *internal* war, an ambiguous aggression that avoids direct and open attack violating international frontiers" (italics his). Apparently, the hardheaded and pragmatic liberals were never divided on the issue of our right to violate international frontiers in reacting to such "internal war." As a prime example of the "kind of critical, searching analysis" that the new, liberal, revitalized State Department was trying to encourage, Hilsman cites a study directed to showing how the United States might have acted more effectively to overthrow the Mossadegh government in Iran. Allen Dulles was "fundamentally right," according to Hilsman, in judging that Mossadegh in Iran (like Arbenz in Guatemala) had come to power (to be sure, "through the usual processes of government") with "the intention of creating a Communist state"—a most amazing statement on the part of the State Department chief of intelligence; and Dulles was fundamentally right in urging support from the United States "to loyal anti-Communist elements" in Iran and Guatemala to meet the danger, even though "no invitation was extended by the *government* in power," obviously. Hilsman expresses the liberal view succinctly in the distinction he draws between the Iranian subversion and the blundering attempt at the Bay of Pigs: "It is one thing . . . to help the Shah's supporters in Iran in their struggle against Mossadegh and his Communist allies, but it is something else again to sponsor a thousand-man invasion against Castro's Cuba, where there was no effective internal opposition." The former effort was admirable; the latter, bound to fail, "is something else again" from the point of view of pragmatic liberalism.

In Vietnam liberal interventionism was not properly conducted, and the situation got out of hand. We learn more about the character of this approach to international affairs by studying a more successful instance. Thailand is a case in point, and a useful perspective on liberal American ideology is given by the careful and informative work of Frank C. Darling, a Kennedy liberal who was a CIA analyst for Southeast Asia and is now chairman of the political science department at DePauw University.[40]

The facts relevant to this discussion, as Darling outlines them, are briefly as follows. At the end of World War II the former British minister, Sir Josiah Crosby, warned that unless the power of the Thai armed forces was reduced, "the establishment of a constitutional government would be doomed and the return of a military dictatorship would be inevitable." American policy in the postwar period was to support and strengthen the armed forces and the police, and Crosby's prediction was borne out.

There were incipient steps towards constitutional government in the immediate postwar period. However, a series of military coups established Phibun Songkhram, who had collaborated with the Japanese during the war, as premier in 1948, aborting these early efforts. The American reaction to the liberal governments had been ambiguous and "temporizing." In contrast, Phibun was immediately recognized by the United States. Why? "Within this increasingly turbulent region Thailand was the only nation that did not have a Communist insurrection within its borders and it was the only country that remained relatively stable and calm. As the United States considered measures to deter Communist aggression in Southeast Asia, a conservative and anti-Communist regime in Thailand became increasingly attractive regardless of its internal policies or methods of achieving power." Phibun got the point. In August 1949, "he stated that foreign pressure had become 'alarming' and that internal Communist activity had 'vigorously increased.'" In 1950, Truman approved a $10 million grant for military aid.

The new rulers made use of the substantial American military aid to convert the political system into "a more powerful and ruthless form of authoritarianism," and to develop an extensive system of corruption, nepotism, and profiteering that helped maintain the loyalty of their followers. At the same time, "American corporations moved in, purchasing large quantities of rubber and tin . . . shipments of raw materials now went directly to the United States instead of through Hong Kong and Singapore."[41] By 1958, "the United States purchased 90 per cent of Thailand's rubber and most of its tin." American investment, however, remained low, because of the political instability as well as "the problems caused by more extensive public ownership and economic planning." To improve matters, the Sarit dictatorship (see below) introduced tax benefits and guarantees against nationalization and competition from government-owned commercial enterprises, and finally banned trade with China and abolished all monopolies, government or private, "in an attempt to attract private foreign capital."

American influence gave "material and moral support" to the Phibun dictatorship and "discouraged the political opposition." It strengthened the executive power and "encouraged the military leaders to take even stronger measures in suppressing local opposition, using the excuse that all anti-government activity was Communist-inspired." In 1954, Pridi Phanomyong, a liberal intellectual who had been the major participant in the overthrow of the absolute monarchy in 1932, had led the Free Thai underground during the war, and had been elected in 1946 when Thai democracy reached "an all-time high," appeared in Communist China; the United States was supporting Phibun, "who had been an ally of the Japanese, while Pridi, who had courageously assisted the OSS, was in Peking cooperating with the Chinese Communists." This was "ironic."

It is difficult to imagine what sort of development towards a constitutional, parliamentary system might have taken place had it not been for American-supported subversion. The liberals were extremely weak in any event, in particular because of the domination of the economy by Western and Chinese enterprises linked with the corrupt governmental bureaucracy. The Coup Group that had overthrown the government "was composed almost entirely of commoners, many of whom had come from the peasantry or low-ranking military and civil service families," and who now wanted their share in corruption and authoritarian control. The opposition "Democrats" were, for the most part, "members of the royal family or conservative landowners who wanted to preserve their role in the government and their personal wealth." Whatever opportunities might have existed for the development of some more equitable society disappeared once the American presence became dominant, however. Surely any Thai liberal reformer must have been aware of this by 1950, in the wake of the coups, the farcical rigged elections, the murder and torture of leaders of the Free Thai anti-Japanese underground, the takeover by the military of the political and much of the commercial system—particularly when he listened to the words of American Ambassador Stanton as he signed a new aid agreement: "The American people fully support this program of aid to Thailand because of their deep interest in the Thai people whose devotion to the ideals of freedom and liberty and wholehearted support of the UN have won the admiration of the American people."

"A notable trend throughout this period was the growing intimacy between the Thai military leaders and the top-level military officials from the United States," who helped them obtain "large-scale foreign aid which in turn bolstered their political power." The head of the American military mission, Colonel Charles Sheldon, stated that Thailand was "threatened by armed aggression by people who do not believe in democracy, who do not believe in freedom or the dignity of the individual man as do the people of Thailand and my country." Adlai Stevenson, in 1953, warned the Thai leaders "that their country was the real target of the Vietminh," and expressed his hope that they "fully appreciate the threat." Meanwhile, United States assistance had built a powerful army and supplied the police with tanks, artillery, armored cars, an air force, naval patrol vessels, and a training school for paratroopers. The police achieved one of the highest ratios of policemen to citizens in the world—about 1 to 400. The police chief meanwhile relied on "his monopoly of the opium trade and his extensive commercial enterprises for the income he needed to support his personal political machine," while the army chief "received an enormous income from the national lottery."

It was later discovered that the chief of police had committed indescribable atrocities; "the extent of the torture and murder committed by the former police chief will probably never be known." What is known is what came to light after Sarit, the army chief, took power in a new coup in 1957. Sarit "stressed the need to maintain a stable government and intensify the suppression of local Communists to 'ensure continued American trust, confidence and aid.'" The Americans were naturally gratified, and the official reaction was very favorable. When Sarit died in 1963 it was discovered that his personal fortune reached perhaps $137 million. Both Darling and Roger Hilsman refer to him as a "benevolent" dictator, perhaps because he "realized that Communism could not be stopped solely by mass arrests, firing squads, or threats of brutal punishment, and launched a development project in the Northeast regions," along with various other mild reforms—without, however, ceasing the former practices, which he felt might "impress the Americans again with the need for more military and economic aid to prevent 'Communist' subversion." He also imposed rigid censorship, abolished trade organizations and labor unions and punished suspected "Communists" without mercy, and, as noted earlier, took various steps to attract foreign investment.

By 1960, "twelve percent of American foreign aid to Thailand since the beginning of the cold war had been devoted to economic and social advancement." The effect of the American aid was clear. "The vast material and diplomatic support provided to the military leaders by the United States helped to prevent the emergence of any competing groups who might check the trend toward absolute political rule and lead the country *back* to a more modern form of government" (italics mine). In fiscal 1963, the Kennedy administration tried to obtain from Congress $50 million in military aid for Thailand, perhaps to commemorate these achievements. The Kennedy administration brought "good intentions and well-founded policy proposals," but otherwise "made no significant modifications in the military-oriented policy in Thailand."

These excerpts give a fair picture of the American impact on Thailand, as it emerges from Darling's account. Naturally, he is not too happy about it. He is disturbed that American influence frustrated the moves towards constitutional democracy and contributed to an autocratic rule responsible for atrocities that sometimes "rivaled those of the Nazis and the Communists." He is also disturbed by our failure to achieve real control (in his terms, "security and stability") through these measures. Thus when Sarit took power in the 1957 coup, "the Americans had no assurance that he would not orient a new regime towards radical economic and social programs as Castro, for example, has done in Cuba. . . . At stake was an investment of about $300 million in military equipment and a gradually expanding economic base which could have been used against American interests in Southeast Asia had it fallen into unfriendly hands." Fortunately, these dire consequences did not ensue, and in place of radical economic and social programs there was merely a continuation of the same old terror and corruption. The danger was real, however.

What conclusions does Darling draw from this record? As he sees it,[42] there are four major alternatives for American foreign policy.

The first would be to "abolish its military program and withdraw American troops from the country." This, however, would be "irrational," because throughout the non-Communist world "respect for American patience and tolerance in dealing with nondemocratic governments would decline"; furthermore, "Thailand's security and economic progress would be jeopardized." To the pragmatic liberal, it is clear that confidence in our commitment to military dictatorships such as that in Thailand must be maintained, as in fact was implied by the moderate scholars' document discussed earlier; and it would surely be unfortunate to endanger the prospects for further development along the lines that were initiated in such a promising way under American influence, and that are now secured by some 40,000 American troops.

A second alternative would be neutralization of Thailand and other nations in Southeast Asia. This also is irrational. For one thing, "the withdrawal of the American military presence would not be matched by the removal of any Communist forces"—there being no nonindigenous Communist forces—and therefore we would gain nothing by this strategy. Furthermore, we could never be certain that there would not be "infiltration of Communist insurgents in the future." And finally, "the Thai leaders have decided to cooperate with the United States," for reasons that are hardly obscure.

A third alternative would be to use our power in Thailand to "push political and economic reforms." But this policy alternative would "do great damage to American strategy in Thailand and other non-Communist nations." And what is more, "extensive interference in the domestic affairs of other nations, no matter how well intentioned, is contrary to American traditions," as our postwar record in Thailand clearly demonstrates.[43]

Therefore, we must turn to the fourth alternative, and maintain our present policy. "This alternative is probably the most rational and realistic. The military policy can be enhanced if it is realized that only American military power is capable of preventing large-scale overt aggression in Southeast Asia, and the proper role for the Thai armed forces is to be prepared to cope with limited guerrilla warfare."

This exposition of United States policy in Thailand and the directions it should take conforms rather well to the general lines of pragmatic liberalism as drawn by Hilsman, among others. It also indicates clearly the hope that we offer today to the countries on the fringes of Asia. Vietnam may be an aberration. Our impact on Thailand, however, can hardly be attributed to the politics of inadvertence.

An interesting sidelight is Darling's explanation in *Thailand and the United States* of how, in an earlier period, "the Western concept of the rule of law" was disseminated through American influence. "Evidence that some officials were obtaining an understanding of the rule of law was revealed" by the statement of a Thai minister who pointed out that "it is essential to the prosperity of a nation that it should have fixed laws, and that nobles should be restrained from oppressing the people, otherwise the latter were like chickens, who instead of being kept for their eggs, were killed off." In its international behavior as well, the Thai government came to understand the necessity for the rule of law: "A growing respect for law was also revealed in the adherence of the Thai government to the unequal restrictions contained in the treaties with the Western nations in spite of the heavy burden they imposed on the finances of the kingdom." This is all said without irony. In fact, the examples clarify nicely what the "rule of law" means to weak nations, and to the exploited in any society.

Darling, Hilsman, and many others whom I have been discussing represent the moderate liberal wing of scholarship on international affairs. It may be useful to sample some of the other views that appear in American scholarship. Consider, for example, the proposals of Thomas R. Adam, professor of political science at New York University.[44]

Adam begins by outlining an "ideal solution" to American problems in the Pacific, towards which we should bend our efforts. The ideal solution would have the United States recognized as "the responsible military protagonist of all Western interests in the area" with a predominant voice in a unified Western policy. United States sovereignty over some territorial base in the area would give us "ideal conditions for extending power over adjoining regions." Such a base would permit the formation of a regional organization, under our dominance, that would make possible "direct intervention in Korea, Vietnam, Laos and Cambodia" without the onus of unilateral intervention ("in the face of brazen communist aggression, it is not the fact of intervention as such that constitutes the issue but rather its unilateral character").

We must understand that for the preservation of Western interests, there is no reasonable alternative to the construction of such a base of power in territories over which we possess direct sovereignty. We cannot maintain the "historic connection" between Asia and the West unless we participate in Asian affairs "through the exercise of power and influence." We must accept "the fact that we are engaged in a serious struggle for cultural survival that involves that continuous presence of Western-oriented communities" in Asia. It is an illusion to believe that we can retreat from Asia and leave it to its own devices, for our own Western culture must be understood as "a minority movement of recent date in the evolution of civilization," and it cannot be taken for granted that Asia will remain

69

"incapable of intervening in our affairs." Thus to defend ourselves, we must intervene with force in the affairs of Asia. If we fail to establish "our industrial enterprise system" universally, we will have to "defend our privileges and gains by means of the continuing, brutalizing, and costly exercise of superior force in every corner of the globe."

Why are we justified in forceful intervention in the affairs of Asia? "One obvious justification for United States intervention in Asian affairs lies in our leadership of the world struggle against communism. Communist political and economic infiltration among a majority of the world's peoples appears to American political leadership to be fatal to our safety and progress; this attitude is supported almost unanimously by public opinion." Pursuing this logic a few steps further, we will soon have the same "obvious justification" for taking out China with nuclear weapons—and perhaps France as well, for good measure.

Further justification is that the defense of our western seaboard "requires that the North Pacific be controlled as a virtual American lake," a fact which "provides one basis for United States intervention in power struggles throughout the region," to preserve the security of this *mare nostrum*. Our "victory over Japan left a power vacuum in Southeast Asia and the Far East that was tempting to communist aggression; therefore, we had to step in and use our military power." "Island possessions, such as Guam, those of the strategic trust territories, and probably Okinawa, remain indispensable, if not to the narrow defense of our shores, certainly to the military posture essential to our total security and world aims."[45] Apart from the magnificent scope of this vision, rarely equaled by our forerunners, the terminology is not unfamiliar.

There are, to be sure, certain restraints that we must observe as we design our policy of establishing an "operational base" for exercise of power in the Far East; specifically, "policy must rest on political and social objectives that are acceptable to, or capable of being imposed upon, all participating elements." Obviously, it would not be pragmatic to insist upon policies that are not capable of being imposed upon the participating elements in our new dominions.

These proposals are buttressed with a brief sketch of the consequences of Western dominion in the past, for example, the "Indian success story," in which "enterprise capital proved a useful incentive to fruitful social change in the subcontinent of India and its environs," a development flawed only by the passivity shown by "traditional Asian social systems" as they imitated "the industrial ideology of their colonial tutor." An important lesson to us is the success of the "neutral Pax Britannica" in imposing order, so that "commerce could flourish and its fruits compensate for vanished liberties."

Adam spares us the observation that the ungrateful natives sometimes fail to appreciate these centuries of solicitude. Thus to a left-wing member of the Congress party in India: "The story is that the British, in the process of their domination over India, kept no limits to brutality and savagery which man is capable of practicing. Hitler's depredations, his Dachaus and Belsens . . . pale into insignificance before this imperialist savagery. . . ."[46] Such a reaction to centuries of selfless and tender care might cause some surprise, until we realize that it is probably only an expression of the enormous guilt felt by the beneficiary of these attentions.

A generation ago, there were other political leaders who feared the effect of Communist gains on their safety and progress, and who, with the almost unanimous support of public opinion, set out to improve the world through forceful intervention—filling power vacuums, establishing territorial bases essential to their total security and world aims, imposing political and social objectives on participating elements. Professor Adam has little to tell us that is new.

II

The examples of counterrevolutionary subordination that I have so far cited have for the most part been drawn from political science and the study of international, particularly Asian, affairs—rather dismal branches of American scholarship, by and large, and so closely identified with American imperial goals that one is hardly astonished to discover the widespread abandonment of civilized norms. In opening this discussion, however, I referred to a far more general issue. If it is plausible that ideology will in general serve as a mask for self-interest, then it is a natural presumption that intellectuals, in interpreting history or formulating policy, will tend to adopt an elitist position, condemning popular movements and mass participation in decision making, and emphasizing rather the necessity for supervision by those who possess the knowledge and understanding that is required (so they claim) to manage society and control social change. This is hardly a novel thought. One major element in the anarchist critique of Marxism a century ago was the prediction that, as Bakunin formulated it:

According to the theory of Mr. Marx, the people not only must not destroy [the state] but must strengthen it and place it at the complete disposal of their benefactors, guardians, and teachers— the leaders of the Communist party, namely Mr. Marx and his friends, who will proceed to liberate [mankind] in their own way. They will concentrate the reins of government in a strong hand, because the ignorant people require an exceedingly firm guardianship; they will establish a single state bank, concentrating in its hands all commercial, industrial, agricultural and even scientific production, and then divide the masses into two armies —industrial and agricultural—under the direct command of the state engineers, who will constitute a new privileged scientific-political estate.[47]

One cannot fail to be struck by the parallel between this prediction and that of Daniel Bell, cited earlier—the prediction that in the new postindustrial society, "not only the best talents, but eventually the entire complex of social prestige and social status, will be rooted in the intellectual and scientific communities."[48] Pursuing the parallel for a moment, it might be asked whether the left-wing critique of Leninist elitism can be applied, under very different conditions, to the liberal ideology of the intellectual elite that aspires to a dominant role in managing the welfare state.

Rosa Luxemburg, in 1918, argued that Bolshevik elitism would lead to a state of society in which the bureaucracy alone would remain an active element in social life—though now it would be the "red bureaucracy" of that State Socialism that Bakunin had long before described as "the most vile and terrible lie that our century has created."[49] A true social revolution requires a "spiritual transformation in the masses degraded by centuries of bourgeois class rule";[50] "it is only by extirpating the habits of obedience and servility to the last root that the working class can acquire the understanding of a new form of discipline, self-discipline arising from free consent."[51] Writing in 1904, she predicted that Lenin's organizational concepts would "enslave a young labor movement to an intellectual elite hungry for power . . . and turn it into an automaton manipulated by a Central Committee."[52] In the Bolshevik elitist doctrine of 1918 she saw a disparagement of the creative, spontaneous, self-correcting force of mass action, which alone, she

73

argued, could solve the thousand problems of social reconstruction and produce the spiritual transformation that is the essence of a true social revolution. As Bolshevik practice hardened into dogma, the fear of popular initiative and spontaneous mass action, not under the direction and control of the properly designated vanguard, became a dominant element of so-called "Communist" ideology.

Antagonism to mass movements and to social change that escapes the control of privileged elites is also a prominent feature of contemporary liberal ideology.[53] Expressed as foreign policy, it takes the form described earlier. To conclude this discussion of counterrevolutionary subordination, I would like to investigate how, in one rather crucial case, this particular bias in American liberal ideology can be detected even in the interpretation of events of the past in which American involvement was rather slight, and in historical work of very high caliber.

In 1966, the American Historical Association gave its biennial award for the most outstanding work on European history to Gabriel Jackson, for his study of Spain in the 1930s.[54] There is no question that of the dozens of books on this period, Jackson's is among the best, and I do not doubt that the award was well deserved. The Spanish Civil War is one of the crucial events of modern history, and one of the most extensively studied as well. In it, we find the interplay of forces and ideas that have dominated European history since the industrial revolution. What is more, the relationship of Spain to the great powers was in many respects like that of the countries of what is now called the Third World. In some ways, then, the events of the Spanish Civil War give a foretaste of what the future may hold, as Third World revolutions uproot traditional societies, threaten imperial dominance, exacerbate great-power rivalries, and bring the world perilously close to a war which, if not averted, will surely be the final catastrophe of modern history. My reason for wanting to investigate an outstanding liberal analysis of the Spanish Civil War is therefore twofold: first, because of the intrinsic interest of these events; and second, because of the insight that this analysis may provide with respect to the underlying elitist bias which I believe to be at the root of the phenomenon of counter-revolutionary subordination.

In his study of the Spanish Republic, Jackson makes no attempt to hide his own commitment in favor of liberal democracy, as represented by such figures as Azaña, Casares Quiroga, Martínez Barrio,[55] and the other "responsible national leaders." In taking this position, he speaks for much of liberal scholarship; it is fair to say that figures similar to those just mentioned would be supported by American liberals, were this possible, in Latin America, Asia, or Africa. Furthermore, Jackson makes little attempt to disguise his antipathy towards the forces of popular revolution in Spain, or their goals.

It is no criticism of Jackson's study that his point of view and sympathies are expressed with such clarity. On the contrary, the value of this work as an interpretation of historical events is enhanced by the fact that the author's commitments are made so clear and explicit. But I think it can be shown that Jackson's account of the popular revolution that took place in Spain is misleading and in part quite unfair, and that the failure of objectivity it reveals is highly significant in that it is characteristic of the attitude taken by liberal (and Communist) intellectuals towards revolutionary movements that are largely spontaneous and only loosely organized, while rooted in deeply felt needs and ideals of dispossessed masses. It is a convention of scholarship that the use of such terms as those of the preceding phrase demonstrates naiveté and muddle-headed sentimentality. The convention, however, is supported by ideological conviction rather than history or investigation of the phenomena of social life. This conviction is, I think, belied by such events as the revolution that swept over much of Spain in the summer of 1936.

The circumstances of Spain in the 1930s are not duplicated elsewhere in the underdeveloped world today, to be sure. Nevertheless, the limited information that we have about popular movements in Asia, specifically, suggests certain similar features that deserve much more serious and sympathetic study than they have so far received.[56] Inadequate information makes it hazardous to try to develop any such parallel, but I think it is quite possible to note long-standing tendencies in the response of liberal as well as Communist intellectuals to such mass movements.

As I have already remarked, the Spanish Civil War is not only one of the critical events of modern history but one of the most intensively studied as well. Yet there are surprising gaps. During the months following the Franco insurrection in July 1936, a social revolution of unprecedented scope took place throughout much of Spain. It had no "revolutionary vanguard" and appears to have been largely spontaneous, involving masses of urban and rural laborers in a radical transformation of social and economic conditions that persisted, with remarkable success, until it was crushed by force. This predominantly anarchist revolution and the massive social transformation to which it gave rise are treated, in recent historical studies, as a kind of aberration, a nuisance that stood in the way of successful prosecution of the war to save the bourgeois regime from the Franco rebellion. Many historians would probably agree with Eric Hobsbawm[57] that the *failure* of social revolution in Spain "was due to the anarchists," that anarchism was "a disaster," a kind of "moral gymnastics" with no "concrete results," at best "a profoundly moving spectacle for the student of popular religion." The most extensive historical study of the anarchist revolution[58] is relatively inaccessible, and neither its author, now living in southern France, nor the many refugees who will never write memoirs but who might provide invaluable personal testimony have been consulted, apparently, by writers of the major historical works.[59] The one published collection of documents dealing with collectivization[60] has been published only by an anarchist press and hence is barely accessible to the general reader, and has also rarely been consulted—it does not, for example, appear in Jackson's bibliography, though Jackson's account is intended to be a social and political, not merely a military, history. In fact, this astonishing social upheaval seems to have largely passed from memory. The drama and pathos of the Spanish Civil War have by no means faded; witness the impact a few years ago of the film *To Die in Madrid*. Yet in this film (as Daniel Guérin points out) one finds no reference to the popular revolution that had transformed much of Spanish society.

I will be concerned here with the events of 1936–1937,[61] and with one particular aspect of the complex struggle involving Franco Nationalists, Republicans (including the Communist party), anarchists, and socialist workers' groups. The Franco insurrection in July 1936 came against a background of several months of strikes, expropriations, and battles between peasants and Civil Guards. The left-wing Socialist leader Largo Caballero had demanded in June that the workers be armed, but was refused by Azaña. When the coup came, the Republican government was paralyzed. Workers armed themselves in Madrid and Barcelona, robbing government armories and even ships in the harbor, and put down the insurrection while the government vacillated, torn between the twin dangers of submitting to

Franco and arming the working classes. In large areas of Spain effective authority passed into the hands of the anarchist and socialist workers who had played a substantial, generally dominant role in putting down the insurrection.

The next few months have frequently been described as a period of "dual power." In Barcelona industry and commerce were largely collectivized, and a wave of collectivization spread through rural areas, as well as towns and villages, in Aragon, Castile, and the Levant, and to a lesser but still significant extent in many parts of Catalonia, Asturias, Estremadura, and Andalusia. Military power was exercised by defense committees; social and economic organization took many forms, following in main outlines the program of the Saragossa Congress of the anarchist CNT in May 1936. The revolution was "apolitical," in the sense that its organs of power and administration remained separate from the central Republican government and, even after several anarchist leaders entered the government in the autumn of 1936, continued to function fairly independently until the revolution was finally crushed between the fascist and Communist-led Republican forces. The success of collectivization of industry and commerce in Barcelona impressed even highly unsympathetic observers such as Borkenau. The scale of rural collectivization is indicated by these data from anarchist sources: in Aragon, 450 collectives with half a million members; in the Levant, 900 collectives accounting for about half the agricultural production and 70 percent of marketing in this, the richest agricultural region of Spain; in Castile, 300 collectives with about 100,000 members.[62] In Catalonia, the bourgeois government headed by Companys retained nominal authority, but real power was in the hands of the anarchist-dominated committees.

The period of July through September may be characterized

as one of spontaneous, widespread, but unconsummated social revolution.[63] A number of anarchist leaders joined the government; the reason, as stated by Federica Montseny on January 3, 1937, was this: ". . . the anarchists have entered the government to prevent the Revolution from deviating and in order to carry it further beyond the war, and also to oppose any dictatorial tendency, from wherever it might come."[64] The central government fell increasingly under Communist control—in Catalonia, under the control of the Communist-dominated PSUC—largely as a result of the valuable Russian military assistance. Communist success was greatest in the rich farming areas of the Levant (the government moved to Valencia, capital of one of the provinces), where prosperous farm owners flocked to the Peasant Federation that the party had organized to protect the wealthy farmers; this federation "served as a powerful instrument in checking the rural collectivization promoted by the agricultural workers of the province."[65] Elsewhere as well, counterrevolutionary successes reflected increasing Communist dominance of the Republic.

The first phase of the counterrevolution was the legalization and regulation of those accomplishments of the revolution that appeared irreversible. A decree of October 7 by the Communist Minister of Agriculture, Vicente Uribe, legalized certain expropriations—namely, of lands belonging to participants in the Franco revolt. Of course, these expropriations had already taken place, a fact that did not prevent the Communist press from describing the decree as "the most profoundly revolutionary measure that has been taken since the military uprising."[66] In fact, by exempting the estates of landowners who had not directly participated in the Franco rebellion, the decree represented a step backward, from the standpoint of the revolutionaries, and it was criticized not only by the CNT but also by the Socialist Federation of Land Workers, affiliated with the UGT. The demand for a much broader decree was unacceptable to the Communist-led ministry, since the Communist party was "seeking support among the propertied classes in the anti-Franco coup" and hence "could not afford to repel the small and medium proprietors who had been hostile to the working class movement before the civil war."[67] These "small proprietors," in fact, seem to have included owners of substantial estates. The decree compelled tenants to continue paying rent unless the landowners had supported Franco, and by guaranteeing former landholdings, it prevented distribution of land to the village poor. Ricardo Zabalza, general secretary of the Federation of Land Workers, described the resulting situation as one of "galling injustice"; "the sycophants of the former political bosses still enjoy a privileged position at the expense of those persons who were unable to rent even the smallest parcel of land, because they were revolutionaries."[68]

To complete the stage of legalization and restriction of what had already been achieved, a decree of October 24, 1936, promulgated by a CNT member who had become Councilor for Economy in the Catalonian Generalitat, gave legal sanction to the collectivization of industry in Catalonia. In this case too, the step was regressive, from the revolutionary point of view. Collectivization was limited to enterprises employing more than a hundred workers, and a variety of conditions were established that removed control from the workers' committees to the state bureaucracy.[69]

The second stage of the counterrevolution, from October 1936 through May 1937, involved the destruction of the local committees, the replacement of the militia by a conventional army, and the re-establishment of the prerevolutionary social and economic system, wherever this was possible. Finally, in

May 1937, came a direct attack on the working class in Barcelona (the May Days).[70] Following the success of this attack, the process of liquidation of the revolution was completed. The collectivization decree of October 24 was rescinded and industries were "freed" from workers' control. Communist-led armies swept through Aragon, destroying many collectives and dismantling their organizations and, generally, bringing the area under the control of the central government. Throughout the Republican-held territories, the government, now under Communist domination, acted in accordance with the plan announced in *Pravda* on December 17, 1936: "So far as Catalonia is concerned, the cleaning up of Trotzkyist and Anarcho-Syndicalist elements there has already begun, and it will be carried out there with the same energy as in the U.S.S.R."[71]—and, we may add, in much the same manner.

In brief, the period from the summer of 1936 to 1937 was one of revolution and counterrevolution: the revolution was largely spontaneous with mass participation of anarchist and socialist industrial and agricultural workers; the counterrevolution was under Communist direction, the Communist party increasingly coming to represent the right wing of the Republic. During this period and after the success of the counterrevolution, the Republic was waging a war against the Franco insurrection; this has been described in great detail in numerous publications, and I will say little about it here. The Communist-led counterrevolutionary struggle must, of course, be understood against the background of the ongoing antifascist war and the more general attempt of the Soviet Union to construct a broad antifascist alliance with the Western democracies. One reason for the vigorous counterrevolutionary policy of the Communists was their belief that England would never tolerate a revolutionary triumph in Spain, where England had substantial commercial interests, as did France and to a lesser extent the United States.[72] I will return to this matter below. However, I think it is important to bear in mind that there were undoubtedly other factors as well. Rudolf Rocker's comments are, I believe, quite to the point:

> . . . the Spanish people have been engaged in a desperate struggle against a pitiless foe and have been exposed besides to the secret intrigues of the great imperialist powers of Europe. Despite this the Spanish revolutionaries have not grasped at the disastrous expedient of dictatorship, but have respected all honest convictions. Everyone who visited Barcelona after the July battles, whether friend or foe of the C.N.T., was surprised at the freedom of public life and the absence of any arrangements for suppressing the free expression of opinion.
>
> For two decades the supporters of Bolshevism have been hammering it into the masses that dictatorship is a vital necessity for the defense of the so-called proletarian interests against the assaults of the counter-revolution and for paving the way for Socialism. They have not advanced the cause of Socialism by this propaganda, but have merely smoothed the way for Fascism in Italy, Germany and Austria by causing millions of people to forget that dictatorship, the most extreme form of tyranny, can never lead to social liberation. In Russia, the so-called dictatorship of the proletariat has not led to Socialism, but to the domination of a new bureaucracy over the proletariat and the whole people. . . .
>
> What the Russian autocrats and their supporters fear most is that the success of libertarian Socialism in Spain might prove to their blind followers that the much vaunted "necessity of a dictatorship" is nothing but one vast fraud which in Russia has led to the despotism of Stalin and is to serve today in Spain to help the counter-revolution to a victory over the revolution of the workers and peasants.[73]

After decades of anti-Communist indoctrination, it is difficult to achieve a perspective that makes possible a serious evalua-

tion of the extent to which Bolshevism and Western liberalism
have been united in their opposition to popular revolution.
However, I do not think that one can comprehend the events in
Spain without attaining this perspective.

With this brief sketch—partisan, but I think accurate—for
background, I would like to turn to Jackson's account of this
aspect of the Spanish Civil War (see note 54).

Jackson presumes (p. 259) that Soviet support for the Republican cause in Spain was guided by two factors: first, concern
for Soviet security; second, the hope that a Republican victory
would advance "the cause of worldwide 'people's revolution'
with which Soviet leaders hoped to identify themselves." They
did not press their revolutionary aims, he feels, because "for the
moment it was essential not to frighten the middle classes or the
Western governments."

As to the concern for Soviet security, Jackson is no doubt
correct. It is clear that Soviet support of the Republic was one
aspect of the attempt to make common cause with the Western
democracies against the fascist threat. However, Jackson's conception of the Soviet Union as a revolutionary power—hopeful
that a Republican victory would advance "the interrupted
movement toward world revolution" and seeking to identify itself with "the cause of the world-wide 'people's revolution'"
—seems to me entirely mistaken. Jackson presents no evidence
to support this interpretation of Soviet policy, nor do I know of
any. It is interesting to see how differently the events were
interpreted at the time of the Spanish Civil War, not only by
anarchists like Rocker but also by such commentators as Gerald
Brenan and Franz Borkenau, who were intimately acquainted
with the situation in Spain. Brenan observes that the counterrevolutionary policy of the Communists (which he thinks was
"extremely sensible") was

the policy most suited to the Communists themselves. Russia is a totalitarian regime ruled by a bureaucracy: the frame of mind of its leaders, who have come through the most terrible upheaval in history, is cynical and opportunist: the whole fabric of the state is dogmatic and authoritarian. To expect such men to lead a social revolution in a country like Spain, where the wildest idealism is combined with great independence of character, was out of the question. The Russians could, it is true, command plenty of idealism among their foreign admirers, but they could only harness it to the creation of a cast-iron bureaucratic state, where everyone thinks alike and obeys the orders of the chief above him.[74]

He sees nothing in Russian conduct in Spain to indicate any interest in a "people's revolution." Rather, the Communist policy was to oppose "even such rural and industrial collectives as had risen spontaneously and flood the country with police who, like the Russian Ogpu, acted on the orders of their party rather than those of the Ministry of the Interior." The Communists were concerned to suppress altogether the impulses towards "spontaneity of speech or action," since "their whole nature and history made them distrust the local and spontaneous and put their faith in order, discipline and bureaucratic uniformity" —hence placed them in opposition to the revolutionary forces in Spain. As Brenan also notes, the Russians withdrew their support once it became clear that the British would not be swayed from the policy of appeasement, a fact which gives additional confirmation to the thesis that only considerations of Russian foreign policy led the Soviet Union to support the Republic.

Borkenau's analysis is similar. He approves of the Communist policy, because of its "efficiency," but he points out that the Communists "put an end to revolutionary social activity, and enforced their view that this ought not to be a revolution but simply the defence of a legal government. . . . communist policy in Spain was mainly dictated not by the necessities of the Spanish fight but by the interests of the intervening foreign power, Russia," a country "with a revolutionary past, not a revolutionary present." The Communists acted "not with the aim of transforming chaotic enthusiasm into disciplined enthusiasm [which Borkenau feels to have been necessary], but with the aim of substituting disciplined military and administrative action for the action of the masses and getting rid of the latter entirely." This policy, he points out, went "directly against the interests and claims of the masses" and thus weakened popular support. The now apathetic masses would not commit themselves to the defense of a Communist-run dictatorship, which restored former authority and even "showed a definite preference for the police forces of the old regime, so hated by the masses." It seems to me that the record strongly supports this interpretation of Communist policy and its effects, though Borkenau's assumption that Communist "efficiency" was necessary to win the anti-Franco struggle is much more dubious—a question to which I return below.[75]

It is relevant to observe, at this point, that a number of the Spanish Communist leaders were reluctantly forced to similar conclusions. Bolloten cites several examples,[76] specifically, the military commander "El Campesino" and Jesús Hernández, a minister in the Caballero government. The former, after his escape from the Soviet Union in 1949, stated that he had taken for granted the "revolutionary solidarity" of the Soviet Union during the Civil War—a most remarkable degree of innocence —and realized only later "that the Kremlin does not serve the interests of the peoples of the world, but makes them serve its own interests; that, with a treachery and hypocrisy without parallel, it makes use of the international working class as a mere pawn in its political intrigues." Hernández, in a speech given shortly after the Civil War, admits that the Spanish Communist leaders "acted more like Soviet subjects than sons of the Spanish people." "It may seem absurd, incredible," he adds, "but our education under Soviet tutelage had deformed us to such an extent that we were completely denationalized; our national soul was torn out of us and replaced by a rabidly chauvinistic internationalism, which began and ended with the towers of the Kremlin."

Shortly after the Third World Congress of the Communist International in 1921, the Dutch "ultra-leftist" Hermann Gorter wrote that the congress "has decided the fate of the world revolution for the present. The trend of opinion that seriously desired world revolution . . . has been expelled from the Russian International. The Communist Parties in western Europe and throughout the world that retain their membership of the Russian International will become nothing more than a means to preserve the Russian Revolution and the Soviet Republic."[77] This forecast has proved quite accurate. Jackson's conception that the Soviet Union was a revolutionary power in the late 1930s, or even that the Soviet leaders truly regarded themselves as identified with world revolution, is without factual support. It is a misinterpretation that runs parallel to the American Cold War mythology that has invented an "international Communist conspiracy" directed from Moscow (now Peking) to justify its own interventionist policies.

Turning to events in revolutionary Spain, Jackson describes the first stages of collectivization as follows: the unions in Madrid, "as in Barcelona and Valencia, abused their sudden authority to place the sign *incautado* [placed under workers' control] on all manner of buildings and vehicles" (p. 279).

Why was this an *abuse* of authority? This Jackson does not explain. The choice of words indicates a reluctance on Jackson's part to recognize the reality of the revolutionary situation, despite his account of the breakdown of Republican authority. The statement that the workers "abused their sudden authority" by carrying out collectivization rests on a moral judgment that recalls that of Ithiel Pool, when he characterizes land reform in Vietnam as a matter of "despoiling one's neighbors," or of Franz Borkenau, when he speaks of expropriation in the Soviet Union as "robbery," demonstrating "a streak of moral indifference."

Within a few months, Jackson informs us, "the revolutionary tide began to ebb in Catalonia" after "accumulating food and supply problems, and the experience of administering villages, frontier posts, and public utilities, had rapidly shown the anarchists the unsuspected complexity of modern society" (pp. 313–14). In Barcelona, "the naïve optimism of the revolutionary conquests of the previous August had given way to feelings of resentment and of somehow having been cheated," as the cost of living doubled, bread was in short supply, and police brutality reached the levels of the monarchy. "The POUM and the anarchist press simultaneously extolled the collectivizations and explained the failures of production as due to Valencia policies of boycotting the Catalan economy and favoring the *bourgeoisie*. They explained the loss of Málaga as due in large measure to the low morale and the disorientation of the Andalusian proletariat, which saw the Valencia government evolving steadily toward the right" (p. 368). Jackson evidently believes that this left-wing interpretation of events was nonsensical, and that in fact it was anarchist incompetence or treachery that was responsible for the difficulties: "In Catalonia, the CNT factory committees dragged their heels on war production, claiming

87

that the government deprived them of raw materials and was favoring the *bourgeoisie*" (p. 365).

In fact, "the revolutionary tide began to ebb in Catalonia" under a middle-class attack led by the Communist party, not because of a recognition of the "complexity of modern society." And it was, moreover, quite true that the Communist-dominated central government attempted, with much success, to hamper collectivized industry and agriculture and to disrupt the collectivization of commerce. I have already referred to the early stages of counterrevolution. Further investigation of the sources to which Jackson refers and others shows that the anarchist charges were not baseless, as Jackson implies. Bolloten cites a good deal of evidence in support of his conclusion that

> In the countryside the Communists undertook a spirited defence of the small and medium proprietor and tenant farmer against the collectivizing drive of the rural wage-workers, against the policy of the labour unions prohibiting the farmer from holding more land than he could cultivate with his own hands, and against the practices of revolutionary committees, which requisitioned harvests, interfered with private trade, and collected rents from tenant farmers.[78]

The policy of the government was clearly enunciated by the Communist Minister of Agriculture: "We say that the property of the small farmer is sacred and that those who attack or attempt to attack this property must be regarded as enemies of the regime."[79] Gerald Brenan, no sympathizer with collectivization, explains the failure of collectivization as follows (p. 321):

> The Central Government, and especially the Communist and Socialist members of it, desired to bring [the collectives] under the direct control of the State: they therefore failed to provide them with the credit required for buying raw materials: as soon as the supply of raw cotton was exhausted the mills stopped

working. . . . even [the munitions industry in Catalonia] were harassed by the new bureaucratic organs of the Ministry of Supply.[80]

He quotes the bourgeois President of Catalonia, Companys, as saying that "workers in the arms factories in Barcelona had been working 56 hours and more each week and that no cases of sabotage or indiscipline had taken place," until the workers were demoralized by the bureaucratization—later, militarization—imposed by the central government and the Communist party.[81] His own conclusion is that "the Valencia Government was now using the P.S.U.C. against the C.N.T.—but not . . . because the Catalan workers were giving trouble, but because the Communists wished to weaken them before destroying them."

The cited correspondence from Companys to Prieto, according to Vernon Richards (p. 47), presents evidence showing the success of Catalonian war industry under collectivization and demonstrating how "much more could have been achieved had the means for expanding the industry not been denied them by the Central Government." Richards also cites testimony by a spokesman for the subsecretariat of munitions and armament of the Valencia government admitting that "the war industry of Catalonia had produced ten times more than the rest of Spanish industry put together and [agreeing] . . . that this output could have been quadrupled as from beginning of September* if Catalonia had had access to the necessary means for purchasing raw materials that were unobtainable in Spanish territory." It is important to recall that the central government had enormous gold reserves (soon to be transmitted to the Soviet Union), so that raw materials for Catalan industry could probably have

---

* The quoted testimony is from September 1, 1937; presumably, the reference is to September 1936.

been purchased, despite the hostility of the Western democracies to the Republic during the revolutionary period (see below). Furthermore, raw materials had repeatedly been requested. On September 24, 1936, Juan Fabregas, the CNT delegate to the Economic Council of Catalonia who was in part responsible for the collectivization decree cited earlier, reported that the financial difficulties of Catalonia were created by the refusal of the central government to "give any assistance in economic and financial questions, presumably because it has little sympathy with the work of a practical order which is being carried out in Catalonia"[82]—that is, collectivization. He "went on to recount that a Commission which went to Madrid to ask for credits to purchase war materials and raw materials, offering 1,000 million pesetas in securities lodged in the Bank of Spain, met with a blank refusal. It was sufficient that the new war industry in Catalonia was controlled by the workers of the C.N.T. for the Madrid Government to refuse any unconditional aid. Only in exchange for government control would they give financial assistance."[83]

Broué and Témime take a rather similar position. Commenting on the charge of "incompetence" leveled against the collectivized industries, they point out that "one must not neglect the terrible burden of the war." Despite this burden, they observe, "new techniques of management and elimination of dividends had permitted a lowering of prices" and "mechanisation and rationalization, introduced in numerous enterprises . . . had considerably augmented production. The workers accepted the enormous sacrifices with enthusiasm because, in most cases, they had the conviction that the factory belonged to them and that at last they were working for themselves and their class brothers. A truly new spirit had come over the economy of Spain with the concentration of scattered enterprises, the simplification of commercial patterns, a significant structure of social projects for aged workers, children, disabled, sick and the personnel in general" (pp. 150–51). The great weakness of the revolution, they argue, was the fact that it was not carried through to completion. In part this was because of the war; in part, a consequence of the policies of the central government. They too emphasize the refusal of the Madrid government, in the early stages of collectivization, to grant credits or supply funds to collectivized industry or agriculture—in the case of Catalonia, even when substantial guarantees were offered by the Catalonian government. Thus the collectivized enterprises were forced to exist on what assets had been seized at the time of the revolution. The control of gold and credit "permitted the government to restrict and prevent the function of collective enterprises at will" (p. 144).

According to Broué and Témime, it was the restriction of credit that finally destroyed collectivized industry. The Companys government in Catalonia refused to create a bank for industry and credit, as demanded by the CNT and POUM, and the central government (relying, in this case, on control of the banks by the socialist UGT) was able to control the flow of capital and "to reserve credit for private enterprise." All attempts to obtain credit for collectivized industry were unsuccessful, they maintain, and "the movement of collectivization was restricted, then halted, the government remaining in control of industry through the medium of the banks . . . [and later] through its control of the choice of managers and directors," who often turned out to be the former owners and managers, under new titles. The situation was similar in the case of collectivized agriculture (pp. 204 f.).

The situation was duly recognized in the West. The *New York Times*, in February 1938, observed: "The principle of

State intervention and control of business and industry, as against workers' control of them in the guise of collectivization, is gradually being established in loyalist Spain by a series of decrees now appearing. Coincidentally there is to be established the principle of private ownership and the rights of corporations and companies to what is lawfully theirs under the Constitution."[84]

Morrow cites (pp. 64–65) a series of acts by the Catalonian government restricting collectivization, once power had shifted away from the new institutions set up by the workers' revolution of July 1936. On February 3, the collectivization of the dairy trade was declared illegal.[85] In April, "the Generalidad annulled workers' control over the customs by refusing to certify workers' ownership of material that had been exported and was being tied up in foreign courts by suits of former owners; henceforth the factories and agricultural collectives exporting goods were at the mercy of the government." In May, as has already been noted, the collectivization decree of October 24 was rescinded, with the argument that the decree "was dictated without competency by the Generalidad," because "there was not, nor is there yet, legislation of the [Spanish] state to apply" and "article 44 of the Constitution declares expropriation and socialization are functions of the State." A decree of August 28 "gave the government the right to intervene in or take over any mining or metallurgical plant." The anarchist newspaper *Solidaridad Obrera* reported in October a decision of the department of purchases of the Ministry of Defense that it would make contracts for purchases only with enterprises functioning "on the basis of their old owners" or "under the corresponding intervention controlled by the Ministry of Finance and Economy."[86]

Returning to Jackson's statement that "In Catalonia, the CNT factory committees dragged their heels on war production, claiming that the government deprived them of raw materials and was favoring the *bourgeoisie*," I believe one must conclude that this statement is more an expression of Jackson's bias in favor of capitalist democracy than a description of the historical facts. At the very least, we can say this much: Jackson presents no evidence to support his conclusion; there is a factual basis for questioning it. I have cited a number of sources that the liberal historian would regard, quite correctly, as biased in favor of the revolution. My point is that the failure of objectivity, the deep-seated bias of liberal historians, is a matter much less normally taken for granted, and that there are good grounds for supposing that this failure of objectivity has seriously distorted the judgments that are rather brashly handed down about the nature of the Spanish revolution.

Continuing with the analysis of Jackson's judgments, unsupported by any cited evidence, consider his remark, quoted above, that in Barcelona "the naïve optimism of the revolutionary conquests of the previous August had given way to feelings of resentment and of somehow having been cheated." It is a fact that by January 1937 there was great disaffection in Barcelona. But was this simply a consequence of "the unsuspected complexity of modern society"? Looking into the matter a bit more closely, we see a rather different picture. Under Russian pressure, the PSUC was given substantial control of the Catalonian government, "putting into the Food Ministry [in December 1936] the man most to the Right in present Catalan politics, Comorera"[87]—by virtue of his political views, the most willing collaborator with the general Communist party position. According to Jackson, Comorera "immediately took steps to end barter and requisitioning, and became a defender of the peasants against the revolution" (p. 314); he "ended requisition,

93

restored money payments, and protected the Catalan peasants against further collectivization" (p. 361). This is all that Jackson has to say about Juan Comorera.

We learn more from other sources: for example, Borkenau, who was in Barcelona for the second time in January 1937—and is universally recognized as a highly knowledgeable and expert observer, with strong anti-anarchist sentiments. According to Borkenau, Comorera represented "a political attitude which can best be compared with that of the extreme right wing of the German social-democracy. He had always regarded the fight against anarchism as the chief aim of socialist policy in Spain. . . . To his surprise, he found unexpected allies for his dislike [of anarchist policies] in the communists."[88] It was impossible to reverse collectivization of industry at that stage in the process of counterrevolution; Comorera did succeed, however, in abolishing the system by which the provisioning of Barcelona had been organized, namely, the village committees, mostly under CNT influence, which had cooperated (perhaps, Borkenau suggests, unwillingly) in delivering flour to the towns. Continuing, Borkenau describes the situation as follows:

> . . . Comorera, starting from those principles of abstract liberalism which no administration has followed during the war, but of which right-wing socialists are the last and most religious admirers, did not substitute for the chaotic bread committees a centralized administration. He restored private commerce in bread, simply and completely. There was, in January, not even a system of rationing in Barcelona. Workers were simply left to get their bread, with wages which had hardly changed since May, at increased prices, as well as they could. In practice it meant that the women had to form queues from four o'clock in the morning onwards. The resentment in the working-class districts was naturally acute, the more so as the scarcity of bread rapidly increased after Comorera had taken office.[89]

In short, the workers of Barcelona were not merely giving way to "feelings of resentment and of somehow having been cheated" when they learned of "the unsuspected complexity of modern society." Rather, they had good reason to believe that they *were* being cheated, by the old dog with the new collar.

George Orwell's observations are also highly relevant:

Everyone who has made two visits, at intervals of months, to Barcelona during the war has remarked upon the extraordinary changes that took place in it. And curiously enough, whether they went there first in August and again in January, or, like myself, first in December and again in April, the thing they said was always the same: that the revolutionary atmosphere had vanished. No doubt to anyone who had been there in August, when the blood was scarcely dry in the streets and militia were quartered in the small hotels, Barcelona in December would have seemed bourgeois; to me, fresh from England, it was liker to a workers' city than anything I had conceived possible. Now [in April] the tide had rolled back. Once again it was an ordinary city, a little pinched and chipped by war, but with no outward sign of working-class predominance. . . . Fat prosperous men, elegant women, and sleek cars were everywhere. . . . The officers of the new Popular Army, a type that had scarcely existed when I left Barcelona, swarmed in surprising numbers . . . [wearing] an elegant khaki uniform with a tight waist, like a British Army officer's uniform, only a little more so. I do not suppose that more than one in twenty of them had yet been to the front, but all of them had automatic pistols strapped to their belts; we, at the front, could not get pistols for love or money. . . .* A deep change had come over the town. There were two facts that were the keynote of all else. One was that the people—the civil population—had lost much of their interest in the war; the other was that the normal division of society into rich and poor, upper class and lower class, was reasserting itself.[90]

* Orwell had just returned from the Aragon front, where he had been serving with the POUM militia in an area heavily dominated by left-wing (POUM and anarchist) troops.

Whereas Jackson attributes the ebbing of the revolutionary tide to the discovery of the unsuspected complexity of modern society, Orwell's firsthand observations, like those of Borkenau, suggest a far simpler explanation. What calls for explanation is not the disaffection of the workers of Barcelona but the curious constructions of the historian.

Let me repeat, at this point, Jackson's comments regarding Juan Comorera: Comorera "immediately took steps to end barter and requisitioning, and became a defender of the peasants against the revolution"; he "ended requisitions, restored money payments, and protected the Catalan peasants against further collectivization." These comments imply that the peasantry of Catalonia was, as a body, opposed to the revolution and that Comorera put a stop to the collectivization that they feared. Jackson nowhere indicates any divisions among the peasantry on this issue and offers no support for the implied claim that collectivization was in process at the period of Comorera's access to power. In fact, it is questionable that Comorera's rise to power affected the course of collectivization in Catalonia. Evidence is difficult to come by, but it seems that collectivization of agriculture in Catalonia was not, in any event, extensive, and that it was not extending in December, when Comorera took office. We know from anarchist sources that there had been instances of forced collectivization in Catalonia,[91] but I can find no evidence that Comorera "protected the peasantry" from forced collectivization. Furthermore, it is misleading, at best, to imply that the peasantry *as a whole* was opposed to collectivization. A more accurate picture is presented by Bolloten (p. 56), who points out that "if the individual farmer viewed with dismay the swift and widespread development of collectivized agriculture, the farm workers of the Anarchosyndicalist CNT and the Socialist UGT saw in it, on the contrary, the commencement of a new era." In short, there was a complex class struggle in the countryside, though one learns little about it from Jackson's oversimplified and misleading account. It would seem fair to suppose that this distortion again reflects Jackson's antipathy towards the revolution and its goals. I will return to this question directly, with reference to areas where agricultural collectivization was much more extensive than in Catalonia.

The complexities of modern society that baffled and confounded the unsuspecting anarchist workers of Barcelona, as Jackson enumerates them, were the following: the accumulating food and supply problems and the administration of frontier posts, villages, and public utilities. As just noted, the food and supply problems seem to have accumulated most rapidly under the brilliant leadership of Juan Comorera. So far as the frontier posts are concerned, the situation, as Jackson elsewhere describes it (p. 368), was basically as follows: "In Catalonia the anarchists had, ever since July 18, controlled the customs stations at the French border. On April 17, 1937, the reorganized carabineros, acting on orders of the Finance Minister, Juan Negrín, began to reoccupy the frontier. At least eight anarchists were killed in clashes with the carabineros." Apart from this difficulty, admittedly serious, there seems little reason to suppose that the problem of manning frontier posts contributed to the ebbing of the revolutionary tide. The available records do not indicate that the problems of administering villages or public utilities were either "unsuspected" or too complex for the Catalonian workers—a remarkable and unsuspected development, but one which nevertheless appears to be borne out by the evidence available to us. I want to emphasize again that Jackson presents no evidence to support his conclusions about the ebbing of the revolutionary tide and the reasons for the disaffection of the Catalonian workers. Once again, I think it fair to attribute his conclusions to the elitist bias of the liberal intellectual rather than to the historical record.

Consider next Jackson's comment that the anarchists "explained the loss of Málaga as due in large measure to the low morale and the disorientation of the Andalusian proletariat, which saw the Valencia government evolving steadily toward the right." Again, it seems that Jackson regards this as just another indication of the naiveté and unreasonableness of the Spanish anarchists. However, here again there is more to the story. One of the primary sources that Jackson cites is Borkenau, quite naturally, since Borkenau spent several days in the area just prior to the fall of Málaga on February 8, 1937. But Borkenau's detailed observations tend to bear out the anarchist "explanation," at least in part. He believed that Málaga might have been saved, but only by a "fight of despair" with mass involvement, of a sort that "the anarchists might have led." But two factors prevented such a defense: first, the officer assigned to lead the defense, Lieutenant Colonel Villalba, "interpreted this task as a purely military one, whereas in reality he had no military means at his disposal but only the forces of a popular movement"; he was a professional officer, "who in the secrecy of his heart hated the spirit of the militia" and was incapable of comprehending the "political factor."[92] A second factor was the significant decline, by February, of political consciousness and mass involvement. The anarchist committees were no longer functioning and the authority of the police and Civil Guards had been restored. "The nuisance of hundreds of independent village police bodies had disappeared, but with it the passionate interest of the village in the civil war. . . . The short interlude of the Spanish Soviet system was at an end" (p. 212). After reviewing the local situation in Málaga and the conflicts in the Valencia government (which failed to provide support or arms for the militia defending Málaga), Borkenau concludes (p. 228): "The Spanish republic paid with the fall of Málaga for the decision of the Right wing of its camp to make an end of social revolution and of its Left wing not to allow that." Jackson's discussion of the fall of Málaga refers to the terror and political rivalries within the town but makes no reference to the fact that Borkenau's description, and the accompanying interpretation, do support the belief that the defeat was due in large measure to low morale and to the incapacity, or unwillingness, of the Valencia government to fight a popular war. On the contrary, he concludes that Colonel Villalba's lack of means for "controlling the bitter political rivalries" was one factor that prevented him from carrying out the essential military tasks. Thus he seems to adopt the view that Borkenau condemns, that the task was a "purely military one." Borkenau's eyewitness account appears to me much more convincing.

In this case too Jackson has described the situation in a somewhat misleading fashion, perhaps again because of the elitist bias that dominates the liberal-Communist interpretation of the Civil War. Like Lieutenant Colonel Villalba, liberal historians often reveal a strong distaste for "the forces of a popular movement" and "the spirit of the militia." And an argument can be given that they correspondingly fail to comprehend the "political factor."

In the May Days of 1937, the revolution in Catalonia received the final blow. On May 3, the councilor for public order, PSUC member Rodríguez Salas, appeared at the central telephone building with a detachment of police, without prior warning or consultation with the anarchist ministers in the government, to take over the telephone exchange. The exchange, formerly the property of IT&T, had been captured by Barcelona workers in July and had since functioned under the control of a UGT-CNT committee, with a governmental delegate, quite in accord with the collectivization decree of October 24, 1936. According to the London *Daily Worker* (May 11, 1937), "Salas sent the armed republican police to disarm the employees there, most of them members of the CNT unions." The motive, according to Juan Comorera, was "to put a stop to an abnormal situation," namely, that no one could speak over the telephone "without the indiscreet ear of the controller knowing it."[93] Armed resistance in the telephone building prevented its occupation. Local defense committees erected barricades throughout Barcelona. Companys and the anarchist leaders pleaded with the workers to disarm. An uneasy truce continued until May 6, when the first detachments of Assault Guards arrived, violating the promises of the government that the truce would be observed and military forces withdrawn. The troops were under the command of General Pozas, formerly commander of the hated Civil Guard and now a member of the Communist party. In the fighting that followed, there were some five hundred killed and over a thousand wounded. "The May Days in reality sounded the death-knell of the revolution, announcing political defeat for all and death for certain of the revolutionary leaders."[94]

These events—of enormous significance in the history of the Spanish revolution—Jackson sketches in bare outline as a marginal incident. Obviously the historian's account must be selective; from the left-liberal point of view that Jackson shares with Hugh Thomas and many others, the liquidation of the revolution in Catalonia was a minor event, as the revolution itself was merely a kind of irrelevant nuisance, a minor irritant diverting energy from the struggle to save the bourgeois government.

The decision to crush the revolution by force is described as follows:

On May 5, Companys obtained a fragile truce, on the basis of which the PSUC councilors were to retire from the regional government, and the question of the Telephone Company was left to future negotiation. That very night, however, Antonio Sesé, a UGT official who was about to enter the reorganized cabinet, was murdered. In any event, the Valencia authorities were in no mood to temporize further with the Catalan Left. On May 6 several thousand *asaltos* arrived in the city, and the Republican Navy demonstrated in the port.[95]

What is interesting about this description is what is left unsaid. For example, there is no comment on the fact that the dispatch of the *asaltos* violated the "fragile truce" that had been accepted by the Barcelona workers and the anarchist and the POUM troops nearby, and barely a mention of the bloody consequences or the political meaning of this unwillingness "to temporize further with the Catalan Left." There is no mention of the fact that along with Sesé, Berneri and other anarchist leaders were murdered, not only during the May Days but in the weeks preceding.[96] Jackson does not refer to the fact that along with the Republican navy, British ships also "demonstrated" in the port.[97] Nor does he refer to Orwell's telling observations about the Assault Guards, as compared to the troops at the front, where he had spent the preceding months. The Assault Guards "were splendid troops, much the best I had seen in Spain. . . . I was used to the ragged, scarcely-armed militia on the Aragon front, and I had not known that the Republic possessed troops like these. . . . The Civil Guards and Carabineros, who were not intended for the front at all, were better armed and far better clad than ourselves. I suspect it is the same in all wars—always the same contrast between the

101

sleek police in the rear and the ragged soldiers in the line."[98]
(See pages 104–5 below.)

The contrast reveals a good deal about the nature of the war,
as it was understood by the Valencia government. Later, Orwell
was to make this conclusion explicit: "A government which
sends boys of fifteen to the front with rifles forty years old and
keeps its biggest men and newest weapons in the rear is manifestly more afraid of the revolution than of the fascists. Hence
the feeble war policy of the past six months, and hence the
compromise with which the war will almost certainly end."[99]
Jackson's account of these events, with its omissions and assumptions, suggests that he perhaps shares the view that the greatest
danger in Spain would have been a victory of the revolution.

Jackson apparently discounts Orwell's testimony, to some extent, commenting that "the readers should bear in mind Orwell's own honest statement that he knew very little about the
political complexities of the struggle." This is a strange comment. For one thing, Orwell's analysis of the "political complexities of the struggle" bears up rather well after thirty years; if it
is defective, it is probably in his tendency to give too much
prominence to the POUM in comparison with the anarchists—
not surprising, in view of the fact that he was with the POUM
militia. His exposure of the fatuous nonsense that was appearing at the time in the Stalinist and liberal presses appears quite
accurate, and later discoveries have given little reason to challenge the basic facts that he reported or the interpretation that
he proposed in the heat of the conflict. Orwell does, in fact, refer
to his own "political ignorance." Commenting on the final defeat of the revolution in May, he states: "I realized—though
owing to my political ignorance, not so clearly as I ought to have
done—that when the Government felt more sure of itself there
would be reprisals." But this form of "political ignorance" has

simply been compounded in more recent historical work.

Shortly after the May Days, the Caballero government fell and Juan Negrín became premier of Republican Spain. Negrín is described as follows, by Broué and Témime: ". . . he is an unconditional defender of capitalist property and resolute adversary of collectivization, whom the CNT ministers find blocking all of their proposals. He is the one who solidly reorganized the carabineros and presided over the transfer of the gold reserves of the Republic to the USSR. He enjoyed the confidence of the moderates . . . [and] was on excellent terms with the Communists."

The first major act of the Negrín government was the suppression of the POUM and the consolidation of central control over Catalonia. The government next turned to Aragon, which had been under largely anarchist control since the first days of the revolution, and where agricultural collectivization was quite extensive and Communist elements very weak. The municipal councils of Aragon were coordinated by the Council of Aragon, headed by Joaquín Ascaso, a well-known CNT militant, one of whose brothers had been killed during the May Days. Under the Caballero government, the anarchists had agreed to give representation to other antifascist parties, including the Communists, but the majority remained anarchist. In August the Negrín government announced the dissolution of the Council of Aragon and dispatched a division of the Spanish army, commanded by the Communist officer Enrique Lister, to enforce the dissolution of the local committees, dismantle the collectives, and establish central government control. Ascaso was arrested on the charge of having been responsible for the robbery of jewelry—namely, the jewelry "robbed" by the Council for its own use in the fall of 1936. The local anarchist press was suppressed in favor of a Communist journal, and in general local anarchist centers were forcefully occupied and closed. The last anarchist stronghold was captured, with tanks and artillery, on September 21. Because of government-imposed censorship, there is very little of a direct record of these events, and the major histories pass over them quickly.[100] According to Morrow, "the official CNT press . . . compared the assault on Aragon with the subjection of Asturias by Lopez Ochoa in October 1934"—the latter, one of the bloodiest acts of repression in modern Spanish history. Although this is an exaggeration, it is a fact that the popular organs of administration were wiped out by Lister's legions, and the revolution was now over, so far as Aragon was concerned.

About these events, Jackson has the following comments:

> On August 11 the government announced the dissolution of the *Consejo de Aragón,* the anarchist-dominated administration which had been recognized by Largo Caballero in December, 1936. The peasants were known to hate the Consejo, the anarchists had deserted the front during the Barcelona fighting, and the very existence of the Consejo was a standing challenge to the authority of the central government. For all these reasons Negrín did not hesitate to send in troops, and to arrest the anarchist officials. Once their authority had been broken, however, they were released.[101]

These remarks are most interesting. Consider first the charge that the anarchists had deserted the front during the May Days. It is true that elements of certain anarchist and POUM divisions were prepared to march on Barcelona, but after the "fragile truce" was established on May 5, they did not do so; no anarchist forces even approached Barcelona to defend the Barcelona proletariat and its institutions from attack. However, a motorized column of 5,000 Assault Guards was sent from the front by the government to break the "fragile truce."[102] Hence the only forces to "desert the front" during the Barcelona fighting were those dispatched by the government to complete the job of dismantling the revolution, by force. Recall Orwell's observations quoted above, pages 101–2.

What about Jackson's statement that "the peasants were known to hate the Consejo"? As in the other cases I have cited, Jackson gives no indication of any evidence on which such a judgment might be based. The most detailed investigation of the collectives is from anarchist sources, and they indicate that Aragon was one of the areas where collectivization was most widespread and successful.[103] Both the CNT and the UGT Land Workers' Federation were vigorous in their support for collectivization, and there is no doubt that both were mass organizations. A number of nonanarchists, observing collectivization in Aragon firsthand, gave very favorable reports and stressed the voluntary character of collectivization.[104] According to Gaston Leval, an anarchist observer who carried out detailed investigation of rural collectivization, "in Aragon 75 percent of small proprietors have voluntarily adhered to the new order of things," and others were not forced to involve themselves in collectives.[105] Other anarchist observers—Augustin Souchy in particular—gave detailed observations of the functioning of the Aragon collectives. Unless one is willing to assume a fantastic degree of falsification, it is impossible to reconcile their descriptions with the claim that "the peasants were known to hate the Consejo"—unless, of course, one restricts the term "peasant" to "individual farm owner," in which case it might very well be true, but would justify disbanding the Council only on the assumption that the rights of the individual farm owner must predominate, not those of the landless worker. There is little doubt that the collectives were economically successful,[106] hardly likely if collectivization were forced and hated by the peasantry.

I have already cited Bolloten's general conclusion, based on very extensive documentary evidence, that while the individual farmer may have viewed the development of collectivized agriculture with dismay, "the farm workers of the Anarchosyndicalist CNT and the Socialist UGT saw in it, on the contrary, the commencement of a new era." This conclusion seems quite reasonable, on the basis of the materials that are available. With respect to Aragon, specifically, he remarks that the "debt-ridden peasants were strongly affected by the ideas of the CNT and FAI, a factor that gave a powerful spontaneous impulse to collective farming," though difficulties are cited by anarchist sources, which in general appear to be quite honest about failures. Bolloten cites two Communist sources, among others, to the effect that about 70 percent of the population in rural areas of Aragon lived in collectives (p. 71); he adds that "many of the region's 450 collectives were largely voluntary," although "the presence of militiamen from the neighbouring region of Catalonia, the immense majority of whom were members of the CNT and FAI" was "in some measure" responsible for the extensive collectivization. He also points out that in many instances peasant proprietors who were not compelled to adhere to the collective system did so for other reasons: ". . . not only were they prevented from employing hired labour and disposing freely of their crops . . . but they were often denied all benefits enjoyed by members" (p. 72). Bolloten cites the attempt of the Communists in April 1937 to cause dissension in "areas where the CNT and UGT had established collective farms by mutual agreement" (p. 195), leading in some cases to pitched battles and dozens of assassinations, according to CNT sources.[107]

Bolloten's detailed analysis of the events of the summer of

1937 sheds considerable light on the question of peasant attitudes towards collectivization in Aragon:

> It was inevitable that the attacks on the collectives should have had an unfavorable effect upon rural economy and upon morale, for while it is true that in some areas collectivization was anathema to the majority of peasants, it is no less true that in others collective farms were organized spontaneously by the bulk of the peasant population. In Toledo province, for example, where even before the war rural collectives existed, 83 per cent of the peasants, according to a source friendly to the Communists, decided in favour of the collective cultivation of the soil. As the campaign against the collective farms reached its height just before the summer harvest [1937] . . . a pall of dismay and apprehension descended upon the agricultural labourers. Work in the fields was abandoned in many places or only carried on apathetically, and there was danger that a substantial portion of the harvest, vital for the war effort, would be left to rot. [P. 196]

It was under these circumstances, he points out, that the Communists were forced to change their policy and—temporarily—to tolerate the collectives. A decree was passed legalizing collectives *"during the current agricultural year"* (his italics) and offering them some aid. This "produced a sense of relief in the countryside during the vital period of the harvest." Immediately after the crops had been gathered, the policy changed again to one of harsh repression. Bolloten cites Communist sources to the effect that "a short though fierce campaign at the beginning of August" prepared the way for the dissolution of the Council of Aragon. Following the dissolution decree, "the newly appointed Governor General, José Ignacio Mantecón, a member of the Left Republican Party, but a secret Communist sympathizer [who joined the party in exile, after the war], . . . ordered the break-up of the collective farms." The means: Lister's division, which restored the old order by force and terror. Bolloten cites Communist sources conceding the excessive harshness of Lister's methods. He quotes the Communist general secretary of the Institute of Agrarian Reform, who admits that the measures taken to dissolve the collectives were "a very grave mistake, and produced tremendous disorganization in the countryside," as "those persons who were discontented with the collectives . . . took them by assault, carrying away and dividing up the harvest and farm implements without respecting the collectives that had been formed without violence or pressure, that were prosperous, and that were a model of organization. . . . As a result, labour in the fields was suspended almost entirely, and a quarter of the land had not been prepared at the time for sowing" (p. 200). Once again, it was necessary to ameliorate the harsh repression of the collectives, to prevent disaster. Summarizing these events, Bolloten describes the resulting situation as follows:

> But although the situation in Aragon improved in some degree, the hatreds and resentments generated by the break-up of the collectives and by the repression that followed were never wholly dispelled. Nor was the resultant disillusionment that sapped the spirit of the Anarchosyndicalist forces on the Aragon front ever entirely removed, a disillusionment that no doubt contributed to the collapse of that front a few months later. . . . after the destruction of the collective farms in Aragon, the Communist Party was compelled to modify its policy, and support collectives also in other regions against former owners who sought the return of confiscated land. . . . [Pp. 200–201]

Returning to Jackson's remarks, I think we must conclude that they seriously misrepresent the situation.[108] The dissolution of the Council of Aragon and the large-scale destruction of the collectives by military force was simply another stage in the eradication of the popular revolution and the restoration of the old order. Let me emphasize that I am not criticizing Jackson

108

for his negative attitude towards the social revolution, but rather for the failure of objectivity when he deals with the revolution and the ensuing repression.

Among historians of the Spanish Civil War, the dominant view is that the Communist policy was in essentials the correct one—that in order to consolidate domestic and international support for the Republic it was necessary to block and then reverse the social revolution. Jackson, for example, states that Caballero "realized that it was absolutely necessary to rebuild the authority of the Republican state and to work in close co-operation with the middle-class liberals." The anarchist leaders who entered the government shared this view, putting their trust in the good faith of liberals such as Companys and believing—naively, as events were to show—that the Western democracies would come to their aid.

A policy diametrically opposed to this was advocated by Camillo Berneri. In his open letter to the anarchist minister Federica Montseny[109] he summarizes his views in the following way: "The dilemma, war or revolution, no longer has meaning. *The only dilemma is this: either victory over Franco through revolutionary war, or defeat*" (his italics). He argued that Morocco should be granted independence and that an attempt should be made to stir up rebellion throughout North Africa. Thus a revolutionary struggle should be undertaken against Western capitalism in North Africa and, simultaneously, against the bourgeois regime in Spain, which was gradually dismantling the accomplishments of the July revolution. The primary front should be political. Franco relied heavily on Moorish contingents, including a substantial number from French Morocco. The Republic might exploit this fact, demoralizing the Nationalist forces and perhaps even winning them to the revolutionary cause by political agitation based on the concrete alternative of pan-Islamic—specifically, Moroc-can—revolution. Writing in April 1937, Berneri urged that the army of the Republic be reorganized for the defense of the revolution, so that it might recover the spirit of popular partici-pation of the early days of the revolution. He quotes the words of his compatriot Louis Bertoni, writing from the Huesca front:

> The Spanish war, deprived of all new faith, of any idea of a social transformation, of all revolutionary grandeur, of any universal meaning, is now merely a national war of independence that must be carried on to avoid the extermination that the international plutocracy demands. There remains a terrible question of life or death, but no longer a war to build a new society and a new humanity.

In such a war, the human element that might bring victory over fascism is lost.

In retrospect, Berneri's ideas seem quite reasonable. Delega-tions of Moroccan nationalists did in fact approach the Va-lencia government asking for arms and matériel, but were refused by Caballero, who actually proposed territorial conces-sions in North Africa to France and England to try to win their support. Commenting on these facts, Broué and Témime ob-serve that these policies deprived the Republic of "the instru-ment of revolutionary defeatism in the enemy army," and even of a possible weapon against Italian intervention. Jackson, on the other hand, dismisses Berneri's suggestion with the remark that independence for Morocco (as for that matter, even aid to the Moroccan nationalists) was "a gesture that would have been highly appreciated in Paris and London." Of course it is correct that France and Britain would hardly have appreciated this development. As Berneri points out, "it goes without saying that one cannot simultaneously guarantee French and British interests in Morocco and carry out an insurrection." But Jackson's comment does not touch on the central issue, namely, whether the Spanish revolution could have been preserved, both from the fascists at the front and from the bourgeois-Communist coalition within the Republic, by a revolutionary war of the sort that the left proposed—or, for that matter, whether the Republic might not have been saved by a political struggle that involved Franco's invading Moorish troops, or at least eroded their morale. It is easy to see why Caballero was not attracted by this bold scheme, given his reliance on the eventual backing of the Western democracies. On the basis of what we know today, however, Jackson's summary dismissal of revolutionary war is much too abrupt.

Furthermore, Bertoni's observations from the Huesca front are borne out by much other evidence, some of it cited earlier. Even those who accepted the Communist strategy of discipline and central control as necessary concede that the repressions that formed an ineliminable part of this strategy "tended to break the fighting spirit of the people."[110] One can only speculate, but it seems to me that many commentators have seriously underestimated the significance of the political factor, the potential strength of a popular struggle to defend the achievements of the revolution. It is perhaps relevant that Asturias, the one area of Spain where the system of CNT-UGT committees was not eliminated in favor of central control, is also the one area where guerrilla warfare continued well after Franco's victory. Broué and Témime observe[111] that the resistance of the partisans of Asturias "demonstrates the depth of the revolutionary élan, which had not been shattered by the reinstitution of state authority, conducted here with greater prudence." There can be no doubt that the revolution was both widespread and deeply rooted in the Spanish masses. It seems quite possible that a revolutionary war of the sort advocated by Berneri would have been successful, despite the greater military force of the fascist armies. The idea that men can overcome machines no longer seems as romantic or naive as it may have a few years ago.

Furthermore, the trust placed in the bourgeois government by the anarchist leaders was not honored, as the history of the counterrevolution clearly shows. In retrospect, it seems that Berneri was correct in arguing that they should not have taken part in the bourgeois government, but should rather have sought to replace this government with the institutions created by the revolution.[112] The anarchist minister García Oliver stated that "we had confidence in the word and in the person of a Catalan democrat and retained and supported Companys as President of the Generalitat,"[113] at a time when in Catalonia, at least, the workers' organizations could easily have replaced the state apparatus and dispensed with the former political parties, as they had replaced the old economy with an entirely new structure. Companys recognized fully that there were limits beyond which he could not cooperate with the anarchists. In an interview with H. E. Kaminski, he refused to specify these limits, but merely expressed his hope that "the anarchist masses will not oppose the good sense of their leaders," who have "accepted the responsibilities incumbent upon them"; he saw his task as "directing these responsibilities in the proper path," not further specified in the interview, but shown by the events leading up to the May Days.[114] Probably, Companys' attitude towards this willingness of the anarchist leaders to cooperate was expressed accurately in his reaction to the suggestion of a correspondent of the *New Statesman and Nation*, who predicted that the assassination of the anarchist mayor of Puigcerdá would lead to a revolt: "[Companys] laughed scornfully and said the anarchists would capitulate as they always had before."[115] As has already been pointed out in some detail, the liberal-Communist Party coalition had no intention of letting the war against Franco take precedence over the crushing of the revolution. A spokesman for Comorera put the matter clearly: "This slogan has been attributed to the P.S.U.C.: 'Before taking Saragossa, it is necessary to take Barcelona.' This reflects the situation exactly. . . ."[116] Comorera himself had, from the beginning, pressed Companys to resist the CNT.[117] The first task of the antifascist coalition, he maintained, was to dissolve the revolutionary committees.[118] I have already cited a good deal of evidence indicating that the repression conducted by the Popular Front seriously weakened popular commitment and involvement in the antifascist war. What was evident to George Orwell was also clear to the Barcelona workers and the peasants in the collectivized villages of Aragon: the liberal-Communist coalition would not tolerate a revolutionary transformation of Spanish society; it would commit itself fully to the anti-Franco struggle only after the old order was firmly re-established, by force, if necessary.[119]

There is little doubt that farm workers in the collectives understood quite well the social content of the drive towards consolidation and central control. We learn this not only from anarchist sources but also from the socialist press in the spring of 1937. On May 1, the Socialist party newspaper *Adelante* had the following to say:

> At the outbreak of the Fascist revolt the labor organizations and the democratic elements in the country were in agreement that the so-called Nationalist Revolution, which threatened to plunge our people into an abyss of deepest misery, could be halted only by a Social Revolution. The Communist Party, however, opposed this view with all its might. It had apparently completely forgotten its old theories of a "workers' and peasants' republic" and a "dictatorship of the proletariat." From its constant repetition of

113

its new slogan of the parliamentary democratic republic it is clear that it has lost all sense of reality. When the Catholic and conservative sections of the Spanish bourgeoisie saw their old system smashed and could find no way out, the Communist Party instilled new hope into them. It assured them that the democratic bourgeois republic for which it was pleading put no obstacles in the way of Catholic propaganda and, above all, that it stood ready to defend the class interests of the bourgeoisie.[120]

That this realization was widespread in the rural areas was underscored dramatically by a questionnaire sent by *Adelante* to secretaries of the UGT Federation of Land Workers, published in June 1937.[121] The results are summarized as follows:

> The replies to these questions revealed an astounding unanimity. Everywhere the same story. The peasant collectives are today most vigorously opposed by the Communist Party. The Communists organize the well-to-do farmers who are on the lookout for cheap labor and are, for this reason, outspokenly hostile to the co-operative undertakings of the poor peasants.
>
> It is the element which before the revolution sympathized with the Fascists and Monarchists which, according to the testimony of the trade-union representatives, is now flocking into the ranks of the Communist Party. As to the general effect of Communist activity on the country, the secretaries of the U.G.T. had only one opinion, which the representative of the Valencia organization put in these words: "It is a misfortune in the fullest sense of the word."[122]

It is not difficult to imagine how the recognition of this "misfortune" must have affected the willingness of the land workers to take part in the antifascist war, with all the sacrifices that this entailed.

The attitude of the central government to the revolution was brutally revealed by its acts and is attested as well in its propaganda. A former minister describes the situation as follows:

The fact that is concealed by the coalition of the Spanish Communist Party with the left Republicans and right wing Socialists is that there has been a successful social revolution in half of Spain. Successful, that is, in the collectivization of factories and farms which are operated under trade union control, and operated quite efficiently. During the three months that I was director of propaganda for the United States and England under Alvarez del Vayo, then Foreign Minister for the Valencia Government, I was instructed not to send out one word about this revolution in the economic system of loyalist Spain. Nor are any foreign correspondents in Valencia permitted to write freely of the revolution that has taken place.[123]

In short, there is much reason to believe that the will to fight Franco was significantly diminished, perhaps destroyed, by the policy of authoritarian centralization undertaken by the liberal-Communist coalition, carried through by force, and disguised in the propaganda that was disseminated among Western intellectuals[124] and that still dominates the writing of history. To the extent that this is a correct judgment, the alternative proposed by Berneri and the left "extremists" gains in plausibility.

As noted earlier, Caballero and the anarchist ministers accepted the policy of counterrevolution because of their trust in the Western democracies, which they felt sure would sooner or later come to their aid. This feeling was perhaps understandable in 1937. It is strange, however, that a historian writing in the 1960s should dismiss the proposal to strike at Franco's rear by extending the revolutionary war to Morocco, on grounds that this would have displeased Western capitalism (see page 110 above).

Berneri was quite right in his belief that the Western democracies would not take part in an antifascist struggle in Spain. In fact, their complicity in the fascist insurrection was not slight.

French bankers, who were generally pro-Franco, blocked the release of Spanish gold to the loyalist government, thus hindering the purchase of arms and, incidentally, increasing the reliance of the Republic on the Soviet Union.[125] The policy of "nonintervention," which effectively blocked Western aid for the loyalist government while Hitler and Mussolini in effect won the war for Franco, was also technically initiated by the French government—though apparently under heavy British pressure.[126]

As far as Great Britain is concerned, the hope that it would come to the aid of the Republic was always unrealistic. A few days after the Franco coup, the foreign editor of *Paris-Soir* wrote: "At least four countries are already taking active interest in the battle—France, which is supporting the Madrid Government, and Britain, Germany and Italy, each of which is giving discreet but nevertheless effective assistance to one group or another among the insurgents."[127] In fact, British support for Franco took a fairly concrete form at the very earliest stages of the insurrection. The Spanish navy remained loyal to the Republic,* and made some attempt to prevent Franco from ferrying troops from Morocco to Spain. Italian and German involvement in overcoming these efforts is well documented;[128] the British role has received less attention, but can be determined from contemporary reports. On August 11, 1936, the *New York Times* carried a front-page report on British naval actions in the Straits of Gibraltar, commenting that "this action helps the Rebels by preventing attacks on Algeciras, where troops from Morocco land." (A few days earlier, loyalist warships had bombarded Algeciras, damaging the British con-

---

* To be more precise, pro-Franco officers were killed, and the seamen remained loyal to the Republic, in many instances.

sulate.) An accompanying dispatch from Gibraltar describes the situation as it appeared from there:

Angered by the Spanish factions' endangering of shipping and neutral Gibraltar territory in their fighting, Great Britain virtually blockaded Gibraltar Harbor last night with the huge battleship Queen Elizabeth in the center of the entrance, constantly playing searchlights on near-by waters.

Many British warships patrolled the entire Strait today, determined to prevent interference with Britain's control over the entrance to the Mediterranean, a vital place in the British "lifeline to the East."

This action followed repeated warnings to the Spanish Government and yesterday's decree that no more fighting would be permitted in Gibraltar Harbor. The British at Gibraltar had become increasingly nervous after the shelling of Algeciras by the Loyalist battleship Jaime I.

Although British neutrality is still maintained, the patrol of the Strait and the closing of the harbor will aid the military Rebels because Loyalist warships cannot attempt to take Algeciras, now in Rebel hands, and completely isolate the Rebels from Morocco. The Rebels now can release some troops, who were rushed back to Algeciras, for duty further north in the drive for Madrid.

It was reported in Gibraltar tonight that the Rebels had sent a transport across the Strait and had landed more troops from Morocco for use in the columns that are marching northward from headquarters at Seville.

This was the second time this year that Britain warned a power when she believed her measure of Mediterranean control was threatened, and it remains to be seen whether the Madrid Government will flout the British as the Italians did. If it attempts to do so, the British gunners of the Gibraltar fort have authority to fire warning shots. What will happen if such shots go unheeded is obvious.

All the British here refer to the Madrid Government as the "Communists" and there is no doubt where British sympathies now lie, encouraged by the statement of General Francisco

117

Franco, leader of the Rebels, that he is not especially cooperating with Italy.

The British Government has ordered Spaniards here to cease plotting or be expelled and has asked Britons "loyally to refrain from either acting or speaking publicly in such a manner as to display marked partiality or partisanship."

The warning, issued in the official Gibraltar Gazette, was signed by the British Colonial Secretary here.

The warning was issued after reports of possible Communist troubles here had reached official ears and after strong complaints that Spanish Rebels were in Gibraltar. It was said Rebels were making headquarters here and entering La Linea to fight. [Italics mine]

I have quoted this dispatch in full because it conveys rather accurately the character of British "neutrality" in the early stages of the war and thenceforth. In May 1938, the British ambassador to Spain, Sir Henry Chilton, "expressed the conviction that a Franco victory was necessary for peace in Spain; that there was not the slightest chance that Italy and/or Germany would dominate Spain; and that even if it were possible for the Spanish Government to win (which he did not believe) he was convinced that a victory for Franco would be better for Great Britain."[129] Churchill, who was at first violently opposed to the Republic, modified his position somewhat after the crushing of the revolution in the summer of 1937. What particularly pleased him was the forceful repression of the anarchists and the militarization of the Republic (necessary when "the entire structure of civilization and social life is destroyed," as it had been by the revolution, now happily subdued).[130] However, his good feelings towards the Republic remained qualified. In an interview of August 14, 1938, he expressed himself as follows: "Franco has all the right on his side because he loves his country. Also Franco is defending Europe against the Communist danger—if you wish to put it in those terms. But I, I am English, and I prefer the triumph of the wrong cause. I prefer that the other side wins, because Franco could be an upset or a threat to British interests, and the others no."[131]

The Germans were quite aware of British sentiments, naturally, and therefore were much concerned that the supervisory committee for the nonintervention agreement be located in London rather than Paris. The German Foreign Ministry official responsible for this matter expressed his view on August 29, 1936, as follows: "Naturally, we have to count on complaints of all kinds being brought up in London regarding failure to observe the obligation not to intervene, but we cannot avoid such complaints in any case. It can, in fact, only be agreeable to us if the center of gravity, which after all has thus far been in Paris because of the French initiative, is transferred to London."[132] They were not disappointed. In November, Foreign Secretary Anthony Eden stated in the House of Commons: "So far as breaches [of the nonintervention agreement] are concerned, I wish to state categorically that I think there are other Governments more to blame than those of Germany and Italy."[133] There was no factual basis for this statement, but it did reflect British attitudes. It is interesting that according to German sources, England was at that time supplying Franco with munitions through Gibraltar and, at the same time, providing information to Germany about Russian arms deliveries to the Republic.[134]

The British left was for the most part in support of the liberal-Communist coalition, regarding Caballero as an "infantile leftist" and the anarchists as generally unspeakable.

The British policy of mild support for Franco was to be successful in preserving British interests in Spain, as the Germans soon discovered. A German Foreign Ministry note of October

1937 to the embassy in Nationalist Spain included the following observation: "That England cannot permanently be kept from the Spanish market as in the past is a fact with which we have to reckon. England's old relations with the Spanish mines and the Generalissimo's desire, based on political and economic considerations, to come to an understanding with England place certain limits on our chances of reserving Spanish raw materials to ourselves permanently."[135]

One can only speculate as to what might have been the effects of British support for the Republic. A discussion of this matter would take us far afield, into a consideration of British diplomacy during the late 1930s. It is perhaps worth mention, now that the "Munich analogy" is being bandied about in utter disregard for the historical facts by Secretary Rusk and a number of his academic supporters, that "containment of Communism" was not a policy invented by George Kennan in 1947. Specifically, it was a dominant theme in the diplomacy of the 1930s. In 1934, Lloyd George stated that "in a very short time, perhaps in a year, perhaps in two, the conservative elements in this country will be looking to Germany as the bulwark against Communism in Europe. . . . Do not let us be in a hurry to condemn Germany. We shall be welcoming Germany as our friend."[136] In September 1938, the Munich agreement was concluded; shortly after, both France and Britain did welcome Germany as "our friend." As noted earlier (see note 99), even Churchill's role at this time is subject to some question. Of course, the Munich agreement was the death knell for the Spanish Republic, exactly as the necessity to rely on the Soviet Union signaled the end of the Spanish revolution in 1937.

The United States, like France, exhibited less initiative in these events than Great Britain, which had far more substantial economic interests in Spain and was more of an independent force in European affairs. Nevertheless, the American record is hardly one to inspire pride. Technically, the United States adhered to a position of strict neutrality. However, a careful look raises some doubts. According to information obtained by Jackson, "the American colonel who headed the Telephone Company had placed private lines at the disposal of the Madrid plotters for their conversations with Generals Mola and Franco,"[137] just prior to the insurrection on July 17. In August, the American government urged the Martin Aircraft Company not to honor an agreement made prior to the insurrection to supply aircraft to the Republic, and it also pressured the Mexican government not to reship to Spain war materials purchased in the United States.[138] An American arms exporter, Robert Cuse, insisted on his legal right to ship airplanes and aircraft engines to the Republic in December 1936, and the State Department was forced to grant authorization. Cuse was denounced by Roosevelt as unpatriotic, though Roosevelt was forced to admit that the request was quite legal. Roosevelt contrasted the attitude of other businessmen to Cuse as follows:

> Well, these companies went along with the request of the Government. There is the 90 percent of business that is honest, I mean ethically honest. There is the 90 percent we are always pointing at with pride. And then one man does what amounts to a perfectly legal but thoroughly unpatriotic act. He represents the 10 percent of business that does not live up to the best standards. Excuse the homily, but I feel quite deeply about it.[139]

Among the businesses that remained "ethically honest" and therefore did not incur Roosevelt's wrath was the Texaco Oil Company, which violated its contracts with the Spanish Republic and shipped oil instead to Franco. (Five tankers that were on the high seas in July 1936 were diverted to Franco, who received six million dollars worth of oil on credit during the

Civil War.) Apparently, neither the press nor the American government was able to discover this fact, though it was reported in left-wing journals at the time.[140] There is evidence that the American government shared the fears of Churchill and others about the dangerous forces on the Republican side. Secretary of State Cordell Hull, for example, informed Roosevelt on July 23, 1936, that "one of the most serious factors in this situation lies in the fact that the [Spanish] Government has distributed large quantities of arms and ammunition into the hands of irresponsible members of left-wing political organizations."[141]

Like Churchill, many responsible Americans began to rethink their attitude towards the Republic after the social revolution had been crushed.[142] However, relations with Franco continued cordial. In 1957, President Eisenhower congratulated Franco on the "happy anniversary" of his rebellion,[143] and Secretary Rusk added his tribute in 1961. Upon criticism, Rusk was defended by the American ambassador to Madrid, who observed that Spain is "a nation which understands the implacable nature of the communist threat,"[144] like Thailand, South Korea, Taiwan, and selected other countries of the Free World.[145]

In the light of such facts as these, it seems to me that Jackson is not treating the historical record seriously when he dismisses the proposals of the Spanish left as absurd. Quite possibly Berneri's strategy would have failed, as did that of the liberal-Communist coalition that took over the Republic. It was far from senseless, however. I think that the failure of historians to consider it more seriously follows, once again, from the elitist bias that dominates the writing of history—and, in this case, from a certain sentimentality about the Western democracies.

The study of collectivization published by the CNT in 1937[146] concludes with a description of the village of Membrilla. "In its miserable huts live the poor inhabitants of a poor province; eight thousand people, but the streets are not paved, the town has no newspaper, no cinema, neither a café nor a library. On the other hand, it has many churches that have been burned." Immediately after the Franco insurrection, the land was expropriated and village life collectivized. "Food, clothing, and tools were distributed equitably to the whole population. Money was abolished, work collectivized, all goods passed to the community, consumption was socialized. It was, however, not a socialization of wealth but of poverty." Work continued as before. An elected council appointed committees to organize the life of the commune and its relations to the outside world. The necessities of life were distributed freely, insofar as they were available. A large number of refugees were accommodated. A small library was established, and a small school of design.

The document closes with these words:

> The whole population lived as in a large family; functionaries, delegates, the secretary of the syndicates, the members of the municipal council, all elected, acted as heads of a family. But they were controlled, because special privilege or corruption would not be tolerated. Membrilla is perhaps the poorest village of Spain, but it is the most just.

An account such as this, with its concern for human relations and the ideal of a just society, must appear very strange to the consciousness of the sophisticated intellectual, and it is therefore treated with scorn, or taken to be naive or primitive or otherwise irrational. Only when such prejudice is abandoned will it be possible for historians to undertake a serious study of

123

the popular movement that transformed Republican Spain in one of the most remarkable social revolutions that history records.

Franz Borkenau, in commenting on the demoralization caused by the authoritarian practices of the central government, observes (p. 295) that "newspapers are written by Europeanized editors, and the popular movement is inarticulate as to its deepest impulses . . . [which are shown only] . . . by acts." The objectivity of scholarship will remain a delusion as long as these inarticulate impulses remain beyond its grasp. As far as the Spanish revolution is concerned, its history is yet to be written.

I have concentrated on one theme—the interpretation of the social revolution in Spain—in one work of history, a work that is an excellent example of liberal scholarship. It seems to me that there is more than enough evidence to show that a deep bias against social revolution and a commitment to the values and social order of liberal bourgeois democracy has led the author to misrepresent crucial events and to overlook major historical currents. My intention has not been to bring into question the commitment to these values—that is another matter entirely. Rather, it has been to show how this commitment has led to a striking failure of objectivity, providing an example of "counterrevolutionary subordination" of a much more subtle and interesting sort—and ultimately, I believe, a far more important one—than those discussed in the first part of this essay.

III

In opening this discussion of the Spanish revolution I referred to the classical left-wing critique of the social role of intellectuals, Marxist or otherwise, in modern society, and to Luxemburg's reservations regarding Bolshevism. Western sociologists have repeatedly emphasized the relevance of this analysis to developments in the Soviet Union,[147] with much justice. The same sociologists formulate "the world revolution of the epoch" in the following terms: "The major transformation is the decline of business (and of earlier social formations) and the rise of intellectuals and semi-intellectuals to effective power."[148] The "ultra-left" critic foresaw in these developments a new attack on human freedom and a more efficient system of exploitation. The Western sociologist sees in the rise of intellectuals to effective power the hope for a more humane and smoothly functioning society, in which problems can be solved by "piecemeal technology." Who has the sharper eye? At least this much is plain: there are dangerous tendencies in the ideology of the welfare state intelligentsia who claim to possess the technique and understanding required to manage our "postindustrial society" and to organize an international society dominated by American superpower. Many of these dangers are revealed, at a purely ideological level, in the study of the counterrevolutionary subordination of scholarship. The dangers exist both insofar as the claim to knowledge is real and insofar as it is fraudulent. Insofar as the technique of management and control exists, it can be used to consolidate the authority of those who exercise it and to diminish spontaneous and free experimentation with new social forms, as it can limit the possibilities for reconstruction of society in the interests of those who are now, to a greater or lesser extent, dispossessed. Where the techniques fail, they will be supplemented by all of the methods of coercion that modern technology provides, to preserve order and stability.

For a glimpse of what may lie ahead, consider the Godkin lectures of McGeorge Bundy, recently delivered at Harvard.[149]

Bundy urges that more power be concentrated in the executive branch of the government, now "dangerously weak in relation to its present tasks." That the powerful executive will act with justice and wisdom—this presumably needs no argument. As an example of the superior executive who should be attracted to government and given still greater power, Bundy cites Robert McNamara. Nothing could reveal more clearly the dangers inherent in the "new society" than the role that McNamara's Pentagon has played for the past half-dozen years. No doubt McNamara succeeded in doing with utmost efficiency that which should not be done at all. No doubt he has shown an unparalleled mastery of the logistics of coercion and repression, combined with the most astonishing inability to comprehend political and human factors. The efficiency of the Pentagon is no less remarkable than its pratfalls.[150] When understanding fails, there is always more force in reserve. As the "experiments in material and human resources control" collapse and "revolutionary development" grinds to a halt, we simply resort more openly to the Gestapo tactics that are barely concealed behind the façade of "pacification."[151] When American cities explode, we can expect the same. The technique of "limited warfare" translates neatly into a system of domestic repression—far more humane, as will quickly be explained, than massacring those who are unwilling to wait for the inevitable victory of the war on poverty.

Why should a liberal intellectual be so persuaded of the virtues of a political system of four-year dictatorship? The answer seems all too plain.

Notes

1. "Politics and the Morality of Scholarship," in Max Black, ed., *The Morality of Scholarship* (Ithaca, N.Y., Cornell University Press, 1967), pp. 59–88.

2. "The War and Its Effects—II," *Congressional Record*, December 13, 1967.

3. *Congressional Record*, July 27, 1967.

4. William A. Nighswonger, *Rural Pacification in Vietnam* (Praeger Special Studies; New York, Frederick A. Praeger, Inc., 1967)—one of a series of "specialized research monographs in U.S. and international economics and politics."

5. Ithiel de Sola Pool, "The Necessity for Social Scientists Doing Research for Governments," *Background*, Vol. 10 (August 1966), p. 111.

6. Max Ways writes in *Fortune* that "McNamara, his systems analysts, and their computers are not only contributing to the practical effectiveness of U.S. action, but *raising the moral level of policy* by a more conscious and selective attention to the definition of its aims" (italics mine). Cited by Andrew Kopkind, "The Future-Planners," *New Republic*, February 25, 1967, p. 23. Comment would be superfluous.

7. Daniel Bell, "Notes on the Post-Industrial Society: Part I," *The Public Interest*, No. 6, 1967, pp. 24–35.

8. Some of the dangers are noted by Richard Goodwin, in a review of Thomas Schelling's *Arms and Influence* in the *New Yorker*, February 17, 1968, pp. 127–34. He observes that "the most profound objection to this kind of strategic theory is not its limited usefulness but its danger, for it can lead us to believe we have an understanding of events and a control over their flow which we do not have." A still more profound objection, I think, is that the pretended objectivity of "strategic theory" can be used to justify the attempt to control the flow of events.

9. Seymour M. Lipset, *Political Man* (Garden City, N.Y., Doubleday & Company, Inc., 1960), p. 406.

10. "Status Politics and New Anxieties," in *The End of Ideology* (New York, The Free Press, 1960), p. 119.

11. "The Necessity and Difficulty of Planning the Future Society," address given at the American Institute of Planners Conference, Washington, D.C., October 3, 1967. Citing this, Senator Fulbright (*op. cit.*) comments aptly that "poverty, which is a tragedy in a poor country, blights our affluent society with something more than tragedy; being unnecessary, it is deeply immoral as well." He also compares "the $904 billion we have spent on military power since World War II" with "the $96 billion we have spent, out of our regular national budget, on education, health, welfare housing, and community development." In his *Challenge to Affluence* (New York, Pantheon Books, 1963), Myrdal concludes that "In society at large there is more equality of opportunity today than there ever was. But for the bottom layer there is less or none" (p. 38). He questions the assumption that "America is still the free and open society of its cherished image and well-established ideals" and remarks that "as less and less work is required of the type that people in the urban and rural slums can offer, they will be increasingly isolated and exposed to unemployment and plain exploitation. There is an ugly smell rising from the basement of the stately American mansion" (p. 49).

12. Adam Ulam, *The Unfinished Revolution* (New York, Vintage Books, 1964), p. 97.

13. In 1965, 20 companies out of 420,000 made 38% of profits after taxes, and earnings on foreign investments were well over three times what they were 15 years earlier. The sales of GM exceeded the GNP of all but nine foreign countries. The 10 largest companies reported profits equal to the next 490. One thousand companies disappeared through merger.

14. "America in the Technetronic Age," *Encounter,* Vol. 30 (January 1968), pp. 16–26.

15. "Marxian Socialism in the United States," in Donald D. Egbert and S. Persons, eds., *Socialism and American Life* (Princeton, N.J., Princeton University Press, 1952), Vol. 1, p. 329.

16. *Op. cit.,* p. 5. Less typical, and more realistic, is his belief that these problems also "seem to defy the social scientist's expertise." For some general discussions of this "generosity," see, for example, David Horowitz, *Hemispheres North and South* (Baltimore, The Johns Hopkins Press, 1966), and many special studies. American public officials do not share this faith in our generosity, by and large. For example, the Assistant Secretary of State for Latin American affairs observed

bluntly that "the State Department is not disposed to favor large loans of public funds to countries not welcoming our private capital" (*State Department Bulletin* No. 22, 1950, cited in Frederick Clairmonte, *Economic Liberalism and Underdevelopment* [Bombay and London, Asia Publishing House, 1960], p. 248). Eugene Black, testifying before Congress on the Asian Development Bank, pointed out that "when the Bank makes loans you have international bids, and I am sure that with our ability and ingenuity in this country, we will get our share of the business. We certainly ought to get more than the small amount we contribute." David Bell testified that "the Bank will play a major role in carrying forward another policy of our own assistance program—strengthening the role of the private sector . . . by identifying particular projects which can attract private capital, by helping to draw up development plans and stimulate policies which will encourage private initiative, and by drawing private capital to the region." Nothing here about "the generosity that characterizes our policy."

Equally revealing is the history of programs such as the Alliance for Progress. As Senator Gore commented, this program "has in large measure come to be a subsidy for American business and American exporters" (*Congressional Record*, July 22, 1966)—a fairly accurate judgment, so it appears. For example, the AID lending program in Latin America, according to former Alliance for Progress official William Rogers (*The Twilight Struggle* [New York, Random House, 1967], p. 205), is based on two elements: "a demonstrated balance of payments needed to increase the nation's ability to import U.S. goods and services, and the adoption of public policies and programs which would insure against capital flight on the international account side or the misuse of domestic resources through inefficient budgeting, reduced local savings or inflation." Commenting on this, Robert Smith notes that "the latter standard included increased tax revenues, reduction of budget deficit, elimination of 'distorting subsidies to public activities,' and the adoption of 'state incentives to private sector investment and growth.'" (*New Politics*, Vol. 6 [Spring 1967], pp. 49–57. For some remarks on the other side of our assistance program, military aid, see the articles by James Petras in this and the preceding issue.)

17. "To Intervene or Not to Intervene," *Foreign Affairs*, Vol. 45 (April 1967), pp. 425–36.

18. *New York Times,* December 20, 1967. The *Times* refers to what is printed as "excerpts," but it is not materially different from the full document. I understand that it has since been signed by many other scholars.

19. See the reviews by Coral Bell and B. R. O'G. Anderson in the *China Quarterly,* No. 28 (October–December 1966), pp. 140–43. It should be noted that opposition to social change, and support for the counterrevolutionary violence that is used to suppress it, are long-standing features of American cultural history. Thus according to American historian Louis Hartz, "there is no doubt that the appearance of even a mild socialism in 1848, of Ledru Rollin and the national workshops, was enough to produce general American dismay. There was no outcry in America against the suppression of the June revolt of the workers in Paris, as there was none over the suppression of the Communards in 1871. Here was violence, and plenty of it, but it was being used for order and law, as one editorial writer put it [in the *New York Journal of Commerce*]." (*The Nature of Revolution,* Testimony before the Senate Committee on Foreign Relations, February 26, 1968 [Washington, Government Printing Office, 1968].)

20. "The Public and the Polity," in Ithiel de Sola Pool, ed., *Contemporary Political Science: Toward Empirical Theory* (New York, Mc-Graw-Hill Book Company, 1967), p. 26.

21. Clairmonte, *op. cit.,* p. 325.

22. Recent confirmatory evidence is given by George M. Kahin, in a memorandum of April 13, 1967, in the *Congressional Record.* He cites the Marine Corps estimate that in this province, the principal area of marine strength, 18 out of 549 hamlets had been "secured."

23. Albert Shaw, editor of the *American Review of Reviews,* commenting, in 1893, on America's failure to acquire colonies. Cited in Ernest R. May, *Imperial Democracy* (New York, Harcourt, Brace & World, Inc., 1961), p. 23.

24. Quoted by Robert Guillain in *Le Monde,* May 25, 1966; reprinted, in English translation, as *Vietnam, the Dirty War* (London, Housmans, 1966).

25. According to Jonathan Randal (*New York Times,* June 11, 1967), "only one officer above the rank of lieutenant colonel did not serve in the French army against the Vietminh in the French Indochina war."

26. Douglas Pike, *Viet Cong,* (Cambridge, Mass., The M.I.T. Press, 1966), pp. 361–62.
27. *Vietnam: A Dragon Embattled* (New York, Frederick A. Praeger, Inc., 1967), Vol. 2, p. 952. See also note 29.
28. *World Communism* (1939; reprinted Ann Arbor, University of Michigan, 1962), p. 24.
29. *Op. cit.,* Vol. 2, p. 856. As Buttinger explains, "Local elections would have given the Vietminh control of most of the rural communities. The Vietminh was not only popular and in effective political control of large regions, but it alone had people with the requisite organizational skills to exploit whatever opportunities for democratic self-expression the regime opened up." He adds that "the NLF was truly the Vietminh reborn," and speaks of "the similarity, or better, near identity, of the Vietminh and the NLF."
30. Roger Hilsman, "Internal War: The New Communist Tactic," in Franklin Mark Osanka, ed., *Modern Guerrilla Warfare* (New York, The Free Press, 1962), p. 460.
31. Alastair Buchan, director of the Institute for Strategic Studies in London, describes the South Koreans as an "organization of Asian 'black and tans'" ("Questions about Vietnam," *Encounter,* Vol. 30 [January 1968], pp. 3–12).

On the reasons for the remarkable success of pacification in Binh Dinh Province, see Bernard Fall, *Last Reflections on a War* (Garden City, N.Y., Doubleday & Company, Inc., 1967), p. 159. This was one of "the areas where American-Korean multidivision operations have literally smothered the opposition" with "vast search-and-destroy operations" and continuing "tight military control"—or so it seemed, until late 1967, and finally February 1968, when the lid blew off. A report on Binh Dinh Province, the "showcase" province for pacification, in the *New York Times,* February 20, tells the story. "The enemy moves in December—which several military men called a 'softening up' for the offensive—resulted in a wave of allied air strikes on villages. Hundreds of homes were destroyed"—the standard American response. An American official reports: "What the Vietcong did was occupy the hamlets we pacified just for the purpose of having the allies move in and bomb them out. By their presence, the hamlets were destroyed." No doubt our psychological warfare specialists are now explaining to the Vietnamese, who seem to have some difficulty understanding these subtleties, that the destruction of the villages is the fault of the Vietcong. In any event, the report continues, "the entire 1968 program for the province has now been shelved" and "the program is now set back anywhere from 14 to 18 months"—that is, back to the time of the initial saturation with American and Korean troops. "It has all gone down the drain," said one gloomy American official.

32. *United States Policy and the Third World* (Boston, Little, Brown and Company, 1967), Ch. 3.

33. Morton H. Halperin, *Contemporary Military Strategy* (Boston, Little, Brown and Company, 1967), pp. 141–2. I am indebted to Herbert P. Bix for bringing this contribution to the social sciences to my attention.

34. Wolf, *op. cit.*, p. 69.

35. There is little point in a lengthy discussion of Wolf's concept of international affairs or his empirical studies. To take a few examples, he assumes without question that North Vietnam's willingness to "disrupt the regime" in the South was motivated in part by "the marked economic and social improvements accomplished by the Diem regime from 1955 to 1960—dramatic by comparison with the economic stagnation in North Vietnam" (for fact rather than fancy on relative development, see Buttinger, *op. cit.*, Vol. 2, pp. 928, 966 f.); and also that India's "moderately successful growth" was part of the motivation behind "China's aggressive actions in October 1962." See also note 36. As to the solidity of Wolf's empirical studies, it is perhaps enough to note that his most significant result, the correlation between higher GNP and higher level of political democracy in Latin America, arises principally from the conclusion (based on data from 1950 to 1960) that Brazil and Argentina (along with Mexico and Chile) rank high on the scale of political democracy (cf. p. 124). The general level of sophistication is illustrated, for example, by a solemn reference to a consultant for having explained that in determining the "total military value" of a set of alternatives, it is not enough to sum up the separate values; one must also weight responses by probability of occurrence.

36. "But in all cases, the primary consideration should be whether the proposed measure is likely to increase the cost and difficulties of insurgent operations and help to disrupt the insurgent organization, rather than whether it wins popular loyalty and support, or whether it contributes to a more productive, efficient, or equitable use of resources" (Wolf, *op. cit.*, p. 69). We must understand that "successful

counterinsurgency programs can be conducted among a rural populace that is passive or even hostile, rather than loyal, to the government." As evidence, Wolf cites his belief that "The growth of the Viet Cong and of the Pathet Lao probably occurred despite the opposition of a large majority of the people in both Vietnam and Laos" (*ibid.,* p. 48). If they can do it, so can we.

In contrast, Robert Scigliano (of the Michigan State University Vietnam Advisory Group) reported that "using the estimate of American officials in Saigon at the end of 1962, about one-half of the South Vietnamese support the NLF" (*South Vietnam: Nation Under Stress* [Boston, Houghton Mifflin Company, 1963], p. 145). Arthur Dommen reports (*Conflict in Laos: The Politics of Neutralization* [New York, Frederick A. Praeger, Inc., 1964]) that "the Pathet Lao needed no propaganda to turn the rural population against the townspeople" (p. 107). The American Mission took care of this, with its lavish aid (½ of 1 percent of which was spent on agriculture, the livelihood of 96 percent of the population) leading to immense corruption, the proliferation of luxurious villas and large automobiles alongside of grinding poverty; and with its constant subversion in support, first of the "pro-Western neutralist" Phoui Sananikone, and then of the military dictator Phoumi Nosavan. As Roger Hilsman puts it, the real Pathet Lao "threat" was "expansion of political control based on winning peasant support in the villages" (*To Move a Nation,* [Garden City, N.Y., Doubleday & Company, Inc., 1967], p. 112). The lack of support for the Pathet Lao was amply demonstrated in the 1958 elections, in which 9 of their 13 candidates won, and Souphanouvong, the leading Pathet Lao figure, received more votes than any other candidate in the country. It was this election victory that set off the American attempts at subversion. As Dommen says, "once again the United States threw its support to the most feudal elements of the society."

To Charles Wolf, all of this demonstrates that counterinsurgency, like insurgency, can succeed without concern for popular loyalty and participation.

37. Cited in Clairmonte, *op. cit.,* p. 92. The ancestors of whom Merivale speaks are those who crushed the Indian textile industry by embargoes and import duties, as was quite necessary. "Had this not been the case, the mills of Paisley and Manchester would have been stopped in their outset, and could scarcely have been again set in motion, even by the power of steam. They were created by the sacri-

fice of Indian manufacturers" (Horace Wilson, 1826, cited by Clairmonte, p. 87).

This is the classic example of the creation of underdevelopment through imperialism. For a detailed study of this process see André Gunder Frank, *Capitalism and Underdevelopment in Latin America,* (New York, Monthly Review Press, 1967).

38. See Robert E. Osgood, *Ideals and Self-Interest in America's Foreign Relations* (Chicago, University of Chicago Press, 1953), pp. 72–73.

39. "Some Reflections on U.S. Policy in Southeast Asia," in William Henderson, ed., *Southeast Asia: Problems of United States Policy* (Cambridge, Mass., The M.I.T. Press, 1963), pp. 249–63. This collection of papers was published with the encouragement of the Asia Society because of "the scholarly quality of the papers and their enlightening contribution to the formation of United States policy in the area."

40. *Thailand and the United States* (Washington, Public Affairs Press, 1965).

41. The Bank of America placed a full-page ad in the Fourth of July edition, 1951, of the *Bangkok Post* saluting the kingdom of Thailand with these words: "In both Thailand and America democracy has gone hand in hand with national sovereignty. Today both nations stand in the forefront of world efforts to promote and defend the democratic way of life."

42. In an article on "U.S.-Thai links" in the *Christian Science Monitor*, October 14, 1967.

43. Just a few paragraphs earlier we read that in the postwar period "the Americans rapidly expanded the Thai armed forces from 50,000 to 100,000 men . . . the United States quickly increased the police forces, and this helped suppress opponents of the government. The technical assistance program was largely converted to military objectives. The internal impact of this policy further strengthened the power and prestige of the Thai military leaders who had seized the government in 1947. The effort to move toward some form of constitutional rule was halted, and the democratic institutions inaugurated by civilian leaders just after the war were abolished. Political parties were suppressed. The press was censored. Power became increasingly centralized in the hands of a few military leaders." All of this, however, did not constitute "interference in the domestic affairs of other nations," and is not "contrary to American traditions."

44. *Western Interests in the Pacific Realm* (New York, Random House, 1967).

45. Of what importance, then, is the fact that the overwhelming majority of Okinawans, including 80% of those whose businesses would be impaired or destroyed by this move, want the island returned to Japan, according to the *Asahi* polls (see *Japan Quarterly*, Vol. 15 [January–March 1968], pp. 42–52)? As to the "strategic trust territories," Adam says, we must also not become overly sentimental: "A strategic trust is based on the assumption of the overriding importance of national defense and the preservation of world order as against the cultural and political freedom of the indigenous inhabitants."

46. H. D. Malaviya, quoted in Clairmonte (*op. cit.*, p. 114), who cites substantial evidence in support of the following evaluation of the consequences of Western dominance: "The systematic destruction of Indian manufacturers; the creation of the Zemindari [landed aristocracy] and its parasitical outgrowths; the changes in agrarian structure; the financial losses incurred by tribute; the sharp transition from a pre-monetised economy to one governed by the international price mechanism—these were some of the social and institutional forces that were to bring the apocalypse of death and famine to millions—with few or no compensatory benefits to the ryot [peasant]" (p. 107). See also note 37.

47. Cited in Paul Avrich, *The Russian Anarchists* (Princeton, N.J., Princeton University Press, 1967), pp. 93–94. A recent reformulation of this view is given by Anton Pannekoek, the Dutch scientist and spokesman for libertarian communism, in his *Workers Councils* (Melbourne, 1950), pp. 36–37:

> It is not for the first time that a ruling class tries to explain, and so to perpetuate, its rule as the consequences of an inborn difference between two kinds of people, one destined by nature to ride, the other to be ridden. The landowning aristocracy of former centuries defended their privileged position by boasting their extraction from a nobler race of conquerors that had subdued the lower race of common people. Big capitalists explain their dominating place by the assertion that they have brains and other people have none. In the same way now especially the intellectuals, considering themselves the rightful rulers of to-morrow, claim their spiritual superiority. They form the rapidly increasing class of university-trained officials and free professions, specialized in mental work, in study of books and of science,

and they consider themselves as the people most gifted with intellect. Hence they are destined to be leaders of the production, whereas the ungifted mass shall execute the manual work, for which no brains are needed. They are no defenders of capitalism; not capital, but intellect should direct labor. The more so, since now society is such a complicated structure, based on abstract and difficult science, that only the highest intellectual acumen is capable of embracing, grasping and handling it. Should the working masses, from lack of insight, fail to acknowledge this need of superior intellectual lead, should they stupidly try to take the direction into their own hands, chaos and ruin will be the inevitable consequence.

48. See note 7. Albert Parry has suggested that there are important similarities between the emergence of a scientific elite in the Soviet Union and the United States, in their growing role in decision making, citing Bell's thesis in support. See the *New York Times,* March 27, 1966, reporting on the Midwest Slavic Conference.

49. Letter to Herzen and Ogareff, 1866, cited in Daniel Guérin, *Jeunesse du socialisme libertaire* (Paris, Librairie Marcel Rivière, 1959), p. 119.

50. Rosa Luxemburg, *The Russian Revolution,* trans. Bertram D. Wolfe (Ann Arbor, University of Michigan Press, 1961), p. 71.

51. Luxemburg, cited by Guérin, *Jeunesse du socialisme libertaire,* pp. 106–7.

52. *Leninism or Marxism,* in Luxemburg, *op. cit.,* p. 102.

53. For a very enlightening study of this matter, emphasizing domestic issues, see Michael Paul Rogin, *The Intellectuals and McCarthy: The Radical Specter* (Cambridge, Mass., the M.I.T. Press, 1967).

54. *The Spanish Republic and the Civil War: 1931–1939* (Princeton, N.J., Princeton University Press, 1965).

55. Respectively, President of the Republic, Prime Minister from May until the Franco insurrection, and member of the conservative wing of the Popular Front selected by Azaña to try to set up a compromise government after the insurrection.

56. It is interesting that Douglas Pike's very hostile account of the National Liberation Front, cited earlier, emphasizes the popular and voluntary element in its striking organizational successes. What he describes, whether accurately or not one cannot tell, is a structure of interlocking self-help organizations, loosely coordinated and developed through persuasion rather than force—in certain respects, of a charac-

ter that would have appealed to anarchist thinkers. Those who speak so freely of the "authoritarian Vietcong" may be correct, but they have presented little evidence to support their judgment. Of course, it must be understood that Pike regards the element of voluntary mass participation in self-help associations as the most dangerous and insidious feature of the NLF organizational structure.

Also relevant is the history of collectivization in China, which, as compared with the Soviet Union, shows a much higher reliance on persuasion and mutual aid than on force and terror, and appears to have been more successful. See Thomas P. Bernstein, "Leadership and Mass Mobilisation in the Soviet and Chinese Collectivization Campaigns of 1929–30 and 1955–56: A Comparison," *China Quarterly*, No. 31 (July–September 1967), pp. 1–47, for some interesting and suggestive comments and analysis.

The scale of the Chinese Revolution is so great and reports in depth are so fragmentary that it would no doubt be foolhardy to attempt a general evaluation. Still, all the reports I have been able to study suggest that insofar as real successes were achieved in the several stages of land reform, mutual aid, collectivization, and formation of communes, they were traceable in large part to the complex interaction of the Communist party cadres and the gradually evolving peasant associations, a relation which seems to stray far from the Leninist model of organization. This is particularly evident in William Hinton's magnificent study *Fanshen* (New York, Monthly Review Press, 1966), which is unparalleled, to my knowledge, as an analysis of a moment of profound revolutionary change. What seems to me particularly striking in his account of the early stages of revolution in one Chinese village is not only the extent to which party cadres submitted themselves to popular control, but also, and more significant, the ways in which exercise of control over steps of the revolutionary process was a factor in developing the consciousness and insight of those who took part in the revolution, not only from a political and social point of view, but also with respect to the human relationships that were created. It is interesting, in this connection, to note the strong populist element in early Chinese Marxism. For some very illuminating observations about this general matter, see Maurice Meisner, *Li Ta-chao and the Origins of Chinese Marxism* (Cambridge, Mass., Harvard University Press, 1967).

I am not suggesting that the anarchist revolution in Spain—with its background of more than thirty years of education and struggle—is being relived in Asia, but rather that the spontaneous and voluntary elements in popular mass movements have probably been seriously misunderstood because of the instinctive antipathy towards such phenomena among intellectuals, and more recently, because of the insistence on interpreting them in terms of Cold War mythology.

57. "The Spanish Background," *New Left Review*, No. 40 (November–December 1966), pp. 85–90.

58. José Peirats, *La C.N.T. en la revolución española* (Toulouse, Ediciones C.N.T., 1951–52), 3 vols. Jackson makes one passing reference to it. Peirats has since published a general history of the period, *Los anarquistas en la crisis política española* (Buenos Aires, Editorial Alfa-Argentina, 1964). This highly informative book should certainly be made available to an English-speaking audience.

59. An exception to the rather general failure to deal with the anarchist revolution is Hugh Thomas' "Anarchist Agrarian Collectives in the Spanish Civil War," in Martin Gilbert, ed., *A Century of Conflict, 1850–1950: Essays for A. J. P. Taylor* (New York, Atheneum Publishers, 1967), pp. 245–63. See note 106 below for some discussion. There is also much useful information in what to my mind is the best general history of the Civil War, *La Révolution et la guerre d'Espagne*, by Pierre Broué and Émile Témime (Paris, Les Éditions de Minuit, 1961). A concise and informative recent account is contained in Daniel Guérin, *L'Anarchisme* (Paris, Gallimard, 1965). In his extensive study, *The Spanish Civil War* (New York, Harper & Row, Publishers, 1961; paperback ed. 1963), Hugh Thomas barely refers to the popular revolution, and some of the major events are not mentioned at all—see, for example, note 97 below.

60. *Collectivisations: l'oeuvre constructive de la Révolution espagnole*, 2nd ed. (Toulouse, Éditions C.N.T., 1965). The first edition was published in Barcelona (Éditions C.N.T.-F.A.I., 1937). There is an excellent and sympathetic summary by the Marxist scholar Karl Korsch, "Collectivization in Spain," in *Living Marxism*, Vol. 4 (April 1939), pp. 179–82. In the same issue (pp. 170–71), the liberal-Communist reaction to the Spanish Civil War is summarized succinctly, and I believe accurately, as follows: "With their empty chatter as to the wonders of Bolshevik discipline, the geniality of Caballero, and the passions of the Pasionaria, the 'modern liberals' merely covered up their real desire for the destruction of all revolutionary possibilities in

the Civil War, and their preparation for the possible war over the Spanish issue in the interest of their diverse fatherlands . . . what was truly revolutionary in the Spanish Civil War resulted from the direct actions of the workers and pauperized peasants, and not because of a specific form of labor organization nor an especially gifted leadership." I think that the record bears out this analysis, and I also think that it is this fact that accounts for the distaste for the revolutionary phase of the Civil War and its neglect in historical scholarship.

61. An illuminating eyewitness account of this period is that of Franz Borkenau, *The Spanish Cockpit* (1938; reprinted Ann Arbor, University of Michigan Press, 1963).

62. Figures from Guérin, *L'Anarchisme,* p. 154.

63. A useful account of this period is given by Felix Morrow, *Revolution and Counter-Revolution in Spain* (1938; reprinted London, New Park Publications, 1963).

64. Cited by Camillo Berneri in his "Lettre ouverte à la camarade Frederica [sic] Montseny," *Guerre de classes en Espagne* (Paris, 1946), a collection of items translated from his journal *Guerra di Classe.* Berneri was the oustanding anarchist intellectual in Spain. He opposed the policy of joining the government and argued for an alternative, more typically anarchist strategy to which I will return below. His own view towards joining the government was stated succinctly by a Catalan worker whom he quotes, with reference to the Republic of 1931: "It is always the old dog with a new collar." Events were to prove the accuracy of this analysis.

Berneri had been a leading spokesman of Italian anarchism. He left Italy after Mussolini's rise to power, and came to Barcelona on July 19, 1936. He formed the first Italian units for the antifascist war, according to anarchist historian Rudolf Rocker (*The Tragedy of Spain* [New York, Freie Arbeiter Stimme, 1937], p. 44). He was murdered, along with his older comrade Barbieri, during the May Days of 1937. (Arrested on May 5 by the Communist-controlled police, he was shot during the following night.) Hugh Thomas, in *The Spanish Civil War,* p. 428, suggests that "the assassins may have been Italian Communists" rather than the police. Thomas' book, which is largely devoted to military history, mentions Berneri's murder but makes no other reference to his ideas or role.

Berneri's name does not appear in Jackson's history.

65. Burnett Bolloten, *The Grand Camouflage: The Communist Con-*

spiracy in the Spanish Civil War (New York, Frederick A. Praeger, Inc., 1961), p. 86. This book, by a UP correspondent in Spain during the Civil War, contains a great deal of important documentary evidence bearing on the questions considered here. The attitude of the wealthy farmers of this area, most of them former supporters of the right-wing organizations that had now disappeared, is well described by the general secretary of the Peasant Federation, Julio Mateu: "Such is the sympathy for us [that is, the Communist party] in the Valencia countryside that hundreds and thousands of farmers would join our party if we were to let them. These farmers . . . love our party like a sacred thing . . . they [say] 'The Communist Party is our party.' Comrades, what emotion the peasants display when they utter these words" (cited in Bolloten, p. 86). There is some interesting speculation about the backgrounds for the writing of this very important book in H. R. Southworth, *Le mythe de la croisade de Franco* (Ruedo Ibérico, Paris, 1964; Spanish edition, same publisher, 1963).

The Communist headquarters in Valencia had on the wall two posters: "Respect the property of the small peasant" and "Respect the property of the small industrialist" (Borkenau, *The Spanish Cockpit*, p. 117). Actually, it was the rich farmer as well who sought protection from the Communists, whom Borkenau describes as constituting the extreme right wing of the Republican forces. By early 1937, according to Borkenau, the Communist party was "to a large extent . . . the party of the military and administrative personnel, in the second place the party of the petty bourgeoisie and certain well-to-do peasant groups, in the third place the party of the employees, and only in the fourth place the party of the industrial workers" (p. 192). The party also attracted many police and army officers. The police chief in Madrid and the chief of intelligence, for example, were party members. In general, the party, which had been insignificant before the revolution, "gave the urban and rural middle classes a powerful access of life and vigour" as it defended them from the revolutionary forces (Bolloten, *op. cit.*, p. 86). Gerald Brenan describes the situation as follows, in *The Spanish Labyrinth* (1943; reprinted Cambridge, Cambridge University Press, 1960), p. 325:

> Unable to draw to themselves the manual workers, who remained firmly fixed in their unions, the Communists found themselves the refuge for all those who had suffered from the excesses of the Revolu-

tion or who feared where it might lead them. Well-to-do Catholic orange-growers in Valencia, peasants in Catalonia, small shopkeepers and business men, Army officers and Government officials enrolled in their ranks. . . . Thus [in Catalonia] one had a strange and novel situation: on the one side stood the huge compact proletariat of Barcelona with its long revolutionary tradition, and on the other the white-collar workers and *petite bourgeoisie* of the city, organized and armed by the Communist party against it.

Actually, the situation that Brenan describes is not as strange a one as he suggests. It is, rather, a natural consequence of Bolshevik elitism that the "Red bureaucracy" should act as a counterrevolutionary force except under the conditions where its present or future representatives are attempting to seize power for themselves, in the name of the masses whom they pretend to represent.

66. Bolloten, *op. cit.*, p. 189. The legalization of revolutionary actions already undertaken and completed recalls the behavior of the "revolutionary vanguard" in the Soviet Union in 1918. Cf. Arthur Rosenberg, *A History of Bolshevism* (1932; republished in translation from the original German, New York, Russell and Russell, Publishers, 1965), Ch. 6. He describes how the expropriations, "accomplished as the result of spontaneous action on the part of workers and against the will of the Bolsheviks," were reluctantly legalized by Lenin months later and then placed under central party control. On the relation of the Bolsheviks to the anarchists in postrevolutionary Russia, interpreted from a pro-anarchist point of view, see Guérin, *L'Anarchisme*, pp. 96–125. See also Avrich, *op. cit.*, Part II, pp. 123–254.

67. Bolloten, *op. cit.*, p. 191.

68. *Ibid.*, p. 194.

69. For some details, see Vernon Richards, *Lessons of the Spanish Revolution* (London, Freedom Press, 1953), pp. 83–88.

70. For a moving eyewitness account, see George Orwell, *Homage to Catalonia* (1938; reprinted New York, Harcourt, Brace & World, 1952, and Boston, Beacon Press, 1955; quotations in this book from Beacon Press edition). This brilliant book received little notice at the time of its first publication, no doubt because the picture Orwell drew was in sharp conflict with established liberal dogma. The attention that it has received as a cold-war document since its republication in 1952 would, I suspect, have been of little comfort to the author.

71. Cited by Rocker, *The Tragedy of Spain*, p. 28.

72. See *ibid.* for a brief review. It was a great annoyance to Hitler that these interests were, to a large extent, protected by Franco.

73. *Ibid.*, p. 35.

74. *Op. cit.*, pp. 324 f.

75. Borkenau, *The Spanish Cockpit*, pp. 289–92. It is because of the essential accuracy of Borkenau's account that I think Hobsbawm (*op. cit.*) is quite mistaken in believing that the Communist policy "was undoubtedly the only one which could have won the Civil War." In fact, the Communist policy was bound to fail, because it was predicated on the assumption that the Western democracies would join the antifascist effort if only Spain could be preserved as, in effect, a Western colony. Once the Communist leaders saw the futility of this hope, they abandoned the struggle, which was not in their eyes an effort to win the Civil War, but only to serve the interests of Russian foreign policy. I also disagree with Hobsbawm's analysis of the anarchist revolution, cited earlier, for reasons that are implicit in this entire discussion.

76. *Op. cit.*, pp. 143–44.

77. Cited by Rosenberg, *op. cit.*, pp. 168–69.

78. Bolloten, *op. cit.*, p. 84.

79. *Ibid.*, p. 85. As noted earlier, the "small farmer" included the prosperous orange growers, etc. (see note 65).

80. Brenan, *op. cit.*, p. 321.

81. Correspondence from Companys to Prieto, 1939. While Companys, as a Catalonian with separatist impulses, would naturally be inclined to defend Catalonian achievements, he was surely not sympathetic to collectivization, despite his cooperative attitude during the period when the anarchists, with real power in their hands, permitted him to retain nominal authority. I know of no attempt to challenge the accuracy of his assessment. Morrow (*op. cit.*, p. 77) quotes the Catalonian Premier, the entrepreneur Juan Tarradellas, as defending the administration of the collectivized war industries against a Communist (PSUC) attack, which he termed the "most arbitrary falsehoods." There are many other reports commenting on the functioning of the collectivized industries by nonanarchist firsthand observers, that tend to support Companys. For example, the Swiss socialist Andres Oltmares is quoted by Rocker (*The Tragedy of Spain*, p. 24) as saying that after the revolution the Catalonian workers' syndicates "in seven

weeks accomplished fully as much as France did in fourteen months after the outbreak of the World War." Continuing, he says:

> In the midst of the civil war the Anarchists have proved themselves to be political organizers of the first rank. They kindled in everyone the required sense of responsibility, and knew how by eloquent appeals to keep alive the spirit of sacrifice for the general welfare of the people.
>
> As a Social Democrat I speak here with inner joy and sincere admiration of my experience in Catalonia. The anti-capitalist transformation took place here without their having to resort to a dictatorship. The members of the syndicates are their own masters, and carry on production and the distribution of the products of labor under their own management with the advice of technical experts in whom they have confidence. The enthusiasm of the workers is so great that they scorn any personal advantage and are concerned only for the welfare of all.

Even Borkenau concludes, rather grudgingly, that industry was functioning fairly well, as far as he could see. The matter deserves a serious study.

82. Quoted in Richards, *op. cit.*, pp. 46–47.

83. *Ibid.* Richards suggests that the refusal of the central government to support the Aragon front may have been motivated in part by the general policy of counterrevolution. "This front, largely manned by members of the C.N.T.-F.A.I., was considered of great strategic importance by the anarchists, having as its ultimate objective the linking of Catalonia with the Basque country and Asturias, i.e., a linking of the industrial region [of Catalonia] with an important source of raw materials." Again, it would be interesting to undertake a detailed investigation of this topic.

That the Communists withheld arms from the Aragon front seems established beyond question, and it can hardly be doubted that the motivation was political. See, for example, D. T. Cattell, *Communism and the Spanish Civil War* (1955; reprinted New York, Russell and Russell, Publishers, 1965), p. 110. Cattell, who in general bends over backwards to try to justify the behavior of the central government, concludes that in this case there is little doubt that the refusal of aid was politically motivated. Brenan takes the same view, claiming that the Communists "kept the Aragon front without arms to spite the Anarchists." The Communists resorted to some of the most grotesque

143

slanders to explain the lack of arms on the Aragon front; for example, the *Daily Worker* attributed the arms shortage to the fact that "the Trotskyist General Kopp had been carting enormous supplies of arms and ammunition across no-man's land to the fascists" (cited by Morrow, *op. cit.*, p. 145). As Morrow points out, George Kopp is a particularly bad choice as a target for such accusations. His record is well known, for example, from the account given by Orwell, who served under his command (see Orwell, *op. cit.*, pp. 209 f.). Orwell was also able to refute, from firsthand observation, many of the other absurdities that were appearing in the liberal press about the Aragon front, for example, the statement by Ralph Bates in the *New Republic* that the POUM troops were "playing football with the Fascists in no man's land." At that moment, as Orwell observes, "the P.O.U.M. troops were suffering heavy casualties and a number of my personal friends were killed and wounded."

84. Cited in *Living Marxism*, p. 172.

85. Bolloten, *op. cit.*, p. 49, comments on the collectivization of the dairy trade in Barcelona, as follows: "The Anarchosyndicalists eliminated as unhygienic over forty pasteurizing plants, pasteurized all the milk in the remaining nine, and proceeded to displace all dealers by establishing their own dairies. Many of the retailers entered the collective, but some refused to do so: 'They asked for a much higher wage than that paid to the workers . . . , claiming that they could not manage on the one allotted to them' [*Tierra y Libertad*, August 21, 1937—the newspaper of the FAI, the anarchist activists]." His information is primarily from anarchist sources, which he uses much more extensively than any historian other than Peirats. He does not present any evaluation of these sources, which—like all others—must be used critically.

86. Morrow, *op. cit.*, p. 136.

87. Borkenau, *The Spanish Cockpit*, p. 182.

88. *Ibid.*, p. 183.

89. *Ibid.*, p. 184. According to Borkenau, "it is doubtful whether Comorera is personally responsible for this scarcity; it might have arisen anyway, in pace with the consumption of the harvest." This speculation may or may not be correct. Like Borkenau, we can only speculate as to whether the village and workers' committees would have been able to continue to provision Barcelona, with or without central administration, had it not been for the policy of "abstract

liberalism," which was of a piece with the general Communist-directed attempts to destroy the Revolutionary organizations and the structures developed in the Revolutionary period.

90. Orwell, *op. cit.*, pp. 109–11. Orwell's description of Barcelona in December (pp. 4–5), when he arrived for the first time, deserves more extensive quotation:

> It was the first time that I had ever been in a town where the working class was in the saddle. Practically every building of any size had been seized by the workers and was draped with red flags or with the red and black flag of the Anarchists; every wall was scrawled with the hammer and sickle and with the initials of the revolutionary parties; almost every church had been gutted and its images burnt. Churches here and there were being systematically demolished by gangs of workmen. Every shop and café had an inscription saying that it had been collectivized; even the bootblacks had been collectivized and their boxes painted red and black. Waiters and shop-walkers looked you in the face and treated you as an equal. Servile and even ceremonial forms of speech had temporarily disappeared. Nobody said "Señor" or "Don" or even "Usted"; everyone called everyone else "Comrade" and "Thou," and said "Salud!" instead of "Buenos dias." Tipping had been forbidden by law since the time of Primo de Rivera; almost my first experience was receiving a lecture from an hotel manager for trying to tip a lift-boy. There were no private motor cars, they had all been commandeered, and all the trams and taxis and much of the other transport were painted red and black. The revolutionary posters were everywhere, flaming from the walls in clean reds and blues that made the few remaining advertisements look like daubs of mud. Down the Ramblas, the wide central artery of the town where crowds of people streamed constantly to and fro, the loud-speakers were bellowing revolutionary songs all day and far into the night. And it was the aspect of the crowds that was the queerest thing of all. In outward appearance it was a town in which the wealthy classes had practically ceased to exist. Except for a small number of women and foreigners there were no "well-dressed" people at all. Practically everyone wore rough working-class clothes, or blue overalls or some variant of the militia uniform. All this was queer and moving. There was much in it that I did not understand, in some ways I did not even like it, but I recognized it immediately as a state of affairs worth fighting for. Also I believed that things were as they appeared, that this was really a workers' State and that the entire bourgeoisie had either fled, been

killed, or voluntarily come over to the workers' side; I did not realize
that great numbers of well-to-do bourgeois were simply lying low and
disguising themselves as proletarians for the time being . . .

. . . waiting for that happy day when Communist power would rein-
troduce the old state of society and destroy popular involvement in the
war.

In December 1936, however, the situation was still as described in
the following remarks (p. 6):

> Yet so far as one can judge the people were contented and hopeful.
> There was no unemployment, and the price of living was still ex-
> tremely low; you saw very few conspicuously destitute people, and
> no beggars except the gipsies. Above all, there was a belief in the
> revolution and the future, a feeling of having suddenly emerged into
> an era of equality and freedom. Human beings were trying to behave
> as human beings and not as cogs in the capitalist machine. In the
> barbers' shops were Anarchist notices (the barbers were mostly An-
> archists) solemnly explaining that barbers were no longer slaves. In
> the streets were coloured posters appealing to prostitutes to stop being
> prostitutes. To anyone from the hard-boiled, sneering civilization of the
> English-speaking races there was something rather pathetic in the
> literalness with which these idealistic Spaniards took the hackneyed
> phrases of revolution. At that time revolutionary ballads of the
> naïvest kind, all about proletarian brotherhood and the wickedness of
> Mussolini, were being sold on the streets for a few centimes each. I
> have often seen an illiterate militiaman buy one of these ballads,
> laboriously spell out the words, and then, when he had got the hang
> of it, begin singing it to an appropriate tune.

Recall the dates. Orwell arrived in Barcelona in late December 1936.
Comorera's decree abolishing the workers' supply committees and the
bread committees was on January 7. Borkenau returned to Barcelona
in mid-January; Orwell, in April.
91. See Bolloten, *op. cit.*, p. 74, citing the anarchist spokesman Juan
Peiró, in September 1936. Like other anarchists and left-wing Social-
lists, Peiró sharply condemns the use of force to introduce collectivization, taking the position that was expressed by most anarchists, as well
as by left-wing socialists such as Ricardo Zabalza, general secretary of
the Federation of Land Workers, who stated, on January 8, 1937: "I
prefer a small, enthusiastic collective, formed by a group of active and
honest workers, to a large collective set up by force and composed of

peasants without enthusiasm, who would sabotage it until it failed. Voluntary collectivization may seem the longer course, but the example of the small, well-managed collective will attract the entire peasantry, who are profoundly realistic and practical, whereas forced collectivization would end by discrediting socialized agriculture" (cited by Bolloten *op. cit.*, p. 59). However, there seems no doubt that the precepts of the anarchist and left-socialist spokesmen were often violated in practice.

92. Borkenau, *The Spanish Cockpit*, pp. 219–20. Of this officer, Jackson says only that he was "a dependable professional officer." After the fall of Málaga, Lieutenant Colonel Villalba was tried for treason, for having deserted the headquarters and abandoned his troops. Broué and Témime remark that it is difficult to determine what justice there was in the charge.

93. Jesús Hernández and Juan Comorera, *Spain Organises for Victory: The Policy of the Communist Party of Spain Explained* (London, Communist Party of Great Britain, n.d.), cited by Richards, *op. cit.*, pp. 99–100. There was no accusation that the phone service was restricted, but only that the revolutionary workers could maintain "a close check on the conversations that took place between the politicians." As Richards further observes, "It is, of course, a quite different matter when the 'indiscreet ear' is that of the O.G.P.U."

94. Broué and Témime, *op. cit.*, p. 266.

95. Jackson, *op. cit.*, p. 370. Thomas suggests that Sesé was probably killed accidentally (*The Spanish Civil War*, p. 428).

96. The anarchist mayor of the border town of Puigcerdá had been assassinated in April, after Negrín's carabineros had taken over the border posts. That same day a prominent UGT member, Roldán Cortada, was murdered in Barcelona, it is presumed by CNT militants. This presumption is disputed by Peirats (*Los Anarquistas:* see note 58), who argues, with some evidence, that the murder may have been a Stalinist provocation. In reprisal, a CNT man was killed. Orwell, whose eyewitness account of the May Days is unforgettable, points out that "One can gauge the attitude of the foreign capitalist Press towards the Communist-Anarchist feud by the fact that Roldán's murder was given wide publicity, while the answering murder was carefully unmentioned" (*op. cit.*, p. 119). Similarly, one can gauge Jackson's attitude towards this struggle by his citation of Sesé's murder as a critical event, while the murder of Berneri goes unmentioned (cf.

147

notes 64 and 95). Orwell remarks elsewhere that "In the English press, in particular, you would have to search for a long time before finding any favourable reference, at any period of the war, to the Spanish Anarchists. They have been systematically denigrated, and, as I know by my own experience, it is almost impossible to get anyone to print anything in their defence" (p. 159). Little has changed since.

97. According to Orwell (*op. cit.*, pp. 153–54), "A British cruiser and two British destroyers had closed in upon the harbour, and no doubt there were other warships not far away. The English newspapers gave it out that these ships were proceeding to Barcelona 'to protect British interests,' but in fact they made no move to do so; that is, they did not land any men or take off any refugees. There can be no certainty about this, but it was at least inherently likely that the British Government, which had not raised a finger to save the Spanish Government from Franco, would intervene quickly enough to save it from its own working class." This assumption may well have influenced the left-wing leadership to restrain the Barcelona workers from simply taking control of the whole city, as apparently they could easily have done in the initial stages of the May Days.

Hugh Thomas comments (*The Spanish Civil War*, p. 428) that there was "no reason" for Orwell's "apprehension" on this matter. In the light of the British record with regard to Spain, it seems to me that Thomas is simply unrealistic, as compared with Orwell, in this respect.

98. Orwell, *op. cit.*, pp. 143–44.

99. *Controversy*, August 1937, cited by Morrow, p. 173. The prediction was incorrect, though not unreasonable. Had the Western powers and the Soviet Union wished, compromise would have been possible, it appears, and Spain might have been saved the terrible consequences of a Franco victory. See Brenan, *op. cit.*, p. 331. He attributes the British failure to support an armistice and possible reconciliation to the fact that Chamberlain "saw nothing disturbing in the prospect of an Italian and German victory." It would be interesting to explore more fully the attitude of Winston Churchill. In April 1937 he stated that a Franco victory would not harm British interests. Rather, the danger was a "success of the trotskyists and anarchists" (cited by Broué and Té-mime, *op. cit.*, p. 172). Of some interest, in this connection, is the recent discovery of an unpublished Churchill essay written in March 1939—six months after Munich—in which he said that England

"would welcome and aid a genuine Hitler of peace and toleration" (see *New York Times*, December 12, 1965).

100. I find no mention at all in Hugh Thomas, *The Spanish Civil War*. The account here is largely taken from Broué and Témime, pp. 279–80.

101. *Op cit.*, p. 405. A footnote comments on the "leniency" of the government to those arrested. Jackson has nothing to say about the charges against Ascaso and others, or the manner in which the old order was restored in Aragon.

To appreciate these events more fully, one should consider, by comparison, the concern for civil liberties shown by Negrín on the second, antifascist front. In an interview after the war he explained to John Whitaker (*We Cannot Escape History* [New York, The Macmillan Company, 1943], pp. 116–18) why his government had been so ineffective in coping with the fifth column, even in the case of known fascist agents. Negrín explained that "we couldn't arrest a man on suspicion; we couldn't break with the rules of evidence. You can't risk arresting an innocent man because you are positive in your own mind that he is guilty. You prosecute a war, yes; but you also live with your conscience." Evidently, these scruples did not pertain when it was the rights of anarchist and socialist workers, rather than fascist agents, that were at stake.

102. Cf. Broué and Témime, p. 262. Ironically, the government forces included some anarchist troops, the only ones to enter Barcelona.

103. See Bolloten, *op. cit.*, p. 55, n. 1, for an extensive list of sources.

104. Broué and Témime cite the socialists Alardo Prats, Fenner Brockway, and Carlo Rosselli. Borkenau, on the other hand, suspected that the role of terror was great in collectivization. He cites very little to substantiate his feeling, though some evidence is available from anarchist sources. See note 91 above.

Some general remarks on collectivization by Rosselli and Brockway are cited by Rudolf Rocker in his essay "Anarchism and Anarcho-syndicalism," n. 1, in Paul Eltzbacher, ed., *Anarchism* (London, Freedom Press, 1960), p. 266:

> Rosselli: In three months Catalonia has been able to set up a new social order on the ruins of an ancient system. This is chiefly due to the Anarchists, who have revealed a quite remarkable sense of proportion, realistic understanding, and organizing ability. . . . All the revolutionary forces of Catalonia have united in a program of Syndicalist-Socialist

character . . . Anarcho-Syndicalism, hitherto so despised, has revealed itself as a great constructive force. I am no Anarchist, but I regard it as my duty to express here my opinion of the Anarchists of Catalonia, who have all too often been represented as a destructive if not a criminal element.

Brockway: I was impressed by the strength of the C.N.T. It was unnecessary to tell me that it is the largest and most vital of the working class organizations in Spain. That was evident on all sides. The large industries were clearly in the main in the hands of the C.N.T.—railways, road transport, shipping, engineering, textiles, electricity, building, agriculture. . . . I was immensely impressed by the constructive revolutionary work which is being done by the C.N.T. Their achievements of workers' control in industry is an inspiration. . . . There are still some Britishers and Americans who regard the Anarchists of Spain as impossible, undisciplined uncontrollables. This is poles away from the truth. The Anarchists of Spain, through the C.N.T., are doing one of the biggest constructive jobs ever done by the working class. At the front they are fighting Fascism. Behind the front they are actually constructing the new workers' society. They see that the war against Fascism and the carrying through of the social revolution are inseparable. Those who have seen them and understood what they are doing must honor them and be grateful to them. . . . That is surely the biggest thing which has hitherto been done by the workers in any part of the world.

105. Cited by Richards, *op. cit.*, pp. 76–81, where long descriptive quotations are given.

106. See Hugh Thomas, "Anarchist Agrarian Collectives in the Spanish Civil War" (note 59). He cites figures showing that agricultural production went up in Aragon and Castile, where collectivization was extensive, and down in Catalonia and the Levant, where peasant proprietors were the dominant element.

Thomas' is, to my knowledge, the only attempt by a professional historian to assess the data on agricultural collectivization in Spain in a systematic way. He concludes that the collectives were probably "a considerable social success" and must have had strong popular support, but he is more doubtful about their economic viability. His suggestion that "Communist pressure on the collectives may have given them the necessary urge to survive" seems quite unwarranted, as does his suggestion that "the very existence of the war . . . may have been responsible for some of the success the collectives had." On the contrary, their success and spontaneous creation throughout Republican Spain suggest that they answered to deeply felt popular sentiments, and both the war and Communist pressure appear to have been highly disruptive factors—ultimately, of course, destructive factors.

Other dubious conclusions are that "in respect of redistribution of wealth, anarchist collectives were hardly much improvement over capitalism" since "no effective way of limiting consumption in richer collectives was devised to help poorer ones," and that there was no possibility of developing large-scale planning. On the contrary, Bolloten (*op. cit.*, pp. 176–79) points out that "In order to remedy the defects of collectivization, as well as to iron out discrepancies in the living standards of the workers in flourishing and impoverished enterprises, the Anarchosyndicalists, although rootedly opposed to nationalization, advocated the centralization—or, socialization, as they called it—under trade union control, of entire branches of production." He mentions a number of examples of partial socialization that had some success, citing as the major difficulty that prevented still greater progress the insistence of the Communist party and the UGT leadership—though apparently not all of the rank-and-file members of the UGT—on government ownership and control. According to Richards (*op. cit.*, p. 82): "In June, 1937 . . . a National Plenum of Regional Federations of Peasants was held in Valencia to discuss the formation of a National Federation of Peasants for the co-ordination and extension of the collectivist movement and also to ensure an equitable distribution of the produce of the land, not only between the collectives but for the whole country. Again in Castille in October 1937, a merging of the 100,000 members of the Regional Federation of Peasants and the 13,000 members in the food distributive trades took place. It represented a logical step in ensuring better co-ordination, and was accepted for the whole of Spain at the National Congress of Collectives held in Valencia in November 1937." Still other plans were under consideration for regional and national coordination —see, for example, D. A. de Santillan, *After the Revolution* (New York, Greenberg Publisher, Inc., 1937), for some ideas.

Thomas feels that collectives could not have survived more than "a few years while primitive misery was being overcome." I see nothing in his data to support this conclusion. The Palestinian experience has shown that collectives can remain both a social and an economic success over a long period. The success of Spanish collectivization, under war conditions, seems amazing. One can obviously not be certain whether these successes could have been secured and extended had it not been for the combined fascist, Communist, and liberal attack, but I can find no objective basis for the almost universal skepticism. Again, this seems to me merely a matter of irrational prejudice.

107. The following is a brief description by the anarchist writer Gaston Leval, *Né Franco, Né Stalin, le collettività anarchiche spagnole nella lotta contro Franco e la reazione staliniana* (Milan, Istituto Editoriale Italiano, 1952), pp. 303 f.; sections reprinted in *Collectivités anarchistes en Espagne révolutionnaire, Noir et Rouge,* undated.

> In the middle of the month of June, the attack began in Aragon on a grand scale and with hitherto unknown methods. The harvest was approaching. Rifles in hand, treasury guards under Communist orders stopped trucks loaded with provisions on the highways and brought them to their offices. A little later, the same guards poured into the collectives and confiscated great quantities of wheat under the authority of the general staff with headquarters in Barbastro. . . . Later open attacks began, under the command of Lister with troops withdrawn from the front at Belchite more than 50 kilometers away, in the month of August. . . . The final result was that 30 percent of the collectives were completely destroyed. In Alcolea, the municipal council that governed the collective was arrested; the people who lived in the Home for the Aged . . . were thrown out on the street. In Mas de las Matas, in Monzon, in Barbastro, on all sides, there were arrests. Plundering took place everywhere. The stores of the cooperatives and their grain supplies were rifled; furnishings were destroyed. The governor of Aragon, who was appointed by the central government after the dissolution of the Council of Aragon—which appears to have been the signal for the armed attack against the collectives—protested. He was told to go to the devil.
>
> On October 22, at the National Congress of Peasants, the delegation of the Regional Committee of Aragon presented a report of which the following is the summary:
>
> "More than 600 organizers of collectives have been arrested. The government has appointed management committees that seized the warehouses and distributed their contents at random. Land, draught animals, and tools were given to individual families or to the fascists who had been spared by the revolution. The harvest was distributed in the same way. The animals raised by the collectives suffered the same

fate. A great number of collectivized pig farms, stables, and dairies were destroyed. In certain communes, such as Bordon and Calaceite, even seed was confiscated and the peasants are now unable to work the land."

The estimate that 30% of the collectives were destroyed is consistent with figures reported by Peirats (*Los anarquistas en la crisis política española*, p. 300). He points out that only 200 delegates attended the congress of collectives of Aragon in September 1937 ("held under the shadow of the bayonets of the Eleventh Division" of Lister) as compared with 500 delegates at the congress of the preceding February. Peirats states that an army division of Catalan separatists and another division of the PSUC also occupied parts of Aragon during this operation, while three anarchist divisions remained at the front, under orders from the CNT-FAI leadership. Compare Jackson's explanation of the occupation of Aragon: "The peasants were known to hate the Consejo, *the anarchists had deserted the front during the Barcelona fighting,* and the very existence of the Consejo was a standing challenge to the authority of the central government" (italics mine).

108. Regarding Bolloten's work, Jackson has this to say: "Throughout the present chapter, I have drawn heavily on this carefully documented study of the Communist Party in 1936–37. It is unrivaled in its coverage of the wartime press, of which Bolloten, himself a UP correspondent in Spain, made a large collection" (p. 363 n.).

109. See note 64. A number of citations from Berneri's writings are given by Broué and Témime. Morrow also presents several passages from his journal, *Guerra di Classe.* A collection of his works would be a very useful contribution to our understanding of the Spanish Civil War and to the problems of revolutionary war in general.

110. Cattell, *op. cit.,* p. 208. See also the remarks by Borkenau, Brenan, and Bolloten cited earlier. Neither Cattell nor Borkenau regards this decline of fighting spirit as a major factor, however.

111. *Op. cit.,* p. 195, n. 7.

112. To this extent, Trotsky took a similar position. See his *Lesson of Spain* (London, Workers' International Press, 1937).

113. Cited in Richards, *op. cit.,* p. 23.

114. H. E. Kaminski, *Ceux de Barcelone* (Paris, Les Éditions Denoël, 1937), p. 181. This book contains very interesting observations on anarchist Spain by a skeptical though sympathetic eyewitness.

115. May 15, 1937. Cited by Richards, *op. cit.*, p. 106.

116. Cited by Broué and Témime, *op. cit.*, p. 258, n. 34. The conquest of Saragossa was the goal, never realized, of the anarchist militia in Aragon.

117. *Ibid.*, p. 175.

118. *Ibid.*, p. 193.

119. The fact was not lost on foreign journalists. Morrow (*op. cit.*, p. 68) quotes James Minifie in the *New York Herald Tribune*, April 28, 1937: "A reliable police force is being built up quietly but surely. The Valencia government discovered an ideal instrument for this purpose in the Carabineros. These were formerly customs officers and guards, and always had a good reputation for loyalty. It is reported on good authority that 40,000 have been recruited for this force, and that 20,000 have already been armed and equipped. . . . The anarchists have already noticed and complained about the increased strength of this force at a time when we all know there's little enough traffic coming over the frontiers, land or sea. They realize that it will be used against them." Consider what these soldiers, as well as Lister's division or the *asaltos* described by Orwell, might have accomplished on the Aragon front, for example. Consider also the effect on the militiamen, deprived of arms by the central government, of the knowledge that these well-armed, highly trained troops were liquidating the accomplishments of their revolution.

120. Cited in Rocker, *The Tragedy of Spain*, p. 37.

121. For references, see Bolloten, *op. cit.*, p. 192, n. 12.

122. Cited in Rocker, *The Tragedy of Spain*, p. 37.

123. Liston M. Oak, "Balance Sheet of the Spanish Revolution," *Socialist Review*, Vol. 6 (September 1937), pp. 7–9, 26. This reference was brought to my attention by William B. Watson. A striking example of the distortion introduced by the propaganda efforts of the 1930s is the strange story of the influential film *The Spanish Earth*, filmed in 1937 by Joris Ivens with a text (written afterwards) by Hemingway— a project that was apparently initiated by Dos Passos. A very revealing account of this matter, and of the perception of the Civil War by Hemingway and Dos Passos, is given in W. B. Watson and Barton Whaley, "The Spanish Earth of Dos Passos and Hemingway," unpublished, 1967. The film dealt with the collectivized village of Fuentidueña in Valencia (a village collectivized by the UGT, incidentally). For the libertarian Dos Passos, the revolution was the dominant

theme; it was the antifascist war, however, that was to preoccupy Hemingway. The role of Dos Passos was quickly forgotten, because of the fact (as Watson and Whaley point out) that "Dos Passos had become anathema to the Left for his criticisms of communist policies in Spain."

124. As far as the East is concerned, Rocker (*The Tragedy of Spain,* p. 25) claims that "the Russian press, for reasons that are easily understood, never uttered one least little word about the efforts of the Spanish workers and peasants at social reconstruction." I cannot check the accuracy of this claim, but it would hardly be surprising if it were correct.

125. See Patricia A. M. Van der Esch, *Prelude to War: The International Repercussions of the Spanish Civil War (1935–1939)* (The Hague, Martinus Nijhoff, 1951), p. 47, and Brenan, *op. cit.,* p. 329, n. 1. The conservative character of the Basque government was also, apparently, largely a result of French pressure. See Broué and Témime, *op. cit.,* p. 172, no. 8.

126. See Dante A. Puzzo, *Spain and the Great Powers: 1936–1941* (New York, Columbia University Press, 1962), pp. 86 f. This book gives a detailed and very insightful analysis of the international background of the Civil War.

127. Jules Sauerwein, dispatch to the *New York Times* dated July 26. Cited by Puzzo, *op. cit.,* p. 84.

128. Cf., for example, Jackson, *op. cit.,* pp. 248 f.

129. As reported by Herschel V. Johnson of the American embassy in London; cited by Puzzo, *op. cit.,* p. 100.

130. See Broué and Témime, *op. cit.,* pp. 288–89.

131. Cited by Thomas, *The Spanish Civil War,* p. 531, no. 3. Rocker, *The Tragedy of Spain,* p. 14, quotes (without reference) a proposal by Churchill for a five-year "neutral dictatorship" to "tranquilize" the country, after which they could "perhaps look for a revival of parliamentary institutions."

132. Puzzo, *op. cit.,* p. 116.

133. *Ibid.,* p. 147. Eden is referring, of course, to the Soviet Union. For an analysis of Russian assistance to the Spanish Republic, see Cattell, *op. cit.,* Ch. 8.

134. Cf. Puzzo, *op. cit.,* pp. 147–48.

135. *Ibid.,* p. 212.

136. *Ibid.,* p. 93.

137. *Op. cit.*, p. 248.

138. Puzzo, *op. cit.*, pp. 151 f.

139. *Ibid.*, pp. 154–55 and n. 27.

140. For some references, see Allen Guttmann, *The Wound in the Heart: America and the Spanish Civil War* (New York, The Free Press, 1962), pp. 137–38. The earliest quasi-official reference that I know of is in Herbert Feis, *The Spanish Story*, (New York, Alfred A. Knopf, 1948), where data is given in an appendix. Jackson (*op. cit.*, p. 256) refers to this matter, without noting that Texaco was violating a prior agreement with the Republic. He states that the American government could do nothing about this, since "oil was not considered a war material under the Neutrality Act." He does not point out, however, that Robert Cuse, the Martin Company, and the Mexican government were put under heavy pressure to withhold supplies from the Republic, although this too was quite legal. As noted, the Texaco Company was never even branded "unethical" or "unpatriotic," these epithets of Roosevelt's being reserved for those who tried to assist the Republic. The cynic might ask just why oil was excluded from the Neutrality Act of January 1937, noting that while Germany and Italy were capable of supplying arms to Franco, they could not meet his demands for oil.

The Texaco Oil Company continued to act upon the pro-Nazi sympathies of its head, Captain Thorkild Rieber, until August 1940, when the publicity began to be a threat to business. See Feis, *op. cit.*, for further details. For more on these matters, see Richard P. Traina, *American Diplomacy and the Spanish Civil War* (Bloomington, Indiana University Press, 1968), pp. 166 f.

141. Puzzo, *op. cit.*, p. 160. He remarks: "A government in Madrid in which Socialists, Communists, and anarchists sat was not without menace to American business interests both in Spain and Latin America" (p. 165). Hull, incidentally, was in error about the acts of the Spanish government. The irresponsible left-wing elements had not been given arms but had seized them, thus preventing an immediate Franco victory.

142. See Jackson, *op. cit.*, p. 458.

143. Cf. Guttmann, *op. cit.*, p. 197. Of course, American liberalism was always proloyalist, and opposed both to Franco and to the revolution. The attitude towards the latter is indicated with accuracy by this comparison, noted by Guttmann, p. 165: "300 people met in Union

Square to hear Liston Oak [see note 123] expose the Stalinists' role in Spain; 20,000 met in Madison Square Garden to help Earl Browder and Norman Thomas celebrate the preservation of bourgeois democracy," in July 1937.

144. *Ibid.,* p. 198.

145. To conclude these observations about the international reaction, it should be noted that the Vatican recognized the Franco government *de facto* in August 1937 and *de jure* in May 1938. Immediately upon Franco's final victory, Pope Pius XII made the following statement: "Peace and victory have been willed by God to Spain . . . which has now given to proselytes of the materialistic atheism of our age the highest proof that above all things stands the eternal value of religion and of the Spirit." Of course, the position of the Catholic Church has since undergone important shifts—something that cannot be said of the American government.

146. See note 60.

147. See, for example, the reference to Machajski in Harold D. Lasswell, *The World Revolution of Our Time: A Framework for Basic Policy Research* (Hoover Institute Studies; Stanford, Calif., Stanford University Press, 1951); reprinted, with extensions, in Harold D. Lasswell and Daniel Lerner, eds., *World Revolutionary Elites: Studies in Coercive Ideological Movements* (Cambridge, Mass., The M.I.T. Press, 1965), pp. 29–96. Daniel Bell has a more extensive discussion of Machajski's critique of socialism as the ideology of a new system of exploitation in which the "intellectual workers" will dominate, in a very informative essay that bears directly on a number of the topics that have been mentioned here: "Two Roads from Marx: The Themes of Alienation and Exploitation, and Workers' Control in Socialist Thought," in *The End of Ideology,* pp. 335–68.

148. Lasswell, *op. cit.,* p. 85. In this respect, Lasswell's prognosis resembles that of Bell in the essays cited earlier.

149. Summarized in the *Christian Science Monitor,* March 15, 1968. I have not seen the text and therefore cannot judge the accuracy of the report.

150. To mention just the most recent example: on January 22, 1968, McNamara testified before the Senate Armed Services Committee that "the evidence appears overwhelming that beginning in 1966 Communist local and guerrilla forces have sustained substantial attrition. As a result, there has been a drop in combat efficiency and morale. . . ."

The Tet offensive was launched within a week of this testimony. See *I. F. Stone's Weekly*, February 19, 1968, for some highly appropriate commentary.

151. The reality behind the rhetoric has been amply reported. A particularly revealing description is given by Katsuichi Honda, a reporter for *Asahi Shimbun*, in *Vietnam—A Voice from the Villages*, 1967, obtainable from the Committee for the English Publication of "Vietnam—a Voice from the Villages," c/o Mrs. Reiko Ishida, 2-13-7, Nishikata, Bunkyo-Ku, Tokyo.

THE REVOLUTIONARY PACIFISM
OF A. J. MUSTE

ON THE BACKGROUNDS
OF THE PACIFIC WAR

INTRODUCTORY COMMENT

The title and subtitle of this essay may seem unrelated; hence
a word of explanation may be useful. The essay was written for
a memorial number of *Liberation* which, as the editor expressed
it, "gathered together a series of articles that deal with some of
the problems with which A. J. struggled." I think that Muste's
revolutionary pacifism was, and is, a profoundly important doctrine, both in the political analysis and the moral conviction that
it expresses. The circumstances of the antifascist war subjected it
to the most severe of tests. Does it survive this test? When I
began working on this article I was not at all sure. I still feel
quite ambivalent about the matter. There are several points that
seem to me fairly clear, however. The American reaction to
Japan's aggressiveness was, in a substantial measure, quite

This essay first appeared in *Liberation*, Vol. 12 (September–October 1967).
I am indebted to Herbert Bix, Louis Kampf, André Schiffrin, and John Viertel
for comments that were useful in revising it to its present form.

159

hypocritical. Worse still, there are very striking, quite distressing similarities between Japan's escapades and our own—both in character and in rationalization—with the fundamental difference that Japan's appeal to national interest, which was not totally without merit, becomes merely ludicrous when translated into a justification for American conquests in Asia.

This essay touches on all of these questions: on Muste's revolutionary pacifism and his interpretation of it in connection with the Second World War; on the backgrounds of Japan's imperial ventures; on the Western reaction and responsibility; and, by implication, on the relevance of these matters to the problems of contemporary imperialism in Asia. No doubt the essay would be more coherent were it limited to one or two of these themes. I am sure that it would be more clear if it advocated a particular "political line." After exploring these themes, I can suggest nothing more than the tentative remarks of the final paragraph.

In a crucial essay written forty years ago,[1] A. J. Muste explained the concept of revolutionary nonviolence that was the guiding principle of an extraordinary life. "In a world built on violence, one must be a revolutionary before one can be a pacifist." "There is a certain indolence in us, a wish not to be disturbed, which tempts us to think that when things are quiet, all is well. Subconsciously, we tend to give the preference to 'social peace,' though it be only apparent, because our lives and possessions seem then secure. Actually, human beings acquiesce too easily in evil conditions; they rebel far too little and too seldom. There is nothing noble about acquiescence in a cramped life or mere submission to superior force." Muste was insistent that pacifists "get our thinking focussed." Their foremost task "is to denounce the violence on which the present system is based, and all the evil—material and spiritual—this entails for the masses of men throughout the world. . . . So long as we are not dealing honestly and adequately with this ninety percent of our problem, there is something ludicrous, and perhaps hypocritical, about our concern over the ten percent of violence employed by the rebels against oppression." Never in American history have these thoughts been so tragically appropriate as today.

The task of the revolutionary pacifist is spelled out more fully in the final paragraph of the essay.

> Those who can bring themselves to renounce wealth, position and power accruing from a social system based on violence and putting a premium on acquisitiveness, and to identify themselves in some real fashion with the struggle of the masses toward the light, may help in a measure—more, doubtless, by life than by words—to devise a more excellent way, a technique of social progress less crude, brutal, costly and slow than mankind has yet evolved.

It is a remarkable tribute to A. J. Muste that his life's work can be measured by such standards as these. His essays are invariably thoughtful and provocative; his life, however, is an inspiration with hardly a parallel in twentieth-century America. Muste believed, with Gandhi, that "unjust laws and practices survive because men obey them and conform to them. This they do out of fear. There are things they dread more than the continuance of the evil." He enriched half a century of American history with a personal commitment to these simple truths. His efforts began in a time when "men believed that a better human order, a classless and warless world, a socialist society, if you please, could be achieved," a time when the labor movement could be described as "that remarkable combination of mass power, prophetic idealism and utopian hope." They continued through the general disillusionment of war and depression and antiradical hysteria, to the days when American sociologists could proclaim that "the realization that escapes no one is that the egalitarian and socially mobile society which the 'free-floating intellectuals' associated with the Marxist tradition have been calling for during the last hundred years has finally emerged in the form of our cumbersome, bureaucratic mass society, and has in turn engulfed the heretics."[2] And finally, still not "engulfed," he persisted in his refusal to be one of the obedient, docile men who are the terror of our time, to the moment when our "egalitarian and socially mobile society" is facing a virtual rebellion from the lower depths, when young men are being faced every day with the questions posed at Nuremberg as their country devotes itself to enforcing the "stability" of the graveyard and the bulldozed village, and when the realization that escapes no one is that something is drastically wrong in American society.

In one of his last published essays, Muste describes himself as an "unrepentant unilateralist, on political as well as moral grounds."[3] In part, he bases his position on an absolute moral commitment that one may accept or reject, but that cannot be profitably debated. In part, he defends it on grounds that seem to me not very persuasive, a psychological principle that "like produces like, kindness provokes kindness," hence an appeal to "the essential humanity of the enemy."[4] It is very difficult to retain a faith in the "essential humanity" of the SS trooper or the commissar or the racist blinded with hate and fear, or, for that matter, the insensate victim of a lifetime of anti-Communist indoctrination. When the enemy is a remote technician programming B-52 raids or "pacification," there is no possibility for a human confrontation and the psychological basis for nonviolent tactics, whatever it may be, simply evaporates. A society that is capable of producing concepts like "un-American" and "peacenik"—of turning "peace" into a dirty word—has advanced a long way towards immunizing the individual against any human appeal. American society has reached the stage of near total immersion in ideology. The commitment has vanished from consciousness—what else can a right-thinking person possibly believe? Americans are simply "pragmatic," and they must bring others to this happy state. Thus an official of the Agency for International Development can write, with no trace of irony, that our goal is to move nations "from doctrinaire reliance on state enterprise to a pragmatic support of private initiative,"[5] and a headline in the *New York Times* can refer to Indian capitulation to American demands concerning the conditions of foreign investment as India's "drift from socialism to pragmatism" (see page 355 below). With this narrowing of the range of the thinkable comes an inability to comprehend how the weak and dispossessed can resist our benevolent manipulation of their lives, an incapacity to react in human terms to the misery that we impose.

The only useful way to evaluate the program of unilateral revolutionary pacifism is to consider what it implies in concrete historical circumstances. As a prescription for the United States in the mid-sixties, it is much too easy to defend. There is no particular merit in being more reasonable than a lunatic; correspondingly, almost any policy is more rational than one that accepts repeated risk of nuclear war, hence a near guarantee of nuclear war in the long run—a "long run" that is unlikely to be very long, given the risks that policy makers are willing to accept. Thus in the Cuban missile crisis, Kennedy was willing (according to Sorensen's memoirs) to accept a probability of

⅓ to ½ of nuclear war, in order to establish that the United States alone has the right to maintain missiles on the borders of a potential enemy.[6] And who knows what "probabilities" the CIA is now providing to the Rostows and the Wheelers who are trying to save something from their Vietnam fiasco by bombing at the Chinese border? Furthermore, it does not require an unusual political intelligence to urge world-wide de-escalation on the great power that by any objective standard is the most aggressive in the world—as measured by the number of governments maintained by force or subverted by intrigue, by troops and bases on foreign soil, by willingness to use the most awesome "killing machine" in history to enforce its concept of world order.

It would be more enlightening to consider the program of revolutionary pacifism in the context of a decade ago, when international gangsterism was more widely distributed, with the British engaged in murderous repression in Kenya, the French fighting the last of their dirty colonial wars, and the Soviet Union consolidating its Eastern European empire with brutality and deceit. But it is the international situation of December 1941 that provides the most severe test for Muste's doctrine. There is a great deal to be learned from a study of the events that led up to an armed attack, by a competing imperialism, on American possessions and the forces defending them, and even more from a consideration of the varying reactions to these events and their aftermath. If Muste's revolutionary pacifism is defensible as a general political program, then it must be defensible in these extreme circumstances. By arguing that it was, Muste isolated himself not only from any mass base, but also from all but a marginal fringe of American intellectuals.

Writing in 1941, Muste saw the war as

a conflict between two groups of powers for survival and domination. One set of powers, which includes Britain and the United States, and perhaps "free" France, controls some 70% of the earth's resources and thirty million square miles of territory. The imperialistic *status quo* thus to their advantage was achieved by a series of wars including the last one. All they ask now is to be left at peace, and if so they are disposed to make their rule mild though firm. . . . On the other hand stands a group of powers, such as Germany, Italy, Hungary, Japan, controlling about 15% of the earth's resources and one million square miles of territory, equally determined to alter the situation in their own favor, to impose their ideas of "order," and armed to the teeth to do that, even if it means plunging the whole world into war.[7]

He foresaw that an Allied victory would yield "a new American empire" incorporating a subservient Britain, "that we shall be the next nation to seek world domination—in other words, to do what we condemn Hitler for trying to do." In the disordered postwar world, we shall be told, he predicts, that "our only safety lies in making or keeping ourselves 'impregnable.' But that . . . means being able to decide by preponderance of military might any international issue that may arise—which would put us in the position in which Hitler is trying to put Germany." In a later essay, he quotes this remark: "The problem after a war is with the victor. He thinks he has just proved that war and violence pay. Who will now teach him a lesson?"[8]

The prediction that the United States would emerge as the world-dominant power was political realism; to forecast that it would act accordingly, having achieved this status by force, was no less realistic. This tragedy might be averted, Muste urged, by a serious attempt at peaceful reconciliation with no attempt to fasten sole war-guilt on any nation, assurance to all peoples of equitable access to markets and essential materials, armament reduction, massive economic rehabilitation, and moves towards international federation. To the American ideologist of

1941 such a recommendation seemed as senseless as the proposal, today, that we support popular revolution. And at that moment, events and policy were taking a very different direction.

Since nothing of the sort was ever attempted, one can only speculate as to the possible outcome of such a course. The accuracy of Muste's forecast unfortunately requires little comment. Furthermore, a plausible case can be made for his analysis of the then existing situation, a matter of more than academic interest in view of developments in Asia since that time.

As I mentioned, the point of view that Muste expressed was a rather isolated one. To see how little the intellectual climate has changed, it is enough to consider the lengthy debate over the decision to drop the bomb. What has been at issue is the question whether this constituted the last act of World War II or the first phase of American postwar diplomacy; or whether it was justified as a means of bringing the war to a quick conclusion. Only rarely has the question been raised whether there was any justification for American victory in the Pacific war; and this issue, where faced at all, has been posed in the context of the Cold War—that is, was it wise to have removed a counterweight to growing Chinese power, soon to become "Communist" power?

A fairly typical American view is probably that expressed by historian Louis Morton:

> In the late summer and autumn of 1945 the American people had every reason to rejoice. Germany and Japan had been defeated, and American troops, victorious everywhere, would soon be returning home. Unprecedented evil had been overcome by the greatest display of force ever marshaled in the cause of human freedom. . . .[9]

It is remarkable that such an attitude should be so blandly expressed and easily accepted. Is it true that in August 1945 the American people "had every reason to rejoice"—at the sight of a Japanese countryside devastated by conventional bombing in which tens of thousands of civilians had been massacred, not to speak of the horrifying toll of two atom bombs (the second being, so it appears, history's most abominable experiment); or at the news of a final gratuitous act of barbarism, trivial in the context of what had just taken place, a thousand-plane raid launched after the Japanese surrender had been announced but, technically, before it was officially received?[10] To Secretary of War Stimson it seemed "appalling that there had been no protest over the air strikes we were conducting against Japan which led to such extraordinarily heavy losses of life"; he felt that "there was something wrong with a country where no one questioned that." What then are we to say of a country that still, twenty years later, is incapable of facing the question of war guilt?

It is not, of course, that the question of war guilt has gone out of fashion. No trip to Germany is complete, even today, without a ritual sigh and wringing of hands over the failure of the German people to face up to the sins of the Nazi era, or the German school texts which glide so easily over the Nazi atrocities and the question of war guilt. This is a sure sign of the corruption of their nature. Just recently, a group of American liberal intellectuals gave their impressions of a tour of West Germany in the *Atlantic Monthly* (May 1967). None failed to raise the question of war guilt. One comments that "however disparate our temperaments or our political emphases, we were plainly a group made coherent by our shared suspicions of Germany's capacity for political health . . . we had not forgotten, nor could we forget, that we were in the country which had been able to devise, and implement, Nazism." The same commentator is impressed with the "dignity and fortitude" with which young Germans "carry an emotional and moral burden unmatched in history: they have to live with the knowledge that their parent generation, and often their own parents, perpetrated the worst atrocities on the record of mankind." Another, a fervent apologist for the American war in Vietnam, asks, "How does a human being 'come to terms' with the fact that his father was a soulless murderer, or an accomplice to soulless murder?" Several "were offended by the way the camp [Dachau] had been fixed up, prettified." (Does the "prettification" of Hiroshima—or, to take a closer analogue, the prettification of Los Alamos—provoke the same response?) To their credit, a few refer to Vietnam; but not once is a question raised —even to be dismissed—as to American conduct in the Second World War, or the "emotional and moral burden" carried by those whose "parent generation" stood by while two atom bombs were used against a beaten and virtually defenseless enemy.

To free ourselves from the conformism and moral blindness that have become a national scandal, it is a good idea occasionally to read the measured reactions of conservative Asians to some of our own exploits. Consider, for example, the words of the Indian justice Radhabinod Pal, the leading Asian voice at the Tokyo Tribunal that assessed the war guilt of the Japanese. In his carefully argued (and largely ignored) dissenting opinion to the decision of the tribunal, he has the following remarks to make:

> The Kaiser Wilhelm II was credited with a letter to the Austrian Kaiser Franz Joseph in the early days of that war, wherein he stated as follows: "My soul is torn, but everything must be put to fire and sword; men, women and children and old men must be

slaughtered and not a tree or house be left standing. With these methods of terrorism, which are alone capable of affecting a people as degenerate as the French, the war will be over in two months, whereas if I admit considerations of humanity it will be prolonged for years. In spite of my repugnance I have therefore been obliged to choose the former system."

This showed his ruthless policy, and this policy of indiscriminate murder to shorten the war was considered to be a crime. In the Pacific war under our consideration, if there was anything approaching what is indicated in the above letter of the German Emperor, it is the decision coming from the allied powers to use the atom bomb. Future generations will judge this dire decision. History will say whether any outburst of popular sentiment against usage of such a weapon is irrational and only sentimental and whether it has become legitimate by such indiscriminate slaughter to win the victory by breaking the will of the whole nation to continue to fight. We need not stop here to consider whether or not "the atom bomb comes to force a more fundamental searching of the nature of warfare and of the legitimate means for the pursuit of military objectives." It would be sufficient for my present purpose to say that if any indiscriminate destruction of civilian life and property is still illegitimate in warfare, then, in the Pacific war, this decision to use the atom bomb is the only near approach to the directives of the German Emperor during the first World War and of the Nazi leaders during the second World War. Nothing like this could be traced to the credit of the present accused.[11]

When we lament over the German conscience, we are demanding of them a display of self-hatred—a good thing, no doubt. But for us the matter is infinitely more serious. It is not a matter of self-hatred regarding the sins of the past. Like the German Kaiser, we believe that everything must be put to fire and sword, so that the war will be more quickly finished—and we act on this belief. Unlike the German Kaiser, our soul is not torn. We manage a relative calm, as we continue, today, to write new chapters of history with the blood of the helpless and innocent.

Returning to Muste's radical pacifism in the context of 1941, recall that the first of his proposals was that there be no attempt "to fasten sole war-guilt on any nation." The second was that measures be taken to assure to all peoples equitable access to markets and essential materials. The immediate cause of the attack on Pearl Harbor was the recognition, by the Japanese military, that it was "now or never." The Western powers controlled the raw materials on which their existence depended, and these supplies were being choked off in retaliation for expansion on the mainland and association with Germany and Italy in the Tripartite Pact. Japan faced an American diplomatic offensive aimed at changing it "from a hostile expansionist empire, with great pride in its destiny and ambitious plans for its future, to a peaceful, contented nation of merchants subcontracting with the United States to aid America's fight against Hitler"[12]—precisely what was achieved by the war, if we replace "Hitler" by "the international Communist conspiracy." To understand the Japanese predicament more fully, to evaluate the claim that Japan represented the forces of "unprecedented evil" arrayed against the American-led "cause of human freedom," and to appreciate the substance of Muste's radical pacifist alternative, it is necessary to look with some care into the backgrounds of Japanese imperialism.

Japan had been opened to Western influence by a threat of force in the mid-nineteenth century, and had then undertaken a remarkably successful effort at modernization. A new plutocracy replaced the old feudal structure, adopting the forms of parliamentary government. Mass participation in the developing political structure was minimal; it is doubtful that the living standards of the peasantry and urban workers rose during the period of transition from a medieval to a modern capitalist society. Japan joined the other imperialist powers in the exploitation of East Asia and took over Formosa, Korea, and parts of southern Manchuria. In short, by the late 1920s, Japan was what in modern political parlance is called a "democracy" and was attempting to play the normal role of a great power.

A portent of danger lay in the virtual independence of the armed forces from the civilian government. The "dual diplomacy" to which this gave rise was shortly to have disastrous consequences.

The great European war of 1914–1918 gave Japan an opportunity to extend its "rights and interests" in China and provided new markets for expanding Japanese industry. The revival of European competition came as a severe blow, and postwar diplomacy attempted vainly to construct a new and stable international system that would integrate Japan with the other imperialist powers. In good faith, Japan accepted the subordinate role assigned it and consented, throughout the twenties, to be a well-behaved member of the imperialist club. The Washington Conference of 1921–1922 established the naval forces of America, England, and Japan in the ratio of 5:5:3, accepting the American position of "equality of security" rather than the Japanese goal of "equality of armaments." As Schroeder comments, "the American argument was that Japan, a state surrounded on all sides by historic enemies and powerful rivals, had a superior natural situation for defense, while the United States, in the midst of two oceans without a powerful enemy on two continents, had defensively an inferior natural endowment."[13]

The Washington Conference arrangements were renegotiated in the London Naval Treaty of 1930 involving Japan, Great Britain, and the United States. The matter is discussed in detail in a study by James Crowley.[14] In the negotiations leading to this treaty, Secretary of State Stimson placed emphasis on "the unusual problems posed by the necessity of the United States to defend two coastlines and on the 'great concessions' which the American government had made at the time of the Washington Conference." Crowley points out that "throughout the 1920's, Japan faithfully adhered to the terms of the Washington Conference treaties." At issue in the subsequent negotiations was the question whether Japan could maintain its primary objective: "supremacy over the American fleet in Japanese home waters." The London Treaty, in effect, required that Japan abandon this objective. The London Treaty "did not render England a second-class naval power, nor did it endanger the safety of the United States or its insular possessions in the Pacific," but it did compromise "the principle of Japanese naval hegemony in Japan's own waters."

The domestic opposition to the treaty in Japan was a very serious matter. It led to a strengthening of the role of the military, which felt, with reason, that the civilian leadership was seriously endangering Japanese security. The treaty also evoked the first of "the series of violent attacks on the legally appointed leaders of Japan which would characterize the political history of that country during the 1930's" when Premier Hamaguchi, who was responsible for the treaty, was shot by "a patriotic youth" in 1930. An immediate consequence of the treaty was the adoption by the opposition party of a platform insisting on "the maintenance of Japan's privileged position in Manchuria, and a foreign policy which discounted the necessity of cooperation with the Anglo-American nations in defense of Japan's continental interests or in the cause of naval armament agreements." In summary, it seems clear that the refusal of the United States to grant to Japan hegemony in its waters (while of course insisting on maintaining its own hegemony in the Western Atlantic and Eastern Pacific) was a significant contributory cause to the crisis that was soon to erupt.

In later years, the Japanese came to feel, with much justice, that they had been hoodwinked more generally in the diplomatic arrangements of the early 1920s, which "embodied the idea that the Far East is essentially a place for the commercial and financial activities of the Western peoples; and . . . emphasized the importance of placing the signatory powers on an equal footing, thus ignoring the desirability of providing special relations between particular countries, especially between Japan and China."[15] A typical Japanese view of the situation was expressed by a delegate to the 1925 conference of the Institute of Pacific Relations (IPR): "Just as [Japan] was getting really skillful at the game of the grab, the other Powers, most of whom had all they wanted anyway, suddenly had an excess of virtue and called the game off."[16] A decade later, a delegate to the 1936 IPR conference was to reiterate:

> The Japanese feel that Western countries are unfair in imposing the *status quo* on Japan and calling it "peace." Their whole conception of diplomatic machinery and collective security is that it is simply a means to maintain that sort of peace, and to that degree the Japanese people are against it. This doesn't mean that Japan would not participate in collective security if some machinery can be devised which provides for "peaceful change." . . . Japan has a legitimate desire to expand. What are the means by which a nation can legitimately expand? Imperialistic advances are apparently out of date, but this is not understood by the Japanese people. The average reasoning of the Japanese people is that Great Britain and the other Western powers have done it, so why shouldn't we? The problem is not so much to determine the aggressor as to provide ample opportunities for the necessary expansion peacefully.[17]

Through the mid-1920s the Japanese were, generally, the most sympathetic of the imperialist powers to the Kuomintang in its attempt to unify China. In 1927, Chiang Kai-shek stated that the Japanese policy differed from the "oppressive" attitude of Britain and the United States, and Eugene Ch'en, then a high Kuomintang official, contrasted Japan's nonparticipation in the imperialist bombardment of Nanking to the "cruelty inherent in the Western civilization"; this "indicated Japan's friendship for China." The goal of Japanese diplomacy was to strengthen the anti-Communist elements in the Kuomintang and, at the same time, to support the rule of the warlord Chang Tso-lin over an at least semi-independent Manchuria. At the time, this seemed not totally unreasonable, although the legal position of Japan was insecure and this policy was sure to come into conflict with Chinese nationalism. According to one authority:

> As of 1927 Manchuria was politically identifiable with China only insofar as its overlord, Chang Tso-lin, was also commander-in-chief of the anti-Kuomintang coalition controlling Peking. But Chang's economic and military base in the Three Eastern Provinces was entirely distinct from China, and in the past he had occasionally proclaimed Manchuria's independence.[18]

To the extent that this assessment is accurate, Japanese diplomacy was not unrealistic in aiming to prevent the growing nationalist movement in China from overwhelming Manchuria, and at the same time to curb the ambitions of the Manchurian warlord to take over all of China. This remained, in essence, the goal of the Japanese civilian governments even through the "Manchurian incident" of 1931–1932.

By 1931, it was becoming fairly clear that the relatively conciliatory diplomacy of the 1920s was unlikely to secure the "rights and interests" regarded as essential for Japan's continued development. The effects of the great depression were immediate and severe (see below). The London Treaty had failed to provide Japan with military security *vis à vis* the other imperialist powers. Manchuria remained independent of the Kuomintang, but Chinese Nationalist pressures for unification were increasing. At the same time, the Soviet Union had significantly expanded its military power on the Manchurian border, a fact that could not fail to concern the Japanese military. Japan had a substantial investment in the South Manchurian Railway and, rightly or wrongly, regarded Manchuria as an extremely important potential source of desperately needed raw materials. Large numbers of Japanese[19] as well as thousands of Korean farmers encouraged by Japan had settled in Manchuria, inflaming Chinese nationalism and, simultaneously, deepening the commitment of the Kwantung Army in Manchuria to "preserve order." The future of the South Manchurian Railway—and with it, the associated investments as well as the welfare of the Japanese and Korean immigrants and residents—was very much in doubt, as Chinese pressures mounted both inside Manchuria and in Nationalist China. "Technically, under a 1905 protocol, China was barred from building any railway lines parallel to the South Manchurian Railway or from constructing any lines which might endanger the commercial traffic along it,"[20] but China was quite naturally disinclined to honor this provision, and Japanese attempts to conduct discussions on railroad construction were frustrated, as the Kuomintang pursued its course of attempting to incorporate Manchuria within China and to eliminate Japanese influence, no doubt with the support of the majority of the Manchurian population. A number of fairly serious incidents of violence occurred involving Korean settlers and the Japanese military. A Japanese officer was murdered in the summer of 1931. In Shanghai, a boycott of Japanese goods was initiated.

Under these conditions, debate intensified within Japan as to whether its future lay in "the political leadership of an East Asia power bloc" guaranteed by military force, or in continuing to abide by "the new rules of diplomacy established by Occidental and satiated powers."[21] The issue was resolved in September 1931, when Kwantung Army officers provoked a clash with Chinese forces (the "Mukden incident") and proceeded to take full control of Manchuria. China, not unexpectedly, refused the Japanese offers to negotiate, insisting that "evacuation is a precondition of direct negotiation."[22] Exercising the right of "self-defense" against Chinese "bandits," the Kwantung Army established control by force, and in August 1932 the Japanese government, under strong military and popular pressure, recognized Manchuria as the new, "independent" state of Manchukuo, under the former Manchu emperor, Pu Yi. As Walter Lippmann commented, the procedure of setting up "local Chinese governments which are dependent upon Japan" was "a familiar one," not unlike the American precedents "in Nicaragua, Haiti, and elsewhere."[23]

The Manchurian events flowed over into China proper and Japan itself, and caused an international crisis. The boycott in Shanghai and a clash between Chinese troops and Japanese marines near the Japanese sector of the international settlement led to a retaliatory aerial bombardment by the Japanese. "This indiscriminate use of air power against a small contingent of Chinese soldiers dispersed among a congested civilian population generated a profound sense of shock and indignation in England and the United States."[24] In Japan, the Shanghai incident was seen rather differently. The Japanese minister to China at the time, Mamoru Shigemitsu, writes in his memoirs[25] that he was responsible for the request that the government dispatch troops to Shanghai "to save the Japanese residents from annihilation." In his view, the thirty thousand Japanese settlers and the Japanese property in Shanghai were at the mercy of the Chinese army, with its rather left-wing tendencies. Furthermore, "Chinese Communists" were starting strikes in Japanese-owned mills. For all of these reasons, Shigemitsu felt justified in requesting troops, which "succeeded in dislodging the Chinese forces from the Shanghai district and restoring law and order"—a "familiar procedure," as Lippmann rightly observed, and not without present-day parallels.[26]

As far as Japan itself is concerned, the events of 1931–1932 were quite serious in their impact. According to the outstanding Japanese political scientist Masao Maruyama, "the energy of radical fascism stored up in the preparatory period now burst forth in full concentration under the combined pressure of domestic panic and international crises such as the Manchurian Incident, the Shanghai Incident, and Japan's withdrawal from the League of Nations."[27] Furthermore, "the issue of the infringement of the supreme command," raised when the civilian leadership had overruled the military leaders and in effect capitulated to the West at the London Naval Conference, "was a great stimulus to the fascist movement" (p. 81). In 1932 a series of assassinations of important political figures (including Prime Minister Inukai) contributed further to the decline of civilian power and the strengthening of the hand of the military.

The international reaction to these events was ambiguous. The League of Nations sent a commission of inquiry, the Lytton Commission, to investigate the Manchurian situation. Its report rejected the Japanese position that Manchukuo should be established as an independent state, and insisted on a loose form of Chinese sovereignty, at which point Japan withdrew from the League of Nations. The United States also found itself somewhat isolated diplomatically, in that the harsh anti-Japanese position taken by Secretary of State Stimson received little support from the other Western powers.

In a careful review of the point of view of the Lytton Commission, the Inukai government, and the central army authorities, Sadako Ogata demonstrates a considerable area of agreement:

> . . . the central army authorities . . . insisted upon the creation of a new local regime with authority to negotiate settlement of Manchurian problems, but under the formal sovereignty of the Chinese National Government, a traditional arrangement. This was the arrangement that the world at large was willing to accept. The Lytton Commission proposed the constitution of a special regime for the administration of Manchuria possessed of a large measure of autonomy but under Chinese jurisdiction. Finally, when the State of Manchukuo declared its independence, the Government of Japan withheld formal recognition and thereby attempted to avoid a head-on collision with the powers, which by then had lined up behind the doctrine of non-recognition of changes caused by Japanese military action in Manchuria. The complete political reconstruction of Manchuria was achieved, then, at the hands of the Kwantung Army in defiance of the opposition of government and central military leaders.[28]

The Lytton Commission report took cognizance of some of the complexities in the situation. The report drew the following conclusion:

> This is not a case in which one country has declared war on another country without previously exhausting the opportunities for conciliation provided in the Covenant of the League of Nations. Neither is it a simple case of the violation of the frontier of one country by the armed forces of a neighboring country, because in Manchuria there are many features without an exact parallel in other parts of the world.

The report went on to point out that the dispute arose in a territory in which both China and Japan "claim to have rights and interests, only some of which are clearly defined by international law; a territory which, although legally an integral part of China, had a sufficiently autonomous character to carry out direct negotiations with Japan on the matters which lay at the roots of this conflict."[29]

It is an open question whether a more conciliatory American diplomacy that took into account some of the real problems faced by Japan might have helped the civilian government (backed by the central army authorities) to prevail over the independent initiative of the Kwantung Army, which ultimately succeeded in bringing the Japanese government to recognize the *fait accompli* of a Manchukuo that was more a puppet of the Kwantung Army than of Japan proper.

In any event, the success of the Kwantung Army in enforcing its conception of the status of Manchuria set Japan and the United States on a collision course. Japan turned to an "independent diplomacy" and reliance on force to achieve its objectives. The Japanese position of the mid-thirties is described as follows by Rōyama. Japan's aim is

> not to conquer China, or to take any territory from her, but instead to create jointly with China and Manchukuo a new order comprising the three independent states. In accordance with this programme, East Asia is to become a vast self-sustaining region where Japan will acquire economic security and immunity from such trade boycotts as she has been experiencing at the hands of the Western powers.[30]

This policy was in conflict with Chinese nationalism and with the long-term insistence of the United States on the Open Door policy in China.

From 1928 there had been an increasing divergence between the policies of the civilian Japanese governments, which attempted to play the game of international politics in accordance with the rules set by the dominant imperialist powers, and the Kwantung Army, which regarded these rules as unfair to Japan and was also dissatisfied with the injustice of domestic Japanese society. The independent initiative of the Kwantung Army was largely that of the young officers of *petit-bourgeois* origin who felt that they represented as well the interests of the soldiers, predominantly of peasant stock. "The Manchurian affair constitutes an external expression of the radical reform movement that was originally inspired by Kita and Okawa,"[31] who had developed the view that Japan represented an "international proletariat," with an emancipating mission for the Asian masses, and who opposed the obvious inequities of modern capitalism. The fundamental law proposed for Manchukuo, in 1932, protected the people from "usury, excessive profit, and all other unjust economic pressure." As Ogata notes,[32] the fundamental law "showed the attempt to forestall the modern forms of economic injustice caused by capitalism." In Japan itself, this program appealed to the Social Democrats, who blamed "Chinese warlords and selfish Japanese capitalists for the difficulties in [Manchuria]" and who demanded "the creation of a socialistic system in Manchuria, one that would benefit 'both Chinese and Japanese living in Manchuria.' "[33]

Ogata cites a great deal of evidence to support the conclusion that the Kwantung Army never expected to establish Japanese supremacy, but rather proposed to leave "wide discretion to the local self-governing Chinese bodies, and intended neither the disruption of the daily lives of the Manchurian people nor their assimilation into Japanese culture" (p. 182). The program for autonomy was apparently influenced by and attempted to incorporate certain indigenous Chinese moves towards autonomy. "In the period immediately preceding the Manchurian Affair, a group of Chinese under the leadership of Chang Ku also attempted to create an autonomous Manchuria based on cooperation of its six largest ethnic groups (Japanese, Chinese, Russians, Mongolians, Koreans, and Manchurians) in order to protect the area from Japanese, Chinese and Soviet encroachment" (p. 40). The governing bodies set up by the Kwantung Army

> were led by prominent Chinese with Japanese support. Reorganization of local administrative organs was undertaken by utilizing the traditional self-governing bodies. . . . Yu Chung-han, a prominent elder statesman of the Mukden Government, . . . was . . . installed as chief of the Self-Government Guiding Board on November 10. Yu had been the leader of the civilian group in Manchuria which, in contrast to the warlords, had held to the principle of absolute *hokyo anmin* (secure boundary and peaceful life). According to him, the protection and prosperity of the Northeastern Provinces assumed priority over all, including the relationship with China proper. Through tax reform, improvement of the wage system of government officials, and abolition of a costly army, the people in Manchuria were to enjoy the benefits of peaceful labor, while defense was to be entrusted to their most powerful neighbor, Japan. [Pp. 118–19]

In general, the Kwantung Army regarded the thirty million people of Manchuria—half of whom had immigrated since the initiation of Japanese development efforts a quarter of a century earlier—as "suffering masses who had been sacrificed to the misrule of warlords and the avarice of wicked officials, masses deriving no benefits of civilization despite the natural abundance of the region."[34] Furthermore, the Army regarded Manchuria as "the fortress against Russian southern advancement, which became increasingly threatening as Soviet influence over the Chinese revolution became more and more apparent."³⁵ With many Japanese civilians, it felt that "Under the leadership of Chiang Kai-shek and with the support of the Western democratic powers which wanted to keep China in a semi-colonial state safe from the continental advance of the Japanese, China was rapidly becoming a military-fascist country"³⁶ and had no right to dominate Manchuria. To use the kind of terminology favored by Secretary Rusk, it was unwilling to sacrifice the Manchurian people to their more powerful or better organized neighbors, and it engaged in serious efforts to win the hearts and minds of the people and to encourage the responsible Chinese leadership that had itself been working for Manchurian independence.³⁷

In fact, a case can be made that "had it not been for Western intervention, which strengthened China, the Tibetans and Mongols would have simply resumed their own national sovereignty after the fall of the Manchu empire" in 1911, as would the Manchurians. With considerable Western prodding, the Nationalist government had abandoned the original demand for union with equality of Chinese, Manchus, Mongols, Moslems, and Tibetans and taken the position that China should rule the outer dominions. The West assumed that China would be under Western guidance and influence; "by confirming a maximum area for China it increased the sphere of future Western investment and exploitation"³⁸ (a fact which adds a touch of irony to current Western complaints about "Chinese expansionism"). From this point of view, the independence of Manchukuo could easily be rationalized as a step towards the emancipation of the peoples of East Asia from Western dominance.

To be sure, the establishment of Japanese hegemony over Manchuria—and later, northern China as well—was motivated by the desire to secure Japanese rights and interests. A liberal professor of American history, Yasaka Takagi, observes that the general support for the Japanese military in 1931 was similar to the Manifest Destiny psychology underlying American expansion into Florida, Texas, California, Cuba, and Hawaii.[39] He describes the bandit-infested, warlord-controlled Manchurian region, then subject to the clash of expansionist Chinese Nationalism and Japanese imperialism, as similar to the Caribbean when the United States justified its Caribbean policy. He asks why there should be a Monroe Doctrine in America and an Open Door principle in Asia, and suggests an international conference to resolve the outstanding problems of the area, noting, however, that few Americans would "entertain even for a moment the idea of letting an international conference define the Monroe Doctrine and review Mexican relations." He points out, quite correctly, that "the peace machinery of the world is in itself primarily the creation of the dominant races of the earth, of those who are the greatest beneficiaries from the maintenance of the *status quo.*"

Nevertheless, it appears that few Japanese were willing to justify the Manchurian incident and subsequent events on the "pragmatic" grounds of self-interest. Rather, they emphasized the high moral character of the intervention, the benefits it would bring to the suffering masses (once the terrorism had been suppressed), and the intention of establishing an "earthly paradise" in the independent state of Manchukuo (later, in China as well), defended from Communist attack by the power of Japan. Maruyama observes that "what our wartime leaders accomplished by their moralizing was not simply to deceive the people of Japan or of the world; more than anyone else they deceived themselves."[40] To illustrate, he quotes the observations of American Ambassador Joseph Grew on the "self-deception and lack of realism" in the upper strata of Japanese society:

. . . I doubt if one Japanese in a hundred really believes that they have actually broken the Kellogg Pact, the Nine-Power Treaty, and the Covenant of the League. A comparatively few thinking men are capable of frankly facing the facts, and one Japanese said to me: "Yes, we've broken every one of these instruments; we've waged open war; the arguments of 'self-defense' and 'self-determination for Manchuria' are rot; but we needed Manchuria, and that's that." But such men are in the minority. The great majority of Japanese are astonishingly capable of really fooling themselves. . . . It isn't that the Japanese necessarily has his tongue in his cheek when he signs the obligation. It merely means that when the obligation runs counter to his own interests, as he conceives them, he will interpret the obligation to suit himself and, according to his own lights and mentality, he will very likely be perfectly honest in so doing. . . . Such a mentality is a great deal harder to deal with than a mentality which, however brazen, knows that it is in the wrong.

In this respect, the analogy to current American behavior in Asia fails; more than one American in a hundred understands that we have actually violated our commitments, not only at Geneva but, more importantly, to the United Nations Charter. However, the general observation remains quite valid in the changed circumstances of today. It *is* very difficult to deal with the mentality that reinterprets obligations to suit self-interest, and may very well be perfectly honest—in some curious sense of the word—in so doing.

Alongside of those who justified the Manchurian intervention on the pragmatic grounds of self-interest, those who spoke of a new Monroe Doctrine "to maintain the peace of East Asia," and those who fantasied about an "earthly paradise,"[41] there were also dissident voices that questioned Japanese policy in a more fundamental way. As the military extended its power, dissidents were attacked—both verbally and physically—for their betrayal of Japan. In 1936, for example, the printing presses of the leading Tokyo newspapers were bombed and Captain Nonaka, who was in command, posted a *Manifesto of the Righteous Army of Restoration* "which identified those groups most responsible for the betrayal of the national polity—the senior statesmen, financial magnates, court officials, and certain factions in the army—proclaiming:

> They have trespassed on the prerogatives of the Emperor's rights of supreme command—among other times, in the conclusion of the London Naval Treaty and in the removal of the Inspector General of Military Education. Moreover, they secretly conspired to steal the supreme command in the March Incident; and they united with disloyal professors in rebellious places. These are but a few of the most notable instances of their villainies. . . .[42]

It is difficult to imagine such a development in the United States today. Difficult, but not impossible. Consider, for example, the column by William H. Stringer on the editorial page of the *Christian Science Monitor* on February 7, 1968, calling for an end to "that violent, discouraged, and anarchic thinking which disrupts government and adds to Washington's already grievous burdens." The final paragraph explains why the "carping and caterwauling from the pseudointellectual establishment" must cease:

> Certainly this time of crucial decisions is a time to uphold the government—President and Congress—with our prayers. Yes, to see that no mist of false doctrine or sleazy upbringing can upset the constitutional order which gives thrust and purpose to our country. And to *remind ourselves and affirm that our leaders have the utilization of ever-present intelligence and wisdom from on high,* that they indeed can perceive and follow the "path which no fowl knoweth." (Job 28) [Italics mine]

One would have to search with some diligence in the literature of totalitarianism to find such a statement. An obscure Japanese military officer condemns the disloyal professors and other betrayers who have trespassed on the imperial prerogatives; a writer for one of our most distinguished and "responsible" newspapers denounces the pseudointellectuals of false doctrine and sleazy upbringing who refuse to recognize that our leaders are divinely inspired. There are, to be sure, important differences between the two situations; thus Captain Nonaka bombed the printing presses, whereas his contemporary equivalent is featured by the responsible American press.

As Toynbee had noted earlier,[43] Japan's

economic interests in Manchuria were not superfluities but vital necessities of her international life. . . . The international position of Japan—with Nationalist China, Soviet Russia, and the race-conscious English-speaking peoples of the Pacific closing in upon her—had suddenly become precarious again.

These special interests had repeatedly been recognized by the United States. Both China and Japan regarded the Root-Takahira Agreement of 1908 as indicating "American acquiescence in the latter's position in Manchuria."[44] Secretary of State Bryan, in 1915, stated that "the United States frankly recognized that territorial contiguity creates special relations between Japan and these districts" (Shantung, South Manchuria, and East Mongolia); and the Lansing-Ishii Notes of 1917 stated that "territorial propinquity creates special relations between countries, and consequently, the Government of the United States recognizes that Japan has special interests in China, particularly in the part to which her possessions are contiguous."[45] In fact, the United States for several years regarded the Kuomintang as in revolt against the legitimate government of China, and even after Chiang's massacre of Communists in 1927, showed little pro-Nationalist sympathy. As late as 1930, the American minister to China saw no difference between the Kuomintang and the warlord rebels in Peking, and wrote that he could not "see any hope in any of the self-appointed leaders that are drifting over the land at the head of odd bands of troops."[46]

At the same time, the United States insisted on preserving its special rights, including the right of extraterritoriality, which exempted American citizens from Chinese law. In 1928, there were more than 5,200 American marines in China protecting these rights (the Japanese army in Manchuria at the time was about 10,000 troops).[47] The other imperialist powers were even more insistent on protecting their rights, and persisted in their anti-Nationalist attitudes right through the Manchurian incident.

In later years, when the Japanese had begun to use force to guarantee their position in China, they still retained the support of the American business community (as long as it did not itself feel threatened by these actions). In 1928, American consuls supported the dispatch of Japanese troops; one reported that their arrival "has brought a feeling of relief . . . even among Chinese, especially those of the substantial class."[48] The business community remained relatively pro-Japanese even after Japanese actions in Manchuria and Shanghai in 1931–1932; "in general, it was felt that the Japanese were fighting the battle of all foreigners against the Chinese who wished to destroy foreign rights and privileges . . . that if the organizing abilities of the Japanese were turned loose in China, it might be a good thing for everybody."[49] Ambassador Grew, on November 20, 1937, entered in his diary a note that the MacMurray Memorandum, just circulated by one of the main American spokesmen on Far Eastern affairs, "would serve to relieve many of our fellow countrymen of the generally accepted theory that Japan has been a big bully and China the downtrodden victim."[50] Commonly the American attitude remained that expressed by Am-

bassador Nelson Johnson, who argued that the American interest dictated that we be neither pro-Chinese nor pro-Japanese
but rather "must have a single eye to the . . . effect of developments in the East . . . upon the future interests of America,"
namely, "the fact that the great population of Asia offers a
valuable outlet for the products of our industries and that as
our industries develop we will be more and more interested in
cultivating an outlet for them".[51] Also typical is his explanation
of the attitude we should adopt "toward these oriental peoples
for whose future we became responsible." What we make of
them will be "peculiarly the product of American idealism"; in
their future "we shall continue to be interested as a father must
be interested in the career of his son long after the son has left
the family nest."[52] He was concerned, in fact, that native American altruism would be too predominant in our treatment of our
Asian wards, and hoped rather that the "new period of American international relations" would be "characterized by the
acquisitive, practical side of American life rather than its idealistic and altruistic side."

As late as 1939 Ambassador Grew, speaking in Tokyo, described the American objection to the New Order as based on
the fact that it included "depriving Americans of their long-
established rights in China" and imposing "a system of closed
economy." Critics noted that nothing was said about the independence of China, and that it might well appear, from his
remarks, that "if the Japanese stopped taking actions that in-
fringed on American rights the United States would not object
to their continued occupation of China."[53] In the fall of 1939,
Secretary of State Hull refused to negotiate a new commercial
treaty with Japan or arrive at a *modus vivendi* "unless Japan
completely changed her attitude and practice towards our
rights and interests in China."[54] Had this condition been met,

so it appears, the situation would have been quite different.

The depression of 1929 marked the final collapse of the attempt of Japanese civilians to live by the rules established by the Western powers. Just as the depression struck, the new Hamaguchi cabinet adopted the gold standard in an attempt to link the Japanese economy more closely with the West, foregoing the previous attempts at unilateral Sino-Japanese "coprosperity." An immediate consequence was a drastic decline in Japanese exports. In 1931, Japan was replaced by the United States as the major exporter to China. Japanese exports to the United States also declined severely, in part as a result of the Smoot-Hawley tariff of June 1930, in part because of the dramatic fall in the price of silk.[55] For an industrialized country such as Japan, with almost no domestic supplies of raw materials, the decline in world trade was an unmitigated disaster. The Japanese diplomat Mamoru Shigemitsu describes the crisis succinctly:

> The Japanese were completely shut out from the European colonies. In the Philippines, Indo-China, Borneo, Indonesia, Malaya, Burma, not only were Japanese activities forbidden, but even entry. Ordinary trade was hampered by unnatural discriminatory treatment. . . . In a sense the Manchurian outbreak was the result of the international closed economies that followed on the first World War. There was a feeling at the back of it that it provided the only escape from economic strangulation.[56]

The infamous Yosuke Matsuoka stated in 1931 that "we feel suffocated as we observe internal and external situations. What we are seeking is that which is minimal for living beings. In other words, we are seeking to live. We are seeking room that will let us breathe."[57] Ten years later he was to describe Japan as "in the grip of a need to work out means of self-supply and self-sufficiency in Greater East Asia." He asks: "Is it for the

United States, which rules over the Western Hemisphere and is expanding over the Atlantic and the Pacific, to say that these ideals, these ambitions of Japan are wrong?"[58]

Western economic policies of the 1930s made an intolerable situation still worse, as was reported regularly in the conferences of the Institute of Pacific Relations (IPR). The report of the Banff conference of August 1933 noted that "the Indian Government, in an attempt to foster its own cotton industry, imposed an almost prohibitive tariff on imported cotton goods, the effects of which were of course felt chiefly by Japanese traders, whose markets in India had been growing rapidly."[59] "Japan, which is a rapidly growing industrial nation, has a special need for . . . [mineral resources] . . . and is faced with a serious shortage of iron, steel, oil, and a number of important industrial minerals under her domestic control, while, on the other hand, the greater part of the supplies of tin and rubber, not only of the Pacific area but for the whole world, are, by historical accident, largely under the control of Great Britain and the Netherlands."[60] The same was true of iron and oil, of course. In 1932, Japanese exports of cotton piece-goods for the first time exceeded those of Great Britain. The Indian tariff, mentioned above, was 75 percent on Japanese cotton goods and 25 percent on British goods. The Ottawa conference of 1932 effectively blocked Japanese trade with the Commonwealth, including India. As the IPR conference report noted, "Ottawa had dealt a blow to Japanese liberalism."

The Ottawa Commonwealth arrangements aimed at constructing an essentially closed, autarchic system; the contemporary American policy of self-sufficiency proceeded in a similar direction. The only recourse available to Japan was to try to mimic this behavior in Manchuria. Liberalism was all very well when Britannia ruled the waves, but not when Lancashire industry was grinding to a halt, unable to meet Japanese competition. The Open Door policy was appropriate to an expanding capitalist economy, but must not be allowed to block American economic recovery. Thus in October 1935, Japan was forced to accept an agreement limiting shipments of cotton textiles from Japan to the Philippines for two years, while American imports remained duty-free. Similarly, revised commercial arrangements with Cuba in 1934 were designed to eliminate Japanese competition in textiles, copper wire, electric bulbs, and cellophane.[61]

The 1936 IPR conference continues the story. Writing on "trade and trade rivalry between the United States and Japan," William W. Lockwood observes that American preponderance in Philippine trade "is attributable in large degree to the Closed Door policy of the United States, which has established American products in a preferential position. Were Japanese business men able to compete on equal terms, there is no doubt but that Japan's share of the trade would advance rapidly."[62] At the same time, American tariffs on many Japanese items exceeded 100 percent.

Japan did not have the resiliency to absorb such a serious shock to its economy. The textile industry, which was hit most severely by the discriminatory policies of the major imperialist powers, produced nearly half of the total value of manufactured goods and about two thirds of the value of Japanese exports, and employed about half of the factory workers. Though industrialized by Asian standards, Japan had only about one seventh the energy capacity per capita of Germany; from 1927 to 1932, its pig-iron production was 44 percent that of Luxemburg and its steel production about 95 percent.[63] It was in no position to tolerate a situation in which India, Malaya, Indochina, and the Philippines erected tariff barriers favoring the mother country, and could not survive the deterioration in its very substantial trade with the United States and the sharp decline in the China trade. It was, in fact, being suffocated by the American and British and other Western imperial systems, which quickly abandoned their lofty liberal rhetoric as soon as the shoe began to pinch.

The situation as of 1936 is summarized as follows by Neumann:

> When an effort to set a quota on imports of bleached and colored cotton cloths failed, President Roosevelt finally took direct action. In May of 1936 he invoked the flexible provision of the tariff law and ordered an average increase of 42 percent in the duty on these categories of imports. By this date Japan's cotton goods had begun to suffer from restrictive measures taken by more than half of their other markets. Japanese xenophobia was further stimulated as tariff barriers [rose] against Japanese goods, like earlier barriers against Japanese immigrants, and presented a convincing picture of western encirclement. The most secure markets were those which Japan could control politically; an argument for further political expansion . . . against an iron ring of tariffs.[64]

It is hardly astonishing, then, that in 1937 Japan again began to expand at the expense of China. From the Japanese point of view, the new government of North China established in 1937 represented the intention of the Japanese to keep North China independent of Nanking and the interest of the Chinese opposed to colonization of the North by the dictatorial Kuomintang.[65] On December 22, 1938, Prince Konoye made the following statement:

> . . . Japan demands that China, in accordance with the principle of equality between the two countries, should recognize the freedom of residence and trade on the part of Japanese subjects in the interior of China, with a view to promoting the economic interests of both peoples; and that, in the light of the historical

and economic relations between the two nations, China should extend to Japan facilities for the development of China's natural resources, especially in the regions of North China and Inner Mongolia.[66]

There were to be no annexations, no indemnities. Thus a new order was to be established, which would defend China and Japan against Western imperialism, unequal treaties, and extraterritoriality. Its goal was not enrichment of Japan, but rather cooperation (on Japanese terms, of course). Japan would provide capital and technical assistance; at the same time, it would succeed in freeing itself from dependence on the West for strategic raw materials.

Japanese leaders repeatedly made clear that they intended no territorial aggrandizement. To use the contemporary idiom, they emphasized that their actions were "not intended as a threat to China" and that "China knows that Japan does not want a wider war," although, of course, they would "do everything they can to protect the men they have there."[67] They were quite willing to negotiate with the recalcitrant Chinese authorities, and even sought third-power intervention.[68] Such Japanese leaders as Tojo and Matsuoka emphasized that no one, surely, could accuse Japan of seeking mere economic gain. In fact, she was spending more on the war in China than she could possibly gain in return. Japan was "paying the price that leadership of Asia demands," they said, attempting "to prevent Asia from becoming another Africa and to preserve China from Communism."[69] The latter was a particularly critical matter. "The Japanese felt that the United Front and the Sino-Soviet pact of 1937 were steps toward the destruction of Nationalist China and the Bolshevization of East Asia."[70] The Japanese were, furthermore, quite willing to withdraw their troops once

193

the "illegal acts" by Communists and other lawless elements were terminated,[71] and the safety and rights of Japanese and Korean residents in China guaranteed.

Such terminology was drawn directly from the lexicon of Western diplomacy. For example, Secretary of State Kellogg had stated United States government policy as: "to require China to perform the obligations of a sovereign state in the protection of foreign citizens and their property" (September 2, 1925). The Washington Treaty powers were "prepared to consider the Chinese government's proposal for the modification of existing treaties in measure as the Chinese authorities demonstrated their willingness and ability to fulfill their obligations and to assume the protection of foreign rights and interests now safeguarded by the exceptional provisions of those treaties," and admonished China of "the necessity of giving concrete evidence of its ability and willingness to enforce respect for the safety of foreign lives and property and to suppress disorders and anti-foreign agitations" as a precondition for the carrying on of negotiations over the unequal treaties (notes of September 4, 1925).[72] Because of this "inability and unwillingness," "none of the Treaty of Washington signatories gave effect to the treaty with respect to extra-territorial rights, intervening in internal Chinese affairs, tariffs, courts, etc., on grounds that their interests were prejudiced by lawlessness and the ineffectiveness of the government of China."[73]

In 1940, Japan established a puppet government in Nanking under the leadership of Wang Ching-wei, who had been a leading disciple of Sun Yat-sen and, through the 1930s, a major figure in the Kuomintang. Its attempt to establish order in China was vain, however, as the United Front continued to resist—in the Japanese view, solely because of outside assistance from the Western imperialist powers. Japan was bogged

down in an unwinnable war on the Asian mainland. The policy
of "crushing blow—generous peace" was failing, because of the
foreign support for the "local authority" of Chiang Kai-shek,
while Japan's real enemy, the Soviet Union, was expanding its
economic and military power.[74] How familiar it all sounds.

With all of the talk about benevolence and generosity, it is
doubtful that Japanese spokesmen ever surpassed the level of
fatuity that characterizes much of American scholarship, which
often seems mired in the rhetoric of a Fourth of July address.
For example, Willard Thorp describes American policy in these
terms: ". . . we do not believe in exploitation, piracy, imperialism or war-mongering. In fact, we have used our wealth to help
other countries and our military strength to defend the independence of small nations"[75] (in the manner indicated in note
62, for example). Many similar remarks might be cited, but it is
depressing to continue.

A wave of revulsion swept through the world as the brutality
of the Japanese attack on China became known. When notified
of the intention of the Japanese government to bomb Nanking,
the United States responded as follows: "The Government is of
the opinion that any bombardment of an extensive zone containing a sizeable population engaged in their peaceful pursuits
is inadmissible and runs counter to the principles of law and
humanity."[76] Now that these principles have been repealed, it
is difficult to recapture the feeling of horror at the events themselves and of contempt for those who had perpetrated them.
For an American today to describe these events in the manner
they deserve would be the ultimate in hypocrisy. For this reason I will say very little about them.

In Manchuria, the Japanese conducted a fairly successful
counterinsurgency operation, beginning in 1931.[77] The record
is instructive. In 1932,

the insurgents who menaced the people and obstructed the attainment of *wangtao* [the perfect way of the ancient kings, or the kingly way] had at one point reached 300,000, but the earnest and brave efforts of various subjugating agencies headed by the Japanese army brought about great results. Thus the number of insurgents declined from 120,000 in 1933, to 50,000 in 1934; 40,000 in 1935; 30,000 in 1936; and 20,000 in 1937. As of September, 1938, the number of insurgents is estimated at 10,000.[78]

The success was achieved in part by contingents of Japanese troops, in part by the national army of Manchukuo, and in part by the police. "Because of the success of these activities [which led to the winning of the support of the masses], the insurgent groups are now in an extremely precarious condition and the attainment of peace seems to be in sight." The "native bandits" and "rebellious troops from the local armies" had been absorbed by the Chinese Communist party during this period, and were, by 1938, "under the Communist hegemony operating with the slogan of 'Oppose Manchukuo and Resist Japan,'" with political leadership supplied from China. The goal of the insurgents was "to destroy the government's pacification efforts" and to win public confidence and disturb public opinion "by opposing Manchukuo and Japan and espousing Communism. Their efforts lead the masses astray on various matters and significantly hamper the development of natural resources and the improvement of the people's livelihood." Through a combination of pacification and propaganda activities, their efforts were being countered and, the report continues, the "nation's economy and culture" preserved.

The report emphasizes the strong distaste of the authorities for forceful means:

The use of military force against the insurgents is the principal means of attaining peace and order, in that it will directly reduce the number of insurgents. But this method is to be used only as a last resort; it is not a method that is compatible with our nation's philosophy, which is the realization of the kingly way (*wangtao*). The most appropriate means suitable for a righteous government is that of liberating the masses from old notions implanted by a long period of exploitative rule by military cliques and feudalistic habits and of dispelling the illusions created by Communist ideology. Furthermore, the philosophy of the state calls for a proper understanding by the masses of the true nature of righteous government, the reasons behind the establishment of the state, and the current state of affairs. The insurgents should be given an opportunity to alter their misconceived notions and to become good citizens. This is why the operation for the inducement of surrender has such grave significance.

A continuing problem was the "nearly universal phenomenon in Manchuria that the insurgent groups return to their original state of operation as soon as the subjugation period is terminated and troops are withdrawn."[79] To counter this tendency, a number of methods were used, with considerable success. Communist groups were heavily infiltrated and alienation was created within the guerrilla groups. The formerly anti-Japanese Korean community was won over by "sociopolitical and accompanying psychological changes" ("revolutionary development," in modern phraseology), specifically, by offering them "the possibility of owning land and escaping from the control of their Chinese landlords" (Lee, p. 23). Among the Chinese, the situation was different, and more difficult.

Through propaganda and example, the guerrillas awakened the patriotism of the people and convinced them that the guerrillas were the only true defenders of their interests. When necessary, the guerrillas terrorized the reluctant elements as a warning to others. An intricate network of anti-Japanese societies, peasant societies, and the like provided the guerrillas both with the necessary supplies and with vital intelligence. Farmers who were located in regions too remote to be protected by the Manchukuo authorities and the Japanese were forced to comply with the guerrillas' demands, even if they had no desire to assist the insurgent cause. [Lee, p. 25]

The obvious answer to this problem was a system of "collective hamlets." By the end of 1937, the Police Affairs Headquarters reported that over 10,000 hamlets had been organized accommodating 5,500,000 people. The collective hamlets, Lee informs us, were set up with considerable ruthlessness.

Families were ordered to move from their farm homes with little or no notice, even if the collective hamlets were not ready. Some farmers were forced to move just before the sowing season, making it impossible for them to plant any seeds that year, while others were ordered to move just before harvest. Many farmhouses seem to have been destroyed by troops engaged in mop-up operations before preparations had been made for the farmers' relocation. The only concern of the military was to cut off the guerrillas' sources of food supply and their contacts with the farmers. [Pp. 26 f.]

There is no point in supplying further details, which will be familiar to anyone who has been reading the American press since 1962.

The collective-hamlet program was fairly successful, though it was necessary to prevent insurgents from "assaulting the weakly protected collective hamlets and . . . plundering food and grain" and to prevent infiltration. According to a report in 1939, many of the residents of the hamlets continued to "sympathize with Communism and secretly plan to join the insurgents," and the Communists continued to exploit the farmers' grievances with skill (Lee, pp. 33 f.). Vice-Governor Itagaki formulated the problem succinctly: "We are not afraid of Communist propaganda; but we are worried because the material for propaganda can be found in the farmers' lives. We are not afraid of the ignition of fire; rather we are afraid of the seeping oil" (p. 34).

The Japanese undertook a number of what are now called "population control methods," including registration of residents, issuance of residence certificates, unscheduled searches, and so on.[80] They also made use of the method of reward and punishment recommended by more recent theorists of pacification (see Lee, pp. 39–40).[81] The Japanese understood that "it was totally unrealistic to expect reforms or innovations to be initiated by those who were already well off" and therefore replaced the former "local gentry" by "young and capable administrative personnel" who were "trained to assist the local administrators through the Hsueh-ho-hui, the government-sponsored organization to recruit mass support for the Manchukuo regime" (p. 46). Many abuses at the village level were also eliminated, in an attempt to wean the villagers from their traditional belief that the government is merely an agency of exploitation. Extensive propaganda efforts were conducted to win the hearts and minds of the villagers (cf. pp. 55 f.). In comparison with American efforts at pacification, the Japanese appear to have achieved considerable success—if these documents can be believed—in part, apparently, because Japan was not committed to guaranteeing the persistence of the old semi-feudal order and was less solicitous of property rights. The reports indicate that by 1940, the Communist guerrillas had been virtually exterminated in Manchuria.

A secret report of the office of information of the government of Manchukuo in April 1939 describes the achievements of pacification in Tunghwa Province in glowing terms:

It must be said that the economic and spiritual impact of the reconstruction activities on the citizens of the province has been very uplifting. We have observed an increase in the areas under cultivation as a result of the recovery of abandoned lands; an increase in agricultural production owing to improvements in

seeds; an increase of farmers' cash incomes as a result of improvement in market facilities; remarkable progress among merchants and industrialists assisted by government loans; and the
winning of public support through medical treatment and the
administration of medicine.[82]

A secret report of November 1939 describes the situation in a
province where "revolutionary development" was not yet quite
so successful and insurgents still operated:

> . . . most atrociously, these insurgents pillage goods, and kill and
> wound men and animals. They are also systematically conducting
> Communist indoctrination operations in various villages. As a
> result, many villagers are led astray by the insurgents' propa-
> ganda and begin to work for the insurgents, passively or politi-
> cally. All this adds to the burden carried by the pacification
> forces.[83]

Farmers were fleeing from "insurgent-infested areas in a continuous stream," though some continued to "sympathize with
Communism." However, plans were being laid to "establish confidence" and destroy insurgent forces, to carry out "relief of
afflicted people," and, in general, to extend the work of nation
building.

I have no knowledge of the reaction in Japan to whatever
information was transmitted to the public about these matters.
No doubt, many Japanese deplored the excesses of the pacification program, though the more reasonable presumably continued to discuss the situation in balanced and unemotional
terms, taking note of the violence carried out on both sides. If
there were vocal advocates of Japanese withdrawal from Manchuria, they could be shown reports of the sort just quoted, and
warned of the atrocities that would be sure to follow were
Japanese troops to be removed and the Communist guerrillas
given a free hand. Obviously, regardless of cost, the Japanese
must continue to use limited means to secure law and order and

to permit the responsible elements of Manchurian society to build an independent nation free from externally directed terror.

No one hated the necessary violence of pacification more than the Japanese officers in charge. Vice-Governor Itagaki described the moral dilemma that they faced in moving words:

> The construction of the defense hamlets must be enforced—with tears. We issue small subsidy funds and severe orders [to the farmers], telling them to move to a designated location by such and such a date and that this is the last order. But it is too miserable [to watch] the farmers destroying their accustomed houses, and [to see] little innocent babies wrapped in rags and smiling on carts that are carrying the household goods away. A few days ago, a girl of sixteen or seventeen made me weep by coming to my office at the prefectural government and kneeling down to beg me to spare her house. She said, "Do we really have to tear down our house, councilor?" She had walked a long way to town thinking, "If I asked the councilor, something could be done." Watching the bony back of the little girl who was quietly led out by the office boy, I closed my eyes and told myself, "You will go to hell." The hardship of the Japanese police officers at the forefront who have to guide the coercive operation directly is beyond imagination. I was told many times while I was on my inspection tours of the front, "I cannot go on with this kind of wretched work. I will quit and go home." These words, uttered [as we sat] around a lamp sipping *kaoliang* gin, sounded as though someone was spitting blood. In each case we had to console and keep telling each other that this was the last hill that needed to be conquered. The program was forced through mercilessly, inhumanely, without emotion—as if driving a horse. As a result, more than 100 defense hamlets were constructed throughout the prefecture. These were built with blood, tears, and sweat.[84]

In Manchuria, the problem of the terrorists and Communist bandits seems to have been solved by 1940. In China itself, pacification continued throughout the Pacific war. Chalmers Johnson summarizes these efforts briefly in a recent study.[85] In

both north and central China "the Japanese suffered from guerrilla attacks and from their inability to distinguish a guerrilla
from a villager." In the north the policy implemented was "the
physical destruction of all life and property in an area where
guerrillas were thought to exist . . . whereas in central China a
policy of establishing so-called Model Peace Zones was pursued
. . . [consisting] of expelling the Communists from certain very
rich agricultural areas and then, following this military phase,
of integrating the cleared area into the Japanese satellite economy." The latter policy was far more successful, and it was
possible to place the government in Chinese hands. There was
also a "strategic hamlet" program, described in the following
terms in a recent Japanese commentary:

> . . . the Japanese Army tried its "Chinghsiang" (Clean Hamlet)
> operations in Soochow in Central China and its "Ailutsun"
> (Railway Defense Village) program in Shangtung Province in
> North China. . . . The concept of "Chinghsiang" lies in making
> the village or hamlet the basis for reforming government at the
> grass-root level; and, by concentrating all military, political, eco-
> nomic and ideological effort on a single village, in building it up
> into a peaceful, stabilized and secure area; then by using this
> village as a model district, in gradually extending security and
> stability to cover the whole "hsien" (county), the whole province
> and eventually the whole country.[86]

However, external interference made it impossible to carry
through this program. With far greater power to enforce their
efforts and a much smaller and weaker enemy, American political scientists were not unreasonable in looking forward to
greater success.

So events proceeded through the terrifying decade of the
1930s. Seeking desperately for allies, Japan joined with Germany and Italy in the Tripartite Pact at a moment when Germany appeared invincible. With the termination of the Japa-

nese-American commercial treaty in January 1940, Japan turned to "other commercial channels," that is, to plans for occupation of French Indochina and the Dutch East Indies, and for gaining "independence" for the Philippines. The expiration of the treaty was the turning point that led many moderates towards support for the Axis powers.[87]

In July 1940, the United States placed an embargo on aviation fuel, which Japan could obtain from no other source,[88] and in September, a total embargo on scrap iron. Meanwhile American aid to China was increasing. In September, the Tripartite Pact was signed, and Japanese troops entered northern Indochina. The goals were basically two: to block the flow of supplies to Chiang Kai-shek and to take steps towards acquisition of petroleum from the Dutch East Indies. On July 2, 1941, a decision was made to move troops to southern Indochina. The decision was known to the American government, since the Japanese diplomatic code had been broken. On July 24, President Roosevelt informed the Japanese ambassador that if Japan would refrain from this step, he would use his influence to achieve the neutralization of Indochina. This message did not reach the Japanese Foreign Ministry until July 27. On July 26, Japan announced publicly its plans to move troops to southern Indochina and the United States government ordered all Japanese assets in the United States to be frozen.[89] On August 1, a total embargo of oil was announced by the United States. At this point, "Japan was denied access to all the vitally needed supplies outside her own control."[90]

What slender hope there now remained to avoid war lay in the Hull-Nomura talks, which had been under way since February. The nature of these talks has been a matter of some dispute. Pal points out that the American position hardened noticeably in the course of the discussions, with respect to all major issues.[91] The United States insisted on making the Axis alliance a major issue, though Japan persistently de-emphasized it. Schroeder argues that the American motive was in part "selling the anticipated war with Japan to the American people," who might not "agree that an attack on non-American soil—on Thailand, Malaya, Singapore, or the Netherlands East Indies—constituted an attack on the United States."[92] It may be that the underlying motive was to justify the forthcoming American involvement in the European war. In any event, the American terms, by November, were such that Japan would have had to abandon totally its attempt to secure "special interests" of the sort possessed by the United States and Britain in the areas under their domination, as well as its alliance with the Axis powers, becoming a mere "subcontractor" in the emerging American world system. Japan chose war—as we now know, with no expectation of victory over the United States but in the hope "that the Americans, confronted by a German victory in Europe and weary of war in the Pacific, would agree to a negotiated peace in which Japan would be recognized as the dominant power in Eastern Asia."[93]

On November 7, 1941, Japan offered to accept "the principle of nondiscrimination in commercial relations" in the Pacific, including China, if this principle "were adopted throughout the world." The qualification was, needless to say, quite unthinkable. Hull's final demand was that the principle be applied in the Japanese occupied areas and that Japan withdraw all forces from China and Indochina. The Western powers could not be expected to respond in kind in their dominions. A few days later came "the day that will live in infamy."

This final exchange points clearly to what had been, for decades, the central problem. Japan had insisted that in its plans for "coprosperity" and then a "new order," it was simply following the precedent established by Great Britain and the United States; it was establishing its own Monroe Doctrine and realizing its Manifest Destiny. It is revealing to study the American response to this claim. Hull professed to be shocked. In his view of the matter, the Monroe Doctrine, "as we interpret and apply it uniformly since 1823 only contemplates steps for our physical safety," whereas Japan is bent on aggression.[94] He deplored the "simplicity of mind that made it difficult for . . . [Japanese generals] . . . to see why the United States, on the one hand, should assert leadership in the Western Hemisphere with the Monroe Doctrine and, on the other, want to interfere with Japan's assuming leadership in Asia," and he asked Nomura, "Why can't the Japanese Government educate the generals" to a more correct understanding of this fundamental distinction?[95]

American scholars were equally offended by the analogy. W. W. Willoughby, in a detailed analysis, concludes that no comparison can be made between the Monroe Doctrine and Japan's plans.[96] The United States, he asserts, has never resorted to the Monroe Doctrine to demand "that it be given special commercial or other economic privileges in the other American States." Rather, "it has exercised its powers of military intervention or of financial administration for the benefit of the peoples of the countries concerned or of those who have had just pecuniary claims against them." He cites with approval the discussion by G. H. Blakeslee in *Foreign Affairs*,[97] which characterizes the main difference between the American and Japanese position in this way:

> The United States is a vast territory with a great population vis-à-vis a dozen Caribbean republics, each with a relatively small area and population. Japan, on the other hand, is a country with a relatively small area and population vis-à-vis the vast territory and great population of China. An attitude which therefore ap-

pears natural for the United States to take toward the Caribbean States does not appear natural for Japan to take toward China.

This contribution to the history of imperialist apologia at least has the merit of originality. To my knowledge, no one had previously argued that attempts by one nation to dominate another are proper to the extent that the victim is smaller and weaker than the power that is bent on subjugating it. However, this argument is perhaps surpassed in acuity by Blakeslee's next explanation of the fundamental error in the Japanese analogy:

> The United States does not need to use military force to induce the Caribbean republics to permit American capital to find profitable investment. The doors are voluntarily wide open.

American willingness to submit to the people's will in the Caribbean was, in fact, nicely illustrated in the fall of 1933, a few months after Blakeslee's article appeared, when Ramón Grau San Martín came into power in Cuba with a program that interrupted what Sumner Welles described as the attempt to secure "a practical monopoly of the Cuban market for American imports." As Welles noted, this government was "highly prejudicial to our interest . . . our own commercial and export interests cannot be revived under this government." Consequently, Roosevelt refused to recognize the Grau government, and Welles commenced his intrigues (which he admitted were "anomalous") with Batista, who was, in his judgment, "the only individual in Cuba today who represented authority. . . . This . . . had rallied to his support the very great majority of the commercial and financial interests in Cuba who are looking for protection" (Welles to Hull, October 4, 1933). The Grau government soon fell, with the result that "the pre-1930 social and economic class structure was retained, and the important place in the Cuban economy held by foreign enterprises was not fundamentally disturbed."[98]

But the basic inadequacy of the Japanese analogy, as Blakes-lee points out, is the difference in aims. The United States

aims to help the backward Caribbean countries to establish and maintain conditions of stability and prosperity. The United States does not wish to seize territory, directly or indirectly, or to assume political or economic control. And when it has seemed necessary to intervene in some revolution-tossed land, it has effected the necessary reorganization and has then withdrawn.

It is this benevolence of intent that the Japanese do not share. Consequently, their appeal to the precedent of American practice is entirely without worth. The matter is simply put in a recent study of postwar American foreign policy, which is very critical of its recent directions: ". . . the American empire came into being by accident and has been maintained from a sense of benevolence." . . . "We engaged in a kind of welfare imperialism, empire-building for noble ends rather than for such base motives as profit and influence." . . . "We have not exploited our empire." ". . . have we not been generous with our clients and allies, sending them vast amounts of money and even sacrificing the lives of our own soldiers on their behalf? Of course we have."[99]

In comparison with this long-standing record of benevolence, Japanese aggression stands exposed as the kind of "unprecedented evil" that fully merited the atom bomb.

This review obviously does not exhaust the issues. But it does serve, I think, to place in context the policy alternatives that were open to the United States in 1941 and in earlier years. The predominant American opinion remains that the only proper response was the one that was adopted. In contrast, "realists" of the Grew-Kennan variety take the position expressed by Schroeder, who argues against the mistake of basing policy on an "emphasis on meting out justice rather than doing good."

The "moralistic" position of Hull, the "too hard and rigid policy with Japan," in Schroeder's view, was not based on "sinister design or warlike intent, but on a sincere and uncompromising adherence to moral principles and liberal doctrines." The "realistic" approach of accommodation favored by Grew would not have been immoral, he argues. "It would have constituted only a recognition that the American government was not then in a position to enforce its principles, reserving for America full freedom of action at some later, more favorable time."[100] Schroeder does not question that we were, in fact, "meting out justice," but argues only that we were wrong, overly moralistic, to do so; he does not question the principles to which the United States adhered, but only our insistence on abiding by these principles at an inappropriate time.

In contrast to the alternatives of "realism" and "moralism," so defined, the revolutionary pacifism of Muste seems to me both eminently realistic and highly moral. Furthermore, even if we were to grant the claim that the United States simply acted in legitimate self-defense, subsequent events in Asia have amply, hideously, confirmed Muste's basic premise that "the means one uses inevitably incorporate themselves into his ends and, if evil, will defeat him." Whether Muste's was in fact the most realistic and moral position at the time may be debated, but I think there is no doubt that its remoteness from the American consciousness was a great tragedy. The lack of a radical critique of the sort that Muste, and a few others, sought to develop was one of the factors that contributed to the atrocity of Hiroshima and Nagasaki, as the weakness and ineffectiveness of such radical critique today will doubtless lead to new and unimaginable horrors.

Notes

1. "Pacifism and Class War," in *The Essays of A. J. Muste,* ed. Nat Hentoff (Indianapolis, The Bobbs-Merrill Co., Inc., 1967), pp. 179–85.

2. Daniel Bell, in "Ideology—A Debate," *Commentary,* Vol. 38 (October 1964), p. 72.

3. "The Movement To Stop the War in Vietnam," *Essays,* pp. 503–13.

4. *Essays,* pp. 180, 287.

5. *Congressional Record,* May 9, 1967.

6. The probabilities are meaningless with respect to the objective situation, but not with respect to the mentalities of those who use them as a guide to action. If anything can be more frightening than the behavior of the self-styled "pragmatic" and "tough-minded" policy makers of the Kennedy administration in this crisis, it is the attitude that remains, long after the crisis has cooled, that this was Kennedy's "finest hour," in which he demonstrated his skill at the game of "nuclear chicken" (cf. historian Thomas Bailey, *New York Times Magazine,* November 6, 1965).

7. "Where Are We Going?" *Essays,* pp. 234–60.

8. "Crisis in the World and in the Peace Movement," *Essays,* pp. 465–78.

9. "The Cold War and American Scholarship," in Francis L. Loewenheim, ed., *The Historian and the Diplomat* (New York, Harper & Row, Publishers, 1967), pp. 123–69. Morton goes on to develop the conventional view that the Soviet Union is solely to blame for the dimming of "the bright hopes for the future," by "the subtle challenge of political subversion and economic penetration" (unthinkable to the West, of course), and by support of revolution, as in Greece, "in violation of allied wartime agreements that had placed Greece in the western sphere of interest." As to the latter, he does not discuss the considerable evidence that indicates, rather, that Stalin was opposed to the Greek rebellion and adhered to the Churchill-Stalin settlement that divided Europe into spheres of influence. He also makes no mention of Truman's statement, immediately after Nagasaki, that Bulgaria and

Rumania, the two countries assigned predominantly to the Russian sphere in the Churchill-Stalin agreement, "are not to be spheres of influence of any one power." Nor is there any reference to the American role except as one of "containment." In a review in the *Political Science Quarterly*, Vol. 82 (December 1967), Arthur Schlesinger describes Morton's essay as "an always intelligent account of the role of history and historians in the era of the cold war," which "will disappoint those looking for a *Studies on the Left* exposé of the corruptions allegedly wrought in the writing of American history by the decision to oppose Communist aggression after 1945."

10. See Wesley F. Craven and James L. Cate, eds., *The Army Air Forces in World War II* (Chicago, University of Chicago Press, 1953), Vol. 5, pp. 732–33:

> Arnold wanted as big a finale as possible, hoping that USASTAF could hit the Tokyo area in a 1,000-plane mission: the Twentieth Air Force had put up 853 B-29's and 79 fighters on 1 August, and Arnold thought the number could be rounded out by calling on Doolittle's Eighth Air Force. Spaatz still wanted to drop the third atom bomb on Tokyo but thought that battered city a poor target for conventional bombing; instead, he proposed to divide his forces between seven targets. Arnold was apologetic about the unfortunate mixup on the 11th and, accepting Spaatz' amendment, assured him that his orders had been "coordinated with my superiors all the way to the top." The teleconference ended with a fervid "Thank God" from Spaatz. . . . From the Marianas, 449 B-29's went out for a daylight strike on the 14th, and that night, with top officers standing by at Washington and Guam for a last-minute cancellation, 372 more were airborne. Seven planes dispatched on special bombing missions by the 509th Group brought the number of B-29's to 828, and with 186 fighter escorts dispatched, USASTAF passed Arnold's goal with a total of 1,014 aircraft. There were no losses, and before the last B-29 returned President Truman announced the unconditional surrender of Japan.

For the reaction of a victim, see Makoto Oda, "The Meaning of 'Meaningless Death.'" *Tenbō*, January 1965, translated in the *Journal of Social and Political Ideas in Japan*, Vol. 4 (August 1966), pp. 75–84.

> In the afternoon of August 14, 1945, thousands of people died during a protracted and intensive aerial bombardment of an arsenal in Osaka. I was a witness to the tragedy. I saw dozens of corpses—loyal subjects literally consumed by service to a government which had already

decided to accept the Potsdam Declaration's demand for unconditional surrender. The only reason these people died was because they happened to have been in the arsenal or environs at the time of the air raid. After what seemed an eternity of terror and anguish, we who were fortunate enough to survive emerged from our shelters. We found the corpses—and the leaflets which American bombers had dropped over the destruction. The leaflets proclaimed in Japanese, "Your Government has surrendered. The war is over!"

11. Radhabinod Pal, *International Military Tribunal for the Far East* (Calcutta, Sanyal and Co., 1953), pp. 620–21.

12. Paul Schroeder, *The Axis Alliance and Japanese-American Relations* (Ithaca, N.Y., Cornell University Press, 1958), p. 87.

13. *Ibid.*, p. 7.

14. *Japan's Quest for Autonomy: National Security and Foreign Policy, 1930–1938* (Princeton, N.J., Princeton University Press, 1966), Ch. 1.

15. Masamichi Rōyama, *Foreign Policy of Japan: 1914–1939* (Tokyo, Japanese Council, Institute of Pacific Relations, 1941), p. 8. He goes on to argue that it was Japanese inexperience that led to passivity and acceptance of the American attempt, with British backing, to attain hegemony in the Pacific—an obvious consequence of "equality" among unequals.

16. Quoted in R. J. C. Butow, *Tojo and the Coming of War* (Princeton, N.J., Princeton University Press, 1961), p. 17.

17. W. C. Holland and K. L. Mitchell, eds., *Problems of the Pacific, 1936* (Chicago, University of Chicago Press, 1936), p. 195.

18. Iriye Akira, *After Imperialism* (Cambridge, Mass., Harvard University Press, 1965), p. 160.

19. According to William L. Neumann, *America Encounters Japan* (Baltimore, The Johns Hopkins Press, 1963), p. 188, "over 200,000 Japanese were living along the South Manchuria Railway and in the Kwantung leased territory." Japanese estimates for Manchuria as a whole are much higher. Yasaka Takagi estimated the number of Japanese in Manchuria as approximately one million ("World Peace Machinery and the Asia Monroe Doctrine," *Pacific Affairs,* Vol. 5 [November 1932], pp. 941–53; reprinted in *Toward International Understanding* [Tokyo, Kenkyusha, 1954]).

20. Crowley, *op. cit.*, p. 103.

21. *Ibid.*, p. 110.

22. *Ibid.*, p. 140.

23. Quoted in *ibid.*, p. 154.

24. *Ibid.*, p. 160. The progress of civilization is indicated by the reaction to the American destruction of cities of the Mekong Delta in early February 1968, for example, the destruction of Ben Tre with thousands of civilian casualties to protect 20 American soldiers (20 had been killed, in a garrison of 40), after the city had been taken over, virtually without a fight, by the NLF forces.

25. *Japan and Her Destiny*, ed. F. S. G. Piggott (New York, E. P. Dutton & Co., Inc., 1958). Shigemitsu describes the Manchurian incident as, in effect, one aspect of an attempted coup, of which the domestic aspect failed. From his viewpoint, "Manchuria was an outlying district belonging to and colonized by China," a "sparsely populated, backward country on the borders of China." By 1930, the "revolutionary diplomacy" of China was attempting to reverse and overthrow the unequal treaties, including long-standing Japanese interests. At a time when the only solution to world problems was free trade, Europe was reverting to a closed autarchic economy and blocking trade between Japan and the colonial possessions of the European powers, and the League of Nations was following the policy of keeping the world static, in the interests of established imperialism. The Kwantung Army acted unilaterally, to protect what they took to be the legitimate interests of Japan in Manchuria. Later steps to defend Manchukuo were determined in part by the threat of ultimate Communist encirclement (by Communist Chinese and the Soviet Union), and in part as an attempt to "counter the world movement to closed economies," which required that the Japanese must attempt "to attain self-sufficiency." This view of the situation, to which I return below, was not unrealistic.

26. Shigemitsu, however, did not escape the Shanghai incident quite so lightly as did, say, American Ambassador to the Dominican Republic W. Tapley Bennett or Presidential Envoy John Bartlow Martin 23 years later, in not dissimilar circumstances. Shigemitsu was severely wounded by a terrorist (an advocate of Korean independence) and had a leg amputated.

27. *Thought and Behaviour in Modern Japanese Politics*, ed. Ivan Morris (New York, Oxford University Press, 1963), p. 30. Maruyama adds that "while there is no doubt that the Manchurian Incident acted as a definite stimulus to Japanese fascism, it must be emphasized that

the fascist movement was not something that suddenly arose after 1931."

28. Sadako Ogata, *Defiance in Manchuria: The Making of Japanese Foreign Policy, 1931–1932* (Berkeley, University of California Press, 1964), p. 178.

29. Quoted in Pal, *op. cit.*, p. 195.

30. *Op. cit.*, pp. 11–12. Rōyama is described by Maruyama (*op. cit.*) as "one of Japan's foremost political scientists and a leading pre-war liberal."

31. Ogata, *op. cit.*, p. 132.

32. *Ibid.*, p. 124. Cf. also p. 185.

33. Crowley, *op. cit.*, p. 138. It should be added that among the complex roots of fascism in Japan was a great concern for the suffering of the poor farmers, particularly after the great depression struck. See Maruyama, *op. cit.*, pp. 44–45, for some relevant quotations and comments.

34. Ogata, *op. cit.*, p. 45, paraphrasing a Kwantung Army research report.

35. *Ibid.*, p. 42.

36. Rōyama, *op. cit.*, p. 11.

37. Comparisons are difficult, but it seems that the Japanese were considerably more successful in establishing a functioning puppet government in Manchuria than the United States has ever been in Vietnam, just as the Germans were more successful in converting French nationalist forces to their ends in occupied and Vichy France than the United States has been in Vietnam. On the insurgency that developed in Manchuria, and the Japanese attempts to suppress it, see below, pages 195–201.

38. Quotes and paraphrase from Owen Lattimore, "China and the Barbarians," in Joseph Barnes, ed., *Empire in the East* (Garden City, N.Y., Doubleday, Doran & Company, Inc., 1934), pp. 3–36.

39. *Op. cit.* See note 19.

40. *Op. cit.*, p. 95.

41. In addition, there were those who opposed any compromise or concession on the grounds that it would then be impossible "to face the myriad spirits of the war dead" (General Matsui, 1941, cited by Maruyama, *op. cit.*, p. 113). It is painful to contemplate the question of how many have died, throughout history, so that others shall not have died in vain.

213

Another crucial factor, according to Maruyama (p. 124), was "the counsel of the Senior Retainers close to the Emperor, who had chosen war abroad in preference to class struggle at home, and who were then less afraid of losing that war than of risking revolution"—also a familiar pattern. See, for example, the discussion of the Spanish Civil War on pages 74–124 above.

42. Crowley, *op. cit.*, p. 245.

43. *Survey of International Affairs* (London, Oxford University Press, 1926), p. 386; cited in Takagi, *op. cit.*

44. A. W. Griswold, *The Far Eastern Policy of the United States* (New York, Harcourt, Brace & Company, 1938; paperback ed., New Haven, Conn., Yale University Press, 1962), p. 130. American scholarship generally agrees that these accords recognized the "special position" of the Japanese in the Manchuria-Mongolia region. See, for example, Robert A. Scalapino in Willard L. Thorp, ed., *The United States and the Far East* (New York, Columbia University Press, 1956), p. 30.

45. Both citations from William C. Johnstone, *The United States and Japan's New Order* (New York, Oxford University Press, 1941), pp. 124, 126. The Lansing-Ishii Notes, however, contained a secret protocol which in effect canceled this concession.

46. Quoted in Iriye, *op. cit.*, p. 271.

47. This is as large a force as the United States maintained in Vietnam in 1962. In late 1937, the Japanese had 160,000 troops in China. One tends to forget, these days, what was the scale of fascist aggression a generation ago.

48. Iriye, *op. cit.*, p. 218.

49. Johnstone, *op. cit.*, p. 214.

50. Cited in Dorothy Borg, *The United States and the Far Eastern Crisis of 1933–1938* (Cambridge, Mass., Harvard University Press, 1964), p. 590.

51. *Ibid.*, p. 42.

52. Officers of the Japanese army in China expressed the same solicitude. General Matsui, departing to take up his post as commander-in-chief of the Japanese expeditionary force in Shanghai in 1937, stated: "I am going to the front not to fight an enemy but in the state of mind of one who sets out to pacify his brother." At the Tokyo Tribunal he defined his task in the following words: "The struggle between Japan and China was always a fight between brothers within the 'Asian

family.' . . . It has been my belief all these years that we must regard this struggle as a method of making the Chinese undergo self-reflection. We do not do this because we hate them, but on the contrary because we love them too much. It is just the same as in a family when an elder brother has taken all that he can stand from his ill-behaved younger brother and has to chastise him in order to make him behave properly." Quoted by Maruyama, *op. cit.*, p. 95.

53. Johnstone, *op. cit.*, p. 290.

54. Quoted in Francis C. Jones, *Japan's New Order in East Asia* (New York, Oxford University Press, 1954), p. 156, from *The Memoirs of Cordell Hull* (New York, The Macmillan Company, 1948), Vol. 1, pp. 725–26.

55. Cf. Iriye, *op. cit.*, pp. 260 f., pp. 278 f., for discussion of these events.

56. Shigemitsu, *op. cit.*, p. 208 (see note 25). The racist American immigration law of 1924 had been a particularly bitter blow to the Japanese. In addition there were immigration barriers in Canada, Latin America, Australia, and New Zealand. It is worthy of mention that the Japanese effort to insert a racial-equality paragraph into the League of Nations resolutions endorsing the "principle of equality of Nations" and "just treatment of their nationals" had been blocked by Britain. Woodrow Wilson, then in the chair, ruled that it should not be instituted "in view of the serious objections of some of us" (Pal, *op. cit.*, pp. 317 f.). Only Britain and the United States failed to vote for this resolution. See Neumann, *op. cit.*, pp. 153–54.

57. Quoted in Ogata, *op. cit.*, p. 35.

58. Quoted in Shigemitsu, *op. cit.*, p. 221.

59. Bruno Lasker and W. L. Holland, eds., *Problems of the Pacific, 1933* (Chicago, University of Chicago Press, 1934), p. 5.

60. *Ibid.*, p. 10.

61. See Robert F. Smith, *The United States and Cuba: Business and Diplomacy, 1917–1960* (New York, Bookman Associates, 1960), p. 159.

62. Holland and Mitchell, *op. cit.*, p. 220. Parenthetically, we may remark that American postwar Philippine policy served to perpetuate what United Nations representative Salvador López calls the prewar "system rooted in injustice and greed" which "required the riveting of the Philippine economy to the American economy through free trade arrangements between the two countries," and which, in "tacit al-

legiance with the Filipino economic elite" led to a "colonial economy of the classical type" ("The Colonial Relationship," in Frank H. Golay, ed., *The United States and the Philippines* [Englewood Cliffs, N.J., Prentice-Hall, Inc., 1966], pp. 7–31). Furthermore, this "shortsighted policy of pressing for immediate commercial advantage" interrupted the Philippine revolution that was under way at the time of the American conquest. This "interruption" continued, for example, with the policies of Magsaysay, who "cleared away the ambivalence which had arisen in the persistent experimentation with public corporations of various kinds by a firm avowal that public policy would reflect faith in and dependence upon private enterprise" (Frank H. Golay, "Economic Collaboration: The Role of American Investment," in *ibid.*, p. 109). One effect of this "improvement" in "the political and economic aspects of the investment climate" was that from 1957 to 1963 "earnings accruing to American foreign investors were in excess of twice the amount of direct foreign investment in the Philippines," an interesting case of foreign aid. In fact, the preferential trade relations forced on the Philippines in 1946 virtually guaranteed American domination of the economy. Two Filipino economists, writing in the same volume, point out that "acceptance of the Trade Act by the Philippines was the price for war damage payments. In view of the prevailing economic circumstances, Filipinos had no alternative but to accept, after considerable controversy and with obvious reluctance" (p. 132). But the "compensating" rehabilitation act was itself something of a fraud, since "the millions of dollars of war damage payments . . . in effect went back to the United States in the form of payments for imports, to the benefit of American industry and labor" (p. 125).

63. Figures from John E. Orchard and H. Foster Bain, in Barnes, *op. cit.*, pp. 39–83, 185–212.

64. *Op. cit.*, pp. 226, 233.

65. Rōyama, *op. cit.*, p. 120. He adds that the new government was "provisional," and willing even to accept members of the Kuomintang if they would join.

66. *Ibid.*, p. 150.

67. Cf. Lyndon B. Johnson, August 18, 1967. In noting the all-too-obvious parallels between Japanese fascism and contemporary American imperialism in Southeast Asia, we should also not overlook the fundamental differences; in particular, the fact that Japan really was

fighting for its survival as a great power, in the face of great-power "encirclement" that was no paranoid delusion.

68. "Despite the vigor of the Japanese government's efforts to convey the idea that they wanted American aid in achieving a quick settlement [in 1937], United States officials again failed to understand the situation" (Borg, *op. cit.,* p. 466). Unfortunately for the Japanese apologists, they were unable to use some of the devices available to their current American counterparts to explain the failure of the Chinese to accept their honorable offers. For example, the director of Harvard's East Asian Research Center, John King Fairbank, thoughtfully explains that "when we offer to negotiate we are making an honorable offer which, in our view, is a civilized and normal thing to do," but the Asian mind does not share our belief "in the supremacy of law and the rights of the individual protected by law through due process" and is thus unable to perceive our honorable intent and obvious sincerity (*Boston Globe,* August 19, 1967). It is only those rather superficial critics who do not understand the Asian mind who insist on taking the North Vietnamese literally when they state that negotiations can follow a cessation of the bombing of North Vietnam, or who point out the moral absurdity of the plea that both the victim and his assailant "cease their violence."

69. Cf. Butow, *op. cit.,* pp. 122, 134.

70. David J. Lu, *From the Marco Polo Bridge to Pearl Harbor* (Washington, Public Affairs Press, 1961), p. 19.

71. Butow, *op. cit.,* pp. 273 f.

72. Cf. Pal, *op. cit.,* p. 212.

73. *Ibid.,* p. 213. The United States was the least offender in this regard, abandoning its control over Chinese tariffs in 1928. Germany and the Soviet Union had relinquished extraterritoriality in the 1920s (the United States did so in 1942). Japan relinquished these rights in the puppet state of Manchukuo.

74. Cf. Shigemitsu, *op. cit.,* p. 190. Also Lu, *op. cit.,* p. 34.

75. In Thorp, *op. cit.,* p. 7. He deplores the fact that this is not well understood by Asians. Thorp, formerly Assistant Secretary of State and member of the UN delegation, and at the time a professor of economics at Amherst, also draws the remarkable conclusion, in 1956, that one of the major international problems is the demonstrated willingness of the Soviet Union to support aggression in Indochina. The conference whose proceedings he was editing concluded finally with

the hope that "the Chinese people will one day regain their liberties and again be free" (p. 225), but did not specify when the people of China had previously possessed their liberties and lived in freedom.

76. September 22, 1937. Quoted in the Documents of the World Conference on Vietnam, Stockholm, July 1967, Bertil Svanhnstrom, chairman.

77. See Chong-sik Lee, *Counterinsurgency in Manchuria: The Japanese Experience*, RAND Corporation Memorandum RM-5012-ARPA, January 1967, unlimited distribution. I am indebted to Herbert Bix for bringing this study to my attention. As is very often the case with RAND Corporation studies, it is difficult to determine whether it was written seriously or with tongue in cheek. There is no reason to question the scholarship, however. The original documents translated in the memorandum are particularly interesting.

78. Pacification Monthly Report of the Office of Information, Government of Manchukuo, October 1938 (Lee, *op. cit.*, pp. 189 f.). The kill ratio is omitted.

79. Report of the Military Advisory Section, Manchukuo, 1937 (Lee, *op. cit.*, p. 12).

80. For an updating of such methods, see William A. Nighswonger, *Rural Pacification in Vietnam* (Praeger Special Studies; New York, Frederick A. Praeger, Inc., 1967).

81. For some discussion, see page 54.

82. Lee, *op. cit.*, p. 305. Such reports illustrate a phenomenon noted by Maruyama, in his analysis of the "theory and psychology of ultra-nationalism": "Acts of benevolence could coexist with atrocities, and the perpetrators were not aware of any contradiction. Here is revealed the phenomenon in which morality is subtly blended with power" (*op. cit.*, p. 11). Again, the reader will have no difficulty in supplying contemporary examples.

83. Lee, *op. cit.*, pp. 307 f.

84. Secret Report of the Office of Information of the Government of Manchukuo, April 1939, entitled: "Pacification Activities in the Communist Bandit Area (Personal Reflections)" (Lee, *op. cit.*, pp. 217 f.).

85. "Civilian Loyalties," in Wilson C. McWilliams, ed., *Garrisons and Governments* (San Francisco, Chandler Publishing Co., 1967), pp. 86–87.

86. Shizuo Maruyama, "The Other War in Vietnam: The Revolutionary Development Program," *Japan Quarterly*, Vol. 14 (July–Septem-

ber 1967), pp. 297-303. The author, a Southeast Asian specialist and editorial writer for *Asahi Shimbun,* notes the similarity to earlier Japanese efforts, but feels that the prospects for the American program are dim for a number of reasons, among them the following: ". . . the wounds inflicted on Nature, so ruthlessly destroyed for this, are too brutal to see. Beautiful grasslands, the verdant forests and the rich crops have all been burned by flame throwers, napalm bombs and chemical defoliants. The great earth has been gouged and dug over. The ugly land, no longer green, has lost its power to attract people and to stir deep in the hearts of people a love for their birthplace and their motherland." There is, he feels, little chance that revolutionary development will succeed "when Nature has been turned into a scorched earth and the system and the traditions born of a race of people have been destroyed."

87. Lu, *op. cit.,* p. 67.

88. Cf. Nobutaka Ike, ed., *Japan's Decision for War: Records of the 1941 Policy Conferences* (Stanford, Calif., Stanford University Press, 1967), p. 11.

89. The timing of these events is given in this order in Lu, *op. cit.,* p. 188. According to Ike, *op. cit.,* p. 108, the order to freeze assets was given on the evening of July 25, the announcement that troops would be moved south at noon on the 26th. The reasons for the delay in transmission of Roosevelt's offer to the Japanese Foreign Ministry are obscure. It appears that there was still some room for diplomatic maneuver at this time.

90. Schroeder, *op. cit.,* p. 53. He quotes General Miles as saying that the United States "today is in a position to wreck completely the economic structure of the Japanese empire," and Admiral Stark as predicting that this move (the freezing of assets) would probably lead directly to war.

91. *Op. cit.,* p. 545.

92. *Op. cit.,* pp. 100 f.

93. Ike, *op. cit.,* Introduction.

94. April 20, 1940; cited by Schroeder, *op. cit.,* p. 170.

95. *Memoirs of Cordell Hull,* Vol. 2, p. 1032.

96. *Japan's Case Examined* (Baltimore, The Johns Hopkins Press, 1940), pp. 128 ff.

97. "The Japanese Monroe Doctrine, "*Foreign Affairs,* Vol. 11 (July 1933), pp. 671–78.

98. Bryce Wood, *The Making of the Good Neighbor Policy* (New York, Columbia University Press, 1962), p. 109.

99. Ronald Steel, *Pax Americana* (New York, The Viking Press, 1967). As Steel observes, this generosity is the price we must pay to enjoy our imperial role. Compare the remarks of H. Merivale, cited on page 58 above. Perhaps the introductory chapters of this book, from which these remarks are selected almost at random, are meant as parody, in which case they serve as witness to, rather than evidence for, the pervasive self-delusion of our highly conformist and ideologically committed society. In American scholarship dealing with the international role of the United States, it is often difficult to determine what is irony and what is sentimentality.

100. Schroeder, *op. cit.*, pp. 203 ff.

THE LOGIC OF WITHDRAWAL

International affairs can be complex, a matter of irreconcila-
ble interests, each with a claim to legitimacy, and conflicting
principles, none of which can be lightly abandoned. The current Middle East crisis is a typical, painful example. American
interference in the affairs of Vietnam is one of the rare excep-
tions to this general rule. The simple fact is that there is no
legitimate interest or principle to justify the use of American
military force in Vietnam.

Since 1954 there has been one fundamental issue in Vietnam:
whether the uncertainty and conflict left unresolved at Geneva
will be settled at a local level, by indigenous forces, or raised to
an international level and settled through great-power involvement. Alone among the great powers, the United States

Parts of this essay appeared as an editorial statement in *Ramparts*, Vol. 5
(September 1967). Originally written in July 1967, it was extended to cover
events of the intervening period in January 1968. The Postscript and a few
interpolated passages date from April 1968.

has insisted on the latter course. It seems clear that if the United States persists on this course, then either the issue will be settled unilaterally through the exercise of American power, in the manner of Nazi Germany in Poland or the Soviet Union in Hungary, or it will develop into a great-power conflict, with unimaginable consequences.

This is the situation to which Howard Zinn has addressed himself in a lucid and compelling study which advocates, very simply, that the United States accept the principle adopted by the other great powers at Geneva in 1954 and agree to turn Vietnam over to the Vietnamese.[1] "The daily toll in Vietnam of innocent people is so terrible that the cessation of our military activity—the bombings, the burning and the shelling of villages, the search and destroy operations—has become no longer debatable or negotiable, but a matter of urgent and unilateral action." And the only action on our part that can mitigate the torture, that can avert the still greater catastrophe that lies in wait, is to remove the military force that bears the primary responsibility. Since, happily, this is the one policy that we can successfully implement, there is a feasible alternative to devastation of Vietnam or a global conflict.

The proposal that the United States withdraw will be dismissed as "extremist." To those who like to describe themselves as "responsible" or "realistic," withdrawal is politically impossible, and the analysis of the situation in Vietnam on which the proposal is based hopelessly naive.

On the issue of domestic politics, Zinn argues that "the so-called 'realists' who urge us to speak softly and so persuade the President are working against the reality, which is that the President responds to self-interest rather than to rational argument. . . . If enough people speak for withdrawal, it can *become* politically feasible." Only a combination of factors can end the war; hence "every citizen must put his full moral weight, his *whole* argument, into the balance." In fact, the government is not a monolith. As the political and military realities in Vietnam emerge through the haze of pretense and deception, the advisability, the desperate urgency of American withdrawal may become correspondingly apparent, to some at least. Consider, for example, the reaction of Senator Young to the news that the South Vietnamese forces are unwilling to do what amounts to police work, so that so-called "pacification" must be taken over by the American army:

> If the South Vietnamese forces of Prime Minister Ky are so inadequate in numbers, intelligence, and training that they cannot handle entirely the pacification program in the villages . . . , then instead of Americans trying to train, indoctrinate, and pacify an alien people, the time is long past due for us to withdraw to our coastal bases and eventually from Vietnam.[2]

This reaction echoes that of Senator Symington after a recent Asian trip:

> If the South Vietnamese do not achieve this pacification, there is no point in this country continuing to pour out lives and treasure in order to protect a government that can neither consolidate nor control what has been taken from them by their own citizens and the North Vietnamese. If the United States decides to become the major factor in this pacification program [as it has since become] as well as in the fighting of the war [as it became long ago], it can only become an extended war of the white man against the Asians, on the mainland of Asia.[3]

Symington's remarks are no doubt accurate, and if past history is any guide, they will soon be forgotten, as Americans become habituated to the new reality. It was, after all, not very long ago that a well-known Asian specialist, with close State Department connections, was able to draw the following conclusion in a review of Southeast Asian affairs:

It is unthinkable that the United States would move into the country directly, take over the conduct of the warfare against the Vietcong, and attempt to build and manage a government for Saigon and the countryside. Apart from other difficulties, this would offer convincing proof of the Communist charge of "imperialism" daily leveled against our government. For the United States to carry the war to the north on any large scale would have the same result.[4]

Observe that the date of this evaluation was February 1965; as we recall, "convincing proof of the Communist charge of imperialism" was not long in coming. And today, there is very good reason to suppose that we will find ourselves in "an extended war of the white man against the Asians, on the mainland of Asia."

Far from being naive, the analysis of the situation that leads to the call for withdrawal—not eventual but immediate—seems to me entirely realistic; and the dimensions of the Vietnamese tragedy are so awesome that whatever the prospects for success may be, the responsible citizen must spare no effort to create the political climate, the background of insight and understanding, in which this call will become a powerful one. The urgency of this matter can hardly be exaggerated. It seems unlikely that the Johnson administration will be willing to face the 1968 elections with an unwinnable war on its hands. The prospects are therefore for sharp escalation, perhaps a forced confrontation with China. What is more, the rapid growth of Chinese nuclear weapon and missile capacity will surely suggest to Pentagon planners the need to act now, before the Chinese are in a position to hold an American army hostage on the fringes of Asia. With this prospect, attempts to predict what may happen next are as irrational as our Vietnamese policy itself.

Zinn gives a concise but persuasive analysis of the political and moral character of the war, the international reaction, the justifications that are offered for persisting in the semiprincipled, semilunatic course of action in which we are now so heavily engaged. His general thesis seems to me entirely correct. The issues are so grave that I would like to go well beyond the bounds of a review and indicate some of the directions in which his discussion might be extended and elaborated.

What is the situation that American policy makers face in mid-1967? The American military takeover of "pacification" is a testimony to the failure, thus far, of the effort to impose a political solution by force on an unwilling population. Its true significance is tersely indicated by an unnamed American official in Saigon who comments: "We've been playing the be-nice-to-the-Asian game for ten years, and it's been a flop. We can't afford it any longer."[5] The American chief of civil operations in the northernmost provinces attributes the failure of the "revolutionary development teams" to the "overwhelming corruption" of Vietnamese official life, to the failure to understand that "until there is a contented peasantry there is no room for the opulent society of the government of Vietnam."[6] The same report in the *Times* goes on to give a dramatic example of the results of this corruption. It comments on the successful attack by a guerrilla force on the province capital of Quang Tri on April 6, and continues: "A few days later, in a series of events that were not fully reported at the time, [the guerrillas] moved virtually unmolested into Hué while the army and the national police fled"—a remarkable event, its significance indicated by the fact that it was kept from the American people at the time and still has not been frankly discussed.

In Saigon itself there are clear indications of the same demoralization or widespread involvement in guerrilla activities. For example, on February 13, 1967, Westmoreland's headquarters in central Saigon were subjected to a mortar attack. As the *New York Times* points out, with considerable understatement, this attack "gives rise to a question of the popular support in Saigon for the South Vietnamese government. . . . It seemed unlikely to observers that the 81mm. mortar and the shells could have been transported to the house, that the roof could have been cut and the weapon set up without detection by someone in the crowded residential district. Until the shells were fired . . . , no one called the police."

Current reports confirm, once again, that "every program to win the allegiance of the countryside for the South Vietnamese government has so far failed, in the opinion of most observers. To this day, 80% of the peasantry . . . falls under Vietcong influence if not outright control."[7] The very terminology of this report gives some insight into the reasons for the recurrent failure; it has yet to be demonstrated that the Americans are correct in their unquestioned assumption that the peasants of Vietnam are objects, incapable of political expression or allegiance, to be "controlled" by one side or the other. The report continues: "If the South Vietnamese themselves cannot achieve support for the government among their own people, it is unlikely that 'giant white foreigners' will be able to do this for them." Yet it is just this attempt to which we are now reduced, with the military takeover. And we can be fairly sure that this latest step will lead to new and glorious reports of success, before the next rude awakening.

The Saigon government has few illusions as to its legitimacy and status. Saigon officials have pointed out repeatedly that they cannot survive in an open political arena, and that therefore the Americans must destroy not only the Vietcong military units but also its political and administrative structure, by such devices as the "pacification" program. A clear and forthright expression of this analysis appears in an interview with "one of the top generals in the junta, a man regarded by U.S. officials as politically the most sophisticated of the group," reported by George M. Kahin in a memorandum to a group of senators.[8] The general describes the situation in the following terms:

> To defeat the communists we must win against them both politically and militarily. But we are very weak politically and without the strong political support of the population which the NLF have. Thus now if we defeat them militarily, they can come to power because of their greater political strength. We now have (thanks to the support of our Allies) a strong military instrument. But we are without a political instrument that can compete with the communists in the south. Such a political instrument we must now begin to create, a process that will take a generation. It is unrealistic to speak of a cease fire until after we have built up our political strength to the point where we can compete with the communists successfully.

He goes on to say that the war must be carried to North Vietnam, with the commitment of a million American troops, then probably to China as well. Finally, he argues that "it might be necessary to move on to World War III so as to insure that communist power was fully removed from Vietnam," a not unrealistic forecast, if the United States continues to insist that its protégés be spared the defeat that they know to be a certainty if the struggle is ever permitted to shift to the political arena, where they lack "the strong political support of the population which the NLF have."

Buddhist leaders appear to share this analysis. In the cited memorandum, Kahin quotes Buddhist spokesmen, obviously unidentified, who point out that the present Saigon regime, dependent for its life on United States support, can do nothing to "win" the war. They plead that the United States lift the tight lid that is clamped on political expression and political activity so that a government with some claim to legitimacy can be established, one that can proceed to make a political settlement with the National Liberation Front. Despite the outrageous suppression of Buddhist political activity, the Buddhists still appear to be confident, as they have been for years, that they can function effectively in cooperation with the NLF. The recent "Policy Statement" published by the Overseas Vietnamese Buddhist Association emphasizes this (as does the touching and pathetic book by Thich Nhat Hanh, *Vietnam: Lotus in a Sea of Fire*), and, in fact, puts forth a program for South Vietnam that is not markedly different from that of the NLF.

American authorities have repeatedly indicated that they share this assessment of the Saigon government and its popular base. Both the present Assistant Secretary of State for Far Eastern Affairs and his predecessor have expressed their belief that neutralization of South Vietnam would lead to a Communist takeover, and it is widely admitted that the American expeditionary force was introduced to stave off what was in essence a political defeat. In his revealing study of the Vietcong, American foreign service officer Douglas Pike concludes, with ample evidence, that the NLF victory in the now long-forgotten civil war was essentially a political and organizational victory, achieved by building a mass movement. The NLF, he states, is the only "truly mass-based political party in South Vietnam." Only the Buddhists—whose political organization was smashed in the spring of 1966—could realistically hope to take part in a coalition with the NLF, in his judgment. General Richard Stilwell, at the time second in command in the Southeast Asian theater, informed Senator Young that we are putting down "an insurrection," and even General Westmoreland, who now asserts that he has seen no signs of insurrection, admitted to Senator Young that the majority of the Vietcong fighting in the Mekong Delta were born and reared there[9]—thus indicating that he may not know the meaning of the word "insurrection."

The basis for the success of the insurrection is not very obscure. Denis Warner, as anti-Communist as any newsman who has worked in Southeast Asia, pointed out years ago that "in hundreds of villages all over South-East Asia the only people working at the grass roots for an uplift in people's living standards are the Communists."[10] And to the Communist agit-prop successes, the Americans have contributed mightily, for example, with the terroristic bombing policy. American sources indicate that in the first year of American bombing of the South, 1965, local recruitment for the Vietcong tripled.[11] The head of the Saigon office of *Asahi Shimbun* concludes that "It is certain that the escalation and spread of the war, even though its results may be advantageous to the Saigon Government itself, only serves to heighten still further opposition to the war among the general population," adding that "The number of draft-dodgers and deserters among young South Vietnamese is a sign of the failure of the war, by and large, to win the support of young people, who tend to view it as an American war."[12] And the situation can only worsen. Saigon authorities indicate that there are now some two million refugees, most of them, according to the reports of war correspondents, victims of American bombardment or forced resettlement. An Associated Press report from Saigon gives the following shattering forecast:

> The United States high command, preoccupied for two years with hunting down North Vietnamese regulars, now is looking more toward the populated valleys and lowlands where the enemy wields potent political influence and gets his sustenance. Quick gains are hoped for by forced resettlement of chronically Communist areas, followed up with scorched-earth operations that deny enemy troops all food, shelter, and material support. Central highlands valleys are being denuded of all living things; people ringing the Communist war zones in the South have been moved.

> Some American observers recently in the Mekong Delta say that the Vietnamese Army, long hated and feared, now is regarded as less of a threat to the countryside than the Americans.[13]

Dozens of such reports can be cited. Those who advocate withdrawal are simply proposing that we eliminate this threat, as only we can do.

It is hardly surprising that the peasantry refuses allegiance to a constituent assembly that could muster 3 votes out of 117 for the one land-reform measure that was introduced, or that even the residents of Saigon are less than enthusiastic about a government so unbelievably corrupt that the secretary of industry in Ky's cabinet seems to be the major supplier of drugs to the Vietcong—of course, after receiving a third of a million dollars in kickbacks from the American and West German suppliers.[14] Nor is it obscure why the American government continues to use its military force to impose on the people of Vietnam the regime of the most corrupt, most reactionary elements in Vietnamese society. There is simply no one else who will do its bidding, and resist the overwhelming popular sentiment for peace and, no doubt, neutralism. The United States government has on occasion indicated that it would not leave if asked to do so "by a left-wing or even neutralist government that, in the U.S. view, did not reflect the true feelings of the South Vietnamese people or military leaders."[15] Furthermore, it will see to it that no such government will arise, and that no such opinions will be publicly expressed. Thus in the last few months, reports from South Vietnam indicate that once again a Buddhist attempt to establish a legal political organization were frustrated and the leaders arrested (Kahin memorandum, cited above, note 8).

Jean Raffaelli, the one Western correspondent who has remained in North Vietnam, has observed that quite apart from any question of politics, there is a human element of grandeur in the resistance of the Vietnamese to the assault launched against them by the world's most advanced technology. In *Le Monde,* a North Vietnamese doctor "of international reputation" is quoted as saying:

> . . . the Americans have demolished everything. All that we have built since 1954 is in ruins: hospitals, schools, factories, new dwellings. We have nothing more to lose, except for independence and liberty. But to safeguard these, believe me, we are ready to endure anything.

In South Vietnam, the American attack has been far more severe, and direct report from its victims is lacking. But some statistics tell the story well enough. According to American sources, the Vietcong are "able to enlist an estimated 7,000 recruits a month."[16] Recently, an extensive propaganda barrage has enthusiastically proclaimed that in March 1967 there were 5,557 defectors from the Vietcong, almost twice as many as in any previous month. Only the careful reader would have noted that of these "defectors" 630 were identified as military men and 301 as political cadres, the rest being peasants, probably coming for a free meal.[17] Seven thousand new recruits and 630 defectors—these figures indicate graphically by what means the American war in Vietnam must be won.

The preceding description is based on reports in early 1967. Rereading it in January 1968, I need hardly emphasize how little the situation has changed. The savage battering of the Vietnamese continues without pause; in scale, it is unique in the history of warfare. We learn that aerial bombardment alone exceeds 100 pounds of explosives per person, 12 tons of explosives per square mile, distributed almost equally between North and South Vietnam. Hundreds of thousands of acres have been subjected to defoliation, with what ultimate consequences no one knows. Refugees in South Vietnam are counted in the millions. Why have they left their homes? ". . . the reason why the people are forced to abandon their villages and their homes is because, in most cases, practically all of the homes are completely burned to the ground by the American forces. However, the people still try to cling to their scorched land, and are removed only by compulsion. . . ."[18] Literate Americans—those who have followed the well-reported horror story of Ben Suc, for example—can supply the details for themselves.[19] Numerous eyewitness reports have given the lie to the cynical pretense that our targets in North Vietnam are purely military, targets of "steel and concrete." The chief editorial writer of *Asahi Shimbun* writes: "I myself walked around and inspected the bombed remains of schools, hospitals, churches, temples, market places, and other peaceful public facilities."[20] Lee Lockwood, Harrison Salisbury, David Schoenbrun, and others have elaborated, for those who wish to know. It is no longer denied that antipersonnel weapons constitute a significant proportion of the bombing.

The political situation remains as before. Elections have been held to legitimize the existing regime in American eyes, at least. To ensure the proper result, the only avowed "peace candidate," Au Truong Thanh, was ruled off the ballot, as was the candidate most likely to be a threat at the polls, General Minh (he had previously been barred from the country). "Communists" and "neutralists" were excluded by electoral law. In the senatorial elections, tickets associated with Tri Quang Buddhists were excluded as "proneutralist," and the trade-union ticket was eliminated because "one candidate lacked certification of his legal status."[21] As anticipated, "the candidates are generally an aristocratic and urban group," including few villagers—"about 90% of them live within Saigon or the surrounding province of

Gia Dinh."[22] The shenanigans involved in deciding who "won" the senatorial elections defy description.[23] Although a number of American political scientists declared themselves satisfied (recalling Dean Rusk's description of the May 1965 provincial elections as "free elections . . . by our standards"), the special committee of the South Vietnamese Constituent Assembly recommended to invalidate; the decision was reversed by a vote of 58–43 in the full Assembly, under police guard, with the director of the national police, General Loan, and his armed bodyguards conspicuously in the gallery. Phan Khac Suu, the conservative landowner who was Assembly Speaker, refused to announce the result, saying, "I am absolutely unwilling to accept the verdict."[24] Shortly after the elections, Truong Dinh Dzu, who surprised everyone by speaking of peace and who placed second in the balloting, was arrested. Also arrested was Au Truong Thanh, "by 79 armed men in combat gear" led by General Loan.[25] Among the charges: he had applied for an exit visa to the United States. "It is up to him to explain why he wants to go abroad," stated General Loan. After being held for eighteen hours, he was returned to house arrest, where apparently he remains, though it is difficult to obtain information. On November 3, the Saigon government freed 6,270 prisoners in an amnesty, including 4,320 "Vietcong suspects," most of them peasants, and 1,120 "political detainees"—"persons who have been held, usually without trial, for periods up to three years." A ranking official said, "It's safe to say that only a tiny fraction of the total was released Wednesday." The government refuses to give further information.

Furthermore, it is by now also clear that the government, in the months since the elections, has fallen into an almost total paralysis, the only noticeable action being the intensive effort by the House to block the attempt to draft South Vietnamese boys of eighteen and nineteen to fight the American war. Tran Van Do, the Foreign Minister, explains that "we are not able to organize South Vietnam politically . . . so we cannot accept the NLF as a political party . . . the integration of the front will be a political way to take over South Vietnam."[26] The Mekong Delta, with 40 percent of the population (and as yet, no North Vietnamese soldiers), continues to be a Vietcong stronghold. Asked why, President Thieu states: "The main reason the Vietcong remain so strongly entrenched in the Mekong Delta is that people there still believe there is little difference between the French whom they called colonialists, and the Americans whom they call imperialists."[27] Another reason is pointed out by Congressman Reid, who notes that "70 percent of the tenant farmers of the lowlands and Mekong Delta now rent from absentee landlords who are living it up in Saigon"[28]—the attempt by Congressmen Reid and Moss to have the government release a detailed study of land measures in South Vietnam by the General Accounting Office has so far been unsuccessful.[29]

Tran Van Do's analysis is confirmed by Hanson Baldwin, who reports that "almost unanimously, . . . U.S. officials in Vietnam view the prospect of imminent negotiations with alarm" because inclusion of the NLF in a coalition would be "the kiss of death."[30] This attitude towards a negotiated settlement reveals itself continually in American diplomacy, with its constant posing of new, more extreme conditions whenever an opportunity for negotiations arises—as in the Ho Chi Minh–Johnson exchange of February 1967, when President Johnson proposed, as a condition for negotiations, that we should stop "augmenting" our forces in South Vietnam after North Vietnam had stopped all infiltration (we, of course, would be free to continue our own supply and "infiltration" operations, for our own far more extensive expeditionary forces, even after the

North Vietnamese desisted totally). Occasionally, spokesmen for the American government have expressed themselves quite clearly about the prospects for negotiations. For example, General Maxwell Taylor stated in August 1965:

> . . . the army is the power in South Vietnam. The generals are completely committed. They've burned all their bridges behind them. They would never tolerate a government that was caught surreptitiously or overtly negotiating with Hanoi or with the Vietcong.[31]

It seems unlikely that either Saigon or Washington will be trapped into negotiations, so long as the political base of those who collaborate with us in South Vietnam remains as weak as it is today.

Corroborating Hanson Baldwin's summary of opinion in Vietnam, Hedrick Smith reports from Washington that "the recent elections did not produce an organized political base for the government," and, in the opinion of United States policy makers, "the Saigon regime lacks sufficient popular support and cohesion to enter . . . a political test of strength with the front."[32] The elections, although they may have temporarily calmed American public opinion, have changed little or nothing in South Vietnam. An internal report of the United States Mission[33] in Saigon reports the gloom of American officials over the "strange drift from reality regarding the U.S. role in Vietnam" among the "South Vietnamese people," as evidenced, for example, in the statement by a group of middle-aged citizens that the new mobilization law had been enacted "at the behest of the Americans, whose real aim is the extermination of as many Vietnamese as possible," or the question of a legislator who asks, "Why should our young men be drafted to serve U.S. interests?"

The mood among Saigon intellectuals is summarized by a

retired professor who is "somewhat to the right in the spectrum of Saigon intellectuals."[34] The problem, he states, is that "at this point the only intellectuals of character who have committed themselves are on the other side." Ho Chi Minh retains his popularity, because "he bridged the gap between Vietnam and the modern world." "Everyone knows and admires Ho." The only hope, as the professor sees it, is for the United States to put aside pretense and to appoint a new "governor or proconsul for Vietnam."

As far as the military situation is concerned, Senator Mansfield, one of the best-informed members of the Senate on Southeast Asian affairs, concluded after General Westmoreland's recent reports in Washington that he saw "very little, if anything, in the pattern of combat operations to indicate any weakening of the ability of the Vietcong to keep on fighting." He believes that the NLF remains "the dominant force in South Vietnam," and points out that its "stronghold" in the Mekong Delta "has hardly been touched." The Front, rather than Hanoi, is "the main factor to be considered in South Vietnam."[35]

There are, to be sure, certain "pacified" areas, some even with few American troops; for example, much of Tay Ninh Province, where the Cao Dai is quite strong. But it is interesting to investigate the details of this success in "pacification." Elizabeth Pond reports that the basis appears to be "a certain accommodation between the Cao Dai and the Viet Cong."[36] Among the Cao Dai intellectuals, the heroes remain those who advocated neutralism—particularly, the former "Cao Dai Pope," Pham Cong Tac, who was exiled under Diem. By some, "the only one who has carried on the tradition of Pham Cong Tac" is considered to be Major Nguyen Thanh Mung, who joined the Vietcong with his Cao Dai troops. The relation between this model area and the Saigon government is one of strong mutual mistrust, according to this report.

There has been no more revealing commentary on the situation in the American-controlled areas of South Vietnam than the testimony elicited by Congressman Donald Riegle from Rutherford Poats, in May 1967, released in September.[37]

Mr. Poats had been, for the preceding three years, "the No. 1 man overseeing our economic program, the so-called 'other war' in Vietnam," and had just been promoted to deputy director of the Agency for International Development. According to this testimony, as Congressman Riegle reports it, "the annual U.S. commodity import program in Vietnam is actually a political ransom paid to powerful South Vietnamese commercial interests to insure political stability in South Vietnam, and insure their continued support of the war." Poats agreed with Congressman Riegle's summary statement that "if we were to withdraw our AID program, . . . the government would likely collapse over there, and for all intents and purposes the war would be over," and that "if this war were conducted in a way that required greater economic sacrifices by certain elements in Vietnam, the political instability is such that the country might fly apart." The situation is such that "there would not be military action by the Vietnamese military forces today had it not been for our provision of commercial imports," because of the resulting "inflation, disruption, and loss of morale." He also agreed that "there is certainly a substantial element of truth" in Congressman Riegle's judgment that without the "ransom," commercial interests in South Vietnam would "get their sympathizers out in the streets and bring down the Government" (though he felt this judgment to be "harsh"). Congressman Riegle concludes that "if we cannot establish some sort of balance between self-sufficiency . . . versus a growing dependency, then we will never get out of this situation. We will be mired down there forever." He adds that "all the evidence that piles up on the military side and on the nonmilitary side" shows a growing dependency. According to Mr. Poats, "that is certainly a danger, and in some instances a fair conclusion." It would follow, then, if this assessment is accurate, that "we will be mired down there forever."

One might compare this testimony with a report by the French resident minister in 1897:

[The only collaborators are] intriguers, disreputable or ignorant, whom we [the French] had rigged out with sometimes high ranks, which became tools in their hands for plundering the country without scruple. . . . Despised, they possessed neither the spiritual culture nor the moral fibre that would have allowed them to understand and carry out their task.[38]

Apart from its rhetorical flair, this might be the testimony of Rutherford Poats today. Mr. Poats's testimony will come as no surprise to those who have been paying attention to the laments of senior American officials in Saigon. In 1959, one such official[39] commented that "in the case of Free Viet-Nam the lack of even a bare minimum of economic self-sufficiency makes enduring political independence only an illusion," and complained that "the majority of the aid is used in a manner that maintains an extravagant standard of living." "The Viet-Minh," he said, ". . . can make a strong case that the United States is effectively replacing France as the new master of Free Viet-Nam." Poats's testimony simply shows how little things have changed. Many additional illustrations of the character of the collaborationist elements might be cited.[40] The whole situation recalls vividly other episodes in the history of colonialism, for example, the situation in the Philippines during the period of the Japanese occupation. The prospects are for deepening misery and still further devastation, so long as the American occupation continues.

Christopher Lydon, the *Boston Globe* correspondent who accompanied General Gavin on his recent trip to Vietnam, concluded a series of articles reporting his impressions with a quotation from Ton That Thien, managing editor of the *Vietnam Guardian,* which was suppressed by the Saigon regime when it printed a report questioning the official claim that Assembly member Tran Van Van was assassinated by the Vietcong. Thien defines what he sees as the only possible American "victory":

> You cannot defeat the other side militarily unless you devote the next 30 or 40 years to it. You can win if you keep killing for a generation. You simply exterminate all the Vietnamese—the way you killed the Indians in America—and there will be no more war.

Lydon comments: "This agony, if not utter desperation, among what seemed to me the most sensitive and patriotic Vietnamese, about the burden of American arms on their country is the overriding impression I carry back from this tortured capital."[41] This agony is shared by the most perceptive observers of the Vietnam tragedy, even those who are basically in support of the American military intervention. Bernard Fall, for example, in one of his last articles warned that "it is Viet-Nam as a cultural and historic entity which is threatened with extinction," as "the countryside literally dies under the blows of the largest military machine ever unleashed on an area of this size."[42] It is appalling beyond words that we permit this to continue.

When one tries to see what lies behind the official government reports, this is the sort of picture that emerges. Of course, it is not the picture that the government seeks to present, nor the one that it succeeds, by and large, in presenting, given the enormous propaganda apparatus at its command. It is to the great credit of the American press that it does still provide information on the basis of which one who is willing to put in the time and effort can arrive at some understanding of what is taking place in Vietnam. But we must recognize that valuable as this is, it has little bearing on the state of American democracy, since the opportunity to do the research that is required to separate fact from propaganda is limited to a privileged few.

In the light of what we have seen in the past three years, it is difficult to become excited over such matters as the ambiguity, or duplicity, of the American government position on the Geneva agreements, or the numerous violations of domestic and international law that have accompanied our intervention in the internal affairs of Vietnam. Nevertheless, these matters, and in particular the reaction as they have become too clear to overlook, are quite revealing for anyone concerned with the American war in Vietnam and its implications for the future. It was, at one time, quite normal to denounce the "Communists" for their disregard of international law and treaty obligations. Now, however, many Americans tend to scoff at such matters as irrelevant, unrealistic. Suddenly, the Constitution and the system of treaties to which we have committed ourselves—the United Nations Charter in particular—have become "outmoded," inappropriate to the complexities of current history, which require a powerful executive, free to react with overwhelming military force to real or alleged "emergencies" and "attacks"—such as the alleged Tonkin Bay attack. In the world-dominant power, this disregard for the formalities must cause very great concern.

Randolph Bourne once warned of the intellectuals who "tell us that our war of all wars is stainless and thrillingly achieving for good"; we have a right to become even more alarmed when they tell us (not in so many words, to be sure, but by the policies they advocate) that our national self-interest requires that we tear to shreds the delicate fabric of international law and disregard our treaty commitments and constitutional processes. Granting the inadequacies and frequent injustice of international law and the institutions set up to give it substance, there is still much truth in the conclusion of the Lawyers Committee on American Policy in Vietnam: ". . . the tragedy in Vietnam reveals that the rules of law, when so flagrantly disregarded, have a way of reasserting the calm wisdom underlying their creation. If international law had been followed, both Vietnam and the American people would have been spared what Secretary General U Thant has described as 'one of the most barbarous wars in history.' "[43]

The disregard for law and treaty was illustrated strikingly by our behavior with respect to the Geneva agreements of 1954. Much has been made of the fact that in a technical sense we did not clearly commit ourselves to uphold these agreements. The record, however, must not be forgotten by those who are concerned to restore a measure of decency to our international behavior. At Geneva, Mr. Bedell Smith did explicitly commit the United States to observe the French-Vietnamese Agreement on Cessation of Hostilities and paragraphs 1–12 of the Final Declaration of the Conference (pointedly omitted was paragraph 13, which provided for consultations "to ensure that the agreements . . . are respected," an interesting omission, in the light of subsequent attempts to achieve a negotiated settlement). The Final Declaration states that "the military demarcation line is provisional and should not in any way be interpreted as constituting a political or territorial boundary," and calls for elections under international control as part of a political settlement based on "the principles of independence, unity and

241

territorial integrity" for all of Vietnam. Apparently, the United States had no intention of fulfilling its Geneva commitment, a fact that is admitted with remarkable frankness. For example, the Honorable Kenneth T. Young, Director of Southeast Asian Affairs in the State Department from 1954 to 1958, writes that in 1954 "our aim was an independent South Vietnam with a strong government responsive to the nationalist aspirations of the population."[44] Thus our aim was to violate our commitment at Geneva. This aim was part of our general program of "trying to safeguard South Vietnam as part of the 'retainment' of all or most of non-communist Asia," "of helping the Vietnamese to create stability, security and prosperity south of the 17th parallel" so as "to deter aggression and subversion from the North"— all in violation of our commitment at Geneva to a unified Vietnam, with supervised elections in 1956. Obviously one could hardly have supposed that "North Vietnam," prior to the scheduled elections in 1956, would carry out "aggression and subversion," and as events were to prove, nothing occurred in those years that could even remotely be construed in such terms, despite the Diemist repression and Diem's refusal (with our support) to undertake the 1955 consultations that were provided for by the Geneva accords.

Secretary Dulles, it will be recalled, went still further in his aims, as when he advised the French ambassador, prior to the conference, that "above all, the deltas of the Red and Mekong rivers must be retained as bases from which a counterattack could recover what was lost to the Viet Minh at the conference table."[45] It would be interesting, though probably impossible, to trace the ways in which the United States and its Saigon ally acted on this concept. Bernard Fall claims, on what evidence he does not say, that "constantly since 1956" small saboteur groups have been parachuted or infiltrated into North Vietnam, though "the casualty rate is very high and successes, if any, are few and far between."[46] Richard Goodwin dates these attempts from 1958.[47] Recall that even according to American propaganda, "There was no serious threat [in South Vietnam] until 1959–60, when North Vietnam set in motion a systematic effort to seize control of South Vietnam by force."[48] In fact, the American government claims only that infiltration of trained South Vietnamese cadres began in 1959; even just prior to the American takeover of the war in early 1965, surveys of Vietcong prisoners and defectors found "most native South Vietnamese guerrillas unaware of any North Vietnamese role in the war, except as a valued ally."[49] A comparative study of the success of the South Vietnamese commandos in North Vietnam and the Northern-trained South Vietnamese cadres sent to South Vietnam in the 1960s might provide an interesting commentary on some of the strange ideas about "revolutionary guerrilla war" that appear in current American propaganda.

It is curious, incidentally, that today only the United States and the "Communists" insist that South Vietnam is a separate and independent entity. The Saigon authorities maintain, in article 1 of the new constitution, that "Vietnam [not South Vietnam] is a territorially indivisible, unified, and independent republic," of which they claim to be the rulers; article 107 of the constitution specifies that article 1 cannot be amended. Hence in their view, even if Ho Chi Minh were to have sent his entire army to South Vietnam, he would not have been guilty of "aggression," but only of insurrection and subversion.

There is, however, a much more dangerous development than the falsification and cynicism of the American government with respect to its international commitments and to domestic and international law, namely, the tolerance by even enlightened American opinion of the notion that we have a perfect right to intervene in the internal affairs of Vietnam, to determine the "legitimate" elements in South Vietnamese society, and to direct the development of social and political institutions of our choice in that unfortunate country. It is shameful but undeniable that the turmoil over the war in the United States would never have risen beyond a whisper had we met with success in our attempt "to strengthen the police and security forces and other institutions contributing to a modern police state" in South Vietnam.[50] One is no longer even surprised to read the recommendation, from a knowledgeable and quite liberal correspondent, that "The United States ought to send [to Vietnam] the best people it has, at this sensitive business of political reorientation," so that the field will not be left to the NLF.[51] As he points out, our Vietnamese "are playing a power game, both locally and in Saigon, for their own special privileges and interest," and they have "little but contempt for the villagers." Therefore, *we* must find a way to win allegiance for them among the peasantry. Imagine how Saville Davis would react on reading such a recommendation in *Pravda*. Both he and his readers take for granted, however, that the United States has the right to carry out "political reorientation" (not to speak of the right to use military force) anywhere in the world.

The Vietnamese revolutionaries may or may not succeed in freeing their country from American domination, but they have already succeeded in shattering American complacency with regard to our international role. American power is so great that no outside force can call us to account; hence the overwhelming urgency of the effort to overcome the effects of a generation of indoctrination and a long history of self-adulation. We will simply compound the tragedy of Vietnam if we do not exploit this opportunity to break loose from the stranglehold of ideology and the tradition of conformism that makes a mockery of the values we pretend to hold.

The first step towards political sanity must be intensive self-examination, exposure not only of what we do and what we represent in the world today, but also of the attitudes that color and distort our perception of our international behavior. A remarkable expression of these attitudes appears in a deservedly famous article by Neil Sheehan, written on his return from three years as a war correspondent in Vietnam.[52] From his direct observations, he concludes that "for its own strategic and political ends, the United States is . . . protecting a non-Communist Vietnamese social structure that cannot defend itself and that perhaps does not deserve to be defended." "Idealism and dedication are largely the prerogative of the enemy"; "in Vietnam, only the Communists represent revolution and social change" and "despite their brutality and deceit, remain the only Vietnamese capable of rallying millions of their countrymen to sacrifice and hardship in the name of the nation and the only group not dependent on foreign bayonets for survival." On our side are the military, and the "mandarins drawn from the merchant and landowning families" who had collaborated with the French just as they collaborate with us.[53] He points out that the existing social system defends privilege and that "many young Vietnamese of peasant origin join the Vietcong because the Communists . . . offer them their best hope of avoiding a life on the rung of the ladder where they began—at the bottom." He describes the new construction in Saigon, virtually all "luxury apartments, hotels and office buildings financed by Chinese businessmen or affluent Vietnamese with relatives or connections within the regime . . . destined to be rented to Americans," while "Saigon's workers live, as they always have, in fetid slums on the city's outskirts." But these are the lucky ones—lucky, that is, in comparison with the more than a million refugees, most of whom have left their homes "because they could no longer bear American and South Vietnamese bombs and shells" or the hundreds of thousands killed and wounded, victims largely of "the extraordinary firepower of American weaponry," often turned against helpless villagers by cynical South Vietnamese officials.[54] He describes the American strategy as one of "creating a killing machine . . . and then turning this machine on the enemy in the hope that over the years enough killing will be done to force the enemy's collapse through exhaustion and despair"[55]—the enemy being, for the most part, the rural population of South Vietnam.

Sheehan concludes this account in the following way: "Despite these misgivings, I do not see how we can do anything but continue to prosecute the war," although he cannot fail to ask himself "whether the United States or any nation has the right to inflict this suffering and degradation on another people for its own ends." The reason: any other course "might undermine our entire position in Southeast Asia."

Many people have commented on the disparity between the contents of this article and the conclusions that Sheehan expresses. But there is a more important point that has received very little attention. Sheehan begins his account by saying that when he arrived in Vietnam he

> believed in what my country was doing in Vietnam. With military and economic aid and a few thousand pilots and Army advisers, the United States was attempting to help the non-Communist Vietnamese build a viable and independent nation-state and defeat a Communist guerrilla insurgency that would subject them to a dour tyranny.

He is disillusioned only because of the devastating consequences, for Vietnam and its people, to which this attempt led.
But he still does not question that we had a perfect right to use
military force to determine the structure of South Vietnamese
society and to defeat an insurgent movement which we had
decided "would subject them to a dour tyranny." There is no
aggressor in history who could not have provided a similar
"justification" for his actions—and many have offered precisely
such justifications. The assumption that we have the right to
impose our will on the Vietnamese (in their best interests, of
course) is almost unchallenged. It is for this reason that one
cannot be too hopeful about the prospects of reaching liberal
American opinion in any fundamental way, on the central issues
of war and peace, freedom, and national self-determination.

There are few who challenge the assumption that we have a
perfect right to determine the legitimate elements in South
Vietnamese society, or to use force to impose the social and
political institutions that we, in our wisdom and benevolence,
have selected for South Vietnam—so long as this attempt is not
too costly to make it worthwhile. The spectrum of "responsible"
opinion extends from those who proclaim openly that we have
this right to those who formulate our goals in a way that pre-
supposes it. As to the latter, consider the final report to Congress by Defense Secretary McNamara, probably as sane a
voice as one is likely to hear in Washington these days. We are
fighting in Vietnam, he says, "to preserve the principle that
political change must not be brought about by externally directed violence and military force." But it is, in his view, perfectly legitimate for "externally directed violence and military
force" to be employed to guarantee political stability—that is,
when it is the United States that exercises this force. In fact, he

goes still further. We even have the right to use our military force to carry out political and social change. Thus the pacification program, which is under American military control, "involves nothing less than the restructuring of Vietnamese society," but it is, in his view, a legitimate, in fact laudable program.[56] Thus the principle that we are fighting to preserve is not the principle of nonintervention by military force in the affairs of other nations. Rather, it is the principle that the United States, and the United States alone, may intervene in the internal affairs of other nations to guarantee political stability and even to restructure their society. Secretary McNamara is of course aware of the fact that the role of North Vietnam in "externally directed violence" has always been, and now remains, far slighter than our own; it is the department that he headed—the Department of Defense—that has provided most of the evidence on this matter. But North Vietnamese interference has been in support of social change of a sort that we define as illegitimate, whereas ours is in support of stability (or occasionally, restructuring) that we have determined to be quite proper. To be concise, we are fighting in Vietnam in fulfillment of our role as international judge and executioner—nothing less.

Secretary McNamara's formulation of our goals in Vietnam is given in calm and measured tones and is for this reason deceptively reassuring. With less subtlety, the same presuppositions are expressed in the words of a congressman from Texas, twenty years ago:

> No matter what else we have of offensive or defensive weapons, without superior air power America is a bound and throttled giant; impotent and easy prey to any yellow dwarf with a pocket knife.[57]

What is important in such statements as this is not the undercurrent of racism—though that is bad enough—but rather the notion that we are "easy prey" to these yellow dwarves with their pocket knives. Obviously, we are "easy prey" to them only in *their* countries, where we have a perfect right to be.

Why do we have this right? The answer has been given by many statesmen and scholars: It is in our national interest. President Johnson has expressed the matter quite clearly on occasion, for example, in the following statement (November 2, 1966):

> There are three billion people in the world and we have only 200 million of them. We are outnumbered 15 to one. If might did make right they would sweep over the United States and take what we have. We have what they want.

Consequently, "we are going to have to stand and say: 'Might doesn't make right' "—as we are doing in South Vietnam, for example. Or in Guatemala, where according to Guatemalan Vice-President Marroquín Rojas, "American planes based in Panama take part in military operations in Guatemala" in which "napalm is frequently used in zones suspected of serving as refuge for the rebels."[58]

When President Johnson pleads that we are defending ourselves against a superior force, that *we* must stand in Vietnam or else *they* will "sweep over the United States and take what we have," he is, unfortunately, representing a substantial, probably dominant body of American opinion. To us today, it may seem difficult to understand how it could be seriously believed, thirty years ago, that a Jewish-Bolshevik conspiracy was threatening the survival of Germany, the bearer of the spiritual values of Western civilization.[59] To others today, it may be equally difficult to take seriously the picture of the strongest, richest nation on earth cowering in terror behind its missiles and nuclear warheads, in fear that "what we have" will be taken away if we allow a tiny country halfway around the world to follow its own course in freedom from American domination. Nevertheless, this characterization is no caricature. People in the so-called "peace movement" have a tendency to regard Lyndon Johnson as an illegitimate usurper who does not represent the mainstream of American opinion. They are probably deluding themselves. Statements such as those just quoted may very well reflect prevailing American attitudes, and one who wishes to think realistically about the American imperial role would do well to bear this in mind—as he should bear in mind the fact that this is a country in which a leading liberal commentator, after all that has happened in the past three years, can describe the American war in Vietnam in these terms:

> [America] is fighting a war now on the principle that military power shall not compel South Vietnam to do what it does not want to do, that man does not belong to the state. This is the deepest conviction of Western Civilization, and rests on the old doctrine that the individual belongs not to the state but to his Creator, and therefore has "inalienable rights" as a person, which no magistrate or political force may violate.[60]

As I have just pointed out, we are not the first nation to have seen itself as fighting to defend the "deepest convictions of Western civilization." When James Reston, with the access to information that he has, can seriously contend that we have been fighting to preserve the inalienable rights of the people of Vietnam against "military power" or "political force," we can see what a long road lies ahead before there is any hope that this country will recover its political sanity.

The colonialist mentality that colors the American perception of the Vietnam war is strikingly evident in the reactions of those who are turning against the war as its monstrous character becomes too plain to hide. Several months ago, for example, the top leaders of the International Voluntary Services resigned—some after almost a decade of work in Vietnamese villages—"because they believed that our military action was proving counterproductive, and threatened to alienate the majority of the Vietnamese from their American saviours."[61] The IVS group paints a grim picture of the consequences of our military intervention in Vietnam, in terms that are not unfamiliar to readers of the American press. Their resignation was intended as a protest against policies which, they predict, can only serve to drive still more of the population into association with the NLF. They assert that our "commitment" in Vietnam has always been to one element of Vietnamese society, "the urban-educated group, which has felt that a noncommunist, independent government would best serve their interests and the interests of their compatriots in the rural villages of South Vietnam." That we had a right to make such a commitment and to act on it is not questioned in their statement. The "tragedy unfolding in Vietnam" to which Senator Morton refers is that we were unable to realize this commitment, to construct a stable government that would represent the interests of the Vietnamese, as these interests are interpreted by "the urban-educated group."

No one would question the sincerity or dedication of the IVS leaders, or their undoubted contributions in their work in South Vietnam. But there is every reason to question their assumption that we have the right to restructure and organize South Vietnamese society, by force if necessary (their resignation came in the fall of 1967), along lines that we have set. In essence, their position is not different from that of Lord Cornwallis, whose "permanent settlement" in India in 1793 restructured village society, creating a landed aristocracy on the British pattern.

There is no reason to doubt the sincerity of his belief that this civilized arrangement could only benefit the Indians in the long run. Of course, the new squirearchy also happened to serve British interests; as the British Governor-General Lord William Bentinck put it: "If security was wanting against popular tumult or revolution, I should say that the 'permanent settlement' . . . has this great advantage . . . of having created a vast body of rich landed proprietors deeply interested in the continuance of British Dominion and having complete command over the mass of the people" (1829). Our reasons for wanting to control Vietnam are not those of the British in India in 1829, but in Vietnam, as in the Philippines and Latin America, our efforts are directed to organizing (or restructuring) the society so as to ensure the domination of those elements that will enter into partnership with us. That we should do so is not surprising, surely not to anyone who is familiar with the history of imperialism. What is extraordinary is that at this late date we should act with so little awareness of what we are doing, that we still find it possible to deceive ourselves, though few others,[62] with the classical rhetoric of long-decayed imperialism.

Before continuing with this sketch of American reactions to the war in Vietnam, I would like to cite another American military source, which gives much insight into the nature of the Vietcong success in the face of the titanic military force with which we have attempted to batter it to the ground:

> The success of this unique system of war depends upon almost complete unity of action of the entire native population. That such unity is a fact is too obvious to admit of discussion; how it is brought about and maintained is not so plain. Intimidation has undoubtedly accomplished much to this end, but fear as the only motive is hardly sufficient to account for the united and apparently spontaneous action of several millions of people. One traitor

in each town would effectually destroy such a complex organization.

This assessment is from a United States War Department report, in the year 1900; the author is Major General Arthur MacArthur, and he is commenting, of course, on the campaign to suppress the Philippine war of national liberation, then actively in progress. These remarks are perfectly apropos today. I quote them to dispel the thought that Vietnam is merely a unique aberration, a blunder, merely a result of "the politics of inadvertence," without roots in our history and without significance for the future.

There is of course a sense in which the liberal critics are correct when they refer to the Vietnam war as an "aberration." In Vietnam, we lost control. The Vietnamese refused to play the game the way they were expected to when the war was simulated on the RAND Corporation computers. They did not realize that they were supposed to yield when the pressure reached a certain point. Therefore, we were forced to escalate beyond any reasonable level, to a stage where our economy and society can hardly bear the cost. In this respect, it is true, Vietnam is an aberration. In all other respects it is a natural consequence of the policy that was described three quarters of a century ago by Brooks Adams, in prophetic words, when he proclaimed: "Our geographical position, our wealth, and our energy pre-eminently fit us to enter upon the development of Eastern Asia and to reduce it to part of our economic system." The suppression of the movement for Philippine independence, shortly after, was only the first attempt to put into practice the policy of reducing Eastern Asia to part of our economic system. At that time, we were defending Christianity from the savage Moros. Now, we are defending the free world from the International Communist Conspiracy. In other respects, little has changed, except for the scale of our attack.

Again, the example of the Philippine war illustrates the need to turn our attention from the problems of Southeast Asia to those of the United States—to the ideological commitments on which American initiatives are based, and the national self-image that permits them to be tolerated with such equanimity; in particular, the unshakable belief in American goodwill and generosity that persists through each calamity—notably, among the self-styled "hardheaded and pragmatic liberals"—and that stultifies political thinking and debases political discourse. We can, for example, learn a great deal about the sources of American Vietnamese policy by observing how American scholarship comes to terms with the suppression of the Philippine struggle for independence—in which, incidentally, there were well over 100,000 Filipino casualties. Thus Louis Halle argues that "we could not hand the Philippines back to the Spanish tyranny, and they were in no condition to govern themselves or encompass their own defense. If we simply got out and came home we would leave chaos behind," with the Germans and Japanese lurking in wait. Therefore, the United States, "having inadvertently become responsible for the Philippines, had no alternative to assuming, itself, the obligation of governing and defending what consequently became the first item of an American overseas empire."[63]

It need hardly be pointed out that it was the American expeditionary force from whom the Filipinos needed "defense." Nor will I discuss the kind of society that we bequeathed them,[64] except to remark that for reasons that are perhaps obvious, the Huk guerrillas once again appear to be in control of large areas of central Luzon, setting the stage for what may be a bloody re-enactment of the tragedy of Vietnam.

We can also learn a good deal from the reactions of American observers to the tensions that have developed between the United States and the Philippines in the postwar period. Consider, for example, the remarks of David Sternberg,[65] who asks "what has happened to the Philippine reservoir of good will and friendship toward Americans" since formal independence was granted to our Philippine colony? To this long-term resident of the Philippines and former AID adviser, it appears that there were "few complex problems" under the American occupation, "once the scars of war had healed and America's good intentions had gained credence" and "the mass of Filipinos were able to relate the realization of their personal hopes and aspirations to a benign American presence." But now, "the commercial American, though still benign employer, is also a potential competitor." The old, mutually satisfactory "mentor-student" relation, suffused by the warmth of the benign employer to his wards, is difficult to reconstruct under the conditions of formal independence. Of course, there is hope, for example, in the "cultural predisposition toward private enterprise" and the existence of "a small but highly competent body of planners and managers at the top level of the private economic sector." The hope is not dimmed by the fact that seventy years after the "benign American presence" was established by force, three quarters of the population live under conditions unchanged since the Spanish occupation, under the continuing rule of a political and economic elite who were "coopted into the colonial regime" and have "an affectionate respect for the American way of life,"[66] a respect not unrelated, perhaps, to the great privileges that they enjoy as a consequence of the American conquest.[67]

It is remarkable to see how easily perceptive and informed commentators succeed in deluding themselves as to the character of American actions and policies. For example, Roger Hilsman, in his recently published study of policy making under the Kennedy administration, *To Move a Nation,* discusses the attempt to concentrate the peasantry in "strategic hamlets" in the early 1960s, maintaining that "the primary role of the strategic hamlet was to provide [the peasants] . . . a free choice between the Viet Cong and the government." As he makes very clear, this "free choice" was to be provided by careful police work inside the hamlets ("for it seemed obvious that putting up defenses around a village would do no good if the defenses enclosed Viet Cong agents"); the failure of the program he attributes to the fact that "there had been no real effort to isolate the population from the Viet Cong by eliminating Viet Cong agents and supporters inside the strategic hamlets and by imposing controls on the movement of people and supplies . . . Viet Cong supporters and agents . . . had no difficulty repenetrating the hamlet and continuing subversion." Thus the program failed "to provide the villager with physical security, so that he has a choice of refusing to cooperate with the Viet Cong," a "free choice" which is obviously denied him as long as Vietcong supporters are permitted to exist in his village.

There is no doubt an important difference between this level of self-deception and that of Marshal Ky, who describes the philosophy of his government as "100 percent social revolutionary,"[68] or CIA analyst George Carver, who tells us of "the genuine social revolution now taking place in the urban areas of South Vietnam."[69] The natural reaction to such pronouncements is one of ridicule, but amusement fades when one begins to calculate the human cost.

Let us return to Howard Zinn's study (cf. note 1), in the light of some of these general observations. Zinn has some apt remarks about the moral blindness that permits America to remain insensitive to the agony of Vietnam. "We listen with the languor of a people who have never been bombed, who have only been the bombardiers." "We have no Hiroshima, no city of the blind and maimed, no professors haggard from long terms in jail . . . we have never been forced . . . to recognize our deeds, to bow, to apologize, to promise a life of peace. We have, in other words, never been caught." Thus protest is muted and diffuse, as "Uncle Sam, the white-gloved financier of counterrevolution has removed his gloves, taken gun in hand, and moved into the jungle," and has slowly composed "an enormous pattern of devastation which, if seen in its entirety, would have to be described as one of the most evil acts committed by any nation in modern times."

There are, I think, certain gaps in Zinn's analysis of the factors that prevent withdrawal of what can only be described as our army of occupation. Consider the matter of prestige. Zinn disposes effectively of the claim that our prestige as a nation would be diminished by withdrawal, noting that this would satisfy a range of opinion that extends from Adenauer to the Japanese left. But there is also the matter of internal prestige—the factor to which Eric Hobsbawm referred when he pointed out that American policy making often seems less concerned with red areas on the map than with red faces in the Pentagon.

Furthermore, it may be that in some respects Zinn underestimates the subtlety of those whose arguments he counters. For example, he remarks that "we see every rebellion as the result of some plot concocted in Moscow or Peking," and that the Russians make the same mistake, attributing revolts "in Hungary or Poznan . . . to bourgeois influence or to American scheming." Although one can, to be sure, become a prisoner of one's own propaganda, it is nevertheless difficult to believe that the Russian leaders so misunderstood the events of 1956; more likely, they were unwilling to tolerate an erosion of their power in a sensitive buffer area and found in "bourgeois influence" and "American scheming" a useful propaganda cover. Similarly, it strains credulity to suppose that our present Secretary of State was simply deluded when he described "the Peiping regime," in 1951, as "a colonial Russian Government—a Slavic Manchukuo on a larger scale." Ample evidence was available to him to show the absurdity of this evaluation, for example, in the State Department White Paper on China published not long before. More likely, as in the case of the Hungarian revolution, it was necessary to find a way to justify a variety of long-range policies: strengthening the Western alliance and rearming Germany, expanding the nuclear arsenal, stemming popular revolutions in the Third World and subverting or strangling those that had taken place. Similarly, it is not easy to convince oneself that the director of the CIA, Allen Dulles, really believed that Mossadegh was willfully "creating a Communist state," or that Assistant Secretary of State for Inter-American Affairs Thomas Mann was so woefully ignorant of world affairs as to suppose that the Dominican revolution in 1965 resulted from the machinations of a "Sino-Soviet military bloc." Rather, one must adapt to current styles of acceptable international behavior. It would not do to use today the phraseology of Secretary of State Philander Knox, who sent marines into Cuba in 1908 saying that "the United States does not undertake first to consult the Cuban Government if a crisis arises requiring a temporary landing somewhere." And in general, the "international Communist conspiracy" is a perfect propaganda device to justify actions that reinforce and extend American hegemony, serving our aims just as "bourgeois influence and American scheming" serve those of Russian imperialism. In both cases there is, of course, a background of fact that gives a superficial plausibility to the fabrications of the propagandist.

Similarly, I think that Zinn does not go far enough in analyzing the justification for the war given by the dissatisfied liberals, a very important matter if one hopes to construct a domestic political base for a policy of disengagement in Vietnam, or more generally, for a significant reorientation of American international behavior away from the policy of repression and "restructuring" on American terms, disguised as "anti-Communism" and "preservation of order." I have already given a number of illustrations of the ideological blinders that must be removed before sensible discussion can even begin. Others can easily be added.

Consider, for example, Richard Goodwin's essay, cited in note 47. Goodwin constructs a powerful argument against the war, but concludes nevertheless that the war is ultimately justified, in part on grounds of American self-interest, in part because of the necessity for "protecting Asia from dominion or conquest by a hostile power." As to the first, "the bedrock vital interest of the United States," which must serve as the "single standard" against which any step in policy making must be tested, is "to establish that American military power, once committed to defend another nation, cannot be driven from the field"—even if, as in the case in question, an American withdrawal would be in the face of an "enemy" that is largely indigenous.[70] If we generalize this "bedrock vital interest" to other great powers, the outlook for the future is dim. The Soviet Union, for example, could have used this argument to justify its military intervention in Hungary (in support of what it regarded as the legitimate government, against rebels incited from the outside and including fascist elements, etc.), or to maintain its missiles in Cuba (there to defend against American invasion), in which case we would not now be discussing Vietnam or anything else.

Still more interesting, however, is the second argument: that we must protect Asia from dominion or conquest by a hostile power. I will not dwell on the fact that all reputable authorities agree that the Vietnamese are strongly anti-Chinese,[71] so that if we were really interested in containing Chinese expansionism, we should presumably be supporting Ho Chi Minh, along with all popular, indigenous forces on the border of China, whatever their domestic character. What seems to me most revealing, however, is the reason that Goodwin cites as underlying our commitment to protect Asia from outside force. It is "the almost idealistic, compelling conviction that the one nation with the power to prevent it should not stand aside while nations unwillingly submit to foreign domination." Thus we must not "undermine the central world purpose of the United States—the creation of an international order of independent states." It does not occur to him that by suppressing a victorious insurrection, we are precisely undermining this "central world purpose" and forcing a nation to "submit to foreign domination." Nor does he take note of the fact that we are unable to form a puppet government with even the legitimacy of those set up by Germany and Japan—we have not, for example, been able to find a national figure of the stature of Pétain or Wang Ching-wei to mask our aggression. This sentimental faith in American benevolence, with its various corollaries ("the politics of inadvertence," "the inscrutability of history"), is a major factor that stands in the way of the realistic and common-sense proposal that Zinn advocates.

Zinn's discussion of the Munich analogy could also be usefully extended by a consideration of the views of the Kennedy liberals. Goodwin, for example, is too sophisticated to accept the Munich analogy, but he goes on to offer a revealing counterthesis. He argues, first of all, that in Vietnam we are combatting not aggression but "internal aggression"—an interesting phrase, which refers apparently to "aggression" by a revolutionary movement against a government maintained in power by foreign arms. And he concludes that what we face is not Munich but rather "another episode . . . in a long, continuing conflict." Other episodes include our "success" in Greece and Turkey, Soviet intervention in Cuba, the invasion of Korea, the bombing of Quemoy and Matsu, subversion in the Congo and the Central African Republic, fighting in Malaya and the Philippines and on the Indian border. And now, he adds, "they are beginning in Thailand."

But with whom are we engaged in this "long, continuing conflict"? Certainly not the Soviet Union, which had little to do with the Sino-Indian border dispute; nor China, which did not start the civil war in Greece; nor Ho Chi Minh, who, for all his sins, is not responsible for subversion in the Congo. Nor is "international Communism" a very convincing devil, in the wake of the Sino-Soviet split, gestures of independence in Eastern Europe and North Korea, the admitted refusal of North Vietnam, even in its present desperate straits, to kowtow to its powerful allies. In fact, there is no identifiable adversary. We are confronted with a mysterious but dangerous force, which cannot be located or specified in any concrete terms, but which is there, threatening us. While rejecting the Munich analogy, Goodwin, the liberal critic, tacitly accepts the assumption on which it is based and which gives it great plausibility. For if this force exists, then surely we must stop it in Vietnam before it lands on the beaches of Florida or Cape Cod.

The unpleasant fact is that if one wishes to pursue the

Munich analogy there is only one plausible contender for the role of Hitler. And if China or Russia do involve themselves in World War III over Vietnam, we can be sure that the memory of Munich will play an important role in their calculations.[72] Arnold Toynbee has put the matter quite succinctly: "The President manifestly feels that he is speaking with Churchill's voice —the Churchill of 1940—but to the ears of peoples who have suffered from Western domination in the past, his voice sounds like the Kaiser's and like Hitler's."

There is surely no greater irony than the demand that to ensure world peace, the United States must develop a strategy for the containment of China. China is surrounded by American missiles and huge military bases supporting an army eight thousand miles from home. It is subject to regular bombardment from an island that is barely off the mainland, not to speak of overflights and commando raids, all under the protection of the Seventh Fleet, admittedly intervening in a civil war. For two years American planes have been bombing the only railroad connecting southwestern China, with its industrial center of Kunming, to the rest of the country—it happens to pass near Hanoi. Yet even a Roger Hilsman, one of the sanest voices commenting on Asian affairs, can speak of the "formidable threat" posed by Communist China, and can conclude that "it certainly served no useful purpose for the United States to reward aggression by recognizing Communist China or by encouraging their being seated in the U.N."[73]

It is illuminating to examine in detail Hilsman's demonstration of "Chinese belligerence." The primary example of "Chinese aggression" (apart from "aggression" in Korea) is the support for the "crude and unsophisticated" insurrections in "Burma, Thailand, Malaya, the Philippines, and French Indochina," which the Chinese succeeded in putting "on a more effective, politically sophisticated course" (p. 285). The history of "Chinese belligerence," of the aggression which we must be careful not to reward, is completed with these instances: (1) the cancellation of trade contacts with Japan when the Kishi government would not allow the Chinese flag to be flown over its mission in Tokyo; (2) various unrealized threats to Hong Kong, including an appeal "to Nationalist leaders to make a deal"; (3) the suppression of the Tibetan revolt; (4) the Sino-Indian border crisis; (5) "encouraging the local communists in a direct use of military force, first in Laos and then in South Vietnam" (pp. 288 f.).

It is not easy to decide which of these is the most telling example of Chinese aggression; perhaps Burma, in which, according to U Thant in 1965, "there has not been a single instance of outside help to the Burmese Communists," during a period when Chinese Nationalist forces roamed northern Burma at great cost to the Burmese. It would also be interesting to discover what evidence was available to the director of intelligence for the State Department regarding Chinese control, or even material assistance, in the cases of Thailand, Malaya, and the Philippines—and also to discover why this evidence has never been made public. "Chinese aggression" in Indochina, in contrast to the responsible and purely defensive posture of the Western powers, is of course well documented. As to Laos, Hilsman himself repeats much of the well-known story of the American attempt to subvert the legitimate government, replacing it by "pro-Western neutralists" and then a right-wing military dictatorship—an attempt which continued until 1962 when Kennedy, in a dramatic and sensible reversal of policy, agreed finally to support the neutralist elements that had previously been backed only by the Communist powers. Quite revealing in this connection is Hilsman's judgment that the real Communist "threat" in Laos "seems more likely to have been an expansion of political control based on winning peasant support in the villages" (p. 112)—a threat rather like that posed by the 1954 Geneva agreements, which, the Vietminh thought, "would give them half of Vietnam for sure and an excellent opportunity to win the other half through political subversion," i.e., an electoral victory (p. 103).

Hilsman also has relevant comments on the Sino-Indian border dispute. He observes (p. 322) that "the Indians unwisely provided the Chinese ample provocation by adopting a forward strategy—establishing isolated outposts *behind* the Chinese outposts that India felt had encroached on what they considered their rightful territory—and Prime Minister Nehru, in the early fall of 1962, announced publicly that the Indian Army had been ordered to clear India's territory of the Chinese aggressors." He points out that the unilateral Chinese pullback of their victorious armies showed that we face "not only a powerful enemy but a politically skillful one" (p. 338). He does not, unfortunately, go into the background of the conflict, but excellent Western sources exist that thoroughly refute the simplistic view—advanced, to my knowledge, by not a single Western scholar—that the border dispute was merely, or even primarily, a matter of "Chinese aggression." The issue of Tibet we need not discuss, since whatever the facts may be—and if Western scholarship is to be trusted, they are not simply what is claimed by American propaganda—Tibet is internationally recognized as a region of China; one might with equal logic accuse the United States of aggression in Watts, or in the Mississippi Delta, where, reports indicate, thousands are starving while Washington plays politics.

Elsewhere, Hilsman demonstrates Chinese aggressiveness on the basis of the principle of *post hoc ergo propter hoc:*

It was in November 1957, following the Soviet Sputnik success, that Mao proclaimed that the "East Wind prevails over the West Wind" and so heralded the shift from the "Bandung" policy of peaceful coexistence back to a hard line. In South Vietnam incidents of guerrilla terrorism and assassination began to mount. [Pp. 418–19]

The same claim is made in connection with his discussion of the difficulties faced by the "pro-Western neutralist" Phoui Sananikone, who came to power through American intrigue in Laos:

Phoui and his policy also had the misfortune to come to the test just when Communist policy was changing away from the "peaceful coexistence" of the Bandung spirit to the hard line enunciated by Mao Tse-tung in his "East Wind Over West Wind" speech in Moscow in November 1957. It was during the next year that Hanoi, following this new hard line, reached the decision to begin the guerrilla war against the South. [P. 119]

The suggestion that it was the Chinese hard line that was responsible for the failure of the American policy of subversion in Laos is a most interesting one. According to the American reporter Arthur Dommen, who appears to be Hilsman's primary source of information on Laos, the Chinese took no action at all in Laos until the end of 1959, despite American violations of the Geneva agreements by the supplying of arms and military training by American officers in civilian clothes;[74] and after that their "interference" consisted of offering support for the neutralist Souvanna Phouma government that the United States was trying desperately to replace, first by the "pro-Western neutralist" Phoui and then by the outright fascist Phoumi Nosavan. However, this is not the point. To Hilsman, the aggressiveness of China and Russia is demonstrated by the fact that they supported the neutralist Souvanna Phouma against the American-sponsored attempt to overthrow his government through continual and intensive subversion.

As to the claim that Hanoi decided to begin guerrilla war in the South on the basis of Mao Tse-tung's new hard line, Hilsman makes no attempt to substantiate this allegation, which is in conflict with whatever is known of the historical record.[75]

Hilsman, recall, was director of intelligence for the State Department and then Assistant Secretary of State for Far Eastern Affairs; he is a Kennedy liberal and an academic expert on international affairs. His treatment of historical events and the reasoning on which he bases conclusions about such matters as "Chinese aggressiveness" can only be described as appalling. Yet it represents the best and most sophisticated thinking that is to be found near the center of power, so the available information indicates. One cannot escape a feeling of alarm on reading Hilsman's study of how policy was set in the Kennedy administration.

In discussing Chinese aggressiveness, we must bear in mind that there is a clear sense in which China has already shown itself to be very aggressive, namely, the following:

> We must recognize that an overt act of war has been committed by an enemy when that enemy builds a military force intended for our eventual destruction, and that the destruction of that force before it can be launched or employed is defensive action and not aggression. As a nation we must understand that an overt act of war has been committed long before the delivery of that first blow.[76]

One wonders how long it will be before the American Air Force undertakes defensive action against such overt acts of war on the part of the Chinese.

It would be wrong to leave this matter of American "containment" of China without reference to a few simple facts that rarely seem to penetrate the American consciousness. There is something peculiarly ugly about the American reaction to the attempt of China to achieve national unity, to raise itself from penury and starvation, to erase a century of degradation. K. S. Karol[77] puts the matter plainly, in words that Americans would do well to ponder:

> . . . by trying to strangle China, which has been permanently on the edge of famine, and by threatening her with bombs, America has helped to "harden" the Chinese and make them what they are today. . . . The American anti-Chinese propaganda . . . boomerangs on occasion. Pharisaic editorial writers like Joseph Alsop and others periodically announce with contemptible pleasure Chinese famines which exist, fortunately, only in their imaginations; but their editorials are often read in countries with pro-American governments where famine actually rages. Sooner or later truth will out, and it is then doubly unfavorable to the Americans, first because it is disgusting to see the world's most overfed country rejoicing that others—even if they are Communist—are suffering from hunger, and secondly because one discovers that it is not in China but in their own camp—in Central or South America, for example—that people are dying of malnutrition . . . today a Kwangtung peasant eats much better than a peasant in Kerala in India—and this is known in Asia.[78]

While sympathizing with China's problems, one may still react with dismay, perhaps even outrage, to the authoritarian and repressive character of the Chinese state, as one may have varying reactions to the society that is developing. But there is nothing to justify our shameful treatment of China in the post-war years.

With all the cynicism of the mid-twentieth century, it is nevertheless startling to see how easily the rhetoric of imperialism comes to American lips, sometimes muted, sometimes entirely overt. Arthur Schlesinger writes that if our killing machine achieves a victory in Vietnam, "we may all be saluting the wisdom and statesmanship of the American government."[79] That an American military victory might be a tragedy—this is unthinkable. Roger Hilsman speaks of "the Korean War, Dienbienphu, the two Laos crises, and Vietnam [as] only the opening guns of what might well be a century-long struggle for Asia."[80] What kind of struggle it will be is clear, if Laos and Vietnam are precedents. The foreign editor of *Look* magazine writes:

> The Far East is now our Far West. The western frontier of American power today stands on the far side of the Pacific Ocean. . . . It stretches through the island chain off the Asian mainland with three toeholds on the continent, Korea, Vietnam and Thailand. . . . We are a Pacific power—the only Pacific power. We are there to stay. . . . This is where we have markets and, except for Japan, no rival producers.[81]

These sentiments are familiar. It has been a long-standing belief, expressed by Cordell Hull, Henry Wallace, Dean Acheson, and many others, that we can escape recurrent economic stagnation or internal regimentation only with ever expanding markets. These words recall the characteristically direct formulations of Harry Truman, who proclaimed in 1947 that "all freedom is dependent on freedom of enterprise. . . . The whole world should adopt the American system. . . . The American system can survive in America only if it becomes a world system."[82]

And the natural counterpart to this doctrine is neatly expressed in the 1967 Prize Essay of the United States Naval Institute, by Professor Harold Rood of Claremont College, who argues as follows:

> The U.S. position in the Pacific is no longer what it was in 1941. The territory which came under direct Japanese attack early in the war, the Hawaiian islands and the Aleutians, are each sov-

ereign states today. . . . Yet Hawaii is closer to Peking than it is to Washington, D.C. The Aleutian islands at their westernmost tip are closer to China than they are to Seattle, Washington. Where once the security of the United States could conveniently, it seemed, rest on Alaska and Hawaii in the Pacific, these two states now have the right to demand the same kind of security which each of them once helped furnish to the continental United States.

Consider the implications. Our allies and our bases in Taiwan, Camranh Bay, Thailand, also have the right to demand the same kind of security which each of them now helps furnish to Alaska and Hawaii. And so on, indefinitely. Of course, we have heard all of this before. Japan once needed Manchuria for survival—without Manchuria, it was a "potted plant," without roots. And to secure Manchuria it was obviously necessary to ensure that North China was "friendly," and then all of China, and Southeast Asia, and on to the Pacific war. Our claim to special rights in Asia is, on grounds of security or economic interest, far weaker than that of Japan. Japan, however, was dwarfed in wealth and power by a colossus across the seas, and we are not.

Along such lines as these, one could develop an instructive sequel to Howard Zinn's discussion of "Munich, dominoes, and containment."

What would be the consequences of a withdrawal of American forces from Vietnam? If past events are any guide, the cessation of aggressive military action by the United States will lead to a disengagement of North Vietnamese units, as happened, apparently, during the bombing pause in January 1966. It is noteworthy that no group in South Vietnam has advocated North Vietnamese involvement in an immediate political solution, and the same North Vietnamese leadership that was willing, a decade ago, to arrange a *modus vivendi* with Diem would very likely agree to negotiate the problems of Vietnam with a government that would at least respond to its diplomatic notes. Just what might emerge from the shattered debris of South Vietnamese society, no one can predict with any confidence. It is clear, however, that under the American occupation there can be only unending tragedy. A few years ago, the Premier of Ceylon commented that "the best form of foreign aid the United States can give to small countries is to abstain from interfering in their affairs." As applied to Vietnam, at least, this grim appraisal is no longer an arguable matter.

Postscript

Shortly before his death, Bernard Fall told an interviewer the story of a Vietnamese who listened to an American general boasting of one of the latest victories of the Vietnam campaign. "Yes, General, I understand," said the Vietnamese, "but aren't your victories coming closer and closer to Saigon?"[83] The preceding essay was completed in January 1968. Within a week, American victories reached Saigon itself. Several months after, it seems that the Tet offensive represents a turning point in the war.

For the past decade there have been two versions of the tragedy of Vietnam. The first is that of the war correspondents. Their message has been that Vietnamese resistance is so deeply embedded in the fabric of Vietnamese society that American "victory" can be achieved only through annihilation. The second is the official story, too familiar to bear repetition. Time after time after time the correspondents' version has been proven correct by events. Now, in the wake of the Tet offensive, there is only one story. Apart from lonely relics like Joseph Alsop and a few Southeast Asian scholars, everyone now seems to understand that there are only two probable endings to the Vietnam tragedy: annihilation or withdrawal of the American army of occupation. Annihilation was the prospect foreseen by Bernard Fall in the interview just mentioned. He quotes a captured prisoner who says, "We will all die, but we will not surrender"; and he concludes that "Vietnam will be destroyed." Spokesmen for the NLF and North Vietnam, however, have long argued that they can win on the battlefield. In the past their estimates have been realistic. It may be that the Tet offensive—which brought home to the American public that the official version of the Vietnamese story was an illusion or a lie—may also have persuaded American policy planners that there are no military options remaining, short of drastically changing the nature of the war and taking a long step towards World War III. If so, this raises the prospects for peace, that is, for withdrawal of the American troops. Withdrawal may be called a "negotiated settlement"; it may be called "victory." What is important is not the words but the substance: the return of Vietnam to the Vietnamese.

It is conceivable, though unlikely, that the Vietnamese resistance will settle for less. One lesson that has been taught them in the past twenty years is that the only victories that last are military ones. The great powers cannot be trusted. They will resort to treachery and subversion to undermine any diplomatic settlement. It seems unlikely that the NLF will lay down their arms so long as they are able to maintain control of substantial parts of South Vietnam, or that they will accept token representation in a coalition, just as it is unlikely that the French resistance twenty-five years ago would have terminated its struggle had it been offered the ministry of health in the Vichy government.

In the last days of January, some 50,000–60,000 Vietcong, about 10 percent North Vietnamese,[84] took over most of the urban areas of South Vietnam, obviously with the cooperation of hundreds of thousands of urban residents. The American response was: destroy. According to the Associated Press, "Heavy bombs, aircraft rockets, naval gunfire, napalm, tear gas and all the usual ground weapons from eight-inch howitzers to tank guns are being used in heavily populated city areas."[85] Robert Shaplen reported from Saigon:

> A dozen separate areas, comprising perhaps sixty or seventy blocks, had been totally burned out. These were almost all residential areas. . . . Most of the damage was the result of rocket attacks by American armed helicopters or other planes, though some of it had been caused by artillery or ground fighting. . . . A modern ten-million-dollar textile plant, containing forty thousand spindles, was entirely destroyed by bombs because it was suspected of being a Vietcong hideout.

The correspondent for *Le Monde*—forced to leave the country soon after—reported that

> in the popular suburbs, the Front has proven that the only way to eliminate its control is through systematic destruction. To dislodge it, the air force had to level many residential areas. Fleeing the bombardments, tens of thousands of refugees have poured into the center of the city.[86]

Hué was virtually destroyed by American troops, block by block, house by house. According to an American military source, 119 American marines were killed in this operation, along with 1,584 "North Vietnamese" and some 3,000 civilians.[87] Charles Mohr reported that "in towns such as Hué, Vinhlong, Bentre and Mytho appalling destruction was wrought when encircled allied forces took the decision to destroy the attacking Vietcong forces by destroying the places they had occupied."[88]

The American political scientist Milton Sacks has only this to say, in an article on these events: "In conventional terms, it now seems clear that the Communists have suffered a military defeat in their Tet offensive. They have expended the lives of thousands of their soldiers without securing a single province or district town of significance"—no word from this Southeast Asian expert about the means by which this "defeat" was accomplished, or its political meaning.[89] American officials on the scene manage a somewhat broader view. One official, quoted by Charles Mohr, stated: "The Government won the recent battles, but it is important to consider how they won. At first the Vietcong had won and held everything in some towns except the American military compound and a South Vietnamese position." Senator Mansfield is also aware of the realities: ". . . the hamlets, villages and the cities are seen to be honeycombed with a National Liberation Front infrastructure which has undoubtedly existed for many years, which is still intact, and which may well be stronger than ever"; there is "not the beginning of a stable political situation" in South Vietnam.[90]

In a broadcast from Saigon, Howard Tuchner of NBC stated that "there is no doubt that the U.S. military position in Vietnam has never been weaker. U.S. officers in Saigon now feel for the first time that the United States can lose the war militarily."[91] The military situation is not widely discussed, but it is indicated by a report that "more than 1000 planes and helicopters are reported destroyed or damaged, principally by Russian-built 122mm. rockets that have a range of eight miles or more." According to an unidentified congressman, "one-third of the U.S. helicopter force in Vietnam has been destroyed or side-lined indefinitely . . . losses were almost as heavy in fixed wing aircraft, particularly in cargo planes." The Navy is reported to have sent a helicopter carrier to the northern part of South Vietnam, in the apparent hope that NLF infiltrators will at least not succeed in penetrating this sanctuary.[92]

In the Mekong Delta, the major cities suffered heavy damage —virtual destruction in some instances—as the Americans decided in case after case "to destroy the town in order to save it," in the words of the American major responsible for the victory at Ben Tre.[93] Still, in April, reports from the countryside are confused. However, the general situation is clear from the fact that the IVS has withdrawn most of its field workers because of "security conditions." A volunteer reported in February: "The number of locations at which we can safely place a volunteer have significantly decreased in recent months"; another said that "we all knew that security in the countryside was getting worse and worse."[94] According to a South Vietnamese senator, Vong A Sang, the government now controls "only one third of the country," the remaining two thirds being occupied by the Vietcong.[95] The nature of the American war is tersely indicated by an American official: "What the Vietcong did was occupy the hamlets we pacified just for the purpose of having the allies move in and bomb them out. By their presence, the hamlets were destroyed."[96] The same report indicates that in Binh Dinh Province—the "showcase" province for pacification—this had been going on, unreported, for months: "The enemy moves in December—which several military men called a 'softening up' for the offensive—resulted in a wave of allied air strikes on villages. Hundreds of homes were destroyed." *Newsweek* summarizes the situation in detail, quoting an IVS worker who reports from Can Tho that almost all of the casualties were caused by United States fire power, in the American counterattack: "As difficult as this may be to believe, not a single Vietnamese I have met in Saigon or in the Delta blames the Viet Cong for the events of the past two weeks."[97] How surprising.

The Tet offensive led to a significant change in the political situation in the United States. President Johnson has indicated that he will not seek re-election. A number of "peace candidates"—who have yet to discuss the fundamental political issues —have received substantial support. For the first time, the American government appears willing to take tentative steps towards serious negotiations. It is a devastating indictment of the state of American democracy that only a major military defeat was able to bring about these changes in the political climate. If the past is any guide, only continuing military setbacks in Vietnam and the threat of serious dislocation at home will succeed in moving the government towards concrete steps that might lead to peace. For the first time, there seems a real hope that the war will end without extermination of the Vietnamese. Nevertheless, those who have devoted themselves to working for peace in Vietnam can only be saddened by the realization that they have failed to create the consciousness in this country that we have no right to win a military victory. It is the miraculous heroism of the Vietnamese resistance that has forced these tentative moves towards peace in Vietnam. To say this is not to make a political judgment with regard to the various forces in Vietnamese society, but only to recognize the bare and inescapable facts. For the so-called "peace movement," the recent events pose a major challenge. The "peace movement" has been getting by for too long with cheap jokes about LBJ and with concentration on peripheral issues such as the bombing of North Vietnam. The challenge it now faces is to create the understanding that we have no right to set any conditions at all on a political settlement in Vietnam; that American military force must be withdrawn from Vietnam, and from the other simmering Vietnams throughout the world; that American power and resources and technical skills must be used to build and not to repress or to "contain" or to destroy.

Notes

1. Howard Zinn, *Vietnam: The Logic of Withdrawal* (Boston, Beacon Press, 1967).
2. *Congressional Record,* June 12, 1967.
3. Quoted in *I. F. Stone's Weekly,* April 3, 1967.
4. William Johnstone, "United States Policy in Southern Asia," *Current History,* Vol. 46 (February 1965), pp. 65–70.
5. *New York Times,* May 13, 1967.
6. *Ibid.,* May 24, 1967.
7. *Christian Science Monitor,* May 26, 1967.
8. *Congressional Record,* April 13, 1967, S5054–7.
9. *Ibid.,* May 3, 1967.
10. Denis Warner, *The Last Confucian* (New York, The Macmillan Company, 1963), p. 312.
11. See Roger Hilsman, *To Move a Nation* (Garden City, N.Y., Doubleday & Company, Inc., 1967), p. 529. Senator Fulbright, using official Pentagon figures, concluded that the Vietcong "had recruited 160,000 during the course of 1965" (*The Truth about Vietnam, Report on the U.S. Senate Hearings of March 1966* [(San Diego, Calif., Greenleaf Classics, Inc., 1966], p. 320). The witness, General Maxwell Taylor, did not question this conclusion. The figure for 1964 is 45,000.
12. Akioka Ieshige, "Youth and Nationalism in Asia: South Vietnam," *Japan Quarterly,* Vol. 14 (January–March 1967), pp. 38–39.
13. *Christian Science Monitor,* April 24, 1967.
14. See Carl Rowan, in a nationally syndicated column, March 26, 1967.
15. "High official" in Washington, explaining a statement to this effect by Ambassador Lodge, *New York Times,* August 13, 1965.
16. John Oakes, *New York Times,* April 3, 1967.
17. *New York Times,* April 6, 1967.
18. Shizuo Maruyama, "The Other War in Vietnam: The Revolutionary Development Program," *Japan Quarterly,* Vol. 14 (July–September 1967), pp. 297–303.
19. The reviews of Jonathan Schell's *The Village of Ben Suc* (New York, Alfred A. Knopf, 1967) have been most remarkable. John

Dillin, in the *Christian Science Monitor,* December 2, 1967, regards the book as "sadly incomplete" because it does not draw "conclusions about the value of these massive and expensive American efforts." He interprets the book as giving "a mild criticism of the American and South Vietnamese roles," a conclusion which can only amaze anyone who has read it, until he realizes that Dillin sees nothing to object to in "evacuation and total destruction of four Viet Cong-controlled villages, including Bensuc," "a thriving village" of farmers who "were healthy and relatively prosperous."

John Mecklin (*New York Times Book Review,* October 29, 1967) at least realizes that the reader is likely to feel "violent disgust as the enormity of Schell's picture begins to sink in," and he has to admit that "much of Schell's indictment . . . is justified, accurate and overdue." But he considers it quite unfair; for example, because it fails to mention the "monstrous handicaps that plague the United States' effort," specifically, the lack of command authority over the Saigon regime (a fact which obviously has no relevance to this purely American operation, conducted without informing the Vietnamese) and "the deplorably short tour of duty . . . of Americans in Vietnam, making it impossible to acquire the kind of experience so badly needed in situations such as Bensuc." He thinks, nevertheless, that the book "should be required reading in the Pentagon . . . because of its rare pinpointing of critical areas where the United States could be doing a better job in Vietnam," presumably, in conducting such operations even more efficiently in the future.

These reactions testify to a kind of creeping Eichmannism, which in fact must also explain the limited reaction to the original *New York Times* report of the Ben Suc operation, January 11, 1967. Pacification in Ben Suc had been a total failure, so "the only military or political solution for this place," according to the American colonel in charge, was forced resettlement. Of course, some of the villagers weren't too happy about it. "I imagine there will be a lot of wailing and gnashing of teeth, but they'll do what they're told," said the colonel. Some might not do what they were told, of course. "41 villagers did not. During the day they were tracked down and killed." The conclusion? "Soon the government will have no need to win the hearts and minds of Bensuc. There will be no Bensuc."

One can hardly decide which is more scandalous, the events themselves or the muted response.

Mecklin, incidentally is responsible for some of the most amazing comments on Vietnam. In a review in the *New York Times Book Review*, June 4, 1967, he attributes to Thich Nhat Hanh the idiotic proposal that "both the Americans and the Communists . . . go away and allow the Vietnamese to work things out." As senior officer in the United States Mission in Saigon from 1962 to 1964, he might, one would think, have perceived that the Vietcong were Vietnamese, particularly since United States officials in Saigon at the end of 1962 estimated that "about one-half of the South Vietnamese support the NLF" (Robert Scigliano, *South Vietnam: Nation Under Stress* [Boston, Houghton Mifflin Company, 1963], p. 145). In his *Mission in Torment* (Garden City, N.Y., Doubleday & Company, Inc. 1965), Mecklin describes the Vietnamese peasant as a man whose "vocabulary is limited to a few hundred words," whose "power of reason . . . develops only slightly beyond the level of an American six-year-old," whose "mind is untrained and therefore atrophies" (p. 76); but strangely, the political and military tactics of the Vietcong, making use of techniques that were "skillfully entwined in the life and character of the Vietnamese peasant," "confounded not only the U.S. Mission but also the aristocratic leaders of the Diem regime" (pp. 78–79). Their forces "were developed to a surprisingly sophisticated degree . . . with jungle arms factories, radio nets, clandestine hospitals, propaganda printing presses, . . . V.C. cameramen filming the action" in ambushes (p. 79); to the Government forces the Vietcong seemed to be "eight feet tall." And so on. For further information on the achievements of these atrophied minds, see Malcolm Browne, *The New Face of War* (Indianapolis, The Bobbs-Merrill Co., Inc., 1965).

20. Kyōzō Mori, "The Logic and Psychology of North Vietnam, *Japan Quarterly*, Vol. 14 (July–September 1967), pp. 286–96. According to Bernard Fall, "it was the hapless refugees," fleeing, for the most part, from "aerial and artillery bombardment," "who account for the whole 5% of the population said to have come under government control" in 1966. See his *Last Reflections on a War* (Garden City, N.Y., Doubleday & Company, Inc., 1967), p. 157. By such means we increase our "control" over the population of South Vietnam.

21. R. W. Apple, *New York Times*, July 22, 1967.

22. *Christian Science Monitor*, July 8, 1967.

23. See the lead story in the *Christian Science Monitor*, September 20, 1967, for an attempt to sort out what happened behind the scenes.

24. For a careful analysis of the elections by an American Southeast Asian expert who has specialized in problems of electoral politics, see *Dr. David Wurfel Reports on Vietnam,* Methodist Division of Peace and World Order, 100 Maryland Ave. N.E., Washington, D.C., September 21, 1967.

25. *New York Times,* September 23, 1967.

26. *Christian Science Monitor,* December 21, 1967.

27. Cited in the *New Republic,* January 6, 1968, p. 29, from an interview with Henry Brandon of the *London Sunday Times.*

28. *New York Times,* December 18, 1967.

29. See the *Christian Science Monitor,* December 18, 1967, for many details.

30. *New York Times,* December 28, 1967.

31. *Congressional Record,* August 24, 1965, S20654.

32. *New York Times,* December 8, 1967.

33. *Ibid.,* December 6, 1967.

34. *Christian Science Monitor,* January 10, 1967.

35. *New York Times,* November 21, 1967.

36. *Christian Science Monitor,* November 24, 1967.

37. See the *Congressional Record,* September 18, 1967, H11979, H12030–8, for a summary.

38. Resident Muselier to the Resident Superior, December 1897, cited in *Vietnam: Fundamental Problems* (Vietnamese Studies, No. 12; Hanoi, Foreign Languages Publishing House, 1966), p. 35.

39. Lawrence Morrison, Chief of Industry Division and Mining, U.S.O.M., Saigon, 1955–1957, in Richard W. Lindholm, ed., *Vietnam: The First Five Years* (East Lansing, Michigan State University Press, 1959), p. 215.

40. See, for example, the report by David Halberstam, "Return to Vietnam," *Harper's,* December 1967, pp. 47-58.

41. *Boston Globe,* January 12, 1967. In May 1968, Ton That Thien was appointed Information Minister in Saigon.

42. *Last Reflections on a War,* pp. 33, 47. Ton That Thien's analogy to the Indian wars appeals to the American military mind, it seems. According to Mecklin (*Mission in Torment,* p. 27), Admiral Felt's headquarters in Honolulu had, posted outside the war room, a notice which purported to be the standing orders of Rogers' Rangers in the French and Indian Wars. Testifying before the Senate Foreign Relations Committee, General Maxwell Taylor described our problem

in Vietnam as basically one of "security": ". . . I have often said it is very hard to plant the corn outside the stockade when the Indians are still around. We have to get the Indians farther away in many of the provinces to make good progress" (*The Truth about Vietnam,* p. 267). See also Anthony Harrigan, *A Guide to the War in Vietnam* (Boulder, Colo., Panther Publications, 1966), for a view of the war that is probably representative of a significant segment of American opinion. He points out that American troops are "regaining a spirit that was characteristic of U.S. troops in the winning of a continent from the turbulent Indian tribes," as they fight a war where "an American can't tell the VC from the 'friendlies,' " where "the smiling face of the farmer on his water buffalo beyond the airstrip fence could be a VC who plans to throw a grenade at you or your airplane," where the Tri Quang Buddhists have "become an instrument in the hands of the enemies of the people of South Viet Nam," where "the agitation over gas is another reminder that protecting a people against communist aggression usually is a thankless job," etc., etc.

43. Richard A. Falk *et al., Vietnam and International Law* (Flanders, N.J., O'Hare Books, 1967), p. 85.

44. "United States Policy and Vietnamese Political Viability," 1954–1967, *Asian Survey,* Vol. 7 (August 1967), pp. 507-14. He adds the obscure remark that if this independent South Vietnam were viable, strong, popular, enlightened, and effective, "then the foreign and diplomatic repercussions of two Vietnams *de facto* would be easier to handle, particularly for regulating the relations between North and South Vietnam in future consultations and elections which we in Washington envisaged coming at some time, perhaps in 1956 or possibly a little later." But the Geneva agreements that we were pledged to uphold say nothing about "two Vietnams *de facto,*" nor about an "independent South Vietnam" as "a strong, viable state." Obviously, it is absurd to speak of a viable, independent state bounded by a provisional demarcation line which "should not in any way be interpreted as constituting a political or territorial boundary." It is interesting, incidentally, that Mr. Young can summarize the American effort to "promote political viability" in Vietnam from 1954 to 1967 with not a mention of what happened to those elections that were "envisaged coming . . . in 1956 or possibly a little later."

Richard Falk has commented on the hypocrisy of the accusation that North Vietnam challenged world order by its "indirect aggression" in South Vietnam in the 1960s, noting that "In Viet Nam Saigon's establishment, rather than the subsequent attempt at its removal, of a political frontier at the seventeenth parallel represented the coercive challenge to world order," since the "political settlement at Geneva in 1954 provided a formula for the nullification (rather than one for the maintenance) of the division" ("International Law and the United States Role in Vietnam," *Yale Law Journal*, Vol. 76 [May 1967], p. 1118). Similarly, the United States effort to build up the military strength of the Saigon regime, which enabled it to crush domestic opposition and institute the "grim dictatorship" that supporters of the American effort were later to deplore, was a clear violation of our pledge at Geneva not to use force or threat of force to disturb the accords. Secretary Dulles was as candid as Kenneth Young about our intention to disregard the Geneva agreements, announcing our intention to build up "the truly independent states of Cambodia, Laos and southern Vietnam" (*Department of State Bulletin*, August 2, 1954, cited in George M. Kahin and John W. Lewis, *The United States and Vietnam* [New York, The Dial Press, 1967], p. 61).

It is, incidentally, remarkable that our professed dissatisfaction with the accords and announced intention not to observe them is often cited today as somehow relieving us from the obligation to honor them, as eliminating any onus for this violation.

45. Cited in R. Scigliano, *op. cit.*, p. 196, from Philippe Devillers and Jean Lacouture, *La Fin d'une guerre: Indochina, 1954* (Paris, Éditions du Seuil, 1960).

46. "Vietnam: the Agonizing Reappraisal," *Current History*, Vol. 48 (February 1965), pp. 95–102. In his *The Two Vietnams*, rev. ed. (New York, Frederick A. Praeger, Inc., 1964), Fall asserts (p. 402) that "the infiltration of guerrilla teams" to the North "has been repeatedly attempted over the past years and has met with dismal failure. . . . Present losses are estimated to run at 85% of the total personnel engaged in such operations." This despite "the air of massive tranquillity" that he himself observed in a visit to North Vietnam in the fall of 1962, when these operations were in progress: ". . . no guards in watchtowers, no airplane patrols. The Hanoi police don't even carry pistols" (*Saturday Evening Post*, November 24, 1962, pp. 18–21). Cf. the recent eyewitness accounts by David Schoenbrun and others, noting the same phenomenon, which Fall characterizes as "one of the most ominous things about North Vietnam."

47. Richard Goodwin, *Triumph or Tragedy* (New York, Vintage Books, 1966), p. 26. There are many other such reports. To mention a recent one, Louis Heren writes in the *London Times,* April 20, 1968, from Washington, that the CIA "did in fact deploy saboteurs in the North from 1959. They were parachuted in or dropped off the coast by patrol boats, and Vice-President Ky commanded the air transport wing of the South Vietnam Air Force in 1962 and 1963. He is known to have been in charge of the parachute drops. The agents were South Vietnamese and were trained by the C.I.A. in Special Forces camps, notably the 77th Special Forces Group. The frogmen were trained at Da Nang. Apart from destroying bridges and other vulnerable points, they were also expected to organize guerrilla warfare, especially in the Catholic areas. Both operations were a complete fiasco, 95 per cent casualties were admitted in 1963, but the opium trade flourished." Heren's report goes on to discuss the possible connection between these operations and the opium trade, and the reports under investigation by a Senate subcommittee that Marshal Ky was dismissed from the operation for his participation in opium smuggling.

48. Dean Rusk, December 5, 1966. Cited in Theodore Draper, *Abuse of Power* (New York, The Viking Press, Inc., 1967), p. 45. It is difficult to exaggerate the startling character of the material that Draper has assembled, particularly with respect to the pronouncements of Dean Rusk.

49. *New York Times,* June 7, 1965. Polls taken for CBS in November 1966 and February 1967 indicate that even "among strong anti-Communist South Vietnamese . . . exposed primarily to government propaganda there still appears to be a rejection of the American idea that the war is a consequence of 'aggression from the North' " (Richard Falk, "International Law and the United States Role in Vietnam," p. 1102 n.). The results are reported in the *Times,* March 22, 1967. Even in this biased sample of South Vietnamese opinion, 83% were in favor of (and 5% opposed to) reunification with the North after the end of the war, and emphasis on negotiations was preferred to extension of military operations to the North by a ratio of 4 to 1.

The poll of Vietcong prisoners cited above showed that "few of them considered themselves Communists or could give a definition of Communism" and confirmed the judgments of most observers that "the Vietcong function far more through persuasion and indoctrination than through the authoritarianism of traditional armies." It has often been emphasized, even by those committed to the American effort in Vietnam, that "it would be a serious mistake to consider Communist power in South Vietnam as based predominantly on terrorism or military strength, or even upon the indifference of an ignorant peasantry" (Scigliano, *op. cit.,* p. 158). There is near unanimity, outside of the State Department, that "the historical fact is that force in the struggle for the South was first used by the Diem regime, not by the Communists," that the latter was, moreover, far more restrained, that although "guidance and assistance from the North" may have been an important factor in the "amazing success" of the NLF, "it would have made little headway without wide popular support," and that "the war started as a civil war in the South," well before the alleged infiltration began (Joseph Buttinger, *Vietnam: A Dragon Embattled* [New York, Frederick A. Praeger, Inc. 1967], Vol. 2, pp. 976 f., 981–82). Buttinger's study is quite interesting, not only for its careful and extensive scholarship but also because he was, for many years, a strong supporter of the Diem regime and the American involvement in support of it. He explains, for example, why Diem was unable to move towards democratic, representative structures: "Local elections would have given the Vietminh control of most of the rural communities. The Vietminh was not only popular and in effective political control of large regions, but it alone had people with the requisite organizational skills to exploit whatever opportunities for democratic self-expression the regime opened up." Thus, "Freely constituted organizations too would have been captured by the Vietminh" (p. 856); he adds that "the NLF was truly the Vietminh reborn" and speaks of "the similarity, or better, near identity, of the Vietminh and the NLF." He also analyzes the much greater economic progress in the North (cf. pp. 928, 966 f.), and notes that repression of dissidence in the North was less severe than in the South, largely, he feels, because dissidence was less dangerous (cf. pp. 964 f.).

50. The thrust of "much of the American effort in Vietnam," according to Scigliano, who served in the Michigan State University Advisory Group in Vietnam (*op. cit.,* 1963, p. 197). In contrast, "precious little of American energies or resources has been devoted to political goals, as contrasted with the military and economic aims." His detailed breakdown of aid figures shows that military aid was overwhelmingly dominant, even

in "economic and social development," and that even true economic aid was largely directed to the relatively affluent. See pp. 135 f. for a summary.

51. Saville Davis, *Christian Science Monitor*, October 21, 1967.

52. "Not a Dove, But No Longer a Hawk," *New York Times Magazine*, October 9, 1966.

53. As to the military, Jonathan Randal points out in the *New York Times*, June 11, 1967, that "only one officer above the rank of lieutenant colonel did not serve in the French army against the Vietminh in the French Indochina war." Perhaps this is part of the reason why the ARVN army has little interest in the war, while "the Vietcong can take the same unwilling recruit and turn him into a tiger in six months" (American regimental adviser), as it may go part way towards explaining the desertion rates that Randal cites for the elite battalions in 1966: 22% for the armed forces as a whole, 31% for the rangers, 33% for the marines, and 45% for the airborne battalions.

54. See Halberstam, *op. cit.*, for some indication of the incredible corruption of those to whom he refers as "our Vietnamese." Their cynicism has continually scandalized American reporters. Malcolm Browne, for example, reports that Vietnamese military officers have ordered hamlets "blown off the map" by American Skyraiders to cover cases of graft (*op. cit.*, p. 210).

55. Kahin, *op. cit.* (see note 8), reports that the medical staff of Hué hospital estimated that "almost 90% of the war casualties were occasioned by American and South Vietnamese army air bombardments and artillery," and that an American working at Quangnai hospital "estimated that about 70% of all civilian war casualties had been inflicted by American, South Korean and South Vietnamese aerial bombardment and artillery." Note that these estimates refer to areas more or less under American control, where victims can hope to reach the hospitals. What is amazing is that any substantial number of casualties in such areas are caused by American and allied forces. Even in Saigon hospital Kahin saw many victims of napalm, mostly children— he was informed by medical students "that it is government policy to disperse as widely as possible napalm casualties that are brought to hospitals so that visitors will not conclude that there are so many of them."

American reactions to such discoveries are often astonishing. For example, Senator Proxmire inserted into the *Congressional Record* (May

26, 1965, S 11799-801) a whitewash of administration policy by Thomas Ross in the *Chicago Sun-Times*, May 23, 1965, to show how real experts support the government. Support the government he does. He also points out that "the Vietcong have achieved a high degree of immunity" and "move freely throughout most of the country with little fear that the local populace will betray them to the government." Military strategy has therefore been forced to shift from counterinsurgency to classical war. But, he observes, "it is still much too soon to tell whether sophisticated weapons and conventional ground troops can succeed where counter-insurgency has failed. In fact, there is some evidence of popular resentment to the expanding use of napalm, a development which is not surprising if one has observed a hospital ward full of bleeding women and children seared from head to toe." While Mr. Ross and Senator Proxmire may await the evidence, others will draw their own conclusions, even before the inevitable study by the RAND Corporation.

56. Excerpts from his secret testimony appear in the *New York Times*, February 2, 1968. The Vietcong will be happy to learn, from his testimony, that we do not "seek the surrender of Vietcong forces; we would be content to see them lay down their arms and take their place as peaceful citizens of South Vietnam, or move to the North if they so desire." Presumably, the distinction between "surrendering" and "laying down one's arms" is explained in the censored part of the testimony.

The remark recalls that of another leading dove, Arthur Goldberg, who announced our position before the United Nations, in what was widely described as a "conciliatory" statement, as being: "No military forces, armed personnel or bases [are] to be maintained in North or South Vietnam except those under the control of the respective governments" (*New York Times*, September 22, 1967). The Vietcong, in other words, need not surrender; we ask only that it go out of existence as a military force. And when the government we have instituted establishes total military control, we will have no further interest in retaining our army in Vietnam. The German High Command could have outlined its goals in France in just the same terms.

57. Lyndon B. Johnson, *Congressional Record*, March 15, 1948, House, p. 2883.

58. Marcel Niedergang in *Le Monde hebdomadaire*, January 18-24, 1968. The same speech was cited by Hugh O'Shaughnessy in the *New Statesman*, December 1, 1967, who goes on to say that "similar things

are happening in Nicaragua, which is virtually a U.S. colony and where guerrilla warfare broke out this year." In the *Nation,* February 5, 1968, pp. 166–67, Norman Diamond reports on the application in Guatemala of "advanced techniques in counterinsurgency being developed in Vietnam," including heavy bombing in large areas of the country, "pacification," even rerouting of rivers "to cover the traces of bombings and massacres, as well as razing forests and bulldozing villages"—all under the paternalistic guidance of the American "advisers." The American press has yet to cover these events. In general, the failure of the press to report events in Latin America is scandalous. The coverage of Latin American events in *Le Monde* is greater in scope (and incomparably greater in depth) than anything to be found in the American press, which, like American scholarship, is little concerned with American-directed violence in other countries so long as it is reasonably successful.

The quoted statement of the Guatemalan Vice-President would very likely cause something of a commotion in liberal circles were it to be published in the American press. However, hardly an eyebrow would be raised at other parts of Niedergang's report, for example, these lines: "According to M. Antonio Palacios, of the Bank of Guatemala, 'two thirds of the population live in a primitive manner; the infant mortality rate is frightful.' 70 percent of those under 20 have never been to school; the average life expectancy is scarcely more than 40 years; hunger and lack of hygiene are a veritable scourge; innumerable clandestine distilleries produce a fiery brandy called 'guaro,' maintaining a destructive alcoholism; 80 percent of doctors practice in the capital; outside begins the rule of the 'sorceror' and the incantations which combine Christianity and the Mayan tradition. Finally, there is 83 percent illiteracy, one of the highest proportions in all of Latin America."

Recall that in 1954 the people of Guatemala were taking some small steps towards extricating themselves from this torment.

59. A picture suggested, for example, in the crabbed and involuted arguments of Martin Heidegger, who, lecturing in 1935, saw Germany as "the nation with the most neighbors and hence the most endangered" by the "great pincers," by the "world character" represented in its crudest form in Russia and America, where "the domination . . . of a cross section of the indifferent mass has become . . . an active onslaught that destroys all rank and every world-creating impulse of

the spirit" (*Introduction to Metaphysics,* trans. Ralph Manheim, [New Haven, Conn., Yale University Press, 1959], pp. 45–46). Germany, "the most metaphysical of nations," must forestall "the peril of world darkening," and, standing "in the center of the Western world," must "take on its historical mission." "If the great decision regarding Europe is not to bring annihilation, that decision must be made in terms of new spiritual energies unfolding historically from out of the center," that is, Germany—in 1935. To Heidegger, in 1935, the cultural mission of Germany is to recapture and advance the "supreme possibility of human being, as fashioned by the Greeks"—which is quite natural, since along with Greek, "the German language is (in regard to its possibilities for thought) at once the most powerful and most spiritual of all languages" (p. 57). Compare Thomas Mann, who left Germany in 1933 because he could not, as "a German writer, made responsible through his habitual use of language, remain silent, quite silent, in the face of all the irreparable evil which has been committed daily, and is being committed in my country, against body, soul and spirit, against justice and truth, against men and man" (quoted in George Steiner, *Language and Silence* [New York, Atheneum Publishers, 1967], p. 102).

60. James Reston, *New York Times,* November 24, 1967. Reston does not question that it is "in defending this doctrine" that men are dying in Vietnam, that this "principle" is in fact what motivates Washington; but he admits that in the "profound spiritual bewilderment" caused by the immense destruction, it is becoming difficult "to believe in the cause." A few days earlier (November 15), he had mused on one of the great "mysteries and tragedies in Vietnam," "the Hanoi Government's continuing refusal to talk about a negotiated settlement." The reason for this "continuing refusal" (which will come as a surprise to those who have been reading the news columns of the *Times* for the past three years) is, he feels, that "Ho Chi Minh and his associates simply cannot believe that the U.S. would make such sacrifices of men and treasure simply to defend the principle of opposing military aggression—and then withdraw when the principle is sustained"; Reston is convinced that "President Johnson is perfectly sincere" in "his offers to make peace and withdraw."

61. Thruston Morton, who inserted the IVS statement "Vietnam: An Inside View," from which quotations follow, in the *Congressional Record,* December 13, 1967, S18499. Senator Morton himself became

disillusioned about the war because our "present military operations" appear to be failing "to win the hearts and minds of the Vietnamese." We cannot succeed in this goal, he feels, when "at least one-third of the total population of Vietnam are refugees who have been driven from their land and their homes by U.S. military action." What is remarkable is that he reacts to this atrocity by raising questions about whether we can succeed, and that he nowhere questions the legitimacy of our attempt to win their hearts and minds.

62. An international Gallup poll released on November 8, 1967, illustrates world opinion on this matter. In eleven countries, people were asked, "Which of these statements comes closest to the way you, yourself, feel about the war in Vietnam?" A. The United States should begin to withdraw its troops; B. The United should carry on its present level of fighting; C. The United States should increase the strength of its attacks against North Vietnam; D. No opinion.

The percentages were as follows:

	A	B	C	D
Finland	81	4	5	10
Sweden	79	10	4	7
Brazil	76	5	5	14
France	72	8	5	15
India	66	4	8	22
West Germany	58	11	14	17
Argentina	57	6	6	31
England	45	15	15	25
Canada	41	16	23	20
United States	31	10	53	6
Australia	29	18	37	16

The poll was mentioned in the *New York Times*, November 27, in an item dealing with a domestic poll headed "Johnson Finds Gain in Poll." The manner in which it was reported was such that few would be aware of these highly significant facts, and the figures were not given. In November, the British *Daily Mail* reported that 66% of those questioned in a poll said Britain should not support the United States, 21% that it should.

It is unfortunate that the press does not see fit to make this information readily available. In countries where the government is somewhat responsive to public opinion, this enormous groundswell of opposition to the United States will sooner or later be translated into diplomatic isolation and, perhaps, an attempt to construct a counterforce to contain American power. The consequences of such a move could be disastrous. No one stands to gain, in the long run, by the concealing of these facts.

63. Louis Halle, "Overestimating the Power of Power," *New Republic*, June 10, 1967, pp. 15–16. Halle's comments are little more than a paraphrase of McKinley's famous statement of how divine guidance led him to the solution of the problem of how to deal with the Philippines:

> I don't know how it was, but it came; 1) that we could not give them back to Spain—that would be cowardly and dishonorable; 2) that we could not turn them over to France or Germany—our commercial rivals in the Orient—that would be bad business and discreditable; 3) that we could not leave them to themselves—they were unfit for self-government—and they would soon have anarchy and misrule over there worse than Spain's was; and 4) that there was nothing left for us to do but to take them all, and to educate the Filipinos, and uplift and *civilize* and *Christianize* them, and by God's grace do the very best we could by them, as our fellowmen for whom Christ also died. And then I went to bed, and went to sleep and slept soundly. . . .

Cited in Hernando J. Abaya, *The Untold Philippine Story* (Quezon City, Philippines, Malaya Books, Inc., 1967), p. 3.

64. See pages 215–16, 316.

65. "The Philippines: Contour and Perspective," *Foreign Affairs*, Vol. 44 (April 1966), pp. 501–11.

66. Onofre D. Corpuz, *The Philippines* (Englewood Cliffs, N.J., Prentice-Hall, Inc., 1965), pp. 66, 70.

67. See the references in note 64.

68. See John Oakes, *New York Times*, April 3, 1967.

69. "The Faceless Viet Cong," *Foreign Affairs*, Vol. 44 (April 1966), pp. 347–72. Carver is here merely identified as a "student of political theory and Asian affairs, with degrees from Yale and Oxford; former officer in the U.S. aid mission in Saigon; author of *Aesthetics and the Problem of Meaning*."

70. Goodwin cites Defense Department estimates "that of a total of about 330,000 Vietcong, dead or alive, only 63,000 have been infiltrators." He does not, however, add that until the American bombings of the North began in February 1965, these infiltrators were overwhelmingly, perhaps exclusively, South Vietnamese and seem to have been

largely unarmed. For a summary of relevant evidence, see Draper, *op. cit.*, and I. F. Stone, "A Reply to the White Paper," in *I. F. Stone's Weekly*, March 8, 1965, reprinted in Marcus G. Raskin and Bernard B. Fall, eds., *The Vietnam Reader* (New York, Vintage, 1965), pp. 155–62. The "White Paper" itself, along with Stone's devastating analysis, is reprinted in Martin E. Gettleman, ed., *Vietnam: History, Documents, and Opinions on a Major World Crisis* (Greenwich, Conn., Fawcett, 1965), pp. 284–316.

71. See for example, P. J. Honey, "The Foreign Policy of North Vietnam," in John D. Montgomery and Albert O. Hirschman, eds., *Public Policy* (Cambridge, Mass., Harvard University Press, 1967), Vol. 16, pp. 160-80. Honey cites as one of the "main requirements of North Vietnamese foreign policy," "to resist Chinese attempts to dominate Vietnam." Similarly, in his *Communism in North Vietnam* (Cambridge, Mass., The M.I.T. Press, 1963), he points out that Pham Van Dong, second in command in North Vietnam, is "no political extremist but rather a cautious moderate" who "has stated that he believes Asia's problems can be solved only through cooperation with the white races," and that Vo Nguyen Giap is violently anti-Chinese— it is for this reason, he goes on to say, that he remains in control of the army. In fact, Honey concludes, "there are excellent grounds for the belief that the principal *raison d'être* of such a powerful army in North Vietnam today is to protect North Vietnam against possible Chinese aggression." Similar views are expressed by just about everyone who has considered the matter. It is particularly interesting that they are shared by Honey, whose militant anti-Communism reaches outlandish levels and frequently leads him to pure fabrication—e.g., his contention that the North Vietnamese refused to agree to negotiations at the beginning of 1965 (*Public Policy*, Vol. 16, p. 180)—and to amazing allegations, for example, that some significant portion of the antiwar activity in Britain and the United States is initiated by the Communist parties and financed by Hanoi—including, as a special reward to loyal supporters, free trips to North Vietnam (*ibid.*, p. 168). One wonders whether his analyses of North Vietnam, which are apparently taken seriously by policy planners, show as much of a sense of reality as his perception of events in Britain and the United States.

72. It is worth recalling that the Soviet Union has much better reasons than we do for taking seriously the lesson of Munich.

73. *Op. cit.*, p. 298.

74. See Arthur J. Dommen, *Conflict in Laos: The Politics of Neutralization* (New York, Frederick A. Praeger, Inc., 1964), p. 136.

75. See Buttinger, *op. cit.;* Kahin and Lewis, *op. cit.* It is interesting to look back to the reports dating from the period in question, before the necessity arose to rewrite history so as to justify later overt American aggression. For example, William Henderson, at the time an executive of the Council on Foreign Relations specializing in Far Eastern affairs, wrote: "From the beginning Diem ran his government along the lines of a police state," with vigorous suppression of political opposition, totalitarian methods to stimulate popular support, and so on. "By the middle of 1956 . . . Diem had still to prove that his professed devotion to the democratic cause represented anything more than a façade to disguise the increasingly plain reality of stern dictatorship." By 1958, there had "been little moderation of the grim dictatorship which Diem has exerted from the beginning." "One result [of this grim dictatorship] has been the growing alienation of the intelligentsia. . . . Another has been the renewal of armed dissidence in the South" (Lindholm, *op. cit.*, pp. 343 f.). In the same volume, David Hotham, correspondent for the *London Times* and the *Economist* in Vietnam from 1955 to 1957, describes the "pacification" methods of the South Vietnamese army: "They consist of killing, or arresting without either evidence or trial, large numbers of persons suspected of being Vietminh or 'rebels' " (p. 359). Possibly these events had as much to do with the renewal of insurgency as Mao's musings about the East and the West Wind.

As to the shift from "peaceful coexistence," it is interesting to note that the Third Party Congress of the Lao Dong party of North Vietnam, in September 1960, announced a major defense cutback to finance economic development. At the time, P. J. Honey summarized the results of this congress as indicating that "Vietnam will follow the Russian policy of peaceful co-existence based on the possibility of avoiding war" ("North Vietnam's Party Congress," *China Quarterly*, No. 4 [October–December 1960], p. 74; cited in Kahin and Lewis, *op. cit.*, p. 116). Bernard Fall makes the same point (*Last Reflections on a War*, p. 203). Now, however, the official line is that at this congress the Lao Dong party set out on its attempt to conquer the South, and, as Hilsman puts it (*op. cit.*, p. 419), the NLF was "duly formed" a few months later. For discussion of the forming of the NLF from somewhat more independent sources, see Buttinger, *op. cit.*, Kahin and Lewis, *op. cit.*, and even Douglas Pike, *Viet Cong* (Cambridge, Mass., The M.I.T. Press, 1966), all of whom present evidence to refute this claim, convenient for the purposes of State Department propaganda but otherwise without merit.

76. *Air Campaigns of the Pacific War,* American Air Force Publication, 1947.

77. *China: The Other Communism* (New York, Hill and Wang, Inc., 1967), pp. 339–40.

78. The fact that this is known in Asia is apparently what frightens American planners like Walt Rostow, who points out that a primary threat posed by China is "the possibility that the Chinese Communists can prove to Asians by progress in China that Communist methods are better and faster than democratic methods"—such as the democratic methods of South Vietnam, Taiwan, and South Korea, for example (Walt W. Rostow and R. W. Hatch, *An American Policy in Asia* [New York, Technology Press and John Wiley & Sons, Inc., 1955], p. 6). The reality of this "threat" is clear from the mixed reactions to China's development in the Asian countries, a combination of fear and admiration. Frederick Clairmonte maintains: "Starting the industrialization race with lower production levels than India, with a ruptured administration frame and a larger population than India's and considerably less foreign aid at its disposal, the dramatic successes that catapulted China into the slipstream of growth signalized the pivotal importance of the agrarian revolution" (*Economic Liberalism and Underdevelopment* [Bombay and London, Asia Publishing House, 1960], p. 309). He cites reports from China by Indian delegations in the mid-1950s which attribute Chinese success in collectivization (which "appeared no less than a miracle") to "a ferment in people's minds," not fear, and he himself concludes that the real success of the Chinese is the construction of a mass base of support, with rural activists from the peasants' associations—a development lacking in India.

The ambivalence of bourgeois Asian reaction to China is nicely reflected in a report of a visit to China by Philippine journalist Carmen Guerrero-Nakpil in the *Asia Magazine,* September 4, 1966. Awed as well as frightened, she describes with evident distaste the ever-present "little figure in blue, never alone," who has emerged "from the invincible chaos of civil war, famine, and social injustice" and is now "not an individual, but the social man," governed in his actions not by terror or the state police but by the fear of "social disgrace," by the very fact "that he is a public man," committed to a vision of "ultimate, uncompromising social truth." The report closes with an interview with a factory manager, who laughs as he discusses commune production and international affairs. "It is discomforting laughter. Why are they so happy?"

79. *The Bitter Heritage: Vietnam and American Democracy* (Boston, Houghton Mifflin Company, 1967), p. 34.

80. *Op. cit.*, p. 150.

81. J. Robert Moskin, "Our New Western Frontier," *Look*, May 30, 1967, pp. 36–37.

82. Quoted in D. F. Fleming, *The Cold War and Its Origins* (Garden City, N.Y., Doubleday & Company, Inc., 1967), Vol. 1, p. 436.

83. Bronson Clark, "With Bernard Fall in Saigon," *The Progressive*, Vol. 31 (May 1967), pp. 34–35.

84. According to Robert Shaplen, "Letter from Saigon," *New Yorker*, March 2, 1968, pp. 44–81.

85. Tom Wicker, *New York Times*, February 20, 1968.

86. Jean-Claude Pomonti, *Le Monde hebdomadaire*, February 4–8, 1968.

87. Reuters, February 25, 1968. The statistics may lack precision. They nevertheless tell us a good deal about the nature of the battle of Hué.

The American press has carried little direct reporting from Hué. Marc Riboud reports in *Le Monde*, April 13, 1968, that in the ten days he spent in Hué in early April he saw two journalists—both Japanese—from an international press corps of 495. He cites as official statistics: 4,100 civilians killed, 4,500 severely wounded, 18,000 of the city's 20,000 houses damaged or destroyed, the majority destroyed. Riboud attempted to see one of the "mass graves" of victims of the North Vietnamese troops that have been reported by the American Mission, but without success. According to the information he could gather, ARVN behavior compared quite unfavorably with that of the North Vietnamese and Vietcong, though the deepest bitterness and resentment is directed against the Americans, whose "blind and systematic bombardment" have turned Hué into "an assassinated city."

88. *New York Times*, February 14.

89. *Boston Globe*, February 24, 1968.

90. *New York Times,* February 12, 1968.
91. *Boston Globe,* February 24, 1968.
92. *Ibid.,* February 25, 1968.
93. See the account by Peter Arnett, AP, February 7, 1968.
94. Bernard Weinraub, *New York Times,* February 20, 1968.
95. *New York Times,* April 4, 1968.
96. *Ibid.,* February 28, 1968.
97. February 19, 1968, p. 39. Because of this report, *Newsweek* was banned from Saigon. The head of its Saigon bureau had already been banned from South Vietnam.

THE BITTER HERITAGE

A REVIEW

As a contribution to our understanding of the Vietnam war, Arthur Schlesinger's *Bitter Heritage* does not seem to me to merit extensive discussion. As a contribution to our understanding of American ideology, it is of somewhat greater importance, as a specimen rather than a commentary. It is common, and quite legitimate, to identify a certain mainstream of political thought (which is, illegitimately, designated "responsible thought") that stays within the rather narrow bounds of the prevailing ideology and does not challenge the conceptions, or the rationalizations, of those who have direct influence over decision making. Schlesinger's position represents one "extreme," the liberal wing of this "responsible approach." He expresses with great clarity the liberal critique of the Vietnam war that developed when it became apparent that American force was probably not going to be able to suppress the Vietnamese

This essay is reprinted, with a few additional remarks, from *Ramparts*, Vol. 5 (April 1967).

insurrection at an "acceptable" cost, to ourselves or to Vietnam. It is of more than historical interest to understand this critique, to determine the assumptions that underlie it, to appreciate the attitude towards the American role in international affairs that it reveals. It has always been possible that the Vietnamese affair might end in a global war or in an attempt by our former allies to construct a counterweight to American power. If the consequences are, on the other hand, something approaching the effective extermination of the Vietnamese (with no international repercussions) or a return of Vietnam to its own population with the withdrawal of the American army of occupation, then it is likely that we will revert to policies that fall within the responsible mainstream of thought and ideology, and that are illuminated by the kind of critique of the aberration of Vietnam —where the situation escaped our control—represented by Schlesinger's analysis.

The essential feature of Schlesinger's critique of the American escalation in Vietnam is that it has a purely tactical basis. Elsewhere in these essays I have quoted his remark that, contrary to his expectations, the American attempt to "suppress the resistance" by widening the war might still meet with success, so that "we may all be saluting the wisdom and statesmanship of the American government." Schlesinger's critique of the policy of escalation is "pragmatic," in that it does not question our ends but only the likelihood of our achieving them. In this sense it is "responsible criticism"; it diverges from the approach of the Johnson administration, or for that matter, the position of the "responsible" critics who take a stronger imperialist position, only in its judgment as to the potential effectiveness of certain methods that are being employed in our attempt to organize Vietnamese society in our perceived interest and in what we determine to be the interests of the Vietnamese. Investigation of this liberal critique shows how remote from the mainstream of American opinion, that opinion which might be influential in decision making, is a point of view that would be considered quite moderate in the spectrum of world opinion: namely, that the United States has no unilateral right to determine by force the course of development of the nations of the Third World.

As a specimen of liberal American ideology, Schlesinger's book also provides some insight into one fairly significant aspect of the complex matter of imperialist expansion. No doubt ideology has its roots in real or at least perceived interests; it is, however, no novel observation that ideology can have a life of its own, contributing to the design and implementation of policy in a way that may, on occasion, even conflict with the interests from which it arose. The postwar American anti-Communist paranoia provides many examples. In part, it provided a convenient—and occasionally plausible—justification for the kind of interventionism that had long characterized American policy, in ever extending domains. In part it no doubt functioned as an almost independent basis for specific policy decisions, leading to actions that go beyond what is demanded by the interests that foreign policy in a general way attempts to serve. Our China policy provides a number of examples of this phenomenon. Another is the behavior of the Eisenhower administration in Cuba in 1960 (as described by Ambassador Philip Bonsal in *Foreign Affairs*, January 1967), when the Castro government demanded that American and British oil refineries process Soviet rather than Venezuelan oil. Although "the companies would probably have reluctantly gone along with the [Castro] government's request," strong pressure from Washington impelled them to refuse, leading to expropriation and a sharp worsening of Cuban-American relations. Such incidents, and there are many, are interesting for those concerned with the dynamics of imperialism in the modern period. Schlesinger's approach to the Vietnam war provides some understanding of the cultural factors that are involved in this complex interaction of real or perceived material interests, ideology, and government initiative.

Schlesinger's critique of current Vietnam policy is also interesting because of the role of its author in the Kennedy administration, when much of the groundwork for the present tragedy in Vietnam was laid. In this respect, it is of some value to "Washington watchers," that is, to those who are interested in determining how American foreign policy develops and how it appears to those involved in its implementation.

It is, for example, of interest to learn of the extent to which Schlesinger attributes our present tribulations to bureaucratic stupidity rather than Machiavellian intent. He raises the question, "which already haunts the American conscience," as to whether we are "really carrying out this policy, as we constantly proclaim, to save the people we are methodically destroying," or are we "doing it for less exalted purposes of our own." The question is not directly answered, but the implication is that stupidity and ignorance, rather than pursuit of self-interest, are to blame for the bitter heritage. Viewing the development of American policy from the outside, it seems not too difficult to construct a rationale. But Schlesinger's judgment must be given weight. After all, he was there.

Still, it is questionable how widely Schlesinger's view of American innocence is shared. For example, he admits that there may appear to be "a gigantic American effort at the encirclement and strangulation of China." But, he asserts, this is not "our view of what we are doing; nor is it in fact what we are doing," though "it really should not astonish us that a crew of dogmatic Marxist-Leninists should so interpret the extraordinary deployment of American armies, navies and military bases thousands of miles from the United States and mobilized . . . against no one but themselves." In fact, one need hardly be a dogmatic Marxist-Leninist to draw the conclusion that we are interested in encircling China. This is precisely, for example, the view of Charles Wolf, senior economist of the RAND Corporation, who regards it as our major foreign policy task to make China "willing to live with this fear" of American encirclement (see the congressional hearings before the Subcommittee on the Far East and the Pacific, January 27, 1966). Schlesinger evidently thinks of his interpretation as consistent with our "philosophical heritage—empirical, pragmatic, ironic, pluralistic, competitive." It just may be, however, that a more appropriate adjective is "inane."

Schlesinger is as aware of what we are doing in Vietnam as any reader of the *New York Times* or *I. F. Stone's Weekly*. He emphasizes that "the war began as an insurrection within South Vietnam which, as it has gathered momentum, has attracted increasing support and direction from the North" and that the result of our bombing of North Vietnam "was to bring North Vietnamese forces south of the border," though on a scale which is dwarfed by our own invasion of the country. He realizes that "if we continue the pursuit of total military victory, we will leave the tragic country gutted and devastated by bombs, burned by napalm, turned into a wasteland by chemical defoliation, a land of ruin and wreck," with its "political and institutional fabric" pulverized. He knows that "our bombers roam over the hapless country, dumping more tonnage of explosives each month than we were dropping per month on all Europe and Africa during the Second World War—more in a year than we dropped on the entire Pacific during the Second World War." And he understands the effects on the civilian population

299

of this attack, unprecedented in scale in the history of warfare. All of this arouses in the author feelings of great compassion— for President Johnson. ("No thoughtful American can withhold sympathy as President Johnson ponders the gloomy choices which lie ahead.")

It is not that Schlesinger is incapable of indignation. He is properly irate about the "warfare in the shadows" of the Viet-cong, their "ambush and assassination and torture, leaving be-hind a trail of burned villages, shattered families and weeping women" (the "trail of burned villages" is not further identified, but perhaps the cast of characters has become confused at this point); and he is not lacking in contempt for those who mob the Secretary of Defense or burn draft cards. One wonders whether he would have been equally offended by a comparable "outpouring of emotion" in Italy in 1935, or Russia in 1956. But as far as American actions are concerned, "it is not only idle but unfair to seek out guilty men." Johnson and Humphrey are mere "sentimental imperialists," fundamentally decent men with an "Asian vision" that is "not dishonorable," interested in "the salvation of Asia."

Not unexpectedly, the Kennedy administration escapes any censure, except for its failure to keep up with the press reports of what was actually taking place. True, Kennedy introduced an army of over 15,000 men, nearly three times the size of the Condor Legion sent by Hitler to "fight Communism" in an ear-lier civil war. But this was simply the "politics of inadvertence." As to the "crisis of credibility," the implication is that this too is a post-Kennedy phenomenon—no one would guess from read-ing this book that a White Paper of December 1961 was entitled "A Threat to the Peace: North Vietnam's Effort to Con-quer South Vietnam." Nor would the reader of *The Bitter Her-itage* be likely to guess that not long before, its author was referring to 1962 as "not a bad year," with "aggression checked in Vietnam," or reiterating, with apparent approval, a characterization of North Vietnam as "the source of aggression" (*A Thousand Days*).

Still, in basic respects, Schlesinger's approach to the conduct of international affairs has a certain internal consistency. He was opposed to the abortive Cuba invasion in 1961, because of his feeling that the planned deception was not likely to succeed, not out of any principled objection to such an action. Similarly, today, he refers with skepticism to Joseph Alsop's prediction that before too long "the Vietnamese war will look successful" from the American point of view, but adds that "we all pray that Mr. Alsop will be right." The liberal view, Schlesinger style, differs from that of Alsop in two important respects: first, in its skepticism as to the immediacy of an American victory; second, in its inability to imagine that any right-thinking American could fail to be in favor of an outright American victory, if only it could be achieved by the means now being employed (which will, to be sure, turn the country into "a land of ruin and wreck"). Thus "we all pray" that American armed might will be successful, but the more sophisticated of us doubt that Alsop's prediction will come true.

Although Schlesinger now insists that "aggression from the North" will hardly do as an explanation for the war in South Vietnam, the old habits break through in his usage of the term "the South Vietnamese." Thus our goal in Vietnam "should be the creation and stabilization of secure areas where the South Vietnamese might themselves undertake social and institutional development." In fact, the areas where the South Vietnamese themselves have undertaken social and institutional development are those where the Vietcong have been in control, for example, in large parts of the Mekong Delta prior to the brutal

American and South Korean campaigns of the last few months. Ample documentation to support this conclusion is presented by Douglas Pike (who, in Schlesinger's judgment, is "the most careful student of the Viet Cong") in his recent book, *Viet Cong*. It would seem, then, that if our goal is to allow the South Vietnamese themselves to undertake social and institutional development, we should simply withdraw, or at the very least permit negotiations among indigenous South Vietnamese forces to the exclusion of outside powers, among which, of course, we ourselves are dominant by an overwhelming margin.

But the South Vietnamese that Schlesinger has in mind are those whose claim to legitimacy is based on American arms (including the "South Vietnamese" in the military junta). Thus, in his lexicon, "South Vietnamese" is to be understood rather in the manner of the Japanese terminology of a quarter of a century ago, in which the "legitimate Chinese government" was that of Wang Ching-wei, the puppet ruler whom they installed (see page 194 above). The only appropriate comments regarding this conception of Rusk, Schlesinger, *et al.* are those of the American note of December 30, 1938, to Japan, which denied "that there is need or warrant for any one Power to take upon itself to prescribe what shall be the terms and conditions of a 'new order' in areas not under its sovereignty and to constitute itself the repository of authority and the agent of destiny in regard thereto."

In the same vein, Schlesinger's "middle course" would offer the Vietcong the prospect of participating in the future political life of Vietnam, "conditioned on their laying down their arms, opening up their territories and abiding by the ground rules of free elections." Since there is no compensating demand that the Americans withdraw and that the Saigon army lay down their arms and open up their territories, Schlesinger's middle course, in essential respects, does not even go as far as the position of the Pentagon, which, on the surface at least, commits us to withdrawal after "Viet Cong military units would be deactivated." Either proposal requests only that the other side surrender, after which we guarantee them political rights.

A true "middle course," demanding capitulation of no faction in the civil struggle, would advocate withdrawal of all foreign troops (American, South Korean, North Vietnamese, and other minor contingents), negotiations among existing political forces in South Vietnam—that is, the National Liberation Front and whatever other forces still have not been crushed by Marshal Ky's American-supported storm troopers—to form a coalition government. As is admitted on all sides, adoption of this middle course would lead to the collapse of the Saigon regime, a fact which, along with the general unwillingness of the Saigon army to fight or even remain in uniform, should lead us, as Schlesinger puts it, to "wonder all the more about the political side of the war."

This course has in fact been repeatedly proposed, by the NLF, despite Schlesinger's blanket assertion that "Hanoi and the Viet Cong will not negotiate so long as they think they can win." It is possible that the repeated Hanoi and NLF initiatives towards negotiation and their demand for a coalition government will prove to be a deception, but there is no doubt that it is a deception simply to deny the existence of these initiatives or to ignore the content of the NLF program—a program which, since 1960, has been calling for the formation of "a broad national democratic coalition administration . . . including representatives of all strata of people, nationalities, political parties, religious communities, and patriotic personalities" (see Kahin and Lewis, *U.S. in Vietnam*, Appendix 6-B).

Similarly, it is a deception to assert blandly, as Schlesinger does, that "Hanoi has put such stress on the withdrawal of American troops as a condition precedent to negotiation," in the face of the frequent insistence from Hanoi that the demand for withdrawal is put forth as "a basis" for negotiations.

Jean Lacouture commented in *Le Nouvel Observateur,* January 1967, that United States government officials are the last people on earth who are unaware of the fundamental elements of the NLF program of 1962. He might have added that Arthur Schlesinger seems the last person on earth to be unaware of the negotiation position of Hanoi and the NLF (stated, for example, by Premier Pham Van Dong; cf. *New York Times,* April 14, 1965), that recognition of the famous four points as "a basis" for a political settlement will create "favorable conditions" for such a settlement and make it "possible to consider the reconvening of an international conference along the pattern of the 1954 Geneva Conference on Vietnam." Neither then nor since has withdrawal of American troops been demanded as a precondition for negotiations.

Thus Schlesinger's "middle course" appears to differ from the approach of the Joint Chiefs and the State Department only in tactical emphasis. All accept the assumption that dispatch of an American expeditionary force of half a million men to take over the conduct of the war is defense of the interests of the South Vietnamese, whereas infiltration from the North is an aggressive attack on South Vietnam. In Schlesinger's case, this assumption takes the form of a proposal that the guerrillas capitulate, after which we will grant them political rights. Analogously, the President and his spokesmen put forth the cynical demand that the North Vietnamese restrict or terminate their activities in the South without any compensating gesture on our side in South Vietnam. This same assumption takes its most ludicrous form when a State Department spokesman refers to resupply efforts by the North Vietnamese during the Tet truce as "extra evidence that they were not sincere in their statement on negotiations," while maintaining that United States logistic operations carried out during the truce period were different because they "did not send men and supplies across the border into North Vietnam but were in South Vietnam only" (*New York Times,* February 17, 1967). To go back to earlier precedents, it is the same attitude that permits Schlesinger (in his *A Thousand Days*) to express his horror at the discovery of Cuban arms cached in Venezuela, but to think nothing of the extensive American military aid that has been used to institute or support repressive regimes throughout the continent. The underlying assumption is that the United States does have a warrant "to take upon itself to prescribe what shall be the terms and conditions of a 'new order' in areas not under its sovereignty and to constitute itself the repository of authority and the agent of destiny in regard thereto."

Every competent observer has pointed out that "the war in South Vietnam has been between the large, professionally trained army of an unpopular government and the amateur military wing of a strong, nationalistically based political movement in which the Communists have formed the spearhead" (Michael Field, *The Prevailing Wind*). For this reason, the Saigon authorities have never wavered from their demand, expressed in a statement of March 1, 1965, that negotiations are unthinkable unless the "Communists" show their sincerity "by withdrawing beforehand their armed units *and their political cadres* from South Vietnamese territory" (italics mine). The demand is appropriate; by their own repeated admission, the Saigon authorities have no hope of maintaining themselves in an open political arena. It is hardly necessary to document the fact that this has been the dominant American position as well, in effect, as Schlesinger himself emphasizes.

Furthermore, Schlesinger has no illusions about the character of the puppet regime in Saigon. He proposes, then, that we should "encourage a pro-peasant regime to come into existence," "a government which enlists enthusiastic popular support in the countryside." He does not raise the question of how this is possible when the country is under American military occupation, or why one should expect the policy makers of the Kennedy-Johnson administrations to be capable of such a total reorientation of approach. But perhaps some light is shed on Schlesinger's conception of democratic processes by his characterization of the 1966 elections in South Vietnam as that "valiant try at self-government" which "excited such idealistic hopes in the United States." He does not see fit to mention that in this valiant try at self-government, Communists and neutralists whose actions might be advantageous to the Communists were, by law, excluded from the ballot, nor does he comment on the conditions, reported widely in the press, under which campaigning and voting took place. In fact, his evaluation of this election recalls the remarks of his occasional adversary Dean Rusk, according to whom the provincial elections of May 1965 "from our point of view . . . were free elections" (August 25, 1965). Under the Rusk-Schlesinger concept of "free elections," it is not unimaginable that "free elections" can be conducted under American military occupation.

Schlesinger grants that the regime we have imposed in Vietnam is that of "a new class of nouveaux mandarins," that it is "pervaded by nepotism, corruption and cynicism," and he admits that our military policy is simply one of devastating the land and annihilating the helpless population. One might suppose, then, that he would suggest American withdrawal. In fact, he says very little about this possibility, dismissing it out of hand because it "would have ominous reverberations throughout Asia," because it would be "humiliating," and because of our "moral obligations" to those whom we have supported and encouraged. The argument is hardly convincing. Our moral obligations, such as they may be, can be met by resettling those whom Schlesinger describes as the "Frankenstein's monsters we delight in creating in our client countries," and their cohorts, say, in Arizona. The "humiliation" of withdrawal hardly compares with the national disgrace of a policy of scorched earth and mass murder. It is difficult to imagine anything more "ominous" for backward Asian countries than a permanent military presence of the sort we are rapidly constructing on the borders of China. Schlesinger's "middle course" is one that, if successful, will leave the United States as dominant as it is in the Philippines, hardly an attractive prospect. If anything will lead this nation to "defile its oldest ideals and disgrace itself in the eyes of the world and its own posterity," it is a willingness to tolerate any barbarism, so long as it can succeed, and to raise our twitters of protest only when total victory seems beyond our grasp.

SOME THOUGHTS ON
INTELLECTUALS AND THE SCHOOLS

In happier times, I would have liked to approach the topic of this symposium in a rather technical and professional way, asking how students might best be exposed to the leading ideas and the most stimulating and penetrating thought in the fields that particularly interest me, how they might be helped to experience the pleasures of discovery and of deepening insight and be given an opportunity to make their own individual contribution to contemporary culture. At this particular historical moment, however, there are other, more pressing matters.

As I write, the radio is bringing the first reports of the bombings of Hanoi and Haiphong. In itself, this is no atrocity by contemporary standards—surely no atrocity, for example, as compared with the American assault on the rural population of

This essay was first printed in the *Harvard Educational Review*, Vol. 36 (Fall 1966), pp. 484–91, in a special issue devoted to a symposium on the topic "American intellectuals and the schools." Copyright © 1966 by the President and Fellows of Harvard College.

South Vietnam for the past year. But the symbolism of this act casts its shadow over any critique of American institutions. When the bombings of North Vietnam began, Jean Lacouture commented aptly that these acts, and the documents produced to justify them, simply reveal that the American leaders regard themselves as having the right to strike where and when they wish. They reveal, in effect, that these leaders regard the world as an American preserve, to be governed and organized in accordance with superior American wisdom and to be controlled, if necessary, by American power. At this moment of national disgrace, as American technology is running amuck in Southeast Asia, a discussion of American schools can hardly avoid noting the fact that these schools are the first training ground for the troops that will enforce the muted, unending terror of the status quo in the coming years of a projected American century; for the technicians who will be developing the means for extension of American power; for the intellectuals who can be counted on, in significant measure, to provide the ideological justification for this particular form of barbarism and to decry the irresponsibility and lack of sophistication of those who will find all of this intolerable and revolting.

Thirty years ago, Franz Borkenau concluded a brilliant study of the crushing of the popular revolution in Spain with this comment: "In this tremendous contrast with previous revolutions one fact is reflected. Before these latter years, counter-revolution usually depended upon the support of reactionary powers, which were technically and intellectually inferior to the forces of revolution. This has changed with the advent of fascism. Now, every revolution is likely to meet the attack of the most modern, most efficient, most ruthless machinery yet in existence. It means that the age of revolutions free to evolve according to their own laws is over."[1]

It would have taken a fair amount of foresight, at that time, to realize that the prediction would be proved accurate, with substitution of "liberal imperialism" for "fascism," and that the United States would, in a generation, be employing the most efficient and most ruthless machinery in existence to ensure that revolutionary movements will not evolve according to their own laws, to guarantee that its own particular concept of civilization and justice and order will prevail. And it would have required considerable insight, in the late 1930s, to realize that before too long a reformist American administration with a "welfare state" domestic orientation would be doing its utmost to prove the correctness of Marx's grim observation about this concept of civilization and justice and order: "The civilization and justice of bourgeois order comes out in its lurid light whenever the slaves and drudges of that order rise against their masters; then this civilization and justice stand forth as undisguised savagery and lawless revenge."

It is conceivable that American actions in Vietnam are simply a single outburst of criminal insanity, of no general or long-range significance except to the miserable inhabitants of that tortured land. It is difficult, however, to put much credence in this possibility. In half a dozen Latin American countries there are guerrilla movements that are approaching the early stages of the second Vietnamese war, and the American reaction is, apparently, comparable. That is, American arms are used to attack guerrilla forces and to "dry up the sea in which they swim," in the Maoist terminology affected by the military; and American "advisers" guide and train the troops which, as Latin American liberals observe, are needed only to occupy their own country in the interests of domestic ruling classes and Northern capital. In these countries it has not yet become necessary, as in Vietnam, to convert the fact of Communist involvement into the myth of

Communist aggression in justification of open United States control of the counterrevolutionary forces, nor has the time yet arrived for application of the full arsenal of terror in support of the regime selected as most favorable to American interests. But it seems that this next step is fully expected. In *Le Nouvel Observateur,* the peasant organizer Francisco Julião was recently quoted as certain of United States intervention when rebellion breaks out in the Brazilian Northeast Provinces. Others, less well known, have expressed themselves similarly. There is little basis, in history or logic, for supposing them to be wrong—little basis, that is, apart from the kind of sentimentality that sees the United States, alone among nations, as a selfless (if rather oafish) public benefactor, devoted only to projects of "international good will," though frequently blundering in an excess of warmhearted generosity. One should no doubt take seriously the insistence of administration spokesmen that one purpose of the present violence is to prove that wars of national liberation cannot succeed; to demonstrate, that is, in the clearest and most explicit terms, that any revolutionary movement that we—unilaterally, as in Vietnam—designate as illegitimate will face the most efficient and ruthless machinery that can be developed by modern technology.

In minor ways, world opinion can serve as some kind of brake on full-scale utilization of the technology of terror and destruction. There has, as yet, been no use of nuclear weapons in Vietnam; and although rural populations are considered fair game for any sort of military attack, urban areas, where the butchery would be more evident to the outside world, are still relatively immune. Similarly, the use of gas attacks and chemical warfare has been extended only slowly, as habituation permits each gradual increment to pass unnoticed.[2] But ultimately, the only effective brake can be popular revulsion on a mass scale in the United States itself. Consequently, the level of culture that can be achieved in the United States is a life-and-death matter for large masses of suffering humanity. This too is a fact that must color any discussion of contemporary American institutions.

It is easy to be carried away by the sheer horror of what the daily press reveals and to lose sight of the fact that this is merely the brutal exterior of a deeper crime, of commitment to a social order that guarantees endless suffering and humiliation and denial of elementary human rights. It is tragic that the United States should have become, in Toynbee's words, "the leader of a world-wide anti-revolutionary movement in defense of vested interests." For American intellectuals and for the schools, there is no more vital issue than this indescribable tragedy.

No one would seriously propose that the schools attempt to deal directly with such contemporary events as the American attack on the rural population of Vietnam or the backgrounds in recent history for the atrocities that are detailed in the mass media. No sane person would have expected the schools in France, for example, to explore the character of and justification for the Algerian war, or the schools in Russia to have dealt honestly with the crushing of the Hungarian revolution, or the schools in Italy to have analyzed the invasion of Ethiopia in an objective way, or the schools in England to have exposed the contemporary suppression of Irish nationalism. But it is perhaps not ridiculous to propose that the schools might direct themselves to something more abstract, to an attempt to offer students some means for defending themselves from the onslaught of the massive government propaganda apparatus, from the natural bias of the mass media, and—to turn specifically to our present topic—from the equally natural tendency of significant

313

segments of the American intellectual community to offer their allegiance, not to truth and justice, but to power and the effective exercise of power.

It is frightening to observe the comparative indifference of American intellectuals to the immediate actions of their government and its long-range policies, and their frequent willingness —often eagerness—to play a role in implementing these policies. This is not the place to illustrate in detail; in any event, I do not command the rhetoric to speak, in the only accurate and appropriate terms, of the actual conduct of the war and the way it has been tolerated at home. But more superficial examples make the point well enough.

Only marginal groups of American academics have reacted to the fact that while the United States stands in the way of the only sort of meaningful negotiations, namely, negotiations among indigenous South Vietnamese political forces to the exclusion of the foreign invaders from the United States and Korea, and (on a vastly different scale) from North Vietnam, it nevertheless is able to persist in its pretense of interest in a "negotiated settlement" with no outcry of protest against this farce. When Secretary Rusk openly admits that we cannot accept the North Vietnamese proposals of April 1965 because they require that the Saigon government be supplanted by a broad, national democratic coalition representing existing political forces in the country, there is no public denunciation of the cynicism of the position he upholds. When the press reports that the electoral law commission in South Vietnam faces the "awesome task" of running "honest elections" while making sure that the Communists do not win and that no Communists or "neutralists whose actions are advantageous to the Communists" appear on the ballot, there is little editorial comment, few letters to the editor, no general dismay. There is little point in multiplying examples. One can only be appalled at the willingness of American intellectuals, who, after all, have access to the facts, to tolerate or even approve of this deceitfulness and hypocrisy. Instead of shocked denunciations, we hear and read mock-serious discussions of the rationality of the American attempt to drive the North Vietnamese by force towards the negotiations that they had been demanding; of the sincere American desire to permit the South Vietnamese people to elect freely the government of their choice (now that the domestic opposition has been crushed and all Communist and neutralist candidates excluded); of the "great complexity" of international affairs (which, strangely, did not seem to justify Russian domination of East Europe or the Japanese attempt to impose a new order in Asia); of the judicious restraint of the administration, presumably, in refraining from genocide at a single stroke; and so on. Or what is worse, we read of the "bedrock vital interest of the United States" in demonstrating that its military power, once committed for whatever reason, cannot be forced to withdraw—a viewpoint which, had it been accepted by the world's second superpower as well, would have brought the history of Western civilization to a close in 1962, and which, if consistently pursued, must lead either to a Pax Americana or to a devastating world conflict.

Traditionally, the role of the intellectual, or at least his self-image, has been that of a dispassionate critic. Insofar as that role has been lost, the relation of the schools to intellectuals should, in fact, be one of self-defense. This is a matter that should be seriously considered. It is, to be sure, ridiculous to propose that the schools, in any country, deal objectively with contemporary history—they cannot sufficiently free themselves from the pressures of ideology for that. But it is not necessarily absurd to suppose that in Western democracies, at least, it should be possible to study in a fairly objective way the national scandals of the past. It might be possible in the United States to study, let us say, the American occupation of the Philippines, leaving implicit its message for the present. Suppose that high school students were exposed to the best of current American scholarship, for example, George Taylor's recent study for the Council on Foreign Relations, *The Philippines and the United States*. Here they would learn how, half a century after the bloody suppression of the native independence movement at a cost of well over 100,000 lives in the years 1898–1900, the country achieved nominal independence and the surface forms of democracy. They would also learn that the United States is guaranteed long-term military bases and unparalleled economic privileges; that for three fourths of the population, living standards have not risen since the Spanish occupation; that 70 percent of the population is estimated to have tuberculosis; that profits flowing to the United States have exceeded new investment in each postwar year; that the democratic forms give a new legitimacy to an old elite, allied now to American interests. They would read that "Colonial policy had tended to consolidate the power of an oligarchy that profited . . . from the free trade relationship and would be likely to respect, after independence, the rights and privileges of Americans"; that economically, "the contrast between the small upper class and the rest of the population . . . [is] . . . one of the most extreme in Asia"; that the consequences of American colonial policy were "that little was done to improve the lot of the average Filipino and that the Philippine economy was tied to the American to the advantage of the few"; and so on. They would then read the book's final recommendation, that we go on with our good work: "In spite of our many shortcomings, the record shows that we are more than equal to the task." It is at least possible that to a young mind, still uncontaminated by cant and sophistry, such a study can teach a revealing lesson, not only about what American dominance is likely to mean concretely, in the Third World, but also about the way in which American intellectuals are likely to interpret this impact.

In general, the history of imperialism and of imperialist apologia, particularly as seen from the point of view of those at the wrong end of the guns, should be a central part of any civilized curriculum. But there are other aspects to a program of intellectual self-defense that should not be overlooked. In an age of science and technology, it is inevitable that their prestige will be employed as an ideological instrument—specifically, that the social and behavioral sciences will in various ways be made to serve in defense of national policy or as a mask for special interest. It is not merely that intellectuals are strongly tempted, in a society that offers them prestige and affluence, to take what is now called a "pragmatic attitude" (in a perverse sense of "pragmatism" which is, sad to say, not without some historical justification, as shown in the Dewey-Bourne interchange during the First World War—see Introduction, pages 5-7), that is, an attitude that one must "accept," not critically analyze or struggle to change, the existing distribution of power, domestic or international, and the political realities that flow from it, and must work only for "slow measures of improvement" in a technological, piecemeal manner. It is not merely that having taken this position (conceivably with some justification, at a particular historical moment), one is strongly tempted to provide it with an ideological justification of a very general sort. Rather, what we must also expect is that political elites will use the terminology of the social and behavioral sciences to protect their actions from critical analysis—the non-specialist does not, after all, presume to tell physicists and engineers how to build an atomic reactor. And for any particular action, experts can certainly be found in the universities who will solemnly testify as to its appropriateness and realism. This is not a matter of speculation; thus we already find, in congressional testimony, the proposal by a leading political scientist that we try to impose mass starvation on a quarter of the human race, if their government does not accept our dictates. And it is commonly argued that the free-floating intellectual, who is now outdated, has no business questioning the conclusions of the professional expert, equipped with the tools of modern science.

This situation again carries a lesson for the schools, one to which teachers in particular should be quite sensitive, bombarded as they have been in recent years by authoritative conclusions about what has been "demonstrated" with regard to human learning, language, and so on. The social and behavioral sciences should be seriously studied not only for their intrinsic interest, but so that the student can be made quite aware of exactly how little they have to say about the problems of man and society that really matter. They should, furthermore, be studied in the context of the physical sciences, so that the student can be brought to appreciate clearly the limits of their intellectual content. This can be an important way to protect a student from the propaganda of the future, and to put him in a position to comprehend the true nature of the means that are sure to be used to conceal the real significance of domestic or international policy.

Suppose, however, that contrary to all present indications, the United States will stop short of using its awesome resources of violence and devastation to impose its passionately held ideology and its approved form of social organization on large areas of the world. Suppose, that is, that American policy ceases to be dominated by the principles that were crudely outlined by President Truman almost twenty years ago, when he observed in a famous and important speech that "all freedom is dependent on freedom of enterprise," that "the whole world should adopt the American system," that "the American system can survive in America only if it becomes a world system." It would nevertheless remain true that the level of culture that can be achieved in the United States is a matter of overwhelming importance for the rest of the world. If we want to be truly utopian, we may consider the possibility that American resources might be used to alleviate the terrorism that seems to be an inevitable correlate of modernization, if we can judge from past and present history. We can conceive of the possibility that the schools, or the intellectuals, might pay serious attention to questions that have been posed for centuries, that they might ask whether society must, indeed, be a Hobbesian *bellum omnium contra omnes,* and might inquire into the contemporary meaning of Rousseau's protest that it is contrary to natural right that "a handful of men be glutted with superfluities while the starving multitude lacks necessities." They might raise the moral issue faced, or avoided, by one who enjoys his wealth and privilege undisturbed by the knowledge that half of the children born in Nicaragua will not reach five years of age, or that only a few miles away there is unspeakable poverty, brutal suppression of human rights, and almost no hope for the future; and they might raise the intellectual issue of how this can be changed. They might ask, with Keynes, how long we must continue to "exalt some of the most distasteful of human qualities into the position of the highest virtues," setting up "avarice and usury and precaution . . . [as] . . . our gods," and pretending to ourselves that "fair is foul and foul is fair, for foul is useful and fair is not." If American intellectuals will be preoccupied with such questions as these, they can have an invaluable civilizing influence on society and on the schools. If, as is more likely, they regard them with disdain as mere sentimental nonsense, then our children will have to look elsewhere for enlightenment and guidance.

Notes

1. *The Spanish Cockpit* (1938; reprinted Ann Arbor, University of Michigan Press, 1963), pp. 288–89.
2. This essay was written in June 1966; it now goes to press again in May 1968. On the use of gas in Vietnam, see Seymour Hersh, "Poison Gas in Vietnam," *New York Review of Books,* May 9, 1968. On current plans for chemical warfare, *Science,* May 24, 1968, contains the following note (p. 863):

> *Expanded Chemical Warfare:* The Air Force has told Congress that it will spend $70.8 million on 10 million gallons of chemicals used for Vietnam defoliation and crop-killing in the fiscal year beginning 1 July, a $24.9 million increase over this year's figure. Next year's expanded efforts are in line with the continuing increase in the U.S. chemical warfare program in Vietnam. In the first 9 months of 1967, 843,606 acres in Vietnam were drenched with defoliants and 121,400 acres with crop-killing chemicals, a figure which slightly exceeded the totals for the whole of 1966.

In its issue of May 10, 1968, *Science* carries a letter by Thomas O. Perry of the Harvard University Forest, who comments as follows on chemical warfare (p. 601):

> The DOD can raise the red herring of "long-term" effects, but there can be no doubt about the short-term effects: 2,4-D and 2,4,5-T kill the green vegetation. When followed by fire bombs, the dead foliage and twigs burn, as they did on some 100,000 acres (about 40,000 hectares) in the "Iron Triangle" last spring.
>
> Through the simple process of starvation, a land without green foliage will quickly become a land without insects, without birds, without animal life of any form. News photographs and on-the-spot descriptions indicate that some areas have been sprayed repeatedly to

assure a complete kill of the vegetation. There can be no doubt that the DOD is, in the short run, going beyond mere genocide to biocide. It commandeered the entire U.S. production of 2,4,5-T for 1967 and 1968 [some 13 to 14 million pounds (6.36 million kilos) according to U.S. Tariff Commission reports]. If one combines this with the other chemicals the DOD concedes it is using, there is a sufficient amount to kill 97 percent of the aboveground vegetation on over 10 million acres of land (about 4 million hectares)—an area so big that it would require over 60 years for a man to walk on each acre.

The long-term effects of spraying such an area may be imponderable, but the short-term effects of using these chemicals are certain: a lot of leaves, trees, rice plants, and other vegetation are dead or dying; and a lot of insects, birds, animals, and a few humans have either migrated or died of starvation. The North Vietnamese are fortunate—they have only bombs to contend with.

THE RESPONSIBILITY OF INTELLECTUALS

Twenty years ago, Dwight Macdonald published a series of articles in *Politics* on the responsibilities of peoples, and specifically, the responsibility of intellectuals. I read them as an undergraduate, in the years just after the war, and had occasion to read them again a few months ago. They seem to me to have lost none of their power or persuasiveness. Macdonald is concerned with the question of war guilt. He asks the question: To what extent were the German or Japanese people responsible for the atrocities committed by their governments? And, quite properly, he turns the question back to us: To what extent are the British or American people responsible for the vicious terror bombings of civilians, perfected as a technique of warfare by the Western democracies and reaching their culmination in

This is a revised version of a talk given at Harvard and published in *Mosaic*, June 1966. It appeared in substantially this form in the *New York Review of Books*, February 23, 1967. The present version is reprinted from Theodore Roszak, ed., *The Dissenting Academy* (New York, Pantheon Books, 1968).

Hiroshima and Nagasaki, surely among the most unspeakable crimes in history? To an undergraduate in 1945–1946—to anyone whose political and moral consciousness had been formed by the horrors of the 1930s, by the war in Ethiopia, the Russian purge, the "China incident," the Spanish Civil War, the Nazi atrocities, the Western reaction to these events and, in part, complicity in them—these questions had particular significance and poignancy.

With respect to the responsibility of intellectuals, there are still other, equally disturbing questions. Intellectuals are in a position to expose the lies of governments, to analyze actions according to their causes and motives and often hidden intentions. In the Western world at least, they have the power that comes from political liberty, from access to information and freedom of expression. For a privileged minority, Western democracy provides the leisure, the facilities, and the training to seek the truth lying hidden behind the veil of distortion and misrepresentation, ideology, and class interest through which the events of current history are presented to us. The responsibilities of intellectuals, then, are much deeper than what Macdonald calls the "responsibility of peoples," given the unique privileges that intellectuals enjoy.

The issues that Macdonald raised are as pertinent today as they were twenty years ago. We can hardly avoid asking ourselves to what extent the American people bear responsibility for the savage American assault on a largely helpless rural population in Vietnam, still another atrocity in what Asians see as the "Vasco da Gama era" of world history. As for those of us who stood by in silence and apathy as this catastrophe slowly took shape over the past dozen years, on what page of history do we find our proper place? Only the most insensible can escape these questions. I want to return to them, later on, after a few scattered remarks about the responsibility of intellectuals and how, in practice, they go about meeting this responsibility in the mid-1960s.

It is the responsibility of intellectuals to speak the truth and to expose lies. This, at least, may seem enough of a truism to pass without comment. Not so, however. For the modern intellectual, it is not at all obvious. Thus we have Martin Heidegger writing, in a pro-Hitler declaration of 1933, that "truth is the revelation of that which makes a people certain, clear, and strong in its action and knowledge"; it is only this kind of "truth" that one has a responsibility to speak. Americans tend to be more forthright. When Arthur Schlesinger was asked by the *New York Times,* in November 1965, to explain the contradiction between his published account of the Bay of Pigs incident and the story he had given the press at the time of the attack, he simply remarked that he had lied; and a few days later, he went on to compliment the *Times* for also having suppressed information on the planned invasion, in "the national interest," as this was defined by the group of arrogant and deluded men of whom Schlesinger gives such a flattering portrait in his recent account of the Kennedy administration. It is of no particular interest that one man is quite happy to lie in behalf of a cause which he knows to be unjust; but it is significant that such events provoke so little response in the intellectual community —no feeling, for example, that there is something strange in the offer of a major chair in humanities to a historian who feels it to be his duty to persuade the world that an American-sponsored invasion of a nearby country is nothing of the sort. And what of the incredible sequence of lies on the part of our government and its spokesmen concerning such matters as negotiations in Vietnam? The facts are known to all who care to know. The press, foreign and domestic, has presented documentation to refute each falsehood as it appears. But the power of the government propaganda apparatus is such that the citizen who does not undertake a research project on the subject can hardly hope to confront government pronouncements with fact.[1]

The deceit and distortion surrounding the American invasion of Vietnam are by now so familiar that they have lost their power to shock. It is therefore well to recall that although new levels of cynicism are constantly being reached, their clear antecedents were accepted at home with quiet toleration. It is a useful exercise to compare government statements at the time of the invasion of Guatemala in 1954 with Eisenhower's admission—to be more accurate, his boast—a decade later that American planes were sent "to help the invaders."[2] Nor is it only in moments of crisis that duplicity is considered perfectly in order. "New Frontiersmen," for example, have scarcely distinguished themselves by a passionate concern for historical accuracy, even when they are not being called upon to provide a "propaganda cover" for ongoing actions. For example, Arthur Schlesinger describes the bombing of North Vietnam and the massive escalation of military commitment in early 1965 as based on a "perfectly rational argument": ". . . so long as the Vietcong thought they were going to win the war, they obviously would not be interested in any kind of negotiated settlement."[3] The date is important. Had the statement been made six months earlier, one could attribute it to ignorance. But this statement appeared after months of front-page news reports detailing the United Nations, North Vietnamese, and Soviet initiatives that preceded the February 1965 escalation and that, in fact, continued for several weeks after the bombing began, after months of soul-searching by Washington correspondents who were trying desperately to find some mitigating circumstances for the startling deception that had been revealed. (Chalmers Roberts, for example, wrote with unconscious irony that late February 1965 "hardly seemed to Washington to be a propitious moment for negotiations [since] Mr. Johnson . . . had just ordered the first bombing of North Vietnam in an effort to bring Hanoi to a conference table where bargaining chips on both sides would be more closely matched."[4]) Coming at this moment, Schlesinger's statement is less an example of deceit than of contempt —contempt for an audience that can be expected to tolerate such behavior with silence, if not approval.[5]

To turn to someone closer to the actual formation and implementation of policy, consider some of the reflections of Walt Rostow, a man who, according to Schlesinger, brought a "spacious historical view" to the conduct of foreign affairs in the Kennedy administration.[6] According to his analysis, the guerrilla warfare in Indochina in 1946 was launched by Stalin,[7] and Hanoi initiated the guerrilla war against South Vietnam in 1958 (*The View from the Seventh Floor*, pp. 39 and 152). Similarly, the Communist planners probed the "free world spectrum of defense" in Northern Azerbaijan and Greece (where Stalin "supported substantial guerrilla warfare"—*ibid.*, pp. 36 and 148), operating from plans carefully laid in 1945. And in Central Europe, the Soviet Union was not "prepared to accept a solution which would remove the dangerous tensions from Central Europe at the risk of even slowly staged corrosion of communism in East Germany" (*ibid.*, p. 156).

It is interesting to compare these observations with studies by scholars actually concerned with historical events. The remark about Stalin's initiating the first Vietnamese war in 1946 does not even merit refutation. As to Hanoi's purported initiative of 1958, the situation is more clouded. But even government sources[8] concede that in 1959 Hanoi received the first direct reports of what Diem referred to[9] as his own Algerian war, and that only after this did they lay their plans to involve themselves in this struggle. In fact, in December 1958 Hanoi made another of its many attempts—rebuffed once again by Saigon and the United States—to establish diplomatic and commercial relations with the Saigon government on the basis of the status quo.[10] Rostow offers no evidence of Stalin's support for the Greek guerrillas: in fact, though the historical record is far from clear, it seems that Stalin was by no means pleased with the adventurism of the Greek guerrillas, who, from his point of view, were upsetting the satisfactory postwar imperialist settlement.[11]

Rostow's remarks about Germany are more interesting still. He does not see fit to mention, for example, the Russian notes of March–April 1952, which proposed unification of Germany under internationally supervised elections, with withdrawal of all troops within a year, *if* there was a guarantee that a reunified Germany would not be permitted to join a Western military alliance.[12] And he has also momentarily forgotten his own characterization of the strategy of the Truman and Eisenhower administrations: "to avoid any serious negotiation with the Soviet Union until the West could confront Moscow with German rearmament within an organized European framework, as a *fait accompli*"[13]—to be sure, in defiance of the Potsdam agreements.

But most interesting of all is Rostow's reference to Iran. The facts are that there was a Russian attempt to impose by force a pro-Soviet government in Northern Azerbaijan that would grant the Soviet Union access to Iranian oil. This was rebuffed by superior Anglo-American force in 1946, at which point the more powerful imperialism obtained full rights to Iranian oil for itself, with the installation of a pro-Western government. We recall what happened when, for a brief period in the early

1950s, the only Iranian government with something of a popular base experimented with the curious idea that Iranian oil should belong to the Iranians. What is interesting, however, is the description of Northern Azerbaijan as part of "the free world spectrum of defense." It is pointless, by now, to comment on the debasement of the phrase "free world." But by what law of nature does Iran, with its resources, fall within Western dominion? The bland assumption that it does is most revealing of deep-seated attitudes towards the conduct of foreign affairs.

In addition to this growing lack of concern for truth, we find, in recent statements, a real or feigned naiveté with regard to American actions that reaches startling proportions. For example, Arthur Schlesinger has recently characterized our Vietnamese policies of 1954 as "part of our general program of international goodwill."[14] Unless intended as irony, this remark shows either a colossal cynicism or an inability, on a scale that defies comment, to comprehend elementary phenomena of contemporary history. Similarly, what is one to make of the testimony of Thomas Schelling before the House Foreign Affairs Committee, January 27, 1966, in which he discusses the two great dangers if all Asia "goes Communist"?[15] First, this would exclude "the United States and what we call Western civilization from a large part of the world that is poor and colored and potentially hostile." Second, "a country like the United States probably cannot maintain self-confidence if just about the greatest thing it ever attempted, namely to create the basis for decency and prosperity and democratic government in the underdeveloped world, had to be acknowledged as a failure or as an attempt that we wouldn't try again." It surpasses belief that a person with even minimal acquaintance with the record of American foreign policy could produce such statements.

It surpasses belief, that is, unless we look at the matter from a more historical point of view, and place such statements in the context of the hypocritical moralism of the past; for example, of Woodrow Wilson, who was going to teach the Latin Americans the art of good government, and who wrote (1902) that it is "our peculiar duty" to teach colonial peoples "order and self-control . . . [and] . . . the drill and habit of law and obedience." Or of the missionaries of the 1840s, who described the hideous and degrading opium wars as "the result of a great design of Providence to make the wickedness of men subserve his purposes of mercy toward China, in breaking through her wall of exclusion, and bringing the empire into more immediate contact with western and Christian nations." Or, to approach the present, of A. A. Berle, who, in commenting on the Dominican intervention, has the impertinence to attribute the problems of the Caribbean countries to imperialism—*Russian* imperialism.[16]

As a final example of this failure of skepticism, consider the remarks of Henry Kissinger in concluding his presentation in a Harvard-Oxford television debate on American Vietnam policies. He observed, rather sadly, that what disturbs him most is that others question not our judgment but our motives—a remarkable comment on the part of one whose professional concern is political analysis, that is, analysis of the actions of governments in terms of motives that are unexpressed in official propaganda and perhaps only dimly perceived by those whose acts they govern. No one would be disturbed by an analysis of the political behavior of Russians, French, or Tanzanians, questioning their motives and interpreting their actions in terms of long-range interests, perhaps well concealed behind official rhetoric. But it is an article of faith that American motives are pure and not subject to analysis (see note 1). Although it is nothing new in American intellectual history—or, for that mat-

ter, in the general history of imperialist apologia—this innocence becomes increasingly distasteful as the power it serves
grows more dominant in world affairs and more capable, therefore, of the unconstrained viciousness that the mass media
present to us each day. We are hardly the first power in history
to combine material interests, great technological capacity, and
an utter disregard for the suffering and misery of the lower
orders. The long tradition of naiveté and self-righteousness that
disfigures our intellectual history, however, must serve as a
warning to the Third World, if such a warning is needed, as to
how our protestations of sincerity and benign intent are to be
interpreted.

The basic assumptions of the "New Frontiersmen" should be
pondered carefully by those who look forward to the involvement of academic intellectuals in politics. For example, I have
referred to Arthur Schlesinger's objections to the Bay of Pigs
invasion, but the reference was imprecise. True, he felt that it
was a "terrible idea," but "not because the notion of sponsoring
an exile attempt to overthrow Castro seemed intolerable in
itself." Such a reaction would be the merest sentimentality, unthinkable to a tough-minded realist. The difficulty, rather, was
that it seemed unlikely that the deception could succeed. The
operation, in his view, was ill-conceived but not otherwise objectionable.[17] In a similar vein, Schlesinger quotes with approval Kennedy's "realistic" assessment of the situation resulting
from Trujillo's assassination: "There are three possibilities in
descending order of preference: a decent democratic regime, a
continuation of the Trujillo regime or a Castro regime. We
ought to aim at the first, but we really can't renounce the second until we are sure that we can avoid the third."[18] The
reason why the third possibility is so intolerable is explained a
few pages later: "Communist success in Latin America would

331

deal a much harder blow to the power and influence of the United States." Of course, we can never really be sure of avoiding the third possibility; therefore, in practice, we will always settle for the second, as we are now doing in Brazil and Argentina, for example.[19]

Or consider Walt Rostow's views on American policy in Asia.[20] The basis on which we must build this policy is that "we are openly threatened and we feel menaced by Communist China." To prove that we are menaced is of course unnecessary, and the matter receives no attention; it is enough that we feel menaced. Our policy must be based on our national heritage and our national interests. Our national heritage is briefly outlined in the following terms: "Throughout the nineteenth century, in good conscience Americans could devote themselves to the extension of both their principles and their power on this continent," making use of "the somewhat elastic concept of the Monroe doctrine" and, of course, extending "the American interest to Alaska and the mid-Pacific islands. . . . Both our insistence on unconditional surrender and the idea of post-war occupation . . . represented the formulation of American security interests in Europe and Asia." So much for our heritage. As to our interests, the matter is equally simple. Fundamental is our "profound interest that societies abroad develop and strengthen those elements in their respective cultures that elevate and protect the dignity of the individual against the state." At the same time, we must counter the "ideological threat," namely "the possibility that the Chinese Communists can prove to Asians by progress in China that Communist methods are better and faster than democratic methods." Nothing is said about those people in Asian cultures to whom our "conception of the proper relation of the individual to the state" may not be the uniquely important value, people who might, for example, be concerned with preserving the "dignity of the individual" against concentrations of foreign or domestic capital, or against semifeudal structures (such as Trujillo-type dictatorships) introduced or kept in power by American arms. All of this is flavored with allusions to "our religious and ethical value systems" and to our "diffuse and complex concepts" which are to the Asian mind "so much more difficult to grasp" than Marxist dogma, and are so "disturbing to some Asians" because of "their very lack of dogmatism."

Such intellectual contributions as these suggest the need for a correction to De Gaulle's remark, in his memoirs, about the American "will to power, cloaking itself in idealism." By now, this will to power is not so much cloaked in idealism as it is drowned in fatuity. And academic intellectuals have made their unique contribution to this sorry picture.

Let us, however, return to the war in Vietnam and the response that it has aroused among American intellectuals. A striking feature of the recent debate on Southeast Asian policy has been the distinction that is commonly drawn between "responsible criticism," on the one hand, and "sentimental" or "emotional" or "hysterical" criticism, on the other. There is much to be learned from a careful study of the terms in which this distinction is drawn. The "hysterical critics" are to be identified, apparently, by their irrational refusal to accept one fundamental political axiom, namely, that the United States has the right to extend its power and control without limit, insofar as is feasible. Responsible criticism does not challenge this assumption, but argues, rather, that we probably can't "get away with it" at this particular time and place.

A distinction of this sort seems to be what Irving Kristol has in mind, for example, in his analysis of the protest over Vietnam policy, in *Encounter*, August 1965. He contrasts the responsible

critics, such as Walter Lippmann, the *New York Times,* and
Senator Fulbright, with the "teach-in movement." "Unlike the
university protesters," he maintains, "Mr. Lippmann engages in
no presumptuous suppositions as to 'what the Vietnamese people really want'—he obviously doesn't much care—or in legalis-
tic exegesis as to whether, or to what extent, there is 'aggression' or 'revolution' in South Vietnam. His is a *realpolitik* point
of view; and he will apparently even contemplate the possibility
of a *nuclear* war against China in extreme circumstances." This
is commendable, and contrasts favorably, for Kristol, with the
talk of the "unreasonable, ideological types" in the teach-in
movement, who often seem to be motivated by such absurdities
as "simple, virtuous 'anti-imperialism.' " who deliver "harangues
on 'the power structure,' " and who even sometimes stoop so
low as to read "articles and reports from the foreign press on
the American presence in Vietnam." Furthermore, these nasty
types are often psychologists, mathematicians, chemists, or
philosophers (just as, incidentally, those most vocal in protest in
the Soviet Union are generally physicists, literary intellectuals,
and others remote from the exercise of power), rather than
people with Washington contacts, who of course realize that
"had they a new, good idea about Vietnam, they would get a
prompt and respectful hearing" in Washington.

I am not interested here in whether Kristol's characterization
of protest and dissent is accurate, but rather in the assumptions
that it expresses with respect to such questions as these: Is the
purity of American motives a matter that is beyond discussion,
or that is irrelevant to discussion? Should decisions be left to
"experts" with Washington contacts—that is, even if we assume
that they command the necessary knowledge and principles to
make the "best" decision, will they invariably do so? And, a
logically prior question, is "expertise" applicable—that is, is

there a body of theory and of relevant information, not in the public domain, that can be applied to the analysis of foreign policy or that demonstrates the correctness of present actions in some way that the psychologists, mathematicians, chemists, and philosophers are incapable of comprehending? Although Kristol does not examine these questions directly, his attitudes presuppose answers, answers which are wrong in all cases. American aggressiveness, however it may be masked in pious rhetoric, is a dominant force in world affairs and must be analyzed in terms of its causes and motives. There is no body of theory or significant body of relevant information, beyond the comprehension of the layman, which makes policy immune from criticism. To the extent that "expert knowledge" is applied to world affairs, it is surely appropriate—for a person of any integrity, quite necessary—to question its quality and the goals that it serves. These facts seem too obvious to require extended discussion.

A corrective to Kristol's curious belief in the administration's openness to new thinking about Vietnam is provided by McGeorge Bundy in a recent article.[21] As Bundy correctly observes, "on the main stage . . . the argument on Viet Nam turns on tactics, not fundamentals," although, he adds, "there are wild men in the wings." On stage center are, of course, the President (who in his recent trip to Asia had just "magisterially reaffirmed" our interest "in the progress of the people across the Pacific") and his advisers, who deserve "the understanding support of those who want restraint." It is these men who deserve the credit for the fact that "the bombing of the North has been the most accurate and the most restrained in modern warfare" —a solicitude which will be appreciated by the inhabitants, or former inhabitants, of Nam Dinh and Phu Ly and Vinh. It is these men, too, who deserve the credit for what was reported by Malcolm Browne as long ago as May 1965: "In the South, huge sectors of the nation have been declared 'free bombing zones,' in which anything that moves is a legitimate target. Tens of thousands of tons of bombs, rockets, napalm and cannon fire are poured into these vast areas each week. If only by the laws of chance, bloodshed is believed to be heavy in these raids."

Fortunately for the developing countries, Bundy assures us, "American democracy has no enduring taste for imperialism," and "taken as a whole, the stock of American experience, understanding, sympathy and simple knowledge is now much the most impressive in the world." It is true that "four-fifths of all the foreign investing in the world is now done by Americans" and that "the most admired plans and policies . . . are no better than their demonstrable relation to the American interest"—just as it is true, so we read in the same issue of *Foreign Affairs,* that the plans for armed action against Cuba were put into motion a few weeks after Mikoyan visited Havana, "invading what had so long been an almost exclusively American sphere of influence." Unfortunately, such facts as these are often taken by unsophisticated Asian intellectuals as indicating a "taste for imperialism." For example, a number of Indians have expressed their "near exasperation" at the fact that "we have done everything we can to attract foreign capital for fertilizer plants, but the American and the other Western private companies know we are over a barrel, so they demand stringent terms which we just cannot meet,"[22] while "Washington . . . doggedly insists that deals be made in the private sector with private enterprise."[23] But this reaction, no doubt, simply reveals once again how the Asian mind fails to comprehend the "diffuse and complex concepts" of Western thought.

It may be useful to study carefully the "new, good ideas about Vietnam" that are receiving a "prompt and respectful hearing" in Washington these days. The United States Government Printing Office is an endless source of insight into the moral and intellectual level of this expert advice. In its publications one can read, for example, the testimony of Professor David N. Rowe, director of graduate studies in international relations at Yale University, before the House Committee on Foreign Affairs (see note 15). Professor Rowe proposes (p. 266) that the United States buy all surplus Canadian and Australian wheat, so that there will be mass starvation in China. These are his words: "Mind you, I am not talking about this as a weapon against the Chinese people. It will be. But that is only incidental. The weapon will be a weapon against the Government because the internal stability of that country cannot be sustained by an unfriendly Government in the face of general starvation." Professor Rowe will have none of the sentimental moralism that might lead one to compare this suggestion with, say, the *Ostpolitik* of Hitler's Germany.[24] Nor does he fear the impact of such policies on other Asian nations, for example Japan. He assures us, from his "very long acquaintance with Japanese questions," that "the Japanese above all are people who respect power and determination." Hence "they will not be so much alarmed by American policy in Vietnam that takes off from a position of power and intends to seek a solution based upon the imposition of our power upon local people that we are in opposition to." What would disturb the Japanese is "a policy of indecision, a policy of refusal to face up to the problems [in China and Vietnam] and to meet our responsibilities there in a positive way," such as the way just cited. A conviction that we were "unwilling to use the power that they know we have" might "alarm the Japanese people very intensely and shake the degree of their friendly relations with us." In fact, a full use of American power would be particularly reassuring to the Japanese, because they have had a demonstration "of the tremen-

337

dous power in action of the United States . . . because they have felt our power directly." This is surely a prime example of the healthy *"realpolitik* point of view" that Irving Kristol so much admires.

But, one may ask, why restrict ourselves to such indirect means as mass starvation? Why not bombing? No doubt this message is implicit in the remarks to the same committee of the Reverend R. J. de Jaegher, regent of the Institute of Far Eastern Studies, Seton Hall University, who explains that like all people who have lived under Communism, the North Vietnamese "would be perfectly happy to be bombed to be free" (p. 345).

Of course, there must be those who support the Communists. But this is really a matter of small concern, as the Honorable Walter Robertson, Assistant Secretary of State for Far Eastern Affairs from 1953 to 1959, points out in his testimony before the same committee. He assures us that "The Peiping regime . . . represents something less than 3 percent of the population" (p. 402).

Consider, then, how fortunate the Chinese Communist leaders are, compared to the leaders of the Vietcong, who, according to Arthur Goldberg, represent about "one-half of one percent of the population of South Vietnam," that is, about one half the number of new Southern recruits for the Vietcong during 1965, if we can credit Pentagon statistics.[25]

In the face of such experts as these, the scientists and philosophers of whom Kristol speaks would clearly do well to continue to draw their circles in the sand.

Having settled the issue of the political irrelevance of the protest movement, Kristol turns to the question of what motivates it—more generally, what has made students and junior faculty "go left," as he sees it, amid general prosperity and under liberal, welfare state administrations. This, he notes, "is a riddle to which no sociologist has as yet come up with an answer." Since these young people are well off, have good futures, etc., their protest must be irrational. It must be the result of boredom, of too much security, or something of this sort.

Other possibilities come to mind. It might be, for example, that as honest men the students and junior faculty are attempting to find out the truth for themselves rather than ceding the responsibility to "experts" or to government; and it might be that they react with indignation to what they discover. These possibilities Kristol does not reject. They are simply unthinkable, unworthy of consideration. More accurately, these possibilities are inexpressible; the categories in which they are formulated (honesty, indignation) simply do not exist for the tough-minded social scientist.

In this implicit disparagement of traditional intellectual values, Kristol reflects attitudes that are fairly widespread in academic circles. I do not doubt that these attitudes are in part a consequence of the desperate attempt of the social and behavioral sciences to imitate the surface features of sciences that really have significant intellectual content. But they have other sources as well. Anyone can be a moral individual, concerned with human rights and problems; but only a college professor, a trained expert, can solve technical problems by "sophisticated" methods. Ergo, it is only problems of the latter sort that are important or real. Responsible, nonideological experts will give advice on tactical questions; irresponsible "ideological types" will "harangue" about principle and trouble themselves over moral issues and human rights, or over the traditional problems of man and society, concerning which "social and behavioral science" have nothing to offer beyond trivialities. Obviously, these emotional, ideological types are irrational, since, being

339

well off and having power in their grasp, they shouldn't worry about such matters.

At times this pseudoscientific posing reaches levels that are almost pathological. Consider the phenomenon of Herman Kahn, for example. Kahn has been both denounced as immoral and lauded for his courage. By people who should know better, his *On Thermonuclear War* has been described "without qualification . . . [as] . . . one of the great works of our time" (Stuart Hughes). The fact of the matter is that this is surely one of the emptiest works of our time, as can be seen by applying to it the intellectual standards of any existing discipline, by tracing some of its "well-documented conclusions" to the "objective studies" from which they derive, and by following the line of argument, where detectable. Kahn proposes no theories, no explanations, no empirical assumptions that can be tested against their consequences, as do the sciences he is attempting to mimic. He simply suggests a terminology and provides a façade of rationality. When particular policy conclusions are drawn, they are supported only by *ex cathedra* remarks for which no support is even suggested (e.g., "The civil defense line probably should be drawn somewhere below $5 billion annually" to keep from provoking the Russians—why not $50 billion, or $5?). What is more, Kahn is quite aware of this vacuity; in his more judicious moments he claims only that "there is no reason to believe that relatively sophisticated models are more likely to be misleading than the simpler models and analogies frequently used as an aid to judgment." For those whose humor tends towards the macabre, it is easy to play the game of "strategic thinking" à la Kahn, and to prove what one wishes. For example, one of Kahn's basic assumptions is that "an all-out surprise attack in which all resources are devoted to counter-value targets would be so irrational that, barring an incredible lack of sophistication or actual insanity among Soviet decision makers, such an attack is highly unlikely." A simple argument proves the opposite. Premise 1: American decision makers think along the lines outlined by Herman Kahn. Premise 2: Kahn thinks it would be better for everyone to be red than for everyone to be dead. Premise 3: If the Americans were to respond to an all-out counter-value attack, then everyone would be dead. Conclusion: The Americans will not respond to an all-out counter-value attack, and therefore it should be launched without delay. Of course, one can carry the argument a step further. Fact: The Russians have not carried out an all-out counter-value attack. It follows that they are not rational. If they are not rational, there is no point in "strategic thinking." Therefore . . .

Of course this is all nonsense, but nonsense that differs from Kahn's only in the respect that the argument is of slightly greater complexity than anything to be discovered in his work. What is remarkable is that serious people actually pay attention to these absurdities, no doubt because of the façade of tough-mindedness and pseudoscience.

It is a curious and depressing fact that the "antiwar movement" falls prey all too often to similar confusions. In the fall of 1965, for example, there was an International Conference on Alternative Perspectives on Vietnam, which circulated a pamphlet to potential participants stating its assumptions. The plan was to set up study groups in which three "types of intellectual tradition" will be represented: (1) area specialists; (2) "social theory, with special emphasis on theories of the international system, of social change and development, of conflict and conflict resolution, or of revolution"; (3) "the analysis of public policy in terms of basic human values, rooted in various theological, philosophical and humanist traditions." The second intellectual tradition will provide "general propositions, derived from social theory and tested against historical, comparative, or experimental data"; the third "will provide the framework out of which fundamental value questions can be raised and in terms of which the moral implications of societal actions can be analyzed." The hope was that "by approaching the questions [of Vietnam policy] from the moral perspectives of all great religions and philosophical systems, we may find solutions that are more consistent with fundamental human values than current American policy in Vietnam has turned out to be."

In short, the experts on values (i.e., spokesmen for the great religions and philosophical systems) will provide fundamental insights on moral perspectives, and the experts on social theory will provide general empirically validated propositions and "general models of conflict." From this interplay, new policies will emerge, presumably from application of the canons of scientific method. The only debatable issue, it seems to me, is whether it is more ridiculous to turn to experts in social theory for general well-confirmed propositions, or to the specialists in the great religions and philosophical systems for insights into fundamental human values.

There is much more that can be said about this topic, but without continuing, I would simply like to emphasize that, as is no doubt obvious, the cult of the expert is both self-serving, for those who propound it, and fraudulent. Obviously, one must learn from social and behavioral science whatever one can; obviously, these fields should be pursued in as serious a way as is possible. But it will be quite unfortunate, and highly dangerous, if they are not accepted and judged on their merits and according to their actual, not pretended, accomplishments. In particular, if there is a body of theory, well tested and verified, that applies to the conduct of foreign affairs or the resolution of domestic or international conflict, its existence has been kept a well-guarded secret. In the case of Vietnam, if those who feel themselves to be experts have access to principles or information that would justify what the American government is doing in that unfortunate country, they have been singularly ineffective in making this fact known. To anyone who has any familiarity with the social and behavioral sciences (or the "policy sciences"), the claim that there are certain considerations and principles too deep for the outsider to comprehend is simply an absurdity, unworthy of comment.

When we consider the responsibility of intellectuals, our basic concern must be their role in the creation and analysis of ideology. And in fact, Kristol's contrast between the unreasonable ideological types and the responsible experts is formulated in terms that immediately bring to mind Daniel Bell's interesting and influential essay on the "end of ideology,"[26] an essay which is as important for what it leaves unsaid as for its actual content. Bell presents and discusses the Marxist analysis of ideology as a mask for class interest, in particular quoting Marx's well-known description of the belief of the bourgeoisie "that the *special* conditions of its emancipation are the *general* conditions through which alone modern society can be saved and the class struggle avoided." He then argues that the age of ideology is ended, supplanted, at least in the West, by a general agreement that each issue must be settled on its own individual terms, within the framework of a welfare state in which, presumably, experts in the conduct of public affairs will have a prominent role. Bell is quite careful, however, to characterize the precise sense of "ideology" in which "ideologies are exhausted." He is referring only to ideology as "the conversion of ideas into social levers," to ideology as "a set of beliefs, infused with passion, . . . [which] . . . seeks to transform the whole of a way of life." The crucial words are "transform" and "convert

343

into social levers." Intellectuals in the West, he argues, have lost interest in converting ideas into social levers for the radical transformation of society. Now that we have achieved the pluralistic society of the welfare state, they see no further need for a radical transformation of society; we may tinker with our way of life here and there, but it would be wrong to try to modify it in any significant way. With this consensus of intellectuals, ideology is dead.

There are several striking facts about Bell's essay. First, he does not point out the extent to which this consensus of the intellectuals is self-serving. He does not relate his observation that, by and large, intellectuals have lost interest in "transforming the whole way of life" to the fact that they play an increasingly prominent role in running the welfare state; he does not relate their general satisfaction with the welfare state to the fact that, as he observes elsewhere, "America has become an affluent society, offering place . . . and prestige . . . to the onetime radicals." Secondly, he offers no serious argument to show that intellectuals are somehow "right" or "objectively justified" in reaching the consensus to which he alludes, with its rejection of the notion that society should be transformed. Indeed, although Bell is fairly sharp about the empty rhetoric of the "New Left," he seems to have a quite utopian faith that technical experts will be able to come to grips with the few problems that still remain; for example, the fact that labor is treated as a commodity, and the problems of "alienation."

It seems fairly obvious that the classical problems are very much with us; one might plausibly argue that they have even been enhanced in severity and scale. For example, the classical paradox of poverty in the midst of plenty is now an ever increasing problem on an international scale. Whereas one might

344

conceive, at least in principle, of a solution within national boundaries, a sensible idea as to how to transform international society in such a way as to cope with the vast and perhaps increasing human misery is hardly likely to develop within the framework of the intellectual consensus that Bell describes.

Thus it would seem natural to describe the consensus of Bell's intellectuals in somewhat different terms than his. Using the terminology of the first part of his essay, we might say that the welfare state technician finds justification for his special and prominent social status in his "science," specifically, in the claim that social science can support a technology of social tinkering on a domestic or international scale. He then takes a further step, proceeding, in a familiar way, to claim universal validity for what is in fact a class interest: he argues that the special conditions on which his claims to power and authority are based are, in fact, the general conditions through which alone modern society can be saved; that social tinkering within a welfare state framework must replace the commitment to the "total ideologies" of the past, ideologies which were concerned with a transformation of society. Having found his position of power, having achieved security and affluence, he has no further need for ideologies that look to radical change. The scholar-expert replaces the "free-floating intellectual" who "felt that the wrong values were being honored, and rejected the society," and who has now lost his political role (now, that is, that the right values are being honored).

Conceivably, it is correct that the technical experts who will (or hope to) manage the "postindustrial society" will be able to cope with the classic problems without a radical transformation of society. Just so, it is conceivably true that the bourgeoisie was right in regarding the special conditions of its emancipation

345

as the general conditions through which alone modern society would be saved. In either case, an argument is in order, and skepticism is justified where none appears.

Within the same framework of general utopianism, Bell goes on to pose the issue between welfare state scholar-experts and Third World ideologists in a rather curious way. He points out, quite correctly, that there is no issue of Communism, the content of that doctrine having been "long forgotten by friends and foes alike." Rather, he says, "the question is an older one: whether new societies can grow by building democratic institutions and allowing people to make choices—and sacrifices— voluntarily, or whether the new elites, heady with power, will impose totalitarian means to transform their countries." The question is an interesting one; it is odd, however, to see it referred to as "an older one." Surely he cannot be suggesting that the West chose the democratic way—for example, that in England during the industrial revolution, the farmers voluntarily made the choice of leaving the land, giving up cottage industry, becoming an industrial proletariat, and voluntarily decided, within the framework of the existing democratic institutions, to make the sacrifices that are graphically described in the classic literature on nineteenth-century industrial society. One may debate the question whether authoritarian control is necessary to permit capital accumulation in the underdeveloped world, but the Western model of development is hardly one that we can point to with any pride. It is perhaps not surprising to find a Walt Rostow referring to "the more humane processes [of industrialization] that Western values would suggest."[27] Those who have a serious concern for the problems that face backward countries and for the role that advanced industrial societies might, in principle, play in development and moderni-

zation must use somewhat more care in interpreting the significance of the Western experience.

Returning to the quite appropriate question, whether "new
societies can grow by building democratic institutions" or only
by totalitarian means, I think that honesty requires us to recognize that this question must be directed more to American intellectuals than to Third World ideologists. The backward countries have incredible, perhaps insurmountable problems, and
few available options; the United States has a wide range of
options, and has the economic and technological resources,
though evidently neither the intellectual nor the moral resources, to confront at least some of these problems. It is easy
for an American intellectual to deliver homilies on the virtues of
freedom and liberty, but if he is really concerned about, say,
Chinese totalitarianism or the burdens imposed on the Chinese
peasantry in forced industrialization, then he should face a task
that is infinitely more significant and challenging—the task of
creating, in the United States, the intellectual and moral climate, as well as the social and economic conditions, that would
permit this country to participate in modernization and development in a way commensurate with its material wealth and
technical capacity. Massive capital gifts to Cuba and China
might not succeed in alleviating the authoritarianism and terror
that tend to accompany early stages of capital accumulation,
but they are far more likely to have this effect than lectures on
democratic values. It is possible that even without "capitalist
encirclement" in its varying manifestations, the truly democratic
elements in revolutionary movements—in some instances so-
viets and collectives, for example—might be undermined by an
"elite" of bureaucrats and technical intelligentsia; but it is a
near certainty that the fact of capitalist encirclement, which all

347

revolutionary movements now have to face, will guarantee this result. The lesson, for those who are concerned to strengthen the democratic, spontaneous, and popular elements in developing societies, is quite clear. Lectures on the two-party system, or even the really substantial democratic values that have been in part realized in Western society, are a monstrous irrelevance in the face of the effort that is required to raise the level of culture in Western society to the point where it can provide a "social lever" for both economic development and the development of true democratic institutions in the Third World—and for that matter, at home as well.

A good case can be made for the conclusion that there is indeed something of a consensus among intellectuals who have already achieved power and affluence, or who sense that they can achieve them by "accepting society" as it is and promoting the values that are "being honored" in this society. And it is also true that this consensus is most noticeable among the scholar-experts who are replacing the free-floating intellectuals of the past. In the university, these scholar-experts construct a "value-free technology" for the solution of technical problems that arise in contemporary society,[28] taking a "responsible stance" towards these problems, in the sense noted earlier. This consensus among the responsible scholar-experts is the domestic analogue to that proposed, in the international arena, by those who justify the application of American power in Asia, whatever the human cost, on the grounds that it is necessary to contain the "expansion of China" (an "expansion" which is, to be sure, hypothetical for the time being)[29]—to translate from State Department Newspeak, on the grounds that it is essential to reverse the Asian nationalist revolutions, or at least to prevent them from spreading. The analogy becomes clear when we look carefully at the ways in which this proposal is formulated.

With his usual lucidity, Churchill outlined the general position in a remark to his colleague of the moment, Joseph Stalin, at Teheran in 1943: ". . . the government of the world must be entrusted to satisfied nations, who wished nothing more for themselves than what they had. If the world-government were in the hand of hungry nations, there would always be danger. But none of us had any reason to seek for anything more. The peace would be kept by peoples who lived in their own way and were not ambitious. Our power placed us above the rest. We were like rich men dwelling at peace within their habitations."[30]

For a translation of Churchill's biblical rhetoric into the jargon of contemporary social science, one may turn to the testimony of Charles Wolf, senior economist of the RAND Corporation, at the congressional committee hearings cited earlier:

> I am dubious that China's fears of encirclement are going to be abated, eased, relaxed in the long-term future. But I would hope that what we do in Southeast Asia would help to develop within the Chinese body politic more of a realism and willingness to live with this fear than to indulge it by support for liberation movements, which admittedly depend on a great deal more than external support . . . the operational question for American foreign policy is not whether that fear can be eliminated or substantially alleviated, but whether China can be faced with a structure of incentives, of penalties and rewards, of inducements that will make it willing to live with this fear.[31]

The point is further clarified by Thomas Schelling: "There is growing experience which the Chinese can profit from, that although the United States may be interested in encircling them, may be interested in defending nearby areas from them, it is, nevertheless, prepared to behave peaceably if they are."[32]

In short, we are prepared to live peaceably within our—to be sure, rather extensive—habitations. And quite naturally, we are offended by the undignified noises from the servants' quarters. If, let us say, a peasant-based revolutionary movement tries to achieve independence from foreign domination or to overthrow semifeudal structures supported by foreign powers, or if the Chinese irrationally refuse to respond properly to the schedule of reinforcement that we have prepared for them, if they object to being encircled by the benign and peace-loving "rich men" who control the territories on their borders as a natural right, then, evidently, we must respond to this belligerence with appropriate force.

It is this mentality that explains the frankness with which the United States government and its academic apologists defend the American refusal to permit a political settlement in Vietnam at a local level, a settlement based on the actual distribution of political forces. Even government experts freely admit that the National Liberation Front is the only "truly mass-based political party in South Vietnam";[33] that the NLF had "made a conscious and massive effort to extend political participation, even if it was manipulated, on the local level so as to involve the people in a self-contained, self-supporting revolution" (p. 374); and that this effort had been so successful that no political groups, "with the possible exception of the Buddhists, thought themselves equal in size and power to risk entering into a coalition, fearing that if they did the whale would swallow the minnow" (p. 362). Moreover, they concede that until the introduction of overwhelming American force, the NLF had insisted that the struggle "should be fought out at the political level and that the use of massed military might was in itself illegitimate. . . . The battleground was to be the minds and loyalties of the rural Vietnamese, the weapons were to be ideas" (pp. 91–92; cf. also pp. 93, 99–108, 155 f.); and correspondingly, that until mid-1964, aid from Hanoi "was largely confined to two areas—doc-

trinal know-how and leadership personnel" (p. 321). Captured
NLF documents contrast the enemy's "military superiority"
with their own "political superiority" (p. 106), thus fully confirming the analysis of American military spokesmen who define
our problem as how, "with considerable armed force but little
political power, [to] contain an adversary who has enormous
political force but only modest military power."[34]

Similarly, the most striking outcome of both the Honolulu
conference in February and the Manila conference in October
was the frank admission by high officials of the Saigon government that "they could not survive a 'peaceful settlement' that
left the Vietcong *political* structure in place even if the Vietcong guerrilla units were disbanded," that "they are not able to
compete *politically* with the Vietnamese Communists."[35] Thus,
Mohr continues, the Vietnamese demand a "pacification program" which will have as "its core . . . the destruction of the
clandestine Vietcong political structure and the creation of an
iron-like system of government political control over the population." And from Manila, the same correspondent, on October
23, quotes a high South Vietnamese official as saying: "Frankly,
we are not strong enough now to compete with the Communists
on a purely political basis. They are organized and disciplined.
The non-Communist nationalists are not—we do not have any
large, well-organized political parties and we do not yet have
unity. We cannot leave the Vietcong in existence." Officials in
Washington understand the situation very well. Thus Secretary
Rusk has pointed out that "if the Vietcong come to the conference table as full partners they will, in a sense, have been
victorious in the very aims that South Vietnam and the United
States are pledged to prevent" (January 28, 1966). Similarly,
Max Frankel reported from Washington: "Compromise has had
no appeal here because the Administration concluded long ago

that the non-Communist forces of South Vietnam could not long survive in a Saigon coalition with Communists. It is for that reason—and not because of an excessively rigid sense of proto-col—that Washington has steadfastly refused to deal with the Vietcong or recognize them as an independent political force."[36]

In short, we will—magnanimously—permit Vietcong repre-sentatives to attend negotiations, but only if they will agree to identify themselves as agents of a foreign power and thus forfeit the right to participate in a coalition government, a right which they have now been demanding for a half-dozen years. We know well that in any representative coalition, our chosen delegates could not last a day without the support of American arms. Therefore, we must increase American force and resist mean-ingful negotiations, until the day when a client government can exert both military and political control over its own population —a day which may never dawn, for as William Bundy has pointed out, we could never be sure of the security of a South-east Asia "from which the Western presence was effectively withdrawn." Thus if we were to "negotiate in the direction of solutions that are put under the label of neutralization," this would amount to capitulation to the Communists.[37] According to this reasoning, then, South Vietnam must remain, perma-nently, an American military base.

All of this is of course reasonable, so long as we accept the fundamental political axiom that the United States, with its traditional concern for the rights of the weak and downtrodden, and with its unique insight into the proper mode of develop-ment for backward countries, must have the courage and the persistence to impose its will by force until such time as other nations are prepared to accept these truths—or simply to aban-don hope.

If it is the responsibility of the intellectual to insist upon the truth, it is also his duty to see events in their historical perspective. Thus one must applaud the insistence of the Secretary of State on the importance of historical analogies, the Munich analogy, for example. As Munich showed, a powerful and aggressive nation with a fanatic belief in its manifest destiny will regard each victory, each extension of its power and authority, as a prelude to the next step. The matter was very well put by Adlai Stevenson, when he spoke of "the old, old route whereby expansive powers push at more and more doors, believing they will open, until, at the ultimate door, resistance is unavoidable and major war breaks out." Herein lies the danger of appeasement, as the Chinese tirelessly point out to the Soviet Union, which they claim is playing Chamberlain to our Hitler in Vietnam. Of course, the aggressiveness of liberal imperialism is not that of Nazi Germany, though the distinction may seem rather academic to a Vietnamese peasant who is being gassed or incinerated. We do not want to occupy Asia; we merely wish, to return to Mr. Wolf, "to help the Asian countries progress toward economic modernization, as relatively 'open' and stable societies, to which our access, as a country and as individual citizens, is free and comfortable."[38] The formulation is appropriate. Recent history shows that it makes little difference to us what form of government a country has as long as it remains an "open society," in our peculiar sense of this term—a society, that is, which remains open to American economic penetration or political control. If it is necessary to approach genocide in Vietnam to achieve this objective, then this is the price we must pay in defense of freedom and the rights of man.

It is, no doubt, superfluous to discuss at length the ways in which we assist other countries to progress towards open societies "to which our access is free and comfortable." One enlightening example is discussed in the recent congressional hearings from which I have now quoted several times, in the testimony of Willem Holst and Robert Meagher, representing the Standing Committee on India of the Business Council for International Understanding.[39] As Mr. Meagher points out: "If it was possible, India would probably prefer to import technicians and know-how rather than foreign corporations. Such is not possible; therefore India accepts foreign capital as a necessary evil." Of course, "the question of private capital investment in India . . . would be no more than a theoretical exercise" had the groundwork for such investment not been laid by foreign aid, and were it not that "necessity has forced a modification in India's approach to private foreign capital." But now, "India's attitude toward private foreign investment is undergoing a substantial change. From a position of resentment and ambivalence, it is evolving toward an acceptance of its necessity. As the necessity becomes more and more evident, the ambivalence will probably be replaced by a more accommodating attitude." Mr. Holst contributes what is "perhaps a typical case history," namely, "the plan under which it was proposed that the Indian Government in partnership with a United States private consortium was to have increased fertilizer production by a million tons per year, which is just double presently installed capacity in all of India. The unfortunate demise of this ambitious plan may be attributed in large part to the failure of both Government and business to find a workable and mutually acceptable solution within the framework of the well-publicized 10 business incentives." The difficulty here was in connection with the percentage of equity ownership. Obviously, "fertilizers are desperately needed in India." Equally obviously, the consortium "insisted that to get the proper kind of control majority ownership was in fact needed." But "the Indian Government officially insisted that they shall have majority ownership," and "in something so complex it was felt that it would be a self-defeating thing."

Fortunately, this particular story has a happy ending. The remarks just quoted were made in February 1966, and within a few weeks, the Indian government had seen the light, as we read in a series of reports in the *New York Times*. The criticism, inside India, that "the American Government and the World Bank would like to arrogate to themselves the right to lay down the framework in which our economy must function," was stilled (April 24); and the Indian government accepted the conditions for resumed economic aid, namely, "that India provide easier terms for foreign private investment in fertilizer plants" and that the American investors "have substantial management rights" (May 14). The development is summarized in a dispatch datelined April 28, from New Delhi, in these terms:

> There are signs of change. The Government has granted easy terms to private foreign investors in the fertilizer industry, is thinking about decontrolling several more industries and is ready to liberalize import policy if it gets sufficient foreign aid. . . . Much of what is happening now is a result of steady pressure from the United States and the International Bank for Reconstruction and Development, which for the last year have been urging a substantial freeing of the Indian economy and a greater scope for private enterprise. The United States pressure, in particular, has been highly effective here because the United States provides by far the largest part of the foreign exchange needed to finance India's development and keep the wheels of industry turning. Call them "strings," call them "conditions" or whatever one likes, India has little choice now but to agree to many of the terms that the United States, through the World Bank, is putting on its aid. For India simply has nowhere else to turn.

The heading of the article refers to this development as India's "drift from socialism to pragmatism."

Even this was not enough, however. Thus we read a few

months later, in the *Christian Science Monitor* (December 5), that American entrepreneurs insist "on importing all equipment and machinery when India has a tested capacity to meet some of their requirements. They have insisted on importing liquid ammonia, a basic raw material, rather than using indigenous naphtha which is abundantly available. They have laid down restrictions about pricing, distribution, profits, and management control." The Indian reaction, I have already cited (see page 336).

In such ways as these, we help India develop towards an open society, one which, in Walt Rostow's words, has a proper understanding of "the core of the American ideology," namely, "the sanctity of the individual in relation to the state." And in this way, too, we refute the simpleminded view of those Asians who, to continue with Rostow's phrasing, "believe or half-believe that the West has been driven to create and then to cling to its imperial holdings by the inevitable workings of capitalist economies."[40]

In fact, a major postwar scandal is developing in India as the United States, cynically capitalizing on India's current torture, applies its economic power to implement India's "drift from socialism to pragmatism."

In pursuing the aim of helping other countries to progress towards open societies, with no thought of territorial aggrandizement, we are breaking no new ground. Hans Morgenthau has aptly described our traditional policy towards China as one of favoring "what you might call freedom of competition with regard to the exploitation of China."[41] In fact, few imperialist powers have had explicit territorial ambitions. Thus in 1784, the British Parliament announced that "to pursue schemes of conquest and extension of dominion in India are measures repugnant to the wish, honor, and policy of this nation." Shortly after, the conquest of India was in full swing. A century later, Britain announced its intentions in Egypt under the slogan "Intervention, Reform, Withdrawal." It is unnecessary to comment on which parts of this promise were fulfilled, within the next half century. In 1936, on the eve of hostilities in North China, the Japanese stated their Basic Principles of National Policy. These included the use of moderate and peaceful means to extend her strength, to promote social and economic development, to eradicate the menace of Communism, to correct the aggressive policies of the great powers, and to secure her position as the stabilizing power in East Asia. Even in 1937, the Japanese government had "no territorial designs upon China." In short, we follow a well-trodden path.

It is useful to remember, incidentally, that the United States was apparently quite willing, as late as 1939, to negotiate a commercial treaty with Japan and arrive at a *modus vivendi* if Japan would "change her attitude and practice towards our rights and interests in China," as Secretary Hull put it. The bombing of Chungking and the rape of Nanking were rather unpleasant, it is true, but what was really important was our rights and interests in China, as the responsible, unhysterical men of the day saw quite clearly. It was the closing of the Open Door by Japan that led inevitably to the Pacific war, just as it is the closing of the Open Door by "Communist" China itself that may very well lead to the next, and no doubt last, Pacific war.

Quite often, the statements of sincere and devoted technical experts give surprising insight into the intellectual attitudes that lie in the background of the latest savagery. Consider, for example, the following comment by economist Richard Lindholm, in 1959, expressing his frustration over the failure of economic development in "free Vietnam": ". . . the use of American aid is determined by how the Vietnamese use their incomes and their savings. The fact that a large portion of the Vietnamese imports financed with American aid are either consumer goods or raw materials used rather directly to meet consumer demands is an indication that the Vietnamese people desire these goods, for they have shown their desire by their willingness to use their piasters to purchase them."[42]

In short, the Vietnamese *people* desire Buicks and air conditioners, rather than sugar-refining equipment or road-building machinery, as they have shown by their behavior in a free market. And however much we may deplore their free choice, we must allow the people to have their way. Of course, there are also those two-legged beasts of burden that one stumbles on in the countryside, but as any graduate student of political science can explain, they are not part of a responsible modernizing elite, and therefore have only a superficial biological resemblance to the human race.

In no small measure, it is attitudes like this that lie behind the butchery in Vietnam, and we had better face up to them with candor, or we will find our government leading us towards a "final solution" in Vietnam, and in the many Vietnams that inevitably lie ahead.

Let me finally return to Macdonald and the responsibility of intellectuals. Macdonald quotes an interview with a death-camp paymaster who bursts into tears when told that the Russians would hang him. "Why should they? What have I done?" he asked. Macdonald concludes: "Only those who are willing to resist authority themselves when it conflicts too intolerably with their personal moral code, only they have the right to condemn the death-camp paymaster." The question "What have I done?"

is one that we may well ask ourselves, as we read, each day, of fresh atrocities in Vietnam—as we create, or mouth, or tolerate the deceptions that will be used to justify the next defense of freedom.

Notes

1. Such a research project has now been undertaken and published as a "Citizens' White Paper": F. Schurmann, P. D. Scott, and R. Zelnik, *The Politics of Escalation in Vietnam* (New York, Fawcett World Library, and Boston, Beacon Press, 1966). For further evidence of American rejection of United Nations initiatives for diplomatic settlement, just prior to the major escalation of February 1965, see Mario Rossi, "The US Rebuff to U Thant," *New York Review of Books*, November 17, 1966. See also Theodore Draper, "How Not To Negotiate," *New York Review of Books*, May 4, 1967. There is further documentary evidence of NLF attempts to establish a coalition government and to neutralize the area, all rejected by the United States and its Saigon ally, in Douglas Pike, *Viet Cong* (Cambridge, Mass., The M.I.T. Press, 1966). In reading material of this latter sort one must be especially careful to distinguish between the evidence presented and the "conclusions" that are asserted, for reasons noted briefly below (see note 33).

It is interesting to see the first, somewhat oblique published reactions to *The Politics of Escalation* by those who defend our right to conquer South Vietnam and institute a government of our choice. For example, Robert Scalapino (*New York Times Magazine*, December 11, 1966) argues that the thesis of the book implies that our leaders are "diabolical." Since no right-thinking person can believe this, the thesis is refuted. To assume otherwise would betray "irresponsibility," in a unique sense of this term—a sense that gives an ironic twist to the title of this chapter. He goes on to point out the alleged central weakness in the argument of the book, namely, the failure to perceive that a serious attempt on our part to pursue the possibilities for a diplomatic settlement would have been interpreted by our adversaries as a sign of weakness.

359

2. *New York Times,* October 14, 1965.

3. *Ibid.,* February 6, 1966.

4. *Boston Globe,* November 19, 1965.

5. At other times, Schlesinger does indeed display admirable scholarly caution. For example, in his introduction to *The Politics of Escalation* he admits that there may have been "flickers of interest in negotiations" on the part of Hanoi. As to the administration's lies about negotiations and its repeated actions undercutting tentative initiatives towards negotiations, he comments only that the authors may have underestimated military necessity and that future historians may prove them wrong. This caution and detachment must be compared with Schlesinger's attitude towards renewed study of the origins of the Cold War: in a letter to the *New York Review of Books,* October 20, 1966, he remarks that it is time to "blow the whistle" on revisionist attempts to show that the Cold War may have been the consequence of something more than mere Communist belligerence. We are to believe, then, that the relatively straightforward matter of the origins of the Cold War is settled beyond discussion, whereas the much more complex issue of why the United States shies away from a negotiated settlement in Vietnam must be left to future historians to ponder.

It is useful to bear in mind that the United States government itself is on occasion much less diffident in explaining why it refuses to contemplate a meaningful negotiated settlement. As is freely admitted, this solution would leave it without power to control the situation. See, for example, note 37.

6. Arthur M. Schlesinger, Jr., *A Thousand Days: John F. Kennedy in the White House* (Boston, Houghton Mifflin Company, 1965), p. 421.

7. Walt W. Rostow, *The View from the Seventh Floor* (New York, Harper & Row, Publishers, 1964), p. 149. See also his *United States in the World Arena* (New York, Harper & Row, Publishers, 1960), p. 244: "Stalin, exploiting the disruption and weakness of the postwar world, pressed out from the expanded base he had won during the Second World War in an effort to gain the balance of power in Eurasia . . . turning to the East, to back Mao and to enflame the North Korean and Indochinese Communists. . . ."

8. For example, the article by CIA analyst George Carver, "The Faceless Viet Cong," in *Foreign Affairs,* Vol. 44 (April 1966), pp. 347–72. See also note 33.

9. Cf. Jean Lacouture, *Vietnam: Between Two Truces* (New York, Random House, 1966), p. 21. Diem's analysis of the situation was shared by Western observers at the time. See, for example, the comments of William Henderson, Far Eastern specialist and executive, Council on Foreign Relations, in Richard W. Lindholm, ed., *Vietnam: The First Five Years* (East Lansing, Michigan State University Press, 1959). He notes "the growing alienation of the intelligentsia," "the renewal of armed dissidence in the South," the fact that "security has noticeably deteriorated in the last two years," all as a result of Diem's "grim dictatorship," and predicts "a steady worsening of the political climate in free Vietnam, culminating in unforeseen disasters."

10. See Bernard Fall, "Vietnam in the Balance," *Foreign Affairs*, Vol. 45 (October 1966), pp. 1–18.

11. Stalin was pleased neither by the Titoist tendencies inside the Greek Communist party nor by the possibility that a Balkan federation might develop under Titoist leadership. It is nevertheless conceivable that Stalin supported the Greek guerrillas at some stage of the rebellion, in spite of the difficulty in obtaining firm documentary evidence. Needless to say, no elaborate study is necessary to document the British or American role in this civil conflict, from late 1944. See D. G. Kousoulas, *The Price of Freedom* (Syracuse, N.Y., Syracuse University Press, 1953), and *Revolution and Defeat* (New York, Oxford University Press, 1965), for serious study of these events from a strongly anti-Communist point of view.

12. For a detailed account, see James Warburg, *Germany: Key to Peace* (Cambridge, Mass., Harvard University Press, 1953), pp. 189 f. Warburg concludes that apparently "the Kremlin was now prepared to accept the creation of an All-German democracy in the Western sense of that word," whereas the Western powers, in their response, "frankly admitted their plan 'to secure the participation of Germany in a purely defensive European community'" (i.e. NATO).

13. *The United States in the World Arena*, pp. 344–45. Incidentally, those who quite rightly deplore the brutal suppression of the East German and Hungarian revolutions would do well to remember that these scandalous events might have been avoided had the United States been willing to consider proposals for neutralization of Central Europe. Some of George Kennan's recent statements provide interesting commentary on this matter, for example, his comments on the falsity, from the outset, of the assumption that the USSR intended to

attack or intimidate by force the Western half of the continent and that it was deterred by American force, and his remarks on the sterility and general absurdity of the demand for unilateral Soviet withdrawal from East Germany together with "the inclusion of a united Germany as a major component in a Western defense system based primarily on nuclear weaponry" (Edward Reed, ed., *Peace on Earth* [New York, Pocket Books, 1965]).

It is worth noting that historical fantasy of the sort illustrated in Rostow's remarks has become a regular State Department specialty. Thus we have Thomas Mann justifying our Dominican intervention as a response to actions of the "Sino-Soviet military bloc." Or, to take a more considered statement, we have William Bundy's analysis of stages of development of Communist ideology in his Pomona College address, February 12, 1966, in which he characterizes the Soviet Union in the 1920s and early 1930s as "in a highly militant and aggressive phase." What is frightening about fantasy, as distinct from outright falsification, is the possibility that it may be sincere and may actually serve as the basis for formation of policy.

14. *New York Times*, February 6, 1966.

15. *United States Policy Toward Asia,* Hearings before the Subcommittee on the Far East and the Pacific of the Committee on Foreign Affairs, House of Representatives (Washington, Government Printing Office, 1966), p. 89.

16. *New York Times Book Review,* November 20, 1966. Such comments call to mind the remarkable spectacle of President Kennedy counseling Cheddi Jagan on the dangers of entering into a trading relationship "which brought a country into a condition of economic dependence." The reference, of course, is to the dangers in commercial relations with the Soviet Union. See Schlesinger, *A Thousand Days,* p. 776.

17. *A Thousand Days,* p. 252.

18. *Ibid.,* p. 769.

19. Though this too is imprecise. One must recall the real character of the Trujillo regime to appreciate the full cynicism of Kennedy's "realistic" analysis.

20. Walt W. Rostow and R. W. Hatch, *An American Policy in Asia* (New York, Technology Press and John Wiley & Sons, Inc., 1955).

21. "End of Either/Or," *Foreign Affairs,* Vol. 45 (January 1967), pp. 189–201.

22. *Christian Science Monitor,* November 26, 1966.
23. *Ibid.,* December 5, 1966.
24. Although, to maintain perspective, we should recall that in his wildest moments, Alfred Rosenberg spoke of the elimination of thirty million Slavs, not the imposition of mass starvation on a quarter of the human race. Incidentally, the analogy drawn here is highly "irresponsible," in the technical sense of this neologism discussed earlier. That is, it is based on the assumption that statements and actions of Americans are subject to the same standards and open to the same interpretations as those of anyone else.
25. *New York Times,* February 6, 1966. What is more, Goldberg continues, the United States is not certain that all of these are voluntary adherents. This is not the first such demonstration of Communist duplicity. Another example was seen in the year 1962, when according to United States government sources 15,000 guerrillas suffered 30,000 casualties. See Arthur Schlesinger, *A Thousand Days,* p. 982.
26. Reprinted in a collection of essays entitled *The End of Ideology: On the Exhaustion of Political Ideas in the Fifties* (New York, The Free Press, 1960), pp. 369–75. I have no intention here of entering into the full range of issues that have been raised in the discussion of the "end of ideology" for the past dozen years. It is difficult to see how a rational person could quarrel with many of the theses that have been put forth, e.g., that at a certain historical moment the "politics of civility" is appropriate, and perhaps efficacious; that one who advocates action (or inaction—a matter less frequently noted) has a responsibility to assess its social cost; that dogmatic fanaticism and "secular religions" should be combated (or if possible ignored); that technical solutions to problems should be implemented, where possible; that *"le dogmatisme idéologique devait disparaître pour que les idées reprissent vie"* (Aron); and so on. Since this is sometimes taken to be an expression of an "anti-Marxist" position, it is worth keeping in mind that such sentiments as these have no bearing on non-Bolshevik Marxism, as represented, for example, by such figures as Luxemburg, Pannekoek, Korsch, Arthur Rosenberg, and many others.
27. Rostow and Hatch, *op. cit.,* p. 10.
28. The extent to which this "technology" is value-free is hardly very important, given the clear commitments of those who apply it. The problems with which research is concerned are those posed by the Pentagon or the great corporations, not, say, by the revolutionaries of

northeast Brazil or by SNCC. Nor am I aware of a research project devoted to the problem of how poorly armed guerrillas might more effectively resist a brutal and devastating military technology—surely the kind of problem that would have interested the free-floating intellectual who is now hopelessly out of date.

29. In view of the unremitting propaganda barrage on "Chinese expansionism," perhaps a word of comment is in order. Typical of American propaganda on this subject is Adlai Stevenson's assessment, shortly before his death (cf. *New York Times Magazine*, March 13, 1966): "So far, the new Communist 'dynasty' has been very aggressive. Tibet was swallowed, India attacked, the Malays had to fight 12 years to resist a 'national liberation' they could receive from the British by a more peaceful route. Today, the apparatus of infiltration and aggression is already at work in North Thailand."

As to Malaya, Stevenson is probably confusing ethnic Chinese with the government of China. Those concerned with the actual events would agree with Harry Miller, in *Communist Menace in Malaya* (New York, Frederick A. Praeger, Inc., 1954), p. 230, that "Communist China continues to show little interest in the Malayan affair beyond its usual fulminations via Peking Radio." There are various harsh things that one might say about Chinese behavior in what the Sino-Indian Treaty of 1954 refers to as "the Tibet region of China," but it is no more proof of a tendency towards expansionism than is the behavior of the Indian government with regard to the Naga and Mizo tribesmen. As to North Thailand, "the apparatus of infiltration" may well be at work, though there is little reason to suppose it to be Chinese—and it is surely not unrelated to the American use of Thailand as a base for its attack on Vietnam. This reference is the sheerest hypocrisy.

The "attack on India" grew out of a border dispute that began several years after the Chinese had completed a road from Tibet to Sinkiang in an area so remote from Indian control that the Indians learned about this operation only from the Chinese press. According to American Air Force maps, the disputed area is in Chinese territory. Cf. Alastair Lamb, *China Quarterly*, No. 23 (July–September 1965), pp. 202–7. To this distinguished authority, "it seems unlikely that the Chinese have been working out some master plan . . . to take over the Indian sub-continent lock, stock and overpopulated barrel." Rather, he thinks it likely that the Chinese were probably unaware that India even claimed the territory through which the road passed. After the Chinese military victory, Chinese troops were, in most areas, withdrawn beyond the McMahon Line, a border which the British had attempted to impose on China in 1914 but which has never been recognized by China (Nationalist or Communist), the United States, or any other government.

It is remarkable that a person in a responsible position could describe all of this as Chinese expansionism. In fact, it is absurd to debate the hypothetical aggressiveness of a China surrounded by American missiles and a still expanding network of military bases backed by an enormous American expeditionary force in Southeast Asia. It is conceivable that at some future time a powerful China may be expansionist. We may speculate about such possibilities if we wish, but it is American aggressiveness that is the central fact of current politics.

30. W. S. Churchill, *The Second World War*, Vol. 5, *Closing the Ring* (Boston, Houghton Mifflin Company, 1951), p. 382.

31. *United States Policy Toward Asia*, p. 104. See note 15.

32. *Ibid.*, p. 105.

33. Douglas Pike, *op. cit.*, p. 110. This book, written by a foreign service officer working at the Center for International Studies, MIT, poses a contrast between our side, which sympathizes with "the usual revolutionary stirrings . . . around the world because they reflect inadequate living standards or oppressive and corrupt governments," and the backers of "revolutionary guerrilla warfare," which "opposes the aspirations of people while apparently furthering them, manipulates the individual by persuading him to manipulate himself." Revolutionary guerrilla warfare is "an imported product, revolution from the outside" (other examples besides the Vietcong are "Stalin's exportation of armed revolution," the Haganah in Palestine, and the Irish Republican Army—see pp. 32–33). The Vietcong could not be an indigenous movement since it has "a social construction program of such scope and ambition that of necessity it must have been created in Hanoi" (p. 76—but on pp. 77–79 we read that "organizational activity had gone on intensively and systematically for several years" before the Lao Dong party in Hanoi had made its decision "to begin building an organization"). On p. 80 we find that "such an effort had to be the child of the North," even though elsewhere we read of the prominent role of the Cao Dai (p. 74), "the first major social group to begin actively opposing the Diem government" (p. 222), and of the Hoa

Hao sect, "another early and major participant in the NLF" (p. 69). Pike takes it as proof of Communist duplicity that in the South the party insisted it was "Marxist-Leninist," thus "indicating philosophic but not political allegiance," whereas in the North it described itself as a "Marxist-Leninist organization," thus "indicating that it was in the main-stream of the world-wide Communist movement" (p. 150). And so on. Also revealing is the contempt for "Cinderella and all the other fools [who] could still believe there was magic in the mature world if one mumbled the secret incantation: solidarity, union, concord"; for the "gullible, misled people" who were "turning the countryside into a bedlam, toppling one Saigon government after another, confounding the Americans"; for the "mighty force of people" who in their mindless innocence thought that "the meek, at last, were to inherit the earth," that "riches would be theirs and all in the name of justice and virtue." One can appreciate the chagrin with which a sophisticated Western political scientist must view this "sad and awesome spectacle."

34. Lacouture, *op. cit.*, p. 188. The same military spokesman goes on, ominously, to say that this is the problem confronting us throughout Asia, Africa, and Latin America, and that we must find the "proper response."

35. Charles Mohr, *New York Times*, February 11, 1966. Italics mine.

36. *New York Times*, February 18, 1966.

37. William Bundy, "The United States and Asia," in Alastair Buchan, ed., *China and the Peace of Asia* (New York, Frederick A. Praeger, Inc., 1965), pp. 29–30.

38. *Op. cit.*, p. 80.

39. *United States Policy Toward Asia*, pp. 191–201, passim.

40. *An American Policy in Asia*, p. 10.

41. *United States Policy Toward Asia*, p. 128.

42. Lindholm, *op. cit.*, p. 322.

ON RESISTANCE

Several weeks after the demonstrations in Washington, I am still trying to sort out my impressions of a week whose quality is difficult to capture or express. Perhaps some personal reflections may be useful to others who share my instinctive distaste for activism, but who find themselves edging towards an unwanted but almost inevitable crisis.

This article first appeared in the *New York Review of Books*, December 7, 1967. It is reprinted with a few revisions. The demonstrations referred to took place at the Justice Department and the Pentagon, on the weekend of October 19–21, 1967. The draft card turn-in at the Justice Department was one of the events that led to the sentencing of Dr. Benjamin Spock, Rev. William Sloane Coffin, Mitchell Goodman, and Michael Ferber to two-year prison sentences for "conspiracy." For details, see Noam Chomsky, Paul Lauter, and Florence Howe, "Reflections on a Political Trial," *New York Review of Books*, August 22, 1968, pp. 23–30. The Pentagon demonstration, which by some estimates involved several hundred thousand people, was a remarkable, unforgettable manifestation of opposition to the war. The spirit and character of the demonstrations are captured, with marvelous accuracy and perception, in Norman Mailer's *The Armies of the Night* (New York, New American Library, 1968).

For many of the participants, the Washington demonstrations symbolized the transition "from dissent to resistance." I will return to this slogan and its meaning, but I want to make clear at the outset that I do feel it to be not only accurate with respect to the mood of the demonstrations but, properly interpreted, appropriate to the present state of protest against the war. There is an irresistible dynamics to such protest. One may begin by writing articles and giving speeches about the war, by helping in many ways to create an atmosphere of concern and outrage. A courageous few will turn to direct action, refusing to take their place alongside the "good Germans" we have all learned to despise. Some will be forced to this decision when they are called up for military service. The dissenting senators, writers, and professors will watch as young men refuse to serve in the armed forces, in a war that they detest. What then? Can those who write and speak against the war take refuge in the fact that they have not urged or encouraged draft resistance, but have merely helped to develop a climate of opinion in which any decent person will want to refuse to take part in a miserable war? It is a very thin line. Nor is it very easy to watch from a position of safety while others are forced to take a grim and painful step. The fact is that most of the one thousand draft cards and other documents turned in to the Justice Department on October 20 came from men who can escape military service but who insisted on sharing the fate of those who are less privileged. In such ways the circle of resistance widens. Quite apart from this, no one can fail to see that to the extent that he restricts his protest, to the extent that he rejects actions that are open to him, he accepts complicity in what the government does. Some will act on this realization, posing sharply a moral issue that no person of conscience can evade.

On Monday, October 16, on the Boston Common I listened as

Howard Zinn explained why he felt ashamed to be an American. I watched as several hundred young men, some of them my students, made a terrible decision which no young person should have to face: to sever their connection with the Selective Service System. The week ended, the following Monday, with a quiet discussion in Cambridge in which I heard estimates, by an academic consultant to the Department of Defense, of the nuclear megatonnage that would be necessary to "take out" North Vietnam ("Some will find this shocking, but . . ."; "No civilian in the government is suggesting this, to my knowledge . . ."; "Let's not use emotional words like 'destruction' "; etc.), and listened to a leading expert on Soviet affairs who explained how the men in the Kremlin are watching very carefully to determine whether wars of national liberation can succeed—if so, they will support them all over the world. (Try pointing out to such an expert that on these assumptions, if the men in the Kremlin are rational, they will surely support dozens of such wars right now, since at a small cost they can confound the American military and tear our society to shreds—you will be told that you don't understand the Russian soul.)

The weekend of the peace demonstrations in Washington left impressions that are vivid and intense, but unclear to me in their implications. The dominant memory is of the scene itself, of tens of thousands of young people surrounding what they believe to be—I must add that I agree—the most hideous institution on this earth and demanding that it stop imposing misery and destruction. Tens of thousands of *young* people. This I find hard to comprehend. It is pitiful but true that by an overwhelming margin it is the young who are crying out in horror at what we all see happening, the young who are being beaten when they stand their ground, and the young who have to decide whether to accept jail or exile, or to fight in a hideous

369

war. They have to face this decision alone, or almost alone. We should ask ourselves why this is so.

Why, for example, does Senator Mansfield feel "ashamed for the image they have portrayed of this country," and not feel ashamed for the image of this country portrayed by the institution these young people were confronting, an institution directed by a sane and mild and eminently reasonable man who can testify calmly before Congress that the amount of ordnance expended in Vietnam has surpassed the total expended in Germany and Italy in World War II? Why is it that Senator Mansfield can speak in ringing phrases about those who are not living up to our commitment to "a government of laws"—referring to a small group of demonstrators, not to the ninety-odd responsible men on the Senate floor who are watching, with full knowledge, as the state they serve clearly, flagrantly violates the explicit provisions of the United Nations Charter, the supreme law of the land? He knows quite well that prior to our invasion of Vietnam there was no armed attack against any state. It was Senator Mansfield, after all, who informed us that "when the sharp increase in the American military effort began in early 1965, it was estimated that only about 400 North Vietnamese soldiers were among the enemy forces in the South which totaled 140,000 at that time"; and it is the Mansfield Report from which we learn that at that time there were 34,000 American soldiers already in South Vietnam, in violation of our "solemn commitment" at Geneva in 1954.

The point should be pursued. After the first International Days of Protest in October 1965, Senator Mansfield criticized the "sense of utter irresponsibility" shown by the demonstrators. He had nothing to say then, nor has he since, about the "sense of utter irresponsibility" shown by Senator Mansfield and others who stand by quietly and vote appropriations as the cities and villages of North Vietnam are demolished, as millions of refugees in the South are driven from their homes by American bombardment. He has nothing to say about the moral standards or the respect for law of those who have permitted this tragedy.

I speak of Senator Mansfield precisely because he is not a breast-beating superpatriot who wants America to rule the world, but is rather an American intellectual in the best sense, a scholarly and reasonable man—the kind of man who is the terror of our age. Perhaps this is merely a personal reaction, but when I look at what is happening to our country, what I find most terrifying is not Curtis LeMay, with his cheerful suggestion that we bomb our "enemies" back into the Stone Age, but rather the calm disquisitions of the political scientists on just how much force will be necessary to achieve our ends, or just what form of government will be acceptable to us in Vietnam. What I find terrifying is the detachment and equanimity with which we view and discuss an unbearable tragedy. We all know that if Russia or China were guilty of what we have done in Vietnam, we would be exploding with moral indignation at these monstrous crimes.

There was, I think, a serious miscalculation in the planning of the Washington demonstrations. It was expected that the march to the Pentagon would be followed by a number of speeches, and that those who were committed to civil disobedience would then separate themselves from the crowd and go to the Pentagon, a few hundred yards away across an open field. I had decided not to take part in civil disobedience, and I do not know in detail what had been planned. As everyone must realize, it is very hard to distinguish rationalization from rationality in such matters. I felt, however, that the first large-scale acts of civil disobedience should be more specifically defined, more

371

clearly in support of those who are refusing to serve in Vietnam, on whom the real burden of dissent must inevitably fall. While appreciating the point of view of those who wished to express their hatred of the war in a more explicit way, I was not convinced that civil disobedience at the Pentagon would be either meaningful or effective.

In any event, what actually happened was rather different from what anyone had anticipated. A few thousand people gathered for the speeches, but the mass of marchers went straight on to the Pentagon, some because they were committed to direct action, many because they were simply swept along. From the speakers' platform where I stood it was difficult to determine just what was taking place at the Pentagon. All we could see was the surging of the crowd. From secondhand reports, I understand that the marchers passed through and around the front line of troops and took up a position, which they maintained, on the steps of the Pentagon. It soon became obvious that it was wrong for the few organizers of the march and the mostly middle-aged group that had gathered near them to remain at the speakers' platform while the demonstrators themselves, most of them quite young, were at the Pentagon. (I recall seeing near the platform Robert Lowell, Dwight Macdonald, Monsignor Rice, Sidney Lens, Benjamin Spock and his wife, Dagmar Wilson, Donald Kalish.) Dave Dellinger suggested that we try to approach the Pentagon. We found a place not yet blocked by the demonstrators, and walked up to the line of troops standing a few feet from the building. Dellinger suggested that those of us who had not yet spoken at the rally talk directly to the soldiers through a small portable sound system. From this point on, my impressions are rather fragmentary. Monsignor Rice spoke, and I followed. As I was speaking, the line of soldiers advanced, moving past me—a rather odd experience. I don't recall just what I was saying. The gist was, I suppose, that we were there because we didn't want the soldiers to kill and be killed, but I do remember feeling that the way I was putting it seemed silly and irrelevant.

The advancing line of soldiers had partially scattered the small group that had come with Dellinger. Those of us who had been left behind the line of soldiers regrouped, and Dr. Spock began to speak. Almost at once, another line of soldiers emerged from somewhere, this time in a tightly massed formation, rifles in hand, and moved slowly forward. We sat down. As I mentioned earlier, I had no intention of taking part in any act of civil disobedience, until that moment. But when that grotesque organism began slowly advancing—more grotesque because its cells were recognizable human beings—it became obvious that one could not permit that thing to dictate what one was going to do. I was arrested at that point by a federal marshal, presumably for obstructing the soldiers (the technical term for this behavior is "disorderly conduct") I should add that the soldiers, so far as I could see (which was not very far), seemed rather unhappy about the whole matter, and were being about as gentle as one can be when ordered (I presume this was the order) to kick and club passive, quiet people who refuse to move. The federal marshals, predictably, were very different. They reminded me of the police officers I had seen in a Jackson, Mississippi, jail several summers ago, who had laughed when an old man showed us a bloody homemade bandage on his leg and tried to describe to us how he had been beaten by the police. In Washington, the ones who got the worst of it at the hands of the marshals were the young boys and girls, particularly boys with long hair. Nothing seemed to bring out the marshals' sadism more than the sight of a boy with long hair. Yet, although I witnessed some acts of violence by the marshals, their behavior largely seemed to range from indifference to petty nastiness. For example, we were kept in a police van for an hour or two with the doors closed and only a few air holes for ventilation—one can't be too careful with such ferocious criminal types.

In the prison dormitory and after my release I heard many stories, which I feel sure are authentic, of the courage of the young people, many of whom were quite frightened by the terrorism that began late at night after the TV cameramen and most of the press had left. They sat quietly hour after hour through the cold night; many were kicked and beaten and dragged across police lines (more "disorderly conduct"). I also heard stories, distressing ones, of provocation of the troops by the demonstrators—usually, it seems, those who were not in the front rows. Surely this was indefensible. Soldiers are unwitting instruments of terror; one does not blame or attack the club that is used to bludgeon someone to death. They are also human beings, with sensibilities to which one can perhaps appeal. There is in fact strong evidence that one soldier, perhaps three or four, refused to obey orders and was placed under arrest. The soldiers, after all, are in much the same position as the draft resisters. If they obey orders, they become brutalized by what they do; if they do not, the personal consequences are severe. It is a situation that deserves compassion, not abuse. But we should retain a sense of proportion in the matter. Everything that I saw or heard indicates that the demonstrators played only a small role in initiating the considerable violence that occurred.

The argument that resistance to the war should remain strictly nonviolent seems to me overwhelming. As a tactic, violence is absurd. No one can compete with the government in this arena, and the resort to violence, which will surely fail, will simply frighten and alienate some who can be reached, and will further encourage the ideologists and administrators of forceful repression. What is more, one hopes that participants in non-violent resistance will themselves become human beings of a more admirable sort. No one can fail to be impressed by the personal qualities of those who have grown to maturity in the civil rights movement. Whatever else it may have accomplished, the civil rights movement has made an inestimable contribution to American society in transforming the lives and characters of those who took part in it. Perhaps a program of principled, nonviolent resistance can do the same for many others, in the particular circumstances that we face today. It is not impossible that this may save the country from a terrible future, from yet another generation of men who think it clever to discuss the bombing of North Vietnam as a question of tactics and cost-effectiveness, or who support our attempt to conquer South Vietnam, with the human cost that they well know, blandly asserting that "our primary motivation is self-interest—the self-interest of our own country in this shrinking world" (Citizens Committee for Peace with Freedom, *New York Times*, October 26, 1967).

Returning to the demonstrations, I must admit that I was relieved to find people whom I had respected for years in the prison dormitory—Norman Mailer, Jim Peck, Dave Dellinger, and a number of others. I think it was reassuring to many of the kids who were there to be able to feel that they were not totally disconnected from a world that they knew and from people whom they admired. It was moving to see that defenseless young people who had a great deal to lose were willing to be jailed for what they believed—young instructors from state universities, college kids who have a very bright future if they are willing to toe the line, many others whom I could not identify.

What comes next? Obviously, that is the question on everyone's mind. The slogan "From Dissent to Resistance" makes sense, I think, but I hope it is not taken to imply that dissent should cease. Dissent and resistance are not alternatives but activities that should reinforce each other. There is no reason why those who take part in tax refusal, draft resistance, and other forms of resistance should not also speak to church groups or town forums, or become involved in electoral politics to support peace candidates or referenda on the war. In my experience, it has often been those committed to resistance who have been most deeply involved in such attempts at persuasion. Putting aside the matter of resistance for a moment, I think it should be emphasized that the days of "patiently explain" are far from over. As the coffins come home and the taxes go up, many people who were previously willing to accept government propaganda will become increasingly concerned to try to think for themselves. The reasons for their change are unfortunate; the opportunities for educational activity are nevertheless very good.

Furthermore, the recent shift in the government's propaganda line offers important opportunities for critical analysis of the war. There is a note of shrill desperation in the recent defense of the American war in Vietnam. We hear less about "bringing freedom and democracy" to the South Vietnamese and more about the "national interest." Secretary Rusk broods about the dangers posed to us by a billion Chinese; the Vice-President tells us that we are fighting "militant Asian Communism" with "its headquarters in Peking" and adds that a Vietcong victory would directly threaten the United States; Eugene Rostow argues that "it is no good building model cities if they are to be bombed in twenty years time," and so on (all of this "a frivolous insult to the United States Navy," as Walter Lippmann rightly commented).

This shift in propaganda makes it much easier for critical analysis to attack the problem of Vietnam at its core, which is in Washington and Boston, not in Saigon and Hanoi. There is something ludicrous, after all, in the close attention that opponents of the war give to the political and social problems of Vietnam. Those who were opposed to the Japanese conquest of Manchuria a generation ago did not place emphasis on the political and social and economic problems of Manchuria, but on those of Japan. They did not engage in farcical debate over the exact degree of support for the puppet emperor, but looked to the sources of Japanese imperialism. Now opponents of the war can much more easily shift attention to the source of the aggression, to our own country, its ideology and institutions. We can ask whose "interest" is served by 100,000 casualties and 100 billion dollars expended in the attempt to subjugate a small country halfway around the world. We can point to the absurdity of the idea that we are "containing China" by destroying popular and independent forces on its borders, and to the cynicism of the claim that we are in Vietnam because "to Americans, peace and freedom are inseparable" and because "suppression of freedom" must not "go unchallenged" (the Citizens Committee again). We can ask why it is that those who make this claim do not suggest that an American expeditionary force be sent to Taiwan, to Rhodesia, to Greece, or to Mississippi, but only to Vietnam, where, they want us to believe, the master aggressor Mao Tse-tung is following a Hitlerian course in his cunning way, committing aggression without troops and announcing world conquest by insisting, through the medium of Lin Piao, that indigenous wars of national liberation can expect little from China beyond applause. We can ask why Secretary McNamara reads such statements as a new *Mein Kampf*—or why those who admit that "a Vietnamese communist regime would probably be . . . anti-Chinese" (Ithiel de Sola Pool, *Asian Survey*, August 1967) nevertheless sign statements which pretend that in Vietnam we are facing the expansionist aggressors from Peking. We can ask what factors in American ideology make it so easy for intelligent and well-informed men to say that we "insist upon nothing for South Vietnam except that it be free to chart its own future" (Citizens Committee) although they know quite well that the regime we imposed excluded all those who took part in the struggle against French colonialism, "and properly so" (Secretary Rusk, 1963); that we have since been attempting to suppress a "civil insurrection" (General Stillwell) led by the only "truly mass-based political party in South Vietnam" (Douglas Pike); that we supervised the destruction of the Buddhist opposition; that we offered the peasants a "free choice" between the Saigon government and the National Liberation Front by herding them into strategic hamlets from which NLF cadres and sympathizers were eliminated by the police (Roger Hilsman); and so on. The story is familiar. And we can emphasize what must be obvious to a person with a grain of political intelligence: that the present world problem is not "containing China" but containing the United States.

More important, we can ask the really fundamental question. Suppose that it were in the American "national interest" to pound into rubble a small nation that refuses to submit to our will. Would it then be legitimate and proper for us to act "in this national interest"? The Rusks and the Humphreys and the Citizens Committee say yes. Nothing could show more clearly how we are taking the road of the fascist aggressors of a generation ago.

We are, of course, in a domestic political environment very different from that of the citizens of Germany or Japan. Here, it takes no heroism to protest. We have many avenues open to us to drive home the lesson that there is not one law for the United States and one for the rest of mankind, that no one has appointed us judge and executioner for Vietnam or anywhere else. Many avenues of political education, on and off the campus, have been explored in the past two years. There can be no question that this effort should continue and grow to whatever limit the degree of commitment permits.

Some seem to feel that resistance will "blacken" the peace movement and make it difficult to reach potential sympathizers through more familiar channels. I don't agree with this objection, but I feel that it should not be lightly disregarded. Resisters who hope to save the people of Vietnam from destruction must select the issues they confront and the means they employ in such a way as to attract as much popular support as possible for their efforts. There is no lack of clear issues and honorable means, surely, hence no reason why one should be impelled to ugly actions on ambiguous issues. In particular, it seems to me that draft resistance, properly conducted (as it has been so far), is not only a highly principled and courageous act, but one that might receive broad support and become politically effective. It might, furthermore, succeed in raising the issues of passive complicity in the war which are now much too easily evaded. Those who face these issues may even go on to free themselves from the mind-destroying ideological pressures of American life, and to ask some serious questions about America's role in the world, and the sources, in American society, for this criminal behavior.

Moreover, I feel that this objection to resistance is not properly formulated. The "peace movement" exists only in the fantasies of the paranoid right. Those who find some of the means employed or ends pursued objectionable can oppose the war in other ways. They will not be read out of a movement that does not exist; they have only themselves to blame if they do not make use of the other forms of protest that are available.

I have left to the end the most important question, the one about which I have least to say. This is the question of the forms resistance should take. We all take part in the war to a greater or lesser extent, if only by paying taxes and permitting domestic society to function smoothly. A person has to choose for himself the point at which he will simply refuse to take part any longer. Reaching that point, he will be drawn into resistance. I believe that the reasons for resistance I have already mentioned are cogent ones: they have an irreducible moral element that admits of little discussion. The issue is posed in its starkest form for the boy who faces induction, and in a form that is somewhat more complex for the boy who must decide whether to participate in a system of selective service that may pass the burden from him to others less fortunate and less privileged. It is difficult for me to see how anyone can refuse to engage himself, in some way, in the plight of these young men. There are many ways to do so: legal aid and financial support; participation in support demonstrations; draft counseling, organization of draft-resistance unions or community-based resistance organizations; assisting those who wish to escape the country; the steps proposed by the clergymen who recently announced that they are ready to share the fate of those who will be sent to prison. About this aspect of the program of resistance I have nothing to say that will not be obvious to anyone who is willing to think the matter through.

Considered as a political tactic, resistance requires careful thought, and I do not pretend to have very clear ideas about it. Much depends on how events unfold in the coming months. Westmoreland's war of attrition may simply continue with no foreseeable end, but the domestic political situation makes this unlikely. If the Republicans do not decide to throw the election again, they could have a winning strategy: they can claim that they will end the war, and remain vague about the means. Under such circumstances, it is unlikely that Johnson will permit the present military stalemate to persist. There are, then, several options. The first is American withdrawal, in whatever terms it would be couched. It might be disguised as a retreat to "enclaves," from which the troops could then be removed. It might be arranged by an international conference, or by permitting a government in Saigon that would seek peace among contending South Vietnamese and then ask us to leave. This policy might be politically feasible; the same public relations firm that invented terms like "revolutionary development" can depict withdrawal as victory. Whether there is anyone in the executive branch with the courage or imagination to urge this course, I do not know. A number of senators are proposing, in essence, that this is the course we should pursue, as are such critics of the war as Walter Lippmann and Hans Morgenthau, if I understand them correctly. A detailed and quite sensible plan for arranging withdrawal along with new, more meaningful elections in the South is outlined by Philippe Devillers in *Le Monde hebdomadaire* of October 26, 1967. Variants can easily be imagined. What is central is the decision to accept the principle of Geneva that the problems of Vietnam be settled by the Vietnamese.

A second possibility would be annihilation. No one doubts that we have the technological capacity for this, and only the sentimental doubt that we have the moral capacity as well. Bernard Fall predicted this outcome in an interview shortly before his death. "The Americans can destroy," he said, "but they cannot pacify. They may win the war, but it will be the victory of the graveyard. Vietnam will be destroyed."

A third option would be an invasion of North Vietnam. This would saddle us with two unwinnable guerrilla wars instead of one, but if the timing is right, it might be used as a device to rally the citizenry around the flag.

A fourth possibility is an attack on China. We could then abandon Vietnam and turn to a winnable war directed against Chinese industrial capacity. Such a move should win the election. No doubt this prospect also appeals to that insane rationality called "strategic thinking." If we intend to keep armies of occupation or even strong military bases on the Asian mainland, we would do well to make sure that the Chinese do not have the means to threaten them. Of course, there is the danger of a nuclear holocaust, but it is difficult to see why this should trouble those whom John McDermott calls the "crisis managers," the same men who were willing, in 1962, to accept a high probability of nuclear war to establish the principle that we, and we alone, have the right to keep missiles on the borders of a potential enemy.

There are many who regard "negotiations" as a realistic alternative, but I do not understand the logic or even the content of this proposal. If we stop bombing North Vietnam we might well enter into negotiations with Hanoi, but there would then be very little to discuss. As to South Vietnam, the only negotiable issue is the withdrawal of foreign troops; other matters can only be settled among whatever Vietnamese groups have survived the American onslaught. The call for "negotiations" seems to me not only empty, but actually a trap for those who oppose the war. If we do not agree to withdraw our troops, the negotiations will be deadlocked, the fighting will continue, American troops will be fired on and killed, the military will have a persuasive argument to escalate, to save American lives. In short, the Symington solution: we offer them peace on our terms, and if they refuse—the victory of the graveyard.

Of the realistic options, only withdrawal (however disguised) seems to me at all tolerable, and resistance, as a tactic of protest, must be designed so as to increase the likelihood that this option will be selected. Furthermore, the time in which to take such action may be very short. The logic of resorting to resistance as a tactic for ending the war is fairly clear. There is no basis for supposing that those who will make the major policy decisions are open to reason on the fundamental issues, in particular the issue of whether we, alone among the nations of the world, have the authority and the competence to determine the social and political institutions of Vietnam. What is more, there is little likelihood that the electoral process will bear on the major decisions. As I have pointed out, the issue may be settled before the next election. Even if it is not, it is hardly likely that a serious choice will be offered at the polls. And if by a miracle such a choice is offered, how seriously can we take the campaign promises of a "peace candidate" after the experience of 1964? Given the enormous dangers of escalation and its hateful character, it makes sense, in such a situation, to search for ways to raise the domestic cost of American aggression, to raise it to a point where it cannot be overlooked by those who have to calculate such costs. One must then consider in what ways it is possible to pose a serious threat. Many possibilities come to mind: a general strike, university strikes, attempts to hamper war production and supply, and so on.

Personally, I feel that disruptive acts of this sort would be justified were they likely to be effective in averting an imminent tragedy. I am skeptical, however, about their possible effectiveness. At the moment, I cannot imagine a broad base for such action, in the white community at least, outside the universities. Forcible repression would not, therefore, prove very difficult.

My guess is that such actions would, furthermore, primarily involve students and younger faculty from the humanities and the theological schools, with a scattering of scientists. The professional schools, engineers, specialists in the technology of manipulation and control (much of the social sciences), would probably remain relatively uninvolved. Therefore the long-range threat, such as it is, would be to American humanistic and scientific culture. I doubt that this would seem important to those in decision-making positions. Rusk and Rostow and their accomplices in the academic world seem unaware of the serious threat that their policies already pose in these spheres. I doubt that they appreciate the extent, or the importance, of the dissipation of creative energies and the growing disaffection among young people who are sickened by the violence and deceit that they see in the exercise of American power. Further disruption in these areas might, then, seem to them a negligible cost.

Resistance is in part a moral responsibility, in part a tactic to affect government policy. In particular, with respect to support for draft resistance, I feel that it is a moral responsibility that cannot be shirked. On the other hand, as a tactic, it seems to me of doubtful effectiveness, as matters now stand. I say this with diffidence and considerable uncertainty.

Whatever happens in Vietnam, there are bound to be significant domestic repercussions. It is axiomatic that no army ever loses a war; its brave soldiers and all-knowing generals are stabbed in the back by treacherous civilians. American withdrawal is likely, then, to bring to the surface the worst features of American culture, and perhaps to lead to a serious internal repression. On the other hand, an American "victory" might well have dangerous consequences both at home and abroad. It might give added prestige to an already far too powerful executive. There is, moreover, the problem emphasized by A. J.

Muste: ". . . the problem after a war is with the victor. He thinks he has just proved that war and violence pay. Who will now teach him a lesson?" For the most powerful and most aggressive nation in the world, this is indeed a danger. If we can rid ourselves of the naive belief that we are somehow different and more pure—a belief held by the British, the French, the Japanese, in their moments of imperial glory—then we will be able honestly to face the truth in this observation. One can only hope that we will face this truth before too many innocents, on all sides, suffer and die.

Finally, there are certain principles that I think must be stressed as we try to build effective opposition to this and future wars. We must not, I believe, thoughtlessly urge others to commit civil disobedience, and we must be careful not to construct situations in which young people will find themselves induced, perhaps in violation of their basic convictions, to commit civil disobedience. Resistance must be freely undertaken. I also hope, more sincerely than I know how to say, that it will create bonds of friendship and mutual trust that will support and strengthen those who are sure to suffer.

SUPPLEMENT TO "ON RESISTANCE"

Following the publication of "On Resistance" in the *New York Review of Books,* a number of very interesting letters were received dealing with several of the questions raised in it. Two appeared, with accompanying comments of mine, in the issue of February 1, 1968. The first, from a college professor whom I will identify here simply as Mr. Y, noted "an undramatic but steady shift of opinion" among middle-class people, many conservative or apolitical, who "are deciding that the war simply isn't worth what it costs." Mr. Y counsels that these people can be convinced, not that the war is wrong, but that it is "damned foolishness," and he suggests that "the patient effort to win over those millions who view the war in pragmatic rather than moral terms may be more significant" than the various forms of resistance which, while perhaps revealing a "pure conscience," may nevertheless "not actually help put an end to war." The second letter is from a former member of "The Resistance," now underground and obviously unidentified, who signs simply: William

X. As he analyzes the situation, "the war will end when the American middle class wants it to" and "what will cause the middle class to want an end to the war will be the *conjunction* of Vietnamese resistance plus the high cost to the middle class in effort and money to deal with taxes, inflation, disruption, and obstruction at home." It follows, then, "that the most effective antiwar activities are those which are the most disruptive, the most costly, those which most undermine the authority of the government domestically and in its war policy"—ghetto rebellions ("those elements of the white middle class opposed to the war must work to protect participants"), demonstrations such as the ones at the Pentagon and at the New York and Oakland induction centers, and others that will cause the government's authority to be questioned and that will "escalate the cost" to the government. He therefore opposes the individual act of "confrontation" and describes the "notion of the alternatives—the military, prison, or exile" sketched in my article as "too limited, constrained by lack of experience and by lack of a full comprehension of what is to be done." "We have work to do, or simply lives to live, and don't intend to make their job easier or our lives more miserable." His advice is "to make them pay the piper, who called the tune. That is what black folks know, who sing and dance all the time."

My own remarks, accompanying these letters, were not intended as an "answer" but simply as a third, somewhat different reaction to the same questions. I have added a few paragraphs for publication here.

Mr. Y and William X agree that middle-class attitudes will be decisive in determining the outcome of the American war in Vietnam, and that these attitudes will be shaped not by moral but by "pragmatic" considerations, considerations of cost. Yet they arrive at diametrically opposed conclusions regarding the appropriate choice of tactics: Mr. Y opposes all forms of resistance and feels that one should try to convince the American people "that the war is damned foolishness," and Mr. X concludes that the "most effective antiwar activities are those which are the most disruptive." Viewing the situation from a rather similar perspective, I nevertheless find myself reaching still different conclusions. This is hardly astonishing. No one can evaluate the effectiveness of various tactics with any precision. Furthermore, no course of action open to us offers much hope of preventing the Vietnam tragedy from assuming still more awesome proportions. We are, unfortunately, discussing tactics of limited effectiveness and partially unpredictable consequences.

I suspect that Mr. Y and Mr. X exaggerate the political significance of middle-class opinion. Even if 65 percent or 99 percent of the American people were convinced "that the war is damned foolishness," there would remain the problem of translating this conviction into politically effective action. It is doubtful that the political system provides this opportunity in a realistic way. Those who feel that an American "victory" in Vietnam would be a political and moral tragedy therefore face two kinds of tactical problem: first, how to bring "pragmatic middle-class opinion" to oppose the war; second, how to give effective political expression to such opposition as exists. I am not convinced that either correspondent is entirely realistic in assessing these matters.

Consider first the matter of dissent. There is no need to try to persuade someone that his taxes are going up, that his neighbor's son was killed, and that he doesn't like it. Rather, I feel, dissent should be concerned with political and moral issues. The American government no doubt commands the resources to end the war through annihilation, and Mr. Y overlooks the fact that those who feel that the war is "damned foolishness" may perfectly well accept this way of bringing it to an end. Suppose, for example, that the military were to decide that the use of tactical nuclear weapons would provide the cheapest means for uprooting the NLF political and administrative structure in the Mekong Delta (with the inevitable solemn statement from Freedom House applauding this exercise of limited means to show that violence doesn't pay). The purpose of dissent is to mobilize opinion against the use of American force to impose a political solution in Vietnam—to the hideous extent it is used today, to the still more barbaric extent of tomorrow, or in fact, to any extent at all—whatever the costs may be. This is the crucial problem that dissent must face with respect to Vietnam as well as all of the other countries where American force is being used directly, or where American arms and military train-ing are contributing to internal repression. Contrary to Mr. Y, then, I feel that dissent *should* aim to convince the American people that the war is wrong, and to explain why this or any similar use of force is wrong.

Consider next the assumption that opposition to the war will mount as its costs visibly increase. It follows that we should attempt to increase these costs. Resistance, properly conducted, can serve to increase the domestic cost of American aggression and can therefore help shape the attitudes of the "pragmatic middle classes" of whom Mr. Y speaks, as it can help shape the decisions of those who must calculate these costs in setting the course of American foreign policy. Mr. Y is surely wrong in supposing that those who undertake resistance do so to preserve their moral purity. Mr. X's letter is ample testimony to the fact that resistance can be, and I feel quite generally is, undertaken as a political act. One may argue that it is misguided, but not that it is apolitical. Of course, the resister must choose his tactics so as to maximize the probability that the developing opposition will take a civilized form—in the case of Vietnam, withdrawal rather than annihilation—and he must accompany his resistance with the kind of dissent that will seek to raise the general level of political and moral consciousness. These, it seems to me, are the conclusions that one should draw from the analysis of the situation that Mr. Y proposes.

To me it seems that draft resistance meets these conditions. The principle is clear and unambiguous. An individual's refusal to carry out the criminal acts of his government sets the stage, in the most effective way possible, for the attempt to demonstrate the criminal nature of these acts. Furthermore, the resistance is "costly," both to the government and to the "pragmatic middle classes." Let us make the matter concrete. Draft resistance is, for the moment, strongest among the students at the best universities. Last month, for example, 320 law school students and several hundred students at Yale signed "We Won't Go" statements. The government will soon have to decide whether to draft graduate students. If the resistance continues to grow, the decision will be a costly one, no matter how it is made. It is politically difficult to give students a blanket exemption, for obvious reasons. On the other hand, an attempt to draft students will, if resistance develops, put the government in the position of tolerating an open violation of the law or of carrying out serious punitive acts against the children of the social and economic elite. One of the costs of the war is the contempt for the government, for its violence and mendacity, felt by many young people. Punishment of resisters will deepen this disaffection, and may channel it in new directions. Involvement of adults in support of resisters increases the costs still more. If we look beyond Vietnam, the costs may be greater still, not only

because of the unpredictable effects of a really large-scale repression of those who are expected to run the society in the
coming years, but also because of the "danger" inherent in the
fact that a citizen dares to ask whether he should mechanically
obey, that he raises questions about the range of meaningful
political action.

There are several ways in which one can hope to affect the
decisions made by the government. One way is to try to influence the choice that will be offered by the two major political
parties and to exercise this choice on Election Day. Another,
very different approach is to try to modify the objective conditions that any elected official must consider when he selects a
course of action. I do not want to go into the general question
of the legitimacy of these alternatives, but rather to make two
points. First, those who are committed to the first method will
naturally regard political action of the latter sort—draft resistance, for example—as a danger, whose cost they must seek to
reduce. Secondly, to be realistic, the parliamentary system at
the moment offers almost no opportunity for meaningful action
on such issues as Vietnam. One cannot be certain, of course.
Nevertheless, we might as well face up to the overwhelming
probability that the choice in November will be between barely
distinguishable policies. Senator McCarthy's candidacy might
be important as an educational effort (it can hardly be regarded as a political effort) *if* McCarthy were to raise serious
issues and break free from the narrow limits of what passes for
political discussion in this country today, but as yet he has not
done so. It is a remarkable fact that in this democracy, not a
single public figure, no segment of the mass media, advocates
the position which, according to the recent international Gallup
polls, is that of the overwhelming majority in most of the "free
world"—that the United States should withdraw from Vietnam.

The basic issues are not discussed in the mass media and are not raised in the political arena. These are the realities that we must face in determining an appropriate mode of political action.

To summarize, draft resistance can make use of the inegalitarian nature of American society as a technique for increasing the cost of American aggression, and it threatens values that are important to those in a decision-making position. (One who shares these values must then ask how they benefit our victims, and what price our victims must pay to secure these values from any risk.) It is difficult to judge how heavily such costs will weigh in the balance, but I think that Mr. Y is not justified in contending that the goal of resistance can only be to safeguard one's purity of conscience.

Of course, resistance might backfire; it might lead the "pragmatic opposition" to demand a harsh and brutal victory. However, the danger seems to me slight. There is no reason why a principled and obviously courageous and highly moral act should have this consequence. Rather, I think it is likely to cause others to consider their own complicity, in their work, in their payment of war taxes, in their preservation of the domestic peace that permits the warmakers to operate freely. Furthermore, it is important to bear in mind that any political act carries with it a potential danger of this sort. For example, it is not unlikely that President Johnson would react to a threat at the polls with a sharp escalation, on the theory (probably correct) that this would gain him at least short-term support. I see no reason to believe that nonviolent resistance is more likely to have this consequence than electoral politics. Quite the contrary.

Although I agree with Mr. X that resistance can be an effective political act, I think his analysis errs in three respects. First, I think he miscalculates the effect that disruptive actions will have on the middle class that he wants to move to opposition. Second, I think he is considering the notion of "cost" in too narrow a sense. And third, I believe that he underestimates the force the government commands. As to the first matter, he fails to take into account the strong likelihood that disruptive acts will increase the urge to win the war by pure terror, with perhaps a violent repression at home as well. As far as costs are concerned, he considers only the matter of "effort and money." But these, I suspect, are negligible costs when we consider the kinds of disruptive acts that might be carried out by the white middle class, students or adults. The million dollars spent by the government on October 21 is a trivial sum for the government—but the substantially greater sums expended to mount the demonstration are not at all trivial, for the "peace movement." Hence if the criterion is cost in this sense, the demonstration would have to be regarded as a serious setback. In general, I think that the important costs that can be increased by student and middle-class resistance are the more abstract ones discussed earlier. These cannot be calculated in dollars and cents, but they are no less real for that.

As to the matter of government force, I think it is surely ample to control, with ease, any disruptive acts that can now be foreseen. As Hans Morgenthau observed recently, there has been a qualitative shift in the balance of force between a government and a massed populace, and this disparity can only increase. A report last June by the Institute of Defense Analysis proposed a great many delightful new ideas for "crowd control" (itching powder, "sticky blobs to glue rioters together," chemical agents, "mechanically spread sticky strings, bands, or adhesives which might slow the movement of the crowd by linking people together or to themselves," foam generators which lead to "psychological distress through loss of contact with the environment," tranquilizing darts, etc.—AP report, November 11, 1967), ideas which give an interesting portent of what is to come and a useful insight into university-sponsored research at its best. My guess is that talk of disruptive acts is a fantasy.

I have said nothing about ghetto rebellions. These may affect the war, in one or another way, but they are not acts undertaken with the end of bringing about American withdrawal from Vietnam and must, I think, be considered in a totally different context.

Although the context today remains quite different, it is still very much to be hoped that resistance against the Vietnam war and the deeper imperialist forces of which it is a manifestation can contribute to the struggle against domestic oppression. No doubt one of the pressures on the government to end the war is the fear that the troops will be needed to occupy American cities and to enforce the status quo at home. The kind of "limited war" mentality that underlies the IDA study just mentioned is revealed even more explicitly by Homer Bigart in the *New York Times,* March 22, 1968, in a long report headed: "Army Helps Police Get 'Hip' on Riots." I quote a few paragraphs, to give the flavor:

> On a piney knoll some 60 city and state policeman and National Guard officers gathered yesterday to watch the testing of "nonlethal agents" that may be used this summer to disperse riotous mobs in the nation's cities. . . . Robins sang, coffee and cookies were served and the post band played "The Stars and Stripes Forever" as the sixth class of the Civil Disobedience Orientation Course climbed out of an Army bus to begin a 20-hour course on the anatomy of a riot . . . [at the] . . . Army's riot control school, an institution hurriedly conceived a few months ago to teach the grim lessons derived from the Detroit and Newark riots. . . .

The report goes on to describe the new, "more devastating" types of tear gas now available, and the ways in which grenades and helicopters can be used to control "the mobs." An accompanying picture shows a "simulated battle between militant civil rights demonstrators and the National Guardsmen." The demonstrators hold a sign saying "We Shall Overcome" and the heavily armed soldiers, with gas masks and fixed bayonets, demonstrate how this slogan can be refuted. The description continues as follows:

> The clash is staged in a Hollywood type mockup of a community called Riotsville. . . . "Baby," a firebrand militant . . . , harangues a crowd, charging policy brutality. The crowd waves signs denouncing war. One sign reads "We Shall Overcome." Bricks and rocks . . . are thrown at the "Mayor" when he tries to placate the mob.
> But here comes the National Guard. Using tear gas, bayonets, an armored personnel carrier, and classic antiriot tactics, the troops prevail. "Baby" is seized and taken off in the armored car, a prisoner.

Presumably the audience breathes a sigh of relief, sipping their coffee and munching on cookies to the strains of "The Stars and Stripes Forever" as the scene fades, secure in the knowledge that those who denounce war and poverty and racism shall not prevail—all of this certainly a reasonable forecast of what the future may hold.

I do agree with Mr. X in his criticism of the tactic of escalating confrontation that was proposed, at one time, by the loosely organized group called "The Resistance." Confrontations will come quickly enough. The real task, for the present, is to organize as large as possible a base of support for resistance—a proliferation of local resistance support groups linked together in a national network, with participation of white and black resisters, with adult middle-class support on and off campus, substantial financial assistance, and personal involvement by people who feel that resistance can be made politically effective, who feel that they have a moral responsibility to give concrete assistance to those who refuse to serve in Vietnam, who wish to increase the political cost of repression by standing alongside the young men who will inevitably suffer most severely. Thinking in still more long-range terms, it may be that the most significant steps towards a reform of American society will prove to be the efforts of the very courageous and unsung few who are devoting themselves to community organizing, often using the draft and its inequities as a point of entry into communities that provide the mass base for American repression, and seeking to create both consciousness and organizational structure for resistance on the part of those who bear the heaviest burdens but who are, for the present, passive victims of an unchallenged coercive ideology. The national RESIST organization is attempting to provide the framework for a range of such activities, using as a basis the *Call To Resist Illegitimate Authority* (most of which appeared as an advertisement in the *New York Review of Books* on October 12, 1967). With all of the necessary qualifications, I feel that involvement in this effort is the most effective form of political action against this and future wars that is now open to a concerned citizen.

Those of us who are not under direct attack and who are relatively free to choose a course of action have a responsibility to the victims of American power that we must face with unwavering seriousness. In considering some tactic of protest or resistance, we must ask what its consequences are likely to be for the people of Vietnam or of Guatemala or of Harlem, and what effect it will have on the building of a movement against war and oppression, a movement that will help to create a society in which one can live without fear and without shame. We have to search for ways to persuade vast numbers of Americans to commit themselves to this task, and we must devise ways to convert this commitment into effective action. The goal may seem so remote as to be a fantasy, but for those who are serious, this is the only strategy that can be considered. Persuasion may involve deeds as well as words; it may involve the construction of institutions and social forms, even if only in microcosm, that overcome the competitiveness and the single-minded pursuit of self-interest that proves a mechanism of social control as effective as that of a totalitarian state. But the goal must be to design and construct alternatives to the present ideology and social institutions that are more compelling on intellectual and moral grounds, and that can draw to them masses of Americans who find that these alternatives satisfy their human needs—including the human need to show compassion, to encourage and to assist those who seek to raise themselves from the misery and degradation that our society has helped to impose and now seeks to perpetuate.

It would be criminal folly to fail to act when there are opportunities to move towards these goals, or to act in such a way as to make them still more distant than they are today. It is not easy to find a way to steer between these dangers. There is no doubt that in the recent past, the error has consistently been on the side of caution and restraint, fear and moral blindness. But one must bear in mind, as tensions mount, that the opposite error is no less serious. It is quite easy to design tactics that will help to consolidate the latent forces of a potential American fascism. To mention just one obvious example, verbal and physical abuse of the police, however great the provocation, can have only this effect. Such tactics may seem "radical" and, in a narrow sense, justified by the magnitude of the infamy and evil that they seek to overcome. They are not.

In fact, it is senseless to speak—as many now do—of tactics and actions as being "radical," "liberal," "conservative," or "reactionary." In itself, an action cannot be placed on a political dimension at all. It may be successful or unsuccessful in achieving an end that can be described in political terms. But it is useful to remember that the same tactics that one man may propose with high conscience and deep commitment to radical social change may also be pressed by a well-placed police spy, bent on destroying such a movement and increasing popular support for the forces of repression. Consider the Reichstag fire, to return to a day that is less remote than one would wish. Or consider the act of a seventeen-year-old Jewish refugee from Poland just thirty years ago—of Herschel Grynszpan, who assassinated a German official in Paris in November 1938. It is difficult to condemn this desperate act, which set off violent pogroms throughout Germany and helped entrench more deeply the Nazi regime of terror; but the victims of Nazi terror would offer no thanks to Herschel Grynszpan. We must not abandon the victims of American power, or play games with their fate. We must not consent to have the same repression imposed on still further helpless victims or the same blind fury unleashed against them. Acts that seem perfectly justified in themselves when regarded in a narrow sense may be very wrong when considered in the light of their probable consequences. And a failure to approach those who can be reached, a failure to act with strength and determination when one can do so in a constructive way, is no less thoughtless and indefensible. These are very general remarks, and not very helpful, perhaps, when we face the concrete question of what we can do right now. Still, I think that such guidelines as these must form the framework for these decisions.

One final remark. The Vietnam war is the most obscene example of a frightening phenomenon of contemporary history— the attempt by our country to impose its particular concept of order and stability throughout much of the world. By any objective standard, the United States has become the most aggressive power in the world, the greatest threat to peace, to national self-determination, and to international cooperation. At the same time, we enjoy a high degree of internal freedom. We can speak and write and organize. Resisters may be punished severely, but they will not be sent to slave-labor camps or gas chambers. Given these facts, resistance is feasible even for those who are not heroes by nature, and it is an obligation, I believe, for those who fear the consequences and detest the reality of the attempt to impose American hegemony. Resistance cannot now significantly deplete the manpower pool that makes possible the use of American power for global repression, nor can it, at the moment, significantly impede the research, production, and supply on which this exercise of power rests. But it can contribute significantly towards raising the domestic costs of this attempt and eliminating the apathy and passivity that may permit it to succeed. It therefore has a potential significance that extends far beyond Vietnam. It may help to save other small countries from the fate of Vietnam, and indeed, to save the world from indescribable catastrophe.

EPILOGUE

As the great peasant revolutions raged in China more than a century ago, Karl Marx wrote in the *New York Tribune* about

> the effect the Chinese revolution seems likely to exercise on the civilized world. It may seem a strange and a very paradoxical assertion that the next uprising of the people of Europe, and their next movement for republican freedom and economy of government, may depend more on what is now passing in the Celestial Empire—the very opposite of Europe—than on any other political cause that now exists. . . . Now, England having brought about the revolution in China, the question is how that revolution will in time react on England, and through England on Europe.

A few years later he discussed the "curious spectacle" of "China sending disorder into the Western world while the Western Powers, by English, French, and American war steamers, are conveying 'order' to Shanghai, Nanking, and the mouths of the Great Canal."

As in other respects, the timetable that Marx envisioned was in error, and the cast of characters has now somewhat changed. Furthermore, what Marx had in mind was the possibility that an economic crisis might be caused in the West by a successful revolution in China, endangering the China trade, the importance of which, in the fashion of most writers on this matter until fairly recently, he tended to exaggerate. Still, it is well to consider today the remarkable spectacle of the disorder created in the Western world as the attempt to convey order to Asian countries—the very opposite of the West—is proving to be beyond the power of Western imperialism. In part, the disorder is rooted in revulsion, and to this extent is a tribute to a strain of decency in Western culture, difficult as it is to pronounce these words amidst the barbarism of the Vietnam war. The disorder spreading through the Western world is not solely or even primarily a reaction to the frustration of Western power in Asia, but there is no doubt that the massive convulsions in Asia, and the heroic Vietnamese resistance to American power, have served as a catalytic agent, releasing forces that might have remained latent. In itself, this disorder is neither good nor bad, a cause neither for hope nor for despair. It remains to be seen whether this disorder can be converted into a force that will revitalize American society, or whether it will settle into deadening repression, or will simply subside, to little effect.

It should be clear to a rational man that the chances for survival, let alone a decent existence, are rather slight if American power continues to be used with such abandon as in the past few years, or even flaunted so freely. The capacity of the national state for violence and coercion, the threat that it poses to the survival of its citizens, are so extreme that other problems seem to fade in comparison. But this violence cannot be met and overcome without regard for its social roots. Just prior to the Second World War, America was in the depths of depression, with nine million unemployed. It is difficult to fault this evaluation of the social and economic policies of the 1930s: "The New Deal failed to solve the problem of depression, it failed to raise the impoverished, it failed to redistribute income, it failed to extend equality and generally countenanced racial discrimination and segregation. It failed generally to make business more responsible to the social welfare or to threaten business' preeminent political power" (Barton J. Bernstein, "The New Deal: The Conservative Achievements of Liberal Reform," in B. J. Bernstein, ed., *Towards a New Past* [New York, Pantheon Books, 1968]). Since the national mobilization of World War II, we have spent over a trillion dollars on "defense." It hardly is necessary to resort to the "new economics" to show that such measures can reduce unemployment and keep the economy functioning, as it requires little political insight to see why the government is likely to expend the resources it commands on research and development that yield no immediate profit, on missiles and "fast-deployment logistic ships" rather than on a mass transportation system that will conflict with the needs of the oil companies and automotive industry, on nerve gas and manned orbital laboratories rather than on farming the oceans (while wealthy farmers and farm industries are subsidized to cut back agricultural production). It is reasonably clear that unless the commercial and industrial system comes under some sort of popular democratic control, political democracy will be a sham and state power will continue to serve inhuman ends. It is easy to say that new thinking and social experimentation are needed to free us from the paralysis and fears that narrow our vision and direct national energies to destruction and waste, that it is necessary to develop social and political consciousness through participation and popular control in decision making. It is also correct. There now exist opportunities for change that are not very likely to recur. In part, they are traceable to the strange and paradoxical touching of extremes to which Marx alluded. The question of how Asian revolutions will in time react on America, and through America on Europe, is very real. It is a question that calls not for speculation, but for commitment and thought and action.